BRANDS AND BRANDING

SAGE was founded in 1965 by Sara Miller McCune to support the dissemination of usable knowledge by publishing innovative and high-quality research and teaching content. Today, we publish over 900 journals, including those of more than 400 learned societies, more than 800 new books per year, and a growing range of library products including archives, data, case studies, reports, and video. SAGE remains majority-owned by our founder, and after Sara's lifetime will become owned by a charitable trust that secures our continued independence.

Los Angeles | London | New Delhi | Singapore | Washington DC | Melbourne

BRANDS AND BRANDING

Stephen Brown

Los Angeles | London | New Delhi
Singapore | Washington DC | Melbourne

Los Angeles | London | New Delhi
Singapore | Washington DC | Melbourne

SAGE Publications Ltd
1 Oliver's Yard
55 City Road
London EC1Y 1SP

SAGE Publications Inc.
2455 Teller Road
Thousand Oaks, California 91320

SAGE Publications India Pvt Ltd
B 1/I 1 Mohan Cooperative Industrial Area
Mathura Road
New Delhi 110 044

SAGE Publications Asia-Pacific Pte Ltd
3 Church Street
#10-04 Samsung Hub
Singapore 049483

Editor: Matthew Waters
Editorial assistant: Lyndsay Aitken
Production editor: Sarah Cooke
Marketing manager: Alison Borg
Cover design: Francis Kenney
Typeset by: C&M Digitals (P) Ltd, Chennai, India
Printed and bound by CPI Group (UK) Ltd,
Croydon, CR0 4YY

Library of Congress Control Number: 2016933262

British Library Cataloguing in Publication data

A catalogue record for this book is available from
the British Library

ISBN 978-1-47391-951-8
ISBN 978-1-47391-952-5 (pbk)

At SAGE we take sustainability seriously. Most of our products are printed in the UK using FSC papers and boards.
When we print overseas we ensure sustainable papers are used as measured by the PREPS grading system.
We undertake an annual audit to monitor our sustainability.

CONTENTS

ABOUT THE AUTHOR

Stephen Brown is Professor of Marketing Research at Ulster University, UK. He has written numerous books including *Fail Better, Free Gift Inside* and *Wizard: Harry Potter's Brand Magic*, the last of which was translated into twelve languages. Once described as 'the Antichrist of Marketing', his articles have appeared in the *Journal of Marketing*, the *Journal of Consumer Research* and the *Harvard Business Review*, among many others. A life-long jogger, who believes Nike is second to none, he writes comic novels in his spare time.

PREFACE
Reasons Why

When persuading people to buy their brands, many managers rely on 'reasons why'. They explain, often with the aid of a snappy slogan or memorable catchphrase, why the purchase is justified. Guinness is Good for You. Benecol Lowers Cholesterol. Domestos Kills All Known Germs. Tunes Help You Breathe More Easily. Olay Fights the Seven Signs of Ageing. Red Bull Gives You Wings. Whether it be sports cars (0–60 in 5.4 seconds), scary movies (chock-a-block with shocks) or cures for the common cold (stops sniffles, sneezes, coughs and wheezes), recounting reasons why is a brand management standby.

There are many, many books about brands and branding. According to one academic authority, around 3,000 branding books are published each year. So why should any-one buy this one? What are the reasons for choosing this particular text when classics like Keller's *Strategic Brand Management*, Aaker's *Building Strong Brands*, de Chernatony's *Creating Powerful Brands* and Elliott and Percy's *Strategic Brand Management* are ready to hand? And ready to second-hand for readers in need of a bargain?

Brands and Branding is worth buying for seven reasons. First, it is *introductory*. Most of the existing textbooks are designed for final-year or postgraduate students, those who are well versed in marketing principles and precepts. Branding, however, is increasingly taught during first or second year, largely because it provides an excellent, student-friendly introduction to marketing management more generally.

There's no suitable textbook, though. Yes, there are plenty of branding-for-beginners books, such as those designed for the *Dummies* demographic. But these are primarily aimed at practitioners and entrepreneurs, not undergraduate students or postgrads without a bachelor's in business studies. *Brands and Branding* assumes nothing more than readers' awareness of, and familiarity with, high-profile brands like McDonald's, Microsoft, Coca-Cola and Chanel.

Second, it is *indicative* rather than comprehensive. It doesn't try to cover every aspect of brands and branding. B&B is a very big subject. So much so, several UK universities offer entire degree programmes on brand management. Many academic disciplines besides marketing, moreover, take a proprietorial interest in the subject. Lawyers, sociologists, anthropologists and accountants – to name but four – have written reams on branding matters. The upshot is that it's easy to get confused, over-whelmed, exasperated. This book focuses on the basics. It deals with big brands that most people know (and sometimes love), though small- and medium-sized opera-tions shall also be mentioned to temper the global focus. More than a few of these will be Irish, albeit regional brands are much the same the world over.

Brands and Branding is indicative in another sense. It is devised with examinations in mind. It's highly likely that readers of this book will be set traditional, essay-style examinations at some stage during their degree programmes. And long lists of facts can be hard to remember. However, with the assistance of indicative acronyms, mnemonics and rhyming couplets, this book will be a boon come exam time. It's a more reliable revision aid than Lucozade.

Third, it is *immersive. Brands and Branding* takes readers on a journey. The chapters are designed to flow naturally into one another, despite dealing with stand-alone topics. Divided into three main sections – Components, Commandments, Constraints – the book has a beginning, a middle and an end, as all stories do. Although there is no time to dawdle, there are diversions along the way. Unlike conventional case studies, these comprise Think Boxes (queries on key issues), Brand Tasks (short reflective challenges) and Recommended Readings (salient articles and texts worth consulting).

Readers must play their part, however, for the full immersive experience. Unlike most other branding textbooks, which are dotted with glossy photos of logos and suchlike, this book works on the assumption that readers have smartphones or tablet computers to hand. And that with one or two taps innumerable Google images of the brands under discussion can be accessed. Ditto Wikipedia entries, newspaper articles and academic publications, if a bit of background on the brand is desired. URLs are invaluable for point-to-point navigation, but stumbling on stuff is very useful too. For that reason the Notes and References section gestures rather than directs.

Fourth, it is *inclusive.* Its sources are many, varied, catholic, eclectic. Contra most books about branding, it doesn't consider academic articles and research reports to be gold standard sources of information on the subject. Academic articles have their place, as do learned research reports. But blogs, novels, newspapers, magazines, mov-ies, reviews, social media, the trade press, comedy routines and bar-room banter can be informative as well. When Stephen King, the bestselling novelist, compares his books to a Big Mac, when a hangover-stricken celebrity calls Coca-Cola 'the black doctor in a red ambulance', when *The Sun* invents spoof slogans for renowned brands like Dulux (437 different ways to say 'white'), Lego (the bane of your foot's existence) and IKEA (we throw in extra parts just to mess with you) then that's worthy of note. Such sources, of course, have to be sifted and stress-tested for truthfulness. But that's true of research reports too.

Fifth, it is *irreverent*. As *The Sun*'s faux slogans show, branding can be tremendous fun. Sure, it's a deadly serious business. Sure, brand owners pour billions into their precious properties. Sure, millions of people are employed by household names and the holding companies that accommodate those names. Sure, there are scores of consultancy firms who strive to calculate how much a brand is worth and how that has changed since the previous calculation. But it is still great fun to find out that Hapi Foods, a Canadian brand of breakfast cereal, changed its name to Holy Crap! because that's what consumers said when they tasted it. There's lots of holy crap in the book you're holding. And lots that's not so holy.

Sixth, it is *intimate*. Books and articles written by academics tend to be stuffed with abstractions. Abstract ideas involving theories, models, flow diagrams and so forth are the coin of the academic realm. The language ordinarily employed is often cold, impersonal and off-putting. It takes a fair bit of time to get used to.

I have found that first- and second-year undergraduates can struggle with the arcane ideas and disembodied language that typify academic textbooks. They like lots and lots of examples relating to the points being made. They want to feel they are dealing with a human being – tutorial style – rather than reading tablets of stone delivered from on high. Therefore, I'll be addressing *you* directly throughout this book as *we* pick *our* way through the sometimes weird but unfailingly wonderful world of brands and branding. I trust you're ready for a fun-filled journey.

More than that, though, I hope you'll find our journey *inspirational*, my final reason why. Branding is never less than fascinating – and laugh-out-loud funny on occasion – but it can also be inspirational from time to time. The achievements of Chain Reaction, a small bicycle repair shop in a remote British village that became one of the world's biggest online bicycling brands, is an inspiration to us all. The never-say-die attitude of Ruth Handler, whose Barbie doll brand was derided by all and sundry only to emerge triumphant in a crowded industry, is something each and every one of us can learn from. The ingenuity of an Irish engineering start-up, at a loss for a name for their brand, is living proof that inspiration can strike when least expected. Exasperated after several hours of fruitless debate, the founder turned to his partners and swore 'In the name of Jesus, Mary and Joseph, will somebody think of a name for this brand!' And lo, JMJ Engineering joined branding's heavenly host.

You'll be joining them too, I trust. My aim with this book is not to tell you everything you need to know about brands and branding. I just want to make you want to find out more about a fabulous, fantastic, never less than fascinating subject.

INTRODUCTION

CHAPTER 1
THE RUDIMENTS OF BRANDING

Overview

We live in a branded world. From dawn to dusk we interact with brands. But what are brands, exactly? Why do we need them? How come companies devote so much time and effort branding their goods and services? This chapter addresses these questions. It shows that brands, like still waters, run deep. They are hard to define. They are subject to all sorts of legal constraints. However, they are immensely valuable and found in ever more sectors of contemporary society, from politics to pop music.

BRANDS SURROUND US

Alpen, Bovril, Cadbury, Dove; eBay, Facebook, Google, *Hello*; Infiniti, Jay-Z, Kodak, Lexus; Marlboro, Nescafé, Oreo, Pepsi; Qantas, Rolex, Sony, Tiffany; Uber, Vodafone, Wrigley, Xbox; YSL, Zegna.

Armani, Beyoncé, Chanel, Dior; Esso, Flora, Gant, Heinz; Intel, Java, Kleenex, Linux; Mercedes, Nikon, Omega, Porsche; Quaker, Radox, Smirnoff, Tetley; Umbro, Visa, Wella, *X Factor*; Yahoo, Zynga.

Apple, Beckham, Cisco, Dell; Emirates, Ferrari, Gucci, Hermès; Iams, Jameson, Kellogg's, Lynx; Microsoft, Netflix, Oracle, Puma; Q-Tips, Rihanna, Samsung, Twitter; Uniqlo, Versace, Wrangler, *X-Men*; Yoplait, Zoopla, Zonga, Zappos, Zoella, Zantac, Zizzi …

Most consumers, if you asked them to name a brand, would likely mention one of the above. Or something very similar: Adidas, Budweiser, Coca-Cola, Duracell, easyJet, Fiat, Guinness, Hollister, etc., etc. Everyone knows what brands are. They are the packaged goods we find in supermarkets. They are the luxury labels that we own, or aspire to own. They are the IT kit we use to keep connected. They are the websites and apps we're connected to. They are the names of the stuff that surrounds us, from Aldi to Zanussi. They are the celebrities with personalized ranges of perfume and apparel. They are what we eat, we drink, we wear, we read, we wash with, we're addicted to, we're entertained by and, as often as not, we work for. They are the things that get us through the day:

> 7.00 a.m. Your clock radio blasts you awake, terminating your recurring MasterCard nightmare. Your eyes, still blurred from sleep, can hardly make out the Sony logo on the radio as you fumble for the off switch, but you dutifully launch yourself from bed and stagger toward the shower. Midway between the L'Oréal shampoo and the Pantene conditioner, you remember that today is the day the jeweller promised your Rolex would be fixed. Even better you remember that today is Casual Friday at the office, so once out of the shower, you bypass the ranks of Brooks Brothers and Armani in your closet and opt for Dockers, your favourite Nikes, and a Gap chambray shirt. Breakfast consists of Maxwell House and a Pop-Tart.[1]

Although brands are fantastic, fascinating, fun-filled things to learn about, they're tricky things to define. It isn't easy to draw a line between 'brand' and 'not-brand'. Here's why.

WHAT IS A BRAND?

A couple of years ago, I did some research on RMS *Titanic*, the 'unsinkable' ship that hit an iceberg on its maiden voyage and sank with enormous loss of life. Countless movies, innumerable novels, hundreds of songs, sermons, poems, paintings, plays, musicals, miniseries, documentaries, exhibitions, websites, smartphone apps and, not least, a veritable tsunami of tie-in merchandise from T-shirts to teabags, have been produced about the terrible events of that unforgettable night.[2]

Whatever way you look at it, the *Titanic* is very big business. And that business was never bigger than in April 2012, the centenary of the sinking. In addition to the magazine articles and newspaper features and television programmes and orchestral recitals and religious ceremonies and black-tie charity galas and deep sea dives to the wreck and general commemorative overkill, every single city with a link to *Titanic* used the connection to promote its tourist attractions. Southampton built a brand new Sea City Museum; Cherbourg constructed its *Cité de la Mer* attraction; Cobh (formerly Queenstown) opened a Tourist Trail and Heritage Centre; and Liverpool, *Titanic*'s port of registration, chose to tell the tragic tale in an enormous work of performance art, a street parade featuring giant puppets of the luckless passengers.

The city of Belfast, my home town, also went overboard for the *Titanic*. It pushed the boat out, big time. A massive, £100 million visitors' centre was constructed beside the slipways where the iconic liner was built by Harland & Wolff, whose giant yellow cranes still scrape the city's skyline. Although many local taxpayers objected to the investment, or wondered whether the building would attract sufficient visitors to cover its cost, Titanic Belfast was duly launched with great branding fanfare and massive worldwide publicity. Just like the original.[3]

Among other things, my research involved interviewing lots of people – from foreign students to *Titanic* tour guides – about 'the unsinkable brand'. Their answers were all over the place. As far as property developers and the local Tourist Board were concerned, Titanic Belfast was nothing less than the 'biggest brand museum in the world', better by far that its nearest Irish rival, the Guinness Storehouse in Dublin. The Tourist Board even produced a 'brand book', advising businesses how best to cash in on the *Titanic* connection.

Ordinary people didn't feel the same way, however. The *Titanic*, for most interviewees, was a majestic ship, an appalling tragedy, an unconsecrated graveyard, an exploitative blockbuster movie by James Cameron. But a brand? Absolutely not! Since when, they said to me, did catastrophes become brands? The very idea was grotesque, disgraceful, sick and twisted.

The most memorable interview, mind you, was with the marketing manager of Harland & Wolff, the shipyard that built the *Titanic* and continues to take a proprietary interest in the wreck. When the b-word came up, he looked at me in a querulous manner and authoritatively announced: 'The *Titanic* is not a brand. Never was, never will be.'

I was dumbfounded. This was a marketing man talking. He, above anyone, must surely be aware that the *Titanic* is a brand with a capital B. He's bound to appreciate its worth, its value, its equity, its vast commercial potential, not least for the closely associated H&W brand. But, no, he didn't. Quite the opposite.

What on earth, I wondered, is going on here?

'The *Titanic* is not a brand,' he then explained, 'because the name cannot be trademarked. It's generic. Anyone can use it. Therefore *Titanic* is not a brand.'

LEGAL INTERVENTION

In one sense, H&W's sales manager is correct. *Titanic*'s standing as a brand is debatable. But only from a strictly legal perspective. Because, if a brand isn't formally registered with the Intellectual Property Office (IPO), pretty much anyone can take the name and make money from it.[4] *The Simpsons* discovered this to their cost with Duff beer – a spoof brand swilled by Homer – which is made and sold in several countries without the TV show's approval.

If, conversely, your surname is McDonald and you are considering opening a fast food restaurant, don't even think of naming it after yourself. Ronald's lawyers will be round with a writ before you can say Happy Meal, never mind Big Mac. Let alone Supersize Me.

The legal side of branding is crucially important, and you ignore it at your peril (Think Box 1). Just ask my local Italian restaurant, the Cipriani. Nice name, I hear you say. However, it's a nice name that's owned by the world-renowned Hotel Cipriani in Venice. And the Cip's attorneys – à la Liam Neeson in *Taken* – look for and find any marketing miscreants who mess with their trademarked entitlement, even unto the ends of the earth.

THINK BOX 1

Some Legal Considerations

Although trademarks have been around since the dawn of civilization, as makers' marks on Greco-Roman pottery prove, the pertinent legal apparatus dates from the late 19th century. The Trade Marks Acts have been amended on several occasions since 1875, as well as harmonized within the EU in accordance with the 1994 Trademarks Directive. Different registration regulations apply in different parts of the world and even within the EC countries. Member states with a common law tradition (where custom and practice give some degree of protection in the absence of registration) operate on a slightly different basis than those with a civil code system.

The legalistic details are less important for present purposes than the simple fact that brands can apply to register their names with the Intellectual Property Office (IPO). At present, applications cost £170 with the proviso that the name isn't already registered by another brand in its particular category. There are forty-two fairly broad categories in the official classification framework, ranging from firearms (class 13) to footwear (class 25). Each category is autonomous to some degree, inasmuch as the name Polo, registered by Volkswagen in class 12, doesn't infringe on the name Polo registered by Ralph Lauren in class 25, or on the Polo mints confectionary registered by Rowntree (now Nestlé) in class 30. When Apple entered the music industry via iTunes, however, the Apple record label established by The Beatles in 1968 sought appropriate legal redress, until common sense prevailed.

Registration applications, as a rule, don't stop at brand names. Signs, symbols, slogans, smells, sounds and just about everything that is used to distinguish the goods and services of one brand from another, are ripe for registration. Applications are often made for several classes, furthermore, since this gives the applicant scope for subsequent brand extensions into contiguous categories. If a global market is aspired to, registrations are routinely sought in multiple national jurisdictions. As each of these applications costs money and as some names may already be in use in certain places – which may necessitate the purchase of the property from its present owner – the seemingly simple act of registering a brand can turn out to be a very expensive process. If patent protection is also sought for inventions (such as Dyson's bagless vacuum cleaner technology) or copyrights (which pertain to literary, dramatic and musical works), the total outlay can be prohibitive. Even more so, if trademark infringement rears its ugly head. Policing patents, trademarks or copyrights doesn't come cheap. Failure to do so, though, can be catastrophic, because legal protection can be lost if it's not actively enforced.

Thinking Outside the Think Box

Taylor Swift, the pop star, is trying to copyright the title of her bestselling album *1989*. Find out why she was moved to do this and, after 'reading around the subject' (aka RATS), assess her chances of success.

But that's daft, some might retort. How in the name of the sainted Ronald McDonald could a tiny trattoria in Belfast adversely affect, much less damage, an iconic Italian haunt of movie stars and A-list celebrities? The answer is that it can't. Of course it can't. That's not the point, though. If Hotel Cipriani fails to police its trademarks assiduously, the brand could lose the legal protection it currently enjoys.

Just ask Colin Mackey, an aspiring Irish entrepreneur who created a brand of flavoursome, freshly-pressed fruit juice, John Appleseed's. Unbeknown to Colin, a near-identical brand named John Appleseed nestled in the bulging product portfolio of AB InBev, one of the biggest brewing conglomerates in the world, whose bedazzling brand-name beverages include Budweiser, Löwenbräu, Corona and Beck's. Even though Colin's ethical, environmentally-friendly social enterprise channels its profits into helping the homeless, his brand duly received a cease and desist letter. Politely worded, no doubt.

Now, Mr Mackey could have told AB InBev to take a hike (and battled it out in the courts thereafter). But most itsy-bitsy brands don't have the time, the money, the managerial resources – not to mention the dedicated legal department – to take the big guys on. As an intellectual property lawyer, asked to comment on the case, made perfectly clear, AB InBev had to act in the way they did because 'What they are doing is taking action to preserve their legal position. It's unfortunate that [Colin] has stepped on the shoes of someone large and sophisticated. But brand is king in today's economy.'[5]

She's right there. And if you're still sceptical, ask the good folks at *Martial Arts Guardian*, an online magazine for kung-fu fighters, which recently aroused the ire of *The Guardian* newspaper for treading on its trademarks.[6] Swatch watches, similarly, is squaring up to Apple, because its supersmart timepiece is called iSwatch and the legal eagles in Cupertino don't like it. Tokyo's Olympics organizing committee isn't best pleased either. Its proposed logo for the 2020 Olympiad was withdrawn, amid much embarrassment, because it was 'plagiarized' by designer Kenjiro Sano from the insignia of a theatre group in Belgium.

Nowhere, however, is the legal side of things better illustrated than in the case of Monopoly, the bazillion selling board game, which is eighty years old and still going strong. Except that it isn't. Eighty years old, that is. According to legend, the board game was invented by Charles Darrow in 1935 and subsequently sold to Parker Brothers, who successfully turned the great game's pretend money into untold millions of the real stuff. Thirty years before Darrow, though, Lizzy Magie came up with the same idea. But she failed to protect her patents properly and lost both fame and fortune as a result. Eighty or 110 years on, depending on your viewpoint, Monopoly remains the undisputed brand leader in its category.[7]

The key point here is that the marketing manager of Harland & Wolff was technically correct when he contended that *Titanic* isn't a 'brand'. However, there's much more to branding than trademarks. The b-word is applied to just about anything and everything these days. We routinely talk about politicians as brands (Brand Obama), about celebrities as brands (Kim Kardashian), about sportspeople as brands (Usain Bolt), about blockbuster movies as brands (*Star Wars*), about cities, countries, colleges, clinics, charities, churches and consumers (like you and me) as brands. Yet comparatively few countries are trademarked. Not too many churches are registered with the IPO. The university I work for doesn't have an ® symbol after its name. Me neither. Do you? Maybe you should, just like those superstar scientists Brian Cox and Stephen Hawking, whose names are trademarked to infinity and beyond. As the *Financial Times* reminds us:

> Once upon a time, children used to want to grow up to be doctors and lawyers. Or, at least, policemen and famous rock stars ... Nowadays, it seems the thing to be, whether you are a person, place or thing, rock star or editor, is a brand.[8]

BRANDING IS EVERYTHING

So, what *exactly* is a brand? This question is more easily asked than answered. There is no consensus on what a brand is or isn't. According to the *OED* definition, the word 'brand' means:

> A piece of burning, smouldering or charred wood; a stigma, a mark of disgrace; a torch, a sword; a kind of blight, leaving leaves with a burnt appearance; a special or characteristic kind (brand of humour); an identifying mark burned on livestock or (formerly) criminals etc. with a hot iron; an iron used for this; a particular make of goods, an identifying trademark, label etc., to designate ownership.

For students of branding, the last of these is the one that counts.[9] Identifying trademarks that designate ownership is essentially the legalistic interpretation employed by Harland & Wolff in relation to *Titanic*. Our learned friends firmly believe that brands are properties. They are private properties for the most part. Those who trespass on legally protected brand properties are liable to prosecution. And as with any other property, brands' 'title deeds' can be bought, sold, traded, bequeathed, etc. Some properties are more valuable than others, depending on size, aspect, position, fertility and the buildings thereon. These buildings can be extended, refurbished, redecorated or reconstructed from the ground up. Many are rented out under lucrative licensing arrangements and, although the precise value of such properties is hard to estimate, that hasn't stopped people trying. Just as estate agents have a pretty fair idea of prevailing house prices, so too branding consultants spend much time and energy calculating the value of the world's leading brands (Think Box 2).

--- **THINK BOX 2** ---

Valuing Brands

Powerful brands are treasure troves, horns of plenty, pots of gold. They are exceptionally valuable corporate assets. More often than not they are included on the balance sheet of the company that owns them. They are bought and sold like any other assets. Bidding battles, such as the recent acquisition of SAB Miller by AB InBev – monster brewers both – are as much about brand ownership as tangible assets like production plants and distribution facilities. Brands and analogous intellectual properties may be intangible, but they are much more valuable, for the most part, than bricks and mortar and the machines that make them.

Unsurprisingly, a great deal of time and attention has been devoted to 'brand equity', calculating the precise value of brands. Like any property, brands are only worth what people are prepared to pay for them. However, several well-established techniques are employed to estimate the financial value of brands. As Lindemann explains, these historically comprise cost-based approaches, consumer-led approaches, price-premium approaches and approaches predicated on the net present value of future expected earnings. More recent innovations include process-orientated approaches (for service sector and B2B brands, mainly) and network-focused approaches (for brand alliances, joint ventures, etc.).

The nitty-gritty of the various schools of thought is less important for present purposes than the simple fact that there are many, many ways of calculating brand equity and equally many consultancy firms which possess proprietary procedures for doing so. Their much-publicized lists of 'Top 100 Brands' often fail to agree, either in relation to the rankings or in terms of the calculated values. Intel, Olins observes, 'is given 8th, 19th and 49th place depending on whose ratings are consulted. Disney is listed as 13th by Interbrand, 43rd by BrandZ and 50th by Brand Finance. Samsung, meanwhile, romps home in 9th, 55th and 6th place respectively.' ... 'No wonder,' he concludes, 'some of us are a little bit sceptical.'[10]

(Continued)

(Continued)

Scepticism notwithstanding and imprecision aside, studies show that brands on average account for more than one-third of shareholder value. This rises to 40% for IBM, 50% for Mercedes and 70% for McDonald's. Little wonder the CEO of Quaker Oats once said, 'If this business were to be split up, I would be glad to take the brands, trademarks and goodwill and you can have all the bricks and mortar – and I would fare better than you.' This statement was considered shocking in its day but few would disagree nowadays.

Thinking Outside the Think Box

Mark Ritson, a distinguished academic, is an outspoken critic of brand valuation. Go online and dig out his blistering articles and speeches. Do you agree with him or is he exaggerating the case for effect?

This preoccupation with property values, however, doesn't reflect the broader interpretation of 'branding' that now prevails. These days, the b-word is employed by police forces, art galleries, utility companies, government departments, NGO quangos, and all sorts of professional service providers from doctors, dentists, designers and divorce lawyers to architects, accountants, archaeologists and archbishops. Branding, what's more, is studied by an ever-widening array of academic disciplines, each with their own angles, agendas, arguments. There are countless thousands of consultancy firms that provide bespoke branding advice, all with their signature tools, techniques and terminologies. There isn't a middle manager in the country who can't pontificate about branding, since brand talk is no longer confined to the marketing department. Consumers too are becoming fluent in 'Brandsperanto', as someone or other once described it.[11] They are exposed to brand chatter in newspapers, magazines, radio programmes, television series and pop songs – rap is replete with brand name-dropping – not to mention mega-selling books by crusading journalists, such as Naomi Klein's *No Logo*, which was a big hit at the beginning of the millennium.[12] So much so, she trademarked the No Logo logo.

As if that weren't enough, another bestselling book by Rachel Greenwald maintains that women who want to find a husband should act like brands and thereby attract the man of their dreams. Segment the market. Develop a USP. Package the product. Promote it in the right places. Turn yourself into a brand worth buying. And so on.[13] Some people might be appalled by Greenwald's antediluvian advice – at least she doesn't recommend giving the customer what he wants – but her hugely successful book is an example of how branding has penetrated most areas of modern life.

The upshot of all this is that the language of branding has proliferated. We don't just talk about brands and branding anymore. We talk about brand audits, brand assets, brand alliances, brand elements, brand essences, brand extensions, brand images, brand identities, brand inventories, brand communities, brand categories, brand concepts. And many more besides. The discourse of branding is a bit like an invasive species. It is the grey squirrel, the cane toad, the kudzu grass, the giant hogweed of 21st century society. Near enough. The meanings of the word have multiplied. It means whatever people want it to mean. It means one thing in Titanic Belfast – the Biggest Brand Museum in the World – and another thing at the head office of Harland & Wolff, less than 500 metres away.

Even esteemed branding specialists, authorities, gurus and what have you can't make up their minds. Yes, they all attempt to define the b-word, often opaquely it has to be said. However their definitions differ dramatically, as Think Box 3 demonstrates. According to the American Marketing Association, the most prestigious professional body in its field, a brand is 'a name, term, sign or design, or a combination of them, intended to identify the goods and services of one seller or group of sellers and to differentiate them from those of competitors'.[14] Pick the bones out of that one.

THINK BOX 3

What is a Brand?[15]

- A brand is any label that carries meaning and associations (*Kotler*).
- A brand is a name and or symbol that is directly used to sell products or services (*Miller and Muir*).
- The most valuable piece of real estate in the world, a corner of someone's mind (*Hegarty*).
- Simply a collection of perceptions held in the mind of the consumer (*Fournier*).
- Brands are a shorthand way of encapsulating what a product is, and what it offers (*Fletcher*).
- The organization of tangible elements that results in a manifestation of a considered plan (*Conley*).
- Brands are relationships (*Schultz and Schultz*).
- A brand is a promise of an experience (*Adams*).
- The packaging of emotion (*Davis*).
- Brands are demonstrably the most important and sustainable asset for any organization (*Hales*).
- Everything that people know about, think about or feel about anything (*Fanning*).
- A brand is a popular idea or set of ideas that people live by (*Grant*).
- A profound manifestation of the human condition (*Olins*).
- The sum of all the parts of a business, product or organization (*Edge and Milligan*).
- A product so desired that a customer would leave a supermarket if it wasn't in stock and go elsewhere for it (*O'Reilly*).

(Continued)

(Continued)

- Brands are there to rescue people from the tyranny of choice (*Taylor*).
- A brand is something you have an unexplained emotional connection to (*Duncan*).
- A product or service plus values and associations (*Edwards and Day*).
- A brand is the semiotic enterprise of the firm, the companion spirit of the firm, a hologram of the firm (*Sherry*).

Thinking Outside the Think Box

Leslie de Chernatony once analysed dozens of definitions and divided them into three basic categories: input, output and time. Read Leslie's interpretation and apply his categories to the above attempts. Do they fit neatly? If not, why not?

Another frequently quoted definition is that of Leslie de Chernatony, a British branding expert and author of several influential books on the subject. He states that a brand is 'an identifiable product, service, person or place, augmented in such a way that the buyer or user perceives relevant and unique added values which match their needs most closely'.[16] Run that past me again.

In fairness to Leslie, the Linnaeus of branding, his attempted definition is admirably comprehensive. It tries to cover all the bases. Other experts are less assiduous. Most opt for aphorisms, the quirkier the better. As students soon discover when they read around the subject, just about everyone who writes about branding feels obliged to come up with a snappy definition, a clever quip, a tweet-worthy epigram. A brand, apparently, is a 'bond', a 'promise', a 'relationship', a 'conversation', a 'prism', a 'pyramid', a 'manifold', an 'onion', a 'gestalt', a 'symbol used to sell', a 'commodity with personality', a 'corner of the customer's mind', a 'label that carries meaning', a 'description of a thing', a 'gut feeling about a product', an 'idea to live by', and 'everything that people know about, think about or feel about anything'. Huh?

Better yet is Jeff Bezos's much-quoted definition of branding. According to the laugh-a-minute boss of Amazon, the mighty online retailer, a brand is 'what people say about you when you aren't in the room'. In his case, I suspect most people are either saying 'How do you pronounce Bezos?' or 'Pay your taxes like the rest of us, Amazon!'

As Think Box 3 indicates, there's an awful lot of blarney in branding. But this doesn't mean that branding is meaningless. Most people, as noted earlier, have a fairly good idea of what brands are, and branding is, if only because the words are flung around so much nowadays. The media likewise make liberal use of them, though they tend to interpret brands and branding in terms of 'look and feel', as do many old-school managers. Alan Sugar, for example, frequently asks his would-be apprentices to create 'brands' of cat food, fruit juice or breakfast cereal. By this he means an attention-grabbing name, an eye-catching package and a toe-curling slogan of excruciating illiteracy. Once again, though, there's more to it than that. Branding isn't just about visual form or clever wordplay. While the look, the logo, the livery, the slogan and so on are crucial, they're not the be all and end all of branding.

Branding, at bottom, is a bit like obscenity. It is easy to recognize but difficult to define. It's a tricky business, albeit an endlessly fascinating one.[17]

WHY BOTHER WITH BRANDING?

Rather than search fruitlessly for a definitive definition of brands and branding – a personal favourite is 'making customers an offer they can't confuse'[18] – it is more productive to focus on *why*. Why do companies and organizations brand their products and services? What advantages come from doing so? What's in it for them?

The principal purpose of branding is to distinguish the goods or services of one producer-provider from the goods or services of all the others in the same class, category or sector. Its competitors, in other words. Branding differentiates. Branding separates. Branding reduces consumers' confusion. It makes life easier for them. It saves consumers time at the supermarket, where there are typically 30,000 competing products to choose from. It likewise lowers the risk of making a bad decision, because big-name brands stand behind their products. Consumers know that Pampers, Persil, Heinz or Hellmann's won't let them down. Or, if they do, a replacement will be forthcoming without any fuss, and with profuse apologies. Customers are aware that customer satisfaction is important to reputable companies and so they learn to trust, adopt and return to dependable brands. As Conley rightly observes:

> Brands offer us mental shortcuts, helping us cut through the clutter of everything we buy ... No one wants to sift through tens of thousands of packaged foods on every trip to the supermarket. Instead, we rely on the brands we know. And branding, when it's consistent, provides us with clarity and simplicity in a progressively hectic world.[19]

In addition to providing convenient shortcuts for busy people with short attention spans and limited time to shop, many brands perform a symbolic function. They are signalling devices. They help consumers show off. They are bling things. They serve as indicators of our exquisite taste, social standing and financial resources. The BMW 7 series, the Louboutin killer heels, the latest 'it' bag by Fendi, the made-to-measure Paul Smith suit, the look-at-me T-shirt from Abercrombie & Fitch, the black 'Centurion' American Express card or the holiday home in Tuscany, Mustique or the Hamptons, are widely understood announcements of who and what we are. They are badges of distinction, emblems of self-expression, markers of meaning that help us stand out from the crowd.[20]

According to Kapferer, a leading marketing authority, brands are the civilian counterpart of military insignia. They are signifiers of consumers' rank, position and place in the pecking order.[21] According to Thompson, an expert on the branding of popular culture, brands are 'a mark of distinction', especially in emerging economies where possessions express sophistication.[22] According to evolutionary psychologists like Miller, brands are the human equivalent of peacocks' tails, signals of health, wealth and good genes. They are the things that determine sexual attraction and selection in 21st century consumer society.[23] Though Tinder might beg to differ.

More to the point, building a brand is beneficial for the businesses behind them.[24] Studies show that powerful brands command premium prices, which simultaneously serve as indicators of quality (Stella Artois – Reassuringly Expensive). Outstanding brands act as a barrier to entry, in that it's difficult for competitors to penetrate the market, much less capture it (cola-flavoured drinks aren't hard to make but competing against Coke or Pepsi is far from easy, as Virgin once discovered). A successful brand can be readily extended into new product categories (Carlsberg, the legendary Danish lager, has recently expanded into the male grooming market – probably – with a range of beer-imbued personal care products including shampoo, conditioner and body lotion), new countries (Zara, the Spanish fast fashion retailer, has outlets in Ecuador, Peru, Taiwan, Tunisia, Thailand and eighty other nations) or new categories and countries both (Manchester United sells a wide range of Red Devils' branded products in dedicated stores all over the world). Highly regarded brands also find it easier to attract and retain talented employees (who wouldn't want to work for Nike or Netflix or Nintendo?), to say nothing of suppliers, distributors, shareholders, stakeholders and so on, all of whom benefit by association.

THE BRAND GRENADE

Such benefits, in truth, tend to exist more in theory than in practice. The conventional wisdom that brands command premium prices is questionable in an era of price-bashing branding behemoths like JD Sports, T.K. Maxx and Poundland. The first of these sells a vast range of famous sporting labels – Puma, Dunlop, Lonsdale, Slazenger, etc. – at a very deep discount. The latter two do likewise in apparel and general merchandise respectively.

Conley's 'mental shortcut' argument is equally questionable these days. Far from reducing consumer confusion, brands often add to it by colonizing every category under the sun. Amazon, for example, started off selling cut-price books by telephone. Look at it now. Google used to be a plain and simple search engine. Recently renamed Alphabet, today's Google boggles the mind. EasyJet once sold low-fare flights to foreign fields. The 'easy' prefix has since been applied to food shops, financial services, pizza delivery, car hire, hotels, cinemas, gyms and buses, to name but a few.

In this regard, there are many horror stories of brands that extended too far and damaged their reputations or ventured into foreign markets only to make a mess of things. Harley-Davidson infamously entered into a host of unedifying licensing arrangements, where its legendary logo and name were attached to anything and everything from underarm deodorant to cake decorating kits. Kellogg's may be one of the most iconic brands in the world but that didn't cut much ice in India, where cereal- and milk-based breakfasts are contrary to cultural and culinary norms. Dasani water, a leading American beverage, launched its brand in Britain with the aid of its US-centric slogan. 'Bottled Spunk' carries slightly different connotations on this side of the Atlantic. UK sales, unsurprisingly, were somewhat underwhelming.

Branding, as the Dasani debacle demonstrates, is a hit and miss affair. Brands can blow up in your face. And often do. Hardly a week goes by without a branding mis-judgement of one kind or another.[25] A couple of years ago, the apparel retailer Gap updated its logo. Many customers of the popular clothing store were infuriated by the sudden loss of the familiar blue box. They soon made their feelings known on social networking platforms. The new look was derided as amateurish and unimaginative. Some even suggested it was a hoax, a joke, a cheap publicity stunt. Suitably chastened, Gap backed down and reverted to its original livery.

In New Zealand, the city of Auckland decided to brand itself with the so-called Big A. The plan was to increase civic pride by persuading inhabitants to salute each other with a hand signal in the shape of the letter A, which was made by joining the thumbs and fingers of both hands. Unfortunately, the signal was identical to the international deaf language sign for AIDS and akin to a singularly offensive gesture directed at women. Irate residents promptly adopted another universally recognized hand signal to anoint the advertising agency behind Auckland's ill-considered branding behaviour.

Critics of a similar disposition came out in force when the brand mascots for the London Olympics were unveiled in May 2010. An unprepossessing pair of personi-fied steel ingots, Wenlock and Mandeville were greeted with universal disdain. The hapless mascots were variously described as 'partially blinded Teletubbies', 'rejects from a Pixar spin-off', 'giant mutated phalluses' and, according to the *Toronto Star* newspaper, 'terrifying one-eyed penis monsters'. Apart from that, everyone loved the little tykes, though the tie-in merchandising featuring their frighteningly phallic faces didn't sell as well as the organizers anticipated, curiously enough.

Such examples are far from unusual. Companies consistently abandon common sense when it comes to branding. Even the biggest brands in the world get things wrong. Way back in 1985, for instance, Coca-Cola shook up their iconic brand. They withdrew the original vanilla-flavoured product and replaced it with a sweeter for-mulation called New Coke. American consumers went berserk. Denied a much-loved national treasure, the entire US population (near enough) rose up against the offend-ers. The Coca-Cola corporation was accused of treason, betrayal, irresponsibility and committing the commercial equivalent of spitting in Uncle Sam's face then kicking him in the *cojones*. Less than three months later, Coca-Cola backtracked on its multi-million dollar reformulation and reintroduced the original flavour, with heartfelt apologies for their error of judgement. To this day, some people think it was a marketing gimmick, because the company's sales rebounded thereafter. If so, New Coke must go down as the most expensive publicity stunt in history.[26]

Stunt or not, the brute reality of branding is that it is challenging. Challenging in a good way. Despite what Alan Sugar seems to believe, it isn't easy to build a brand. Slapping a logo on something and calling it a brand is a one-way ticket to oblivion. Branding takes persistence, patience and not a little perspicacity. But when it works, when it clicks, when it all comes together, 'branding is the most fun you can have in business'.[27]

TOO MUCH MUCH-OF-A-MUCHNESS

The intriguing thing about branding today is that it is becoming increasingly challenging, yet at the same time ever more important. The reasons for this are twofold. In the first instance, there are more and more products and services competing for customers, in every conceivable category of goods. The choice of toothbrushes or tissues or toasters or televisions or tumble driers, or tablet PCs or training shoes or tennis rackets or tea towels or tablecloths or trampolines or treadmills or trouser presses or theme parks or travel agents or Twitter streams or tongue scrapers is vast. And getting vaster by the day. Second, there is very little to choose between the various toothbrushes, toasters, torches, televisions, and the like. They are all pretty good. They do the job. They are, to all intents and purposes, functionally indistinguishable. As the novelist Jonathan Coe wryly notes about Britain's surfeit of identikit stand-up comedians:

> He opened the package from Amazon which his overworked postman had delivered earlier. It contained two DVDs, which bore a striking resemblance to one another. The cover of the first showed a young, tousled, slightly overweight white man wearing a loose brightly coloured shirt, untucked at the trouser. He was talking into a microphone ... The cover of the second showed another young, tousled, slightly overweight white man wearing a loose brightly coloured shirt, untucked at the trouser. He too was talking into a microphone.[28]

This observation does not mean that there are *no* differences between stand-ups or indeed DVDs or digital cameras or coffee makers or cosmetic surgeons or detox clinics or price comparison websites, never mind tongue scrapers. Marketers have long distinguished between downmarket, upmarket and midmarket brands in the same product category. Nevertheless, in strictly functional or performance terms, it's worthwhile posing the following questions: Is your £3,000 Hermès Birkin bag really *one hundred times* better at holding your bits and pieces than a cheap and cheerful handbag from H&M? Is your vintage Omega wristwatch really *seventy-five times* better at telling the time than my seen-better-days Sekonda? Is the ride in your brand new S-class Mercedes really *thirty times better* than that in my clapped-out Citroën C3?

It probably is, come to think of it. Okay, I'll give you that one ...

The key point here is not that price premiums are hard to justify in performance terms, but that one of the principal purposes of branding is to persuade consumers that functionally identical products and services *aren't* as identical as they appear to be. Irrespective of the category – be it eggs, sausages, bacon, body wash, face cream, hairdryers, energy drinks, electric kettles, washing machines, laptop computers, mobile phones, microwave ovens, credit cards, insurance policies, small family hatchbacks, low-cost airlines or computer chip-controlled tongue scrapers – the main aim of branding is to separate the inseparable, differentiate the identikit, make the similar dissimilar and pull almost indistinguishable products ever-further apart in consumers' minds. As Russell Hanlin, the CEO of Sunkist, once observed, 'An orange is an orange is an orange ... unless that orange happens to be Sunkist, a name 80% of consumers know and trust.'[29]

So, how do brand managers do it? How do they persuade consumers that identical oranges aren't the same? How do they convince consumers that *their* oranges are much better than other oranges? So much better, in fact, that consumers are prepared to pay a 10%, 20%, 50% or even 100% price premium for them?

Well, they paint consumers a picture. They tell consumers a story. They inform consumers that their oranges are more fresh, more ripe, more tasty, more tangy, more healthy, more vitamin filled, more environmentally-friendly (no nasty pesticides), more socially responsible (growers get a fair price), more lovingly cultivated (because the best fertilizer by far is L-U-R-V-E) than all the other unloved and unlovely oranges on sale in the friendly neighbourhood supermarket or farmers' market stall with its faux-organic offerings.

Now, some of you might say you'd never fall for such hyperbole. That's your prerogative. However, the evidence indicates that there's nothing as powerful as a good story well told.[30] And successful brands are nothing if not good storytellers, as we shall see in due course.

WATER, WATER EVERYWHERE

For now, it's sufficient to note that branding works. MRI scans of consumers' brains show that branded versions of products like cola beat unbranded equivalents hands down, even when the actual drinks being tested are identical.[31] Scientifically conducted studies of classic French wines reveal that the label *really does* make a difference to the perceived quality of the beverages people imbibe, even those who consider themselves connoisseurs.[32]

If oenophiles don't convince you, reflect on the world's biggest and most brilliantly successful brand: Apple. By common consent the coolest, hottest, most marketing savvy brand bar none, Apple has had more than its fair share of disasters. It launched the iPhone 5 with much-ballyhooed Touch ID fingerprint identification, a pretty neat feature that bypassed the need for annoying passcodes. Unfortunately, all it took to hack the system was 'a fingerprint photographed from a glass surface or scanned on an everyday office printer'.[33] And then, of course, there was the 'bendgate' issue with the iPhone 6, which was wont to warp. And then there was the 'antennagate' problem with the iPhone 4, where the signal got lost if it was held in a ham-fisted way.

And as for the Apple Watch, it too is stricken with issues: complicated to set up, difficult to recharge, drains the iPhone battery, wristbands don't lock and can cause irritation, tattoos on the user's arm or wrist adversely affect its performance and, in order to get the little screen to light up, exaggerated arm and hand movements are sometimes required. The inhabitants of Auckland, thankfully, are well placed in that regard. Provided they don't have tattoos.

But, did any of this damage the iPhone brand? Not really. If anything, it increased consumers' adoration. Imperfections are endearing in iconic brands.[34] Even the recent revelation that Tesco's Hudl, a cheap-as-chips tablet, not only outperforms the latest iPad Air but outperforms it by a considerable margin on every imaginable dimension from speed to screen resolution, doesn't make a blind bit of difference to Apple's all-conquering dominion. As Interbrand's annual calculation of brand value makes clear, Apple is the most valuable brand on the planet at present, ahead of Google, Coca-Cola, Microsoft and the once imperious IBM.

Should further proof be required, look no further than the market for bottled water. In the western world, there is no need to buy bottled water. The mains supplies are perfectly adequate. They are often superior to the stuff sold in plastic bottles. Blind taste tests reveal that consumers can't tell the difference between tap water and bottled water. Yet the market for the latter is ginormous and getting bigger by the year. Water bottling is damaging for the environment, what's more, both in terms of depleted aquifers and the costs of packaging, distributing, refrigerating and disposing of purportedly 'recyclable' containers. According to Gleick, bottled water is one thousand times more expensive, on average, than the public supply in America and Western Europe.[35] It's more expensive, pro rata, than petroleum. Some brands give Chanel No 5 a run for its money. The morality of drinking such stuff when millions of people in the developing world go without, is debatable to say the least.

Even more pertinently from our perspective, branded bottled water is sold at a wide variety of price points. These range from the economical own-label brands at your local Tesco Express, through heavily advertised midmarket brands like Evian, Volvic, Vittel, Badoit, Perrier and San Pellegrino, all the way up to eye-wateringly expensive brands like Fiji (beloved by Hollywood A-listers), 90H20 (beloved by wannabe Hollywood A-listers), ARTY (painstakingly extracted from Californian artichokes) and Finé (sourced from groundwater beneath Japan's Mount Fuji).

In addition, there are countless speciality brands of ultra-premium-priced 'enhanced' water. Examples include diet water, vitamin water, medicinal water, magnetized water, oxygenated water, sports performance water and spiritually uplifting water like the celebrated Kabbalah brand beloved by Madonna and Britney Spears. The beverages are functionally indistinguishable. The price differences defy belief. Branding is the reason that these differences are sustainable. Although the spread of branded water prices seems to have narrowed since the great recession – consumers, presumably, are wising up – there's still a vast gulf between Sainsbury's own-label spring water and 80 Degrees North Iceberg Water. The latter is 'harvested from chunks of icebergs formed over 15,000 years ago in the Arctic polar icecaps, which have been locked away safely and therefore untouched by pollutants and toxins created by civilisation'.

Do you think Captain Smith of the *Titanic* would buy a story like that? Probably. He fell for the one about the unsinkable ship, don't forget.

BRAND TASK

Reflect on your own consumption of bottled water. Or non-consumption, as the case may be. What way do you take your water? What brand, or brands, do you prefer? Why is that? Has it always been that way? Write a little biographical note about your relationship with water in general and brands of bottled water in particular.

RECOMMENDED READINGS

John F. Sherry, 'Brand Meaning', in A.M. Tybout and T. Calkins, eds., *Kellogg on Branding* (John Wiley: New York, 2005, 40–69). Sherry is one of the best writers around and this chapter on branding is as good an introduction to the subject as you'll find among the outpourings of academia.

Jan Lindemann, 'Brand Valuation', in R. Clifton and J. Simmons, *Brands and Branding* (Bloomberg Press: Princeton, NJ, 2003, 27–45). The entire book is worth reading, but Lindemann's chapter on the valuation of brands is an especially clear summary of a complex branding issue.

Lucas Conley, *OBD: Obsessive Branding Disorder* (PublicAffairs: New York, 2008). Sometimes the best books on a topic are written by those with an axe to grind. A journalist for *Fast Company*, Conley is no fan of branding. However, his insights are never less than astute.

Richard Wilk, 'Bottled Water: The Pure Commodity in the Age of Branding', *Journal of Consumer Culture*, 6 (3), 2006, 303–325. Richard Wilk is a cultural anthropologist who often writes on marketing, branding and consumer behaviour. This is a particularly eloquent article on the politics of bottled water.

PART I
COMPONENTS

CHAPTER 2
BRAND NAMES MATTER

Overview

Brands are made up of ten key components. The first and most fundamental of these is the name. Naming may seem like a trivial thing but, partly on account of legal considerations, it can prove quite complicated. All sorts of brand names exist, from the simple descriptive (Sofa.com) to the strange (Mojang) and charmed (Elf). This chapter brings order to the confusion and explains where brand names come from.

THE NAME GAME

Way back in the early days of the internet, a New York merchant banker took a punt on the future of the 'information superhighway'. He quit his job in the Big Apple and drove west while working up a business plan for an online retail operation. He didn't know what category of products to sell. But he was determined to sell something through this new-fangled channel of distribution. After weighing up the options, the banker finally settled on books. And, by the time he got to Seattle, he'd come up with a cute name for his bookselling dotcom: Cadabra.

Cadabra's cuteness came partly from its derivation, the much-loved fairytale word 'abracadabra'. It also benefitted from its initial consonant, the magic 'k' sound that's integral to many memorable brand names including Kinko's, Kit-Kat, Krispy Kreme, Coca-Cola, Calvin Klein, the Kardashian Kollection and kountless others. The only problem was that when potential investors, suppliers or customers telephoned the start-up, they misheard the company's name as 'cadaver'. Clearly, there's a world of difference between Cadaver.com and Cadabra.com, though the former might work quite well for sellers of body parts, embalming fluid and autopsy equipment. Chastened by his cadaverous encounter, the former merchant banker promptly changed the name of the brand to Amazon.com. The rest is history.[1]

Jeff Bezos is just one among many. The history of branding is riddled with stories about badly chosen or near-miss brand names. The mighty company we now know as Apple was almost given the unprepossessing brand name Executech. And Matrix Electronics was another serious contender. The great glorious giant that goes by the name Google was initially called BackRub. However its founders, Sergey Brin and Larry Page, feared it might get mistaken for a porn site, so they rapidly backed off BackRub. At a loss for a name that captured the essence of his social media site, Noah Glass gave due consideration to Throb, Vibrate, Tremble, Quickly and FriendStalker, before settling on the rather less salacious term Twitter. No such anguish beset the legendary Ralph Lauren. He knew only too well that he had to change his surname if he wanted to sell fashionable apparel. You might do the same if you were called Ralph Lifshitz.

Name changes, of course, are not unusual among celebrities, or those who aspire to celebrity status. Katheryn Hudson, Christopher Bridges, Margaret Hyra, Demetria Guynes and Shawn Corey Carter, to name but a few, are better known as Katy Perry, Ludacris, Meg Ryan, Demi Moore and Jay-Z respectively. Classic works of popular culture often get new names along the way. The movie *Pretty Woman* was originally called *3,000*, Orwell's novel *1984* began life as *The Last Man in Europe*, and The Smiths' classic album *The Queen is Dead* once went by the even more alarming *Margaret on the Guillotine*. Unpleasantly named species of fish, such as Slimehead, Mud Bug and Pollock, are routinely rebranded to make them more palatable to consumers, as are towns, cities, countries and colleges *à la* Beaver University, Pennsylvania, which was renamed Arcadia U. in 2001.[2] But you already knew that.

But did you know that Netflix was originally called Kibble? Or that the Barbie doll is named after a German sex worker? Or that the timeless Swatch watch, which originally went by the tremulous moniker Delirium Tremens, was released under the demeaning name Vulgaris? Or that Phil Knight, former athlete and distributor of Tiger sneakers in the US, came up with a terrific name for his own brand of training shoes: Fourth Dimension. In the event, he was outvoted by the fledgling company's 48 employees, all of whom had thrown naming suggestions into a hat. The winner was Nike. Phil wasn't very happy with the decision but he had to live with it.[3] He wasn't best pleased with the swoosh logo either, which was designed for $35 by local art college student Carolyn Davidson. That's another story, though.

WHAT'S IN A NAME?

Rather a lot is the answer to that one. Most authorities agree that names are the most important component part of a brand. They aren't the only component, as we shall see, but they are a crucial one. According to Morris, they are 'the key to a company's fortune'.[4] For Blackett, the name provides 'enormous competitive advantage and is a powerful marketing tool'.[5] Danesi, a Canadian semiotician, contends that they are 'primary constituents in the product's signification system'.[6] Al Ries, the world famous branding guru, sagaciously observes that 'the most important decision you can make is what to name the product'.[7] An eminent consultant from Interbrand likewise confirms that 'this wee little thing is arguably the most important element of the branding mix'.[8] His American counterpart concurs:

> In the process of branded product development, the selection of a name can be the most creative and the most critical part of the process. If your brand name is distinctive and memorable, it can and will make the difference in winning at the shelf. It can and will make a major contribution to the longevity of the overall concept. It can and will make your advertising dollars work harder, and it will create more attention and provide more value to your consumer.[9]

So there you have it, names are the bees' knees of branding. There are several reasons for this. The most significant and perhaps the most obvious one is: 'where would we be without them?' If we didn't have names for things they'd be very difficult to tell apart. The first thing we do with new-born babies is give them names. Names that distinguish them from all the other new-borns and give notice that they are separate, clearly identifiable individuals. Indeed, if you share a name – as I do – with someone famous or infamous you'll know only too well that names matter.[10]

Names, furthermore, are the often the first point of contact for many consumers. They are the portal through which people encounter brands, Kapferer claims, thanks to the word-of-mouth recommendations of friends and relatives.[11] Engaging names, like Build a Bear, can draw biddable consumers into their orbit or, conversely, give them serious pause for thought, as in the case of Screaming Sphincter, an extra hot chilli sauce.[12]

There's also a more practical reason why names are vital. They tend to remain unchanged. All the other parts of the branding mix are updated on a regular basis – logos get tweaked, packaging is refreshed, slogans are replaced, prices are slashed and the management is purged on a fairly regular basis. But names, by and large, stay put. Ford, Shell, Philips, Heinz, Bayer, Persil, Pears, Chanel and Levi Strauss, for example, are more than a century old. Their longevity adds to the product's allure.

True, names *do* get changed from time to time, often as a consequence of corporate mergers (e.g. Orange to EE) or a global brand's desire to coordinate its activities across multiple markets (Ulay to Olay). For the most part, though, they're retained. Not least because loyal consumers can get very, *very* upset when a familiar brand is renamed. To this day, consumers complain about Marathon, a popular chocolate bar, which was renamed Snickers in 1990. For many well-bred Brits, the new name carried unfortunate connotations of ladies' underwear. There was no telling them that Snickers was the name of the brand owner's racehorse. There's no telling fans of

Hull City football club either, who bitterly oppose the proposed name change to Hull Tigers. So much so, some carry protest banners to home games claiming Hull City AFC is 'A Club Not a Brand'.

Another reason why names matter relates to litigation. Trade names, as noted in chapter 1, are ordinarily registered with the IPO. And any brand that infringes on a legally-protected name can be – and often is – litigated against. The courts are full of ongoing battles over brand names. Budweiser and Budweiser slugged it out with each other for decades until the giant American brewer bought a Czech upstart that shared its name.[13] Liverpool's Cavern Club and The Hard Rock Café are having a hard day's night over the rights to the name of The Beatles' musical birthplace. A brand of tongue-in-cheek toys called Haute Diggity Dog, whose spoof products include Chewy Vuiton, Dog Perignon, Jimmy Chews, Furcedes, Starbarks and Chewnel Number 5, soon discovered that the legal team at Louis Vuitton didn't share their sense of humour. And the one and only World Wildlife Fund once went head to head – *Kung Fu Panda*-style – with the World Wrestling Federation for the rights to the initials WWF.

Face-offs and smack-downs notwithstanding, the key consideration used to determine infringement is consumer confusion. If the courts believe that the names are sufficiently similar to bewilder buyers of the brand being infringed, then the copycat is ruled illegal. The advent of search engines, which enable legal eagles to identify name-nappers more easily than before, has been a godsend to our learned friends.[14] As someone who once tangled with Harry Potter's people, I know whereof I speak.[15]

WHICH NAMES WORK BEST?

Harry Potter is a terrific brand name. It comprises two two-syllable words with twin letters. It trips off the tongue, as do many of the fabulous fictional brand names in Rowling's fantastic books. Names like Fizzing Whizbees, Canary Creams, Cockroach Clusters, Ogden's Old Firewhisky, Sleekeazy Hair Potion, Dr Ubbly's Oblivious Unction and the incomparable Bertie Bott's Beans. But what, many wonder, makes a good brand name?

Well, according to the prestigious *New Yorker* magazine, the best brand names are profoundly poetic.[16] They compress a range of resonant meanings and evocative associations into one or two words. Elizabeth Arden, for example, was born Florence Nightingale Graham in a small town outside Toronto, but her pseudonymous brand of beauty products got its euphonious name from an artful blend of Good Queen Bess, a monarch who wore makeup, and *As You Like It*, Shakespeare's crowd-pleaser play set in the Forest of Arden.[17]

Zeiss is likewise much loved by photography aficionados and knowledgeable brandmeisters, not least on account of its expressive name. As one of them artfully observes:

Does Zeiss make great lenses? Who knows? But the name makes the lenses 'sound' great. The word 'Zeiss' has hits of 'glass' and 'precise', and evokes thoughts of German technological superiority. The name works so well that it can stretch to include high-end sunglasses and other precision products without the risk of breaking.[18]

Viagra is even better. According to Frankel, the letters *vi-* stand for vitality, vigour and virility; *-agra* means to catch or grasp; and *Viagra* has connotations of Niagara, a place with a prodigiously powerful waterfall that was once a popular destination for newlyweds. More than that, though:

Viagra had the feeling of an older name, one that called to mind Italian frescoes and the marketplace – the Greek agora. It is not jarring but familiar-sounding, in the same way that the scents imbued in fabric softeners can make one subconsciously comprehend a springtime field of flowers that one had never actually seen or smelled. It's a subtle name, maybe that of a space-age aphrodisiac dropped off on earth by a set of roving aliens. It's a Trojan horse of words, ready to disgorge meaning if necessary.[19]

Apple is another outstanding moniker. Not only did it help the company stand out from the IT crowd. But the word carries all sorts of associations that add immeasurably to Apple's incredible allure. These include the association with childhood and schooling, bringing an apple for the teacher; the association with Sir Isaac Newton, who discovered gravity when an apple dropped on his head; and the association with Adam and Eve, picking an apple from the Tree of Knowledge then taking that fateful bite (as the brand's logo is testament). More than that, Johnson observes:

The deeper power of the name Apple comes from our everyday experiences with actual apples. They are, in a sense, the perfect consumer commodity: they're ubiquitous and inexpensive, you grasp them in your hand and literally consume them, and they're delicious. For almost everyone, they're old childhood friends: cut into little pieces and cooked into sauce for babies, put into school lunch boxes and toted around, and baked into pies. It's these deeply rooted sensory memories of apples that make Apple a great name. Nothing is more familiar, more accessible, and less intimidating than an apple.[20]

Much of this is retrospective rationalization. It's unlikely that Steve Jobs had such things in mind when he came up with the immortal, beloved A-word. A marketing genius he may have been, but his brand naming record was patchy at best. He wanted to call the Macintosh the Apple Bicycle, never forget, and the iMac was originally called Macman, a pitiful pun on Pacman, the pioneering video game. Still, Jobs' obsession with aesthetics – he studied calligraphy at college – encouraged others to take the art of branding more seriously, names included.

Nowadays there are books and websites aplenty on brand naming best practice. So we won't discuss the process at length.[21] Suffice it to say that exponents of phono-aesthetics delve deeply into onomatopoeia, sound symbolism and the nuances of language more generally. They tell us that rhyming brand names like Fitbit, Hobnobs, Hubba Bubba, Curly Wurly and Reese's Pieces are more persuasive than the great unrhymed; that alliterative brand names like Burt's Bees, Nobby's Nuts, Dunkin' Donuts, Circuit City and Shake Shack are pretty persuasive too; that 'k' is king when it comes to memorability (e.g. Costco, Kickers, Costa Coffee, Kall Kwik, Clarice Cliff, Cath Kidston, Kellogg's Corn Flakes, *Candy Crush Saga*); and that short names are better than long ones.

They also inform us of the strange but true 'name halo' effect.[22] This refers to people's propensity to buy brands that share their initials. That is to say, Tom is more likely to buy a Toyota than Jack, who is more inclined to lease a Jaguar than Mary, who is a serial Mazda owner and proud of it. A form of nominative determinism, where people's names reflect the jobs they do – such as Mr Salmon, the fishmonger, Mr Phibbs, the solicitor, William Wordsworth, the poet, Donald Trump, the casino impresario, Tom Kitchin, the Scottish restaurateur – the brand name halo effect is bizarre. But it exists.[23]

THE BIG PICTURE

The nuances of brand names are never less than fascinating and placing them under the microscope provides a steady income for many marketing consultants. Some, moreover, try to make sense of the big picture by studying the vast array of names that have been pressed into branding service. As far as Rivkin and Sutherland are concerned, brand names can be divided into three basic types: *descriptive*, *allusive* and *coined*.[24]

Descriptive names, do exactly what it says on the tin. They describe what the brand does. No more, no less. The Restaurant Group, as the name makes crystal clear, has a range of restaurants in its portfolio; 475 to be precise. These include well-known chains like Chiquito, Garfunkels, Coast to Coast and Frankie & Benny's, as well as a bunch of stand-alone gastro-pubs and coffee houses. All things considered, The Restaurant Group sums things up pretty well.

Consider also Cookie Box, Burger King, the Card Factory, Webuyanycar.com or The Country Garage, which is literally a big garage way out in the middle of the Irish countryside. A garage, mind you, that sells BMWs hand over fist, making it one of the brand's most successful dealerships in the British Isles.

Notonthehighstreet.com sells bespoke items that aren't available in high street stores. People Will Always Need Plates does something similar. The names tell us all we need to know.

Allusive brand names are proper words, such as Dove or Lynx. However, the words don't refer directly to the business the brand owner is in. They drop hints instead. They give consumers a sense, a rough idea, of what the brand's about. Visa, the credit card company, is a classic example. The word has no direct connection to matters financial, nor is it a stamp of approval that gets people past surly immigration officials. But a Visa card grants access, in its own way, to all sorts of desirable products, exotic places, upscale hotels, restaurants and retail stores.

Merlin Entertainments is an equally good example. Second only to Disney in its sector, Merlin operates more than one hundred themed attractions, including Madame Tussauds, London Dungeon, Alton Towers, Thorpe Park and Legoland, which deliver magical experiences to millions of holiday makers. The name captures that pretty successfully, though Cadabra would work just as well. Or maybe not ...

Mojang is another allusive brand name, though you need to be Swedish to appreciate what the makers of *Minecraft*, the massively popular computer game, are alluding to. It means something like 'thingamajig' or 'whatchamacallit'.

Coined names are new-to-the-world words, neologisms concocted by those responsible for the brand or by the ever-growing numbers of naming consultants. Without doubt, the best-known neologism in branding is Kodak. It was coined more than a century ago by George Eastman, the inventor of the beloved Box Brownie camera, who explained his nomenclatural rationale as follows:

> I knew a trade name must be short, vigorous, incapable of being misspelled to an extent that will destroy its identity and, in order to satisfy trademark laws, it must mean nothing. The letter K had been a favourite with me – it seemed a strong, incisive sort of letter. Therefore, the word I wanted had to start with K. Then it became a question of trying out a great number of combinations of letters that made words starting and ending with K. The word Kodak is the result.[25]

Pentium is almost on a par with Eastman's marvellous mashup. Created for Intel by Lexicon, the world's preeminent naming agency, Pentium is the brand name given to the company's 586 (and subsequent) microprocessors. *Pente* means five in Greek, as in pentagram, so that was a natural starting point for Lexicon's wonderful word wranglers. However, it was the phoneme 'ium', sourced from the Periodic Table of the Elements, that turned out to be the key ingredient. At the time, admittedly, one of Intel's executives disdainfully declared that Pentium 'sounds like a toothpaste'. Few people take that view nowadays:

> Pentium, Pentium! That is a great word ... Let me just list a few things I think about when I hear Pentium. It sounds like it's out of a James Bond movie. It feels hard and elemental. It sounds like some rare element, something that can be found on the periodic table of the elements alongside titanium and selenium. It's like some substance that has to be mined in Africa and sells for $500 an ounce. It gleams.[26]

ZzzQuil is pretty good too. It's the name of a sleeping tablet made by P&G, itself a resonant brand name.

THE Ps AND Qs OF BRAND NAMES

The DAC classification of brand names is fine as far as it goes. But a threefold division into *Descriptive*, *Allusive* and *Coined* doesn't go very far. It fails to capture the full spectrum of branding possibilities. So here's something more useful, something that's easy to remember when examination time rolls round. It's an eight-category typology consisting of four words beginning with the letter P and four starting with the letter Q. The Ps consist of brands named after *People*, *Places*, *Products* and what I call *Pacts*. The Qs comprise *Quaint*, *Quant*, *Quirks* and *Quips*. Stand back and form a circle while I explain how to mind your Ps and Qs.

People

According to a study of the top 100 brands in the world, more than half are named after people. These include Disney, McDonald's, Kellogg's, Heineken, Heinz, Mercedes-Benz, Harley-Davidson, Procter & Gamble, Goldman Sachs, Morgan Stanley, Merrill Lynch, L'Oréal, Lidl, Pfizer and lots, lots more. Eponyms are especially common in the luxury goods sector – Chanel, Gucci, Pucci, Prada, Louis Vuitton, Tommy Hilfiger, Tom Ford, Donna Karan – where they carry connotations of master craftsmen, the creative artiste herself, busy at work in an untidy atelier. It's also the norm in professional services like lawyers, architects, merchant bankers and advertising agencies, where long strings of surnames such as Tragos, Bonnange, Wiesendanger and Ajroldi (TWBA) have become something of a standing joke within the industry. They're no less common among local butchers, neighbourhood bakers, and bespoke candlestick makers, as well as the white van men and women of this world (Fred Bloggs Builders, Paula Peters Plumbers, Mark Sparks Electrician, Joe Doe Painting and Decorating).

Familiar family-favourites like Birdseye, Tupperware, Tresemmé, Toblerone, Chevrolet, Hallmark, Mars and Biro are also named after their founders, though most consumers seem to have forgotten the connection. The same can't be said about brands built around superstar celebrities like David and Victoria Beckham or Maria Sharapova, whose own-brand candy collection 'Sugarpova' caused consternation among advocates of healthy eating. Fictional characters are fodder for the branding machine, furthermore. Uncle Ben, Aunt Jemima, Dr Pepper, Captain Morgan and John Hollister, the 'founder' of the casual So-Cal fashion chain, are just as fictional as Homer Simpson, Bruce Wayne, Peppa Pig, Miss Marple and Dr Who, no mean brand names themselves.

Places

Although people comprise the single biggest category of brand names, places run them close. Singapore Airlines, Waterford Crystal, American Express, Danske Bank, Canadian Dry, Heidelberg University, *Washington Post*, *China Daily*, Sydney Swans,

Real Madrid, Mecca Cola, Oxford Marmalade, *Paris Match*, Highland Spring, River Island, Mountain Warehouse, Western Union, Southern Comfort, Chicago Pizza, Tokyo Laundry, Philadelphia Cream Cheese, Bombay Sapphire Gin. The list goes on and on. There's Amazon and Iceland and Everest and Buckfast and Rockport and Marathon and Vauxhall and Nokia and Hitachi and Pringles and Patagonia and Pall Mall and Fane Valley and Mont Blanc and Mountain Dew and Maxwell House and Norwich Union and Scottish Widows and Bloomsbury Publishing and Thames & Hudson and Land O'Lakes and Banana Republic and The Olive Garden and The North Face and Urban Decay and, of course, all those world-renowned casinos along Las Vegas Boulevard – the Luxor, the Venetian, the Paris, the Rio, the Bellagio, the Riviera, the Monte Carlo, the Mandalay Bay, the Barbary Coast, the Treasure Island, New York New York and the fabled, fearsome, possibly apocryphal, Hell Casino (Think Box 4).

THINK BOX 4

Hell's Bells

Dateline Las Vegas. Megacorp recently announced plans for a new, entirely below ground, hotel/casino/theme park here to be called 'Hell'. Having already themed Pharonic Egypt, the Roman Empire, Caribbean Pirates, South Sea Volcanic Isles, the Land of Oz, New York City, Paris, Venice, Monte Carlo, Bellagio, medieval castles, and other exotic locales and eras, it was perhaps only a matter of time before one of the corporations in Las Vegas tumbled to Hell. The resort ties in nicely with the city's annual Helldorado celebration as well as its well-entrenched association with the mortal sins of greed, lust, drunkenness, debauchery, and bad taste. With the catchy ad slogans Megacorp is trumpeting – 'Go to Hell,' 'You'll be Dying to Get Here,' 'The Devil Made Me Do It,' and 'Damned Good Fun' – Hell seems destined to become the latest and greatest attraction in this city of excess. With Hell's promised spectacle of ever-flaming fire and brimstone, the Mirage's periodically erupting volcano is likely to seem tame. Planned theme rides like The Drop of Doom, From Here to Eternity, and The Bottomless Pit promise much more profound and frightening adventures than the roller coasters and log flumes of other Strip resorts. What's a wave pool when you can swim in boiling oil? What's a barge on the Nile when you can be ferried across the River Styx by Charon? And what's gambling for money when you can play 'You Bet Your Life'? If the Secrets of the Luxor appeal to those fascinated with New Age occultism, imagine the Satanic possibilities of tititlating torture in Hell. Demonic and devilishly costumed employees will be fittingly called the croupiers from Hell, the cocktail waitresses from Hell, and the pit bosses from Hell. The new resort's president is to be addressed as His Royal

(Continued)

(Continued)

Satanic Majesty. And to attract aging baby boomers, Megacorp has already signed Mick Jagger to play the big room, doing 'Sympathy for the Devil,' along with warm-up acts Kiss ('Hotter than Hell') and Meatloaf ('Bat out of Hell'), while a succession of heavy metal bands will appear as lounge acts. It comes as little surprise that the resort's restaurants will feature flame-broiled dinners, devilled eggs, soul food and devils food cake to guests seated in hand baskets. Shops in the resort's attached shopping arcade include Needful Things, Souls on Fire Discotheque, Hallmark Cards, Save My Sole Shoes, Rosemary's Baby Shop, Devil May Care Clothing, Hellraiser's Bar, Beetlejuice Julius, Paradise Lost Luggage, Inferno Hot Tubs, S&M Candies, Purgatory Pete's Pets, Club Limbo, Death Watch Dinner Theater (featuring the 'Corpses on Parade' musical revue), Hell's Angels Insignia Wear, the Faustus Follies, Hard Rock and a Hard Place, and Beelzebub's Brew Pub. In the future Las Vegas's rumored underworld connections are likely to have entirely new meanings.[27]

Thinking Outside the Think Box

Although it was written as a spoof, Belk's article about Hell Casino proved prescient. Recent years have seen the rise of 'dark tourism', travel to sites of death and destruction. Read up on the subject, select a dark attraction and evaluate its branding.

For Danesi, the semiotician, a crucial distinction must be made between totalizing brand names like Universal Studios or Globo-Gym (the megalomaniacal fitness chain run by Ben Stiller in *Dodgeball*) and locally-focused brand names like Made in Belfast, a Northern Irish restaurant, or the magical Macaskill Arms (the one-horse hotel owned by Denis Lawson in *Local Hero*).[28] But brand names aren't constrained by earthly considerations. Where would we be without Sky satellite television, Venus razor blades, Mercury mobile phones, Saturn motor cars, Sun Microsystems software and Milky Way chocolate bars, not to mention imaginary places like Arcadia, Valhalla, Avalon, Camelot, Elysium, Utopia and the immersive *World of Warcraft*?

Products

Place-based names are notoriously hard to trademark, as Blackett explains,[29] and that's why so many geo-brands have the product category attached in addition: British Airways, American Apparel, Australian Automobile Association. Brands named after the products they sell, or services provided, are a commonplace too. They are descriptive brand names par excellence. If, during the past decade, you've strolled along any high street, tarried in any shopping mall or stumbled on an e-commerce operation, you must have encountered scores of them. The Perfume Shop, the Suit Shop, Pizza

Express, Toys R Us, Dunkin' Donuts, PC World, Insure and Go, Spaghetti Factory, Office Depot, Sunglasses Hut, Key Travel, Hotels.com, Pet World, Movie House, Tile Market, Furniture Village, *Better Homes and Gardens* and many more besides.

Some product-led names are more allusive than others, admittedly. Airbus, Body Shop, SlimFast, Paperchase, Weight Watchers, Head & Shoulders, Foot Locker, Staples, Dreams, Lean Cuisine, Holiday Inn, Travel Lodge, Volkswagen, PlayStation, Facebook, YouTube, Specsavers, Superdrug, Pret a Manger are rather less flagrant than Eat, The Beer Store, Sofa.com, never mind Sweaty Betty. But it's not hard to work out what to expect in In-N-Out Burger or Wash & Go or U-Haul or Prontaprint or Dollar Shave or Payless Shoes or Karrimor luggage or Kwik-Fit or Speedy Cleaners or Vision Express or Bed, Bath and Beyond or Whole Foods Market or, for that matter, from batteries like Ever Ready, Duracell and Die Hard.

Pact

The product–place combination is all fine and dandy. But it can end up as a bit of a mouthful; viz. the British Broadcasting Corporation, Svenska Aeroplanaktiebolaget, Hongkong and Shanghai Banking Corporation, Fabbrica Italiana Automobili Torino. Brevity is better, by and large, and brand owners have never been reluctant to recast their names in an abbreviated manner (Pact, of course, being short for Compact). Hence, BBC, SAAB, FIAT, HSBC. Sometimes these combinations of initial letters form catchy acronyms, such as SPAR (Samenwerken Profiteren Allen Regelmatig), BART (Bay Area Rapid Transport), BEBO (Blog Early Blog Often), IKEA (Ingvar Kamprad Elmtaryd Agunnaryd) and AGFA (Aktien Gesellschaft fur Anilin-Fabrikation).[30] But more often than not, the capital letters are articulated individually, as in the case of BT (British Telecom), HP (Hewlett-Packard), BMW (Bayerische Motoren Werke), DKNY (Donna Karan New York), JCB (Joseph Cyril Bamford), AIB (Allied Irish Bank), MTV (Music Television), IBM (International Business Machines), BAA (British Airports Authority), DFS (Direct Furniture Shipments), BVD (Bradley Voorhees & Day), and ICI as was (Imperial Chemical Industries). Portmanteau pacts are popular too as in the case of Asda, which melds Associated and Dairies, as do Aldi (Albrecht Diskont), Texaco (Texas Company), Haribo (Hans Riegel, Bonn), Nabisco (National Biscuit Company), Ambev (American Beverage Company), Fed-Ex (Federal Express), Nat-West (National Westminster Bank), Consarc (Consulting Architects) and Muji (Mujirushi Ryōhin, meaning 'no label quality goods').[31]

Pacts 'n' paraphrases, if truth be told, are not popular with branding consultants or advertising agencies. 'Initials say nothing,' one snorts, 'and tend to be anonymous and difficult to remember.'[32] However, they are very much in tune with our FYI, LOL, BTW world of tweets, texts and micro-messages. More than that, they can be very helpful when a brand outgrows its original function. KFC no longer carries the unhealthy connotations of Fried Chicken. WPP, the global advertising and communications conglomerate, has moved far beyond wire and paper products. Zappos, the online footwear retailer, changed its name from ShoeSite for fear of getting stuck in feet. Apple Computers recently dropped the Computers for Inc., since it sells a lot more than IT nowadays. Many of Poundland's products, meanwhile, cost more than one pound. Is change a-comin' there too?

Quaint

It may be some time before Poundland changes its name to £&, but it would certainly stand out from the Poundwises, Poundstretchers, Poundcrushers and Poundworlds of this world. When it comes to naming, Taylor notes, the best strategy is to do the exact opposite of what every other brand in the category is doing.[33] That is, to zag when the rest zig. The telecoms sector was transformed by Orange back in 1994; Egg rewrote the brand name rule book in banking; Mother and St. Luke's did likewise with the alphabet soup of advertising agencies. Looking to the past rather than revolutionizing the present is another tempting possibility, not least because edgy can become embarrassing. Carphone Warehouse anyone? Quaint names are those that pertain to the past. These include old names abandoned at some point in time, often as a consequence of mergers and acquisitions. Caffrey's Irish Ale languished in the Bass beer portfolio for decades, before being re-released to great acclaim in 1998. Ditto Mitchell & Butlers. The TSB, an old faithful British bank and subsidiary of Lloyds, was reactivated in the wake of recent financial scandals. HSBC's Midland Bank is making a comeback, some say, for much the same reasons. Many iconic car brands have been disinterred of late (Mini, Beetle, Vauxhall Viva). The same is true of long lost fashion labels (Biba, Penguin, Schiaparelli) and mega-blockbuster movie franchises (*Jurassic Park*, *Star Wars*, *Sherlock Holmes*).

By far the most popular source of pastness, however, is myth and legend. Hermès (luxury goods), Oracle (software), Osiris (sunglasses), Orion (movie production), Mazda (motor cars), Ajax (scouring powder), Aramis (toiletries), Argos (catalogue retailing), Janus (financial services) and Cerberus (investment banking) all hail from prehistory, as do Olympus (cameras), Athena (books), Pandora (jewellery), Setanta (satellite television), Thales (defence systems), Taranis (fighter drones), Subaru (pickup trucks), Aesop (skin-care products) and Isis (Belgian chocolate). The last, understandably, has caused consternation since the rise of Islamic State, with some brands choosing to retain (Isis Energy, Isis Interiors, Isis Automation) and others deciding to abandon (Isis Pharmaceuticals to Ionis) the Ancient Egyptian goddess.

Quant

Another renowned brand that dropped its name is the Minnesota Mining and Manufacturing Company. Now called 3-M it is best known for Post-it Notes, all sorts of industrial adhesives and its ethos of incessant innovation. More than that, though, its name is numerical. Numbers are a perennial brand name standby, often in alpha-numeric forms such as CK1, Jet 2, Y3, E4, VO5, iOS6, EA7, Q8, K-9 and Oxy10. (And let us not forget GB12, 15Love, Club 18-30, 23andMe, WD40, 42 Below, Colt 45, Fly53, Heinz 57, Bud 66, Zantac 75, Haircut 100, Xbox 360, Airbus 380, Levi's 501, Boeing 757 and Porsche 911.) Stand-alone numerals are rather less common than alphanumeric, but they're not unknown. Notable examples include 3, the mobile phone network, 7-Eleven, the convenience store, 43, the Spanish liquor, 888, the gambling website, 1664, the French lager, 118 118, the directory enquiries provider, Intel's aforementioned pre-Pentium ranges of microchips, and a gone but not forgot-ten brand of eau de cologne, 4-7-11.[34] Numerical names, like pacts, are especially well suited to today's short-form age – it's easier to type 1D or PS4 than One Direction and PlayStation 4 – and even the most old-fashioned consumer would surely agree that the original name for a popular American beverage, Bib-Label Lithiated Lemon-Lime Soda, isn't a patch on its present much-loved moniker, 7 Up.

Seven, in fairness, is the world's favourite number, though 1, 2 and 3 are pretty popular too.[35] Thirteen is studiously avoided by many people, as are 666 and 4, which sounds like 'death' in Mandarin. Eight, on the other hand, is considered lucky in many Asian countries. And heavy metal, needless to say, wouldn't be heavy metal without 11. Whether it's First Direct bank, Second Life virtual world, Third Space fitness club, Four Seasons luxury hotels, Five Guys gourmet burgers, Six Flags theme parks, Seven Seas vitamin pills or Eight O'Clock whole bean coffee, brands can't get enough of quantification. Whatever happened to Love Potion Number 9, by the way?

Quirks

Google too is named after a number, albeit a quirky one. Ten raised to the hun-dredth power, to be precise, though there are no googols of anything in the known universe, neither atoms nor stars. Odd eh? Almost as odd as Cillit Bang, the ghastly grime, lime-scale and soap-scum remover made by the equally oddly named Reckitt Benckiser. Regularly voted the most hated brand in Britain – where there's no short-age of competition – Cillit Bang is sold around the world under a wide range of oddball names including Easy-Off Bang, Easy-Off Bam, Lime Cleaner Trigger and Power Grime.[36] Like it or loathe it, Cillit is a classic case of a brand that stands tall in a crowded, highly competitive market by dint of its daftness, its difference and, not least, its barking mad spokesperson, BARRY SCOTT! Cillit Bang is so bad it's good, as is Smucker's jam which advertises itself with the deathless slogan 'With a name like Smucker's, it's got to be good'. Häagen-Dazs is equally offbeat, because the brand has no connection whatsoever to Denmark or Holland or any European language using umlauts (it was founded in the Bronx in 1961).[37]

When it comes to quirkiness, though, it's hard to beat the nomenclatural out-pourings of the brand consultancy constituency, who've come up with countless quirky classics from Accenture, Altria and Allante to Zeneca, Zostavax and Zixoryn. Nor can we forget Corus, Capita, Centrica, Carillion, Claritin, Ceridian and the roundly-detested Consignia, which briefly replaced Royal Mail before public out-rage persuaded the British postal service to think again. True, there are very good reasons for the rise of names that sound like badly translated Elvish excerpts from *Lord of the Rings*. They are relatively easy to trademark and provide blank canvases for brand managers, market researchers, corporate identity developers, etc. But as PwC's widely ridiculed name change to Strategy&, and the unpronounceable com-puter peripherals maker Zzyzx bear eloquent witness, the outcomes are often odd and frequently farcical:

> Titles should be specific and transparent, even engaging, rather than mysterious acronyms or Esperanto-like nouns put together at great expense by branding con-sultants who have persuaded their clients that they need to be called by a word that can be spoken as easily in Swahili as in Mandarin.[38]

Quips

Farces of course can be funny if you're not the manager or naming consultant respon-sible. When PwC Computing changed its name to Monday, everyone's least favourite day of the week, the laughter was loud and long and Monday was duly dropped like the proverbial hot potato, as was Thus, which briefly anointed Scottish Power with its jocose connotations of thistles (th) and togetherness (us). Hilarity, it's fair to say, gets short shrift from brand naming gurus. When hard-headed, hatchet-faced, stony-hearted corporate chiefs are spending squillions on new names, they tend to react negatively to irreverent suggestions like Unperhaps, Forty Blinks, Shocking Beige, World on Toast or indeed Hot Potato. For the most part, though, funny, punning, parody names are very popular outside the blue-chip brand bubble. One of the earli-est known brand names – found on several bottles of Vesuvinum wine excavated at Pompeii – was a pun on Vesuvius, the volcano and *vinium*, Latin for vine.[39]

Indeed, if you saunter down to your local shopping precinct you'll pass any num-ber of tongue-in-cheek chippies (Assalt and Battery), hair salons (Curl Up and Dye), oriental restaurants (Wok This Way), record stores (Vinyl Resting Place), hobby shops (Sew What), pet beauticians (Doggy Style), dry cleaners (Crease Lightning), taxi firms (Chariots of Hire), chimney sweeps (Ash Wipe), photographers (Flash Gordon), door stores (Knobs & Knockers), gift shops (Soap and Glory), fishmongers (Fish You Were Here), video rentals (Planet of the Tapes) and public houses (The Bar With No Name).[40] Trekking through drugstore aisles can be no less diverting (e.g. Clean On Me, Shave to Love, Dry Hard) and the supermarket is fun-filled too (Gü, Too Good to be True, Oat So Simple, I Hate the French Vanilla, I Can't Believe It's Not Butter).

It would be remiss of us, what is more, to overlook Ben & Jerry's pun-filled flavours, including Cherry Garcia, Phish Food, Chunky Monkey and, Barack Obama's personal favourite, Yes Pecan.

WHERE DO NAMES COME FROM?

A sense of humour always helps when in need of a brand name. However, it isn't the only source of inspiration. Serendipity also works. Etsy, the online craft shop, came from a simple misunderstanding of an Italian phrase. eBay, by contrast, was chosen by default, because Pierre Omidyar's preferred alternative, EchoBay, was already taken.[41] Desperation isn't unknown either, as in the case of Tom Tom, the Dutch satnav brand. Tech giant Ericsson gave the founders 12 hours to come up with a workable name for their joint venture. Harold Goddijn wracked his brains but could only manage Tom singular. Then he discovered that it was trademarked already. Tom Tom wasn't, though. Better yet, as the term alluded to drumming, an ancient mode of communication and wayfinding, Tom Tom proved fortuitously appropriate. Their Swedish partners weren't best pleased, mind you, retorting, 'what do you think we're selling, teddy bears?' But it was Goddijn who went to the picnic, selling 60 million satnavs in less than a decade.[42]

Rather than rely on flashes of inspiration, many namers rely on good old-fashioned methods like dictionaries (Twitter), telephone books (Pringles), employee suggestions (Aviva), customer recommendations (Hovis), computer searches (Elf petroleum) and the names of their children (Mercedes) or pets (Zynga). Failing that, there's always Latin and Greek, as Omega (watches), Delta (airlines), Oculus (headsets), Audi (meaning 'listen'), Volvo ('it rolls') and the ASICS acronym ('a healthy mind in a healthy body') are testament. Popular culture is another important source of brand names. Classics include Starbucks (*Moby-Dick*), Yahoo (*Gulliver's Travels*), Ariel (*The Tempest*), Ask Jeeves (P.G. Wodehouse), Rohan clothing (*Lord of the Rings*), Phileas Fogg snacks (*Around the World in Eighty Days*), Ivory soap (The Holy Bible), Warby Parker, an online seller of eyewear (named after Jack Kerouac characters) and of course Zara, which was originally going to be called Zorba (after the 1964 movie *Zorba the Greek*). However, a bar in Amancio Ortega's home town, La Coruña, was already called Zorba, so he settled on Zara instead.

Yet another powerful fountainhead is market research. Widely employed by the major brand naming consultancies, the denotations, connotations and sound symbolism of proposed brand names are scrutinized to an extraordinary degree (Think Box 5). Hundreds are typically suggested, sorted, sifted and tested to death. BlackBerry is a famous case in point. Originally called PocketLink, the handheld device was temporarily tagged with Airwire, Banter, Gameplan, Outrigger, Waterfall and Riff, before Blackberry got the nod.[43] Esso, similarly, spent more than $100 million back in 1972 to find a new name for themselves. Three years after the study started, the petroleum giant was proudly renamed Exxon, much to the annoyance of linguistic purists who objected vociferously to the double X. Consumers didn't seem to mind, though, something that can't be said for the most infamous naming debacle bar none. More than 300 consultants were brought in by Ford to come up with a suitable name for their spanking new model, which debuted in 1957. These included the modernist poet Marianne Moore, who threw Utopian Turtletop, Bullet Cloisonné and Mongoose Civique into the mix. In the end, they settled on the forename of Henry Ford's only son. Although its name wasn't the worst of the Ford Edsel's problems – one wag, on seeing the strangely shaped front grille, described it as an Oldsmobile sucking a lemon – Morris rightly concludes that 'Edsel today remains synonymous with "really bad product name" '.[44]

THINK BOX 5

Going Corporate

In many SMEs, the company and the brand are synonymous. Coco Mojo Ltd sells a range of healthy fruit drinks called Coco Mojo. Big Shot Ltd retails caffeine-free, tourine-free, no e-number energy drinks named Little Big Shot. Feckin Irish Whiskey, as the name implies, made feckin Irish whiskey in its feckin Irish distillery until the company was acquired by Cooley, a larger concern.

But, as regional brands develop a national or international presence, it's not unusual for the company to adopt a separate name, an allusive name that appeals to the stock market and financial institutions rather than the man or woman in the street. Diageo, for instance, is the corporate entity that shelters world-renowned beverage brands such as Smirnoff, Tanqueray and Johnnie Walker. Alphabet, likewise, is the recently adopted corporate appellation for Google's many and varied services.

The pros and cons of corporate branding are much debated. Some high-profile brands, like Virgin and Apple, have consistently resisted the separation temptation. Regardless of the rationale, it illustrates the thinking behind the brand naming process, especially the neologisms that are coined by specialist consultancies.

A selection of these have been analysed by Muzellec, who explains the reasoning behind a range of corporate rebrands.[45] That is, the organization's account of what, exactly, their newly-coined brand name refers to. Accenture, the consultancy firm, claims its name 'connotes putting an accent on the future'. Altria, the tobacco giant formerly known as William Morris, takes its name from 'the Latin word *altus*, meaning high'. Aviva, the insurance group, 'brings with it associations of life, vitality and living well'. Novartis, the pharmaceutical company, 'comes from the Latin term *novae artes*, meaning "new arts"'. Verizon, the telecommunications corporation, 'is derived from the combination of *veritas*, which means truth in Latin, and horizon'. Vivendi, France's foremost media operation, is a Latin gerundive, meaning 'vivacity and mobility'.

Thinking Outside the Think Box

In a notorious renaming debacle, the Royal Mail changed its name to Consignia. Then swiftly changed it back again. But what's so bad about Consignia, especially compared to some of the above? Should they have stuck with it?

Market research costs money and entrepreneurs are notoriously reluctant to stump up. Luckily, there's a cheap alternative. Copy someone else. When a brand takes off, imitators attach themselves to its nomenclatural undercarriage. Coca-Cola's ascent inspired countless copycats including Co Kola, Coke-Ola, Okla-Cola, Sola-Cola, Carbo-Cola, Klu-Ko Cola and even Celery-Cola. The world's first supermarket was called Piggly Wiggly – don't ask – and before long the brand was joined by Helpy Selfy, Hoggly Woggly, Savy Wavy, Handy Andy and Jitney Jungle, among others. The suffix -ex was popular in the 1930s (Pyrex, Kleenex), -master had its moment in the 1940s (Mixmaster, Toastmaster), -o-matic came to the fore in the 1950s (Cruise-o-matic), as did -tastic (Snacktastic), -tacular (Sportacular), -ola (Mazola) and o-rama (Beef-o-rama).[46] Latterly, there's been a rise in lower case capital letters (iTunes, eBay), a trend toward intra-nominative capitalizations (PlayStation, YouTube), a fashion for dropped vowels, 'e' in particular (Tumblr, Flickr), a penchant for the letter X, with all its connotations of edginess and X-treme sports (Xbox, SpaceX) and a cascade of.com appendages. Some of the latter inadvertently failed to take account of the 'web gap', where spaces between words are omitted in URLs. This led to red faces on a site for fountain pen lovers, Pen Island, on a site for occupational therapists, Therapist Finder, on a site for stock market followers, Investors Exchange, and on an environmentally-friendly site devoted to garden moles, Mole Station.

Name fails also occur when they're exported to foreign climes, like the nippy Vauxhall Nova (nova means 'won't go' in Spanish), Clairol's deodorant Mist Stick ('mist' is German for manure) and Mitsubishi's cack-handed Pajero (in Spain 'pajero' is a slang term for, um, pleasuring oneself excessively). Foreign brands too can come a cropper, as Pee Cola, Pet Sweat, Man Goo, Only Puke, Bonka coffee, Plopp chocolate, Barf detergent, Pschitt lemonade and Krapp, a Swedish toilet tissue brand, attest.[47]

Tissue issues notwithstanding, names can be overtaken by events. BP considered a name change in the United States after the Deepwater Horizon oil spill. Ivory soap is seen in a very different light now that poaching has decimated elephant and rhino populations. If Andersen Consulting hadn't changed its name to Accenture, it would have been tainted by association with the Enron financial scandal. The Kia Provo was all set to go in Britain and Ireland until someone pointed out who the Provos are. Impact Reduction Apparel unsettled more than a few with its abbreviation, furthermore.

BRAND TASK

Doddle is the name of a parcel delivery service, which possesses pick-up and drop-off points in major railway stations. Think about the connotations and denotations of Doddle's brand name, then draw up a list of pros and cons, as you perceive them. Do likewise with Kibble, the name that was almost given to Netflix. It was abandoned for an erogenous reason. Find out why.

RECOMMENDED READINGS

Alex Frankel, *Word Craft* (Crown: New York, 2004). Brand naming is a fascinating topic and this is one of the best books on the subject. Written by a *New York Times* journalist, it tells all manner of amazing stories about much-admired, blue-chip brands.

John Colapinto, 'Famous Names: Does it Matter What a Product is Called?', *The New Yorker*, October 3, 2011. If you can't be bothered with an entire book on brand names, have a gander at this well-written and free-to-download article from the preeminent literary magazine in America (www.newyorker.com).

Bill Bryson, *Made in America* (Minerva: London, 1995). A humorist by profession, Bill Bryson is an American expat who writes very funny travelogues about Great Britain. From time to time, he expatiates on his homeland and this book contains many gems, not least a fabulous chapter on branding and advertising.

Evan Morris, *From Altoids to Zima* (Simon & Schuster: New York, 2004). This is one of those 'fun reading' books that big publishers churn out for the Christmas gift market. But it tells terrific stories about the naming of numerous famous brands in a handy A–Z format.

CHAPTER 3

LOGOS, SLOGANS, MASCOTS AND MORE

Overview

Much has been written about logos and a lot of hot air is talked on the topic. Important as the visual side of branding is, the verbal side is crucial too (slogans, taglines), as are sensory aspects of branding more generally (smell, touch, taste, sound). Packaging, mascots and of course the product or service itself – the offer – are key components of the branding mix. All are given their due in this chapter.

LOGOS A-GO-GO

Designed by Jim Schindler in 1960, McDonald's golden arches is one of the best known logos in the world. Emblazoned on 31,000 restaurants in 116 countries – to say nothing of innumerable posters, flyers, web pages, staff uniforms, packaging materials and television adverts – it is as famous as the Statue of Liberty.[1] One place that remains arches free, though, is the fashion show, the runway, the catwalk.

Until 2014, that is. The sensation of the summer season's Parisian collections was Moschino's McDonaldized makeover. A giant golden M was embroidered on the Italian fashion label's coats, dresses, bags, casuals and accessories, most notably an iPhone cover in the familiar form of a French Fries carton. Fashionistas, needless to say, went wild for Moschino's fast food fashion, as did the media. Although many commentators condemned haute couture's celebration of obesity-inducing junk food – especially in light of the industry's obscene obsession with size zero – the social media storm that followed didn't bother the irreverent Italian fashion brand, nor the Happy Meals people for that matter. As a McDonald's spokesperson flatly stated, 'We've signed a license agreement with Moschino that allows them to use McDonald's intellectual property on the merchandise.'[2]

Regardless of the rights and wrongs of Moschino's behaviour, McDonald's is only one among many logos lifted and repurposed by high fashion's finest. A recent D&G men's wear collection featured jackets and jumpers covered in Fanta, Disney and Coca-Cola insignia. Anya Hindmarch, famous for her 'this is not a bag' bag, retails a range of totes, clutches, baguettes and backpacks fashioned on Kellogg's celebrated spokes-characters Tony the Tiger, Coco the Monkey and Cornelius, the cockerel from the Corn Flakes box. Even Karl Lagerfeld got in on the act. His couture collection of March 2014 comprised a giant supermarket filled with Chanel-styled Perrier bottles, Pringles containers, Nutella jars and multipacks of purses. The shopping baskets came complete with Chanel's signature chain-link handles. The only thing missing was a Chanellogg's breakfast cereal box depicting Cornelius in an LBD.

Although Karl missed a trick when he failed to include Coco Pops boxes – Coco Chanel Pops boxes, more like – his megabrand's homage to branding's greatest hits speaks volumes about the logo-filled world we live in. Just as pop music was once accused of eating itself, so too branding is nibbling its own backside. According to Naomi Klein, she of the *No Logo* logo, corporate emblems, insignia, labels et al. are the nearest thing we have to a universal language.[3] Whether it be Nike's affirmative swoosh, Starbucks' twin-tailed mermaid, Legal & General's multi-coloured umbrella, Disney's magical castle, Shell's celebrated cowrie, Playboy's bowtie-wearing bunny, London Underground's bright red roundel or Amnesty International's barbed wire-wrapped candle, logos are more than encapsulations of the organizations they represent. They symbolize consumer society. They are emblems of western capitalism triumphant.[4]

UNDERSTANDING EMBLEMS

The logo is what most people think about when they think about branding.[5] And it's easy to understand why. Also known as emblems – I'll be using the terms synonymously – logos are the most visible part, the most omnipresent part, of most brands. They are the things plastered on every product sold or service delivered. They are unfailingly found on letterheads, homepages, carrier bags, mouse mats, ballpoint pens, baseball caps, business cards, press releases, annual reports, delivery vehicles, head office blocks and, in strictly old-school organizations, the managing director's necktie, cufflinks and buttonhole.

MDs, moreover, tend to be very protective toward the sigils of corporate life. Many a time I've listened to chief executives expatiating on their insignia. Without much prompting, they wax lyrical about deep meanings, profound symbolism, suggestive subtleties and suchlike. I'm sometimes tempted to say, 'It's only a squiggle, mate' or 'There's more to brands than logos, sunshine'. But one doesn't wish to offend. As a celebrity CEO once said to two marketing management gurus, 'You can do anything you want with the brand, just don't fuck with the logo.'[6]

Managers' protective attitude toward their 'precious' is as nothing compared to the preciousness of graphic designers. Never reluctant to sermonize about their art, they are happy to pontificate on the personalities of fonts, rhapsodize about the bevelling of this, complain about the kerning of that, and disparage the running colour of the other.[7] Like heraldic officials of old, they make hair-splitting distinctions between emblems and monograms and wordmarks and logotypes and symbols and icons and so on.[8] And they find more philosophical profundities in an ovoid than philosophers do in Ovid. MasterCard's three circles, 'reflect the company's unique, three-tiered business model as a franchisor, processor and advisor'. Who knew? LG's letters logo symbolizes 'the World, Future, Youth, Humanity and Technology'. Well, I never! Huawei's fan-like emblem reflects the Chinese tech giant's 'principles of customer focus, innovation, steady and sustainable growth and harmony'. Strewth!![9]

As for those pesky golden arches:

> At a primary level the arches form the letter M, the first letter in the McDonald's brand name. But at a secondary level, arches are mythic structures that seem to beckon people to march through them triumphantly into a paradise of cleanliness, friendliness, hospitality and family values. Like the arches of ancient cities, they symbolize tradition and allegiance ... In modern day households, meals are routinely consumed separately by the members. The home has become a place where people now tend to eat apart. Enter McDonald's to the rescue![10]

When we read stuff like that, it's easy to become cynical about graphic design. There's no denying, though, that logos are a key component of the branding mix. In the hierarchy of humankind's five senses, vision is first by some distance.[11] It is more ancient and, arguably, more essential than its verbal counterpart. For cognitive psychologists, visual thinking is the primal, the default mode of comprehending the world. Hence the Mercedes star, the Tuborg crown, the Wella wave, the Prudential rock, the Republican Party elephant ...

According to Evamy's analysis of 1,300 logos in 75 different sectors, there are three basic types of brand emblem: *symbols*, *representations* and *logotypes*:

> *Symbols* are the basic geometric figures – squares, triangles, circles, crosses – that are deeply meaningful for many cultures. Examples include Esso's oval, Amex's blue box, Mitsubishi's three diamonds, Bayer's cross inside a circle and the very first trademarked logo, Bass brewery's bright red triangle.

> *Representations* are stylized depictions of the many and varied things that surround us – plants, animals, flames, feathers, buildings, body parts and so on. Disney's castle,

Hollister's seagull, Montblanc's snowflake, Shiseido's camellia, Rolling Stones' lolling tongue, and the Conservative Party's flaming torch are typical of the breed, as is Aer Lingus's signature shamrock.

Logotypes spell out brand names in distinctive typefaces, which judiciously combine the verbal and the visual. Coca-Cola's cursive script is the all-time classic logotype, though Ford's, Kellogg's, Cadbury's, Cartier's, H&M's and Harrods' 'handwritten' fonts are almost as famous. Not every logotype is cursive of course. Kodak, eBay, RAC, Lego, CNN, MTV, Dell, Braun, Dunhill and Pirelli, with its famous stretched P, are just some of the more striking logotypes out there.

Now, Evamy's classification of emblems is admirable in many respects.[12] But, as noted in the previous chapter, tripartite typologies can be a bit baggy. The categories tend to be too broad for pedagogic purposes (such as answering examination questions). Therefore I have formulated a fuller framework which might help you think things through and isn't too hard to remember (Think Box 6). Instead of Evamy's symbols, representations and logotypes, it consists of ten separate categories each beginning with the letter A.

―――――――――― **THINK BOX 6** ――――――――――

Typology of Brand Emblems[13]

Category	Content	Examples
Alphabetic	Letters, characters, punctuation marks	McDonald's, IBM, Seat, Unilever, Facebook, MTV, Vodafone, PlayStation
Autographic	'Hand-written' logotypes	Cartier, *Esquire*, Virgin, Davidoff, Paul Smith, Grolsch, Lindt, Chopard
Astronomy	Globes, suns, stars, galaxies	BT, BP, Texaco, AT&T, Mercedes, Heineken, Converse, NASA, P&G
Anatomy	Hearts, heads, faces, eyes, body parts, people	CBS, LG, Innocent, National Lottery, KFC, Walls, Arm & Hammer, I♥NY
Architecture	Buildings, houses, monuments, castles	UCL, Lands' End, Aviva, *Sesame Street*, Capitol music, Castle lager

Category	Content	Examples
Arboreal	Trees, plants, vegetation, landscape	Timberland, Aer Lingus, Adidas, Apple, Prudential, Toblerone, Air Canada
Ancestral	Shields, crowns, heraldic symbols, mythical figures	UPS, Harley-Davidson, Rolex, Tuborg, Starbucks, BrewDog, KLM, BMW
Animal	Birds, fish, dogs, cats, insects, etc.	Jaguar, NBC, WWF, Qantas, Puma, Nestlé, Skoda, Hollister, Camel
Abstract	Geometric shapes, arrows, stripes, waves, patterns	Wrigley, Fedex, Citroën, Chevron, Audi, Renault, Target, Wella, BuzzFeed
A.N. Other	Flames, flags, keys, arcs, harps, blobs, rays of light	Nectar, Nike, UBS, P&O, Walmart, Guinness, Ascis, Nikon, British Gas

Thinking Outside the Think Box

Go online and get hold of the latest Interbrand list of most valuable brands. Take the top 100 and classify their logos according to the above typology. Identify those that 'don't fit' (and end up in A.N. Other). Modify the typology with two new categories.

Before you get stuck in, however, bear one thing in mind. Logos are the visual equivalent of brand names. At their very best, they encapsulate what a brand is all about. They ensure it stands out from the crowd. And, as with brand names, emblems change from time to time. These can be radical changes, such as Pepsi's abandonment of its elaborate cursive logotype for a simple red, white and blue-striped roundel, or BP's infamous switch from a combat green heraldic shield to an eco-friendly efflorescent sunburst (which proved ironically inappropriate after the Gulf oil spill).[14]

More often than not, though, logos are tweaked, refreshed, touched up, given a graphic makeover to maintain their relevance (as Google's new and improved homepage, Microsoft's redesign of its four-tile symbol and eBay's recently refreshed logotype bear witness). These incremental updates, like necessary nip 'n' tuck surgery on celebrities, can completely change the look of a logo over time. Just consider the evolution of the Apple, Opel, Renault, Siemens or Xerox insignia, the current versions of which are vastly different from the originals.[15]

Logos are a moveable feast, albeit a repast that's hard to stomach when graphic designers are dishing out the discourse.

OTHER ORGANS

The human brain is hard wired for vision and marketing communications reflect this fact. Research reveals that more than 80% of marketing communication is visual.[16] Verbal communication, comparatively speaking, doesn't get a look in. However there's so much visual clutter these days that consumers are increasingly ignoring brands' look-at-me overkill. Large-scale sporting events, for instance, are swamped with logo litter. Emblems of one sort or another are plastered on the players, on the pitch, on the hoardings, on the grandstands, on the post-match interview backdrops, on the match ball, on the big screens, on the ticket stubs, on the replica shirts worn by fans and, as often as not, on the exterior of the stadium itself, courtesy of the sponsoring brand – Emirates, Reebok, Aviva, etc. As Lindstrom rightly observes, 'We are more visually stimulated than ever before. And studies have shown that the more stimulated we are, the harder it is to capture our attention.'[17]

There are other senses besides sight and recent years have seen the rise of sensory marketing or, to be more precise, brand organoleptics. Organoleptic refers to anything that affects or stimulates the senses, be it *tactile, olfactory, auditory*, or *gustatory*.

Tactile

Luxury brands are the petting zoo of consumer society. The sensuous feel of a Hermès silk scarf, the buttery leather of a Belstaff biker jacket, the exquisite texture of Louis Vuitton's lozine-trimmed luggage, the delicious fit of Tod's slip-on driving shoes, the perfect nestle-in-the-hand heft of a Bang & Olufsen channel changer, the touchscreen triumph of the Galaxy S6 smartphone, with its beautiful bevelled edges, are nothing less than tactile testaments to the power of touch. Consumers want to have and to hold, to hug, to clutch, to caress, to squeeze, to fondle their favourite brands.

It's not just luxury goods, either. For older consumers among us, the convenience of squirting Heinz tomato ketchup from a plastic container doesn't compare to the kinaesthetic thrill of thumping the bottom of the iconic glass bottle, with all the attendant risks of sudden discharge and overspill overkill:

> We in Britain love stuff that doesn't work. And we miss having a sauce bottle that refuses to deliver its contents. That's why we buy so many Gillette razors, because they come in a packet that can only be opened with Semtex. Today, Heinz sells its tomato ketchup in squeezy bottles and that's no good at all. We need glass bottles with a neck that is precisely 2mm narrower than the width of the average kitchen knife. And the contents need to have a viscosity that enables them to sit completely still unless you hit the bottom of the bottle with a force slightly greater than the breaking point of the human trapezoid bone.[18]

As an impressionable adolescent, what's more, I was lucky enough to attend the worldwide launch of the legendary DeLorean sports car, beloved by fans of *Back to the Future*. Beautiful as its glorious gull-wing doors undoubtedly were – and remain to this day – the thing that really captivated petrol-heads back then was the brand's brushed-steel bodywork. Everyone wanted to touch it. In no time at all, the car was covered in sticky fingerprints. DMC employees were placed on permanent polishing duty, but the pawing, patting and heavy-handed petting couldn't be stopped. They roped the car off in the end.

Olfactory

The DMC smelled beautiful too, as all new cars do. Despite Lindstrom's revelation that the 'new car smell' comes from a can, car owners can't get enough of it.[19] Nor are they inured to the insidious aroma of Johnson's Baby Powder, Bewley's coffee bars, Singapore Airlines' singular scent, Krispy Kreme's freshly-baked doughnuts, Crayola Crayons' olfaction satisfactions, Thomas Pink's peerless tailored shirts, which are suffused with the bouquet of freshly-laundered cotton, let alone the pungent rush of Lush's organic bath bombs, bubble bars and body lotions. The less said about sniffing UHU glue, the better.

Smell, neuroscience informs us, is the sense that stirs the strongest emotions, because the brain's olfactory bulb sends signals directly to the limbic system, the hippocampus, the instinctual core of the cerebellum.[20] Canny brand managers have cottoned on to that fact. There's more to contemporary scentology, however, than the lemony zest of Flash floor cleaner or the floral aroma of Surf Tropical Lily washing powder, or the manly whiff of Molton Brown's black pepper shower gel or the womanly waft of Jo Malone's wood, sage and sea salt candles or the hot buttered popcorn pong that's pumped into movie theatres by the Vues, Odeons and AMCs of this world. Just as every brand worth its salt has a logo, so too proprietary smells are de rigueur for today's airlines, hotels, spas, retail stores, glossy magazines and every product you can think of from tissues, hairdryers and mobile phones to nappies, trainers and motor car tyres. Yes, motor car tyres. Seriously.

Outdoor advertising is also getting in on the olfactory act. Select bus shelters in Britain disburse the delicious smell of McCain's oven chips to patiently waiting passengers, who slaver at the heaven-sent scent. It would appear that Pavlov's dogs, are alive and well, without the sound of a bell to unsettle them.[21]

Auditory

According to Beckerman's recent book *Sonic Boom*, human beings react much faster to sound than any other sensory stimulus.[22] It's an inbuilt defence mechanism that evolved in Palaeolithic times when small groups of hunter-gatherers battled with woolly mammoths, sabre-toothed tigers and, if blockbuster movies are anything to go by, vicious velociraptors.

Movie makers, in fairness, are masters of sonic marketing. The dum dum dum of *Jaws*, the eeek eeek eeek of *Psycho*, the dah dah dah dah of 20th Century Fox's fantastic fanfare and the unforgettable anthems in innumerable Disney movies, from *Hey Ho* to *Let It Go*, are ever-present reminders of sound's unerring ability to impose itself upon us.

Share-of-ear is the new frontier for brand managers and they're competing for it vigorously. Sonic logos, like Intel's iconic 'wave', McDonald's I'm Lovin' It whistle, Nokia's famously infuriating ringtone and of course the potato-potato-potato exhaust note of Harley-Davidson motorcycles are as distinctive as – arguably more distinctive than – their visual counterparts. Can you recall Nokia's logo? Or Harley's for that matter? Me neither. But I'd recognize the MGM lion's roar anywhere, or the come-ye-all chimes of Mr Softee's ice cream vans, or the big C Major that greets Macbook owners when they switch on, or the supremely satisfying click when Lego bricks lock together, or British Airways' theme tune, the Flower Duet from Delibes' *Lakmé*, which was abandoned for a while then reinstated after passenger protests.

Sound, in certain respects, is the secret weapon of brand managers. Whether it be jolly jingles that lodge forever in the memory ('We Buy Any Car Dotcom' – once heard, never forgotten), the attention-grabbing, appetite-stimulating sound of sizzling fajitas in Chili's chain restaurants (they call it 'the Fajita effect'), or the solid scientific evidence that in-store shopper behaviour is directly affected by the type and tempo of background music (up-tempo, we move faster; downbeat, we take our time), consumers are suckers for sonics.[23] Literally, because judiciously chosen background music makes food and drink taste better. Guinness may or may not be good for you, but its flavour is enhanced by the lively jigs, swirling reels and stately laments served up in Irish theme pubs.

Gustatory

Guinness, of course, is an 'acquired taste', something that takes time and effort and suspension of disbelief to achieve. The same is often said of Marmite, Vegemite, Spam, Bovril and Red Bull, which has been known to trigger the gag reflex among some first-time drinkers. True or not, such claims serve as markers of distinction, living proof that the consumer is special, sophisticated, a connoisseur. Taste, Ackerman explains, is an overwhelmingly social sense, the sense that serves to bind the tribe, the family, the nation:

> Throughout the world, the stratagems of business take place over meals; weddings end with a feast; friends reunite at celebratory dinners; children herald their birthdays with ice cream and cake; religious ceremonies offer food in fear, homage and sacrifice; wayfarers are welcomed with a meal ... If an event is meant to matter emotionally, symbolically or mystically, food will be close at hand to sanctify and bind it. Every culture uses food as a sign of approval or commemoration, and some foods are even credited with supernatural powers.[24]

It serves to separate too, insofar as consumers who can't acquire the taste don't 'belong', not least in a metaphorical sense where 'bad taste' in our choice of car marques, household furnishings, dietary regimes, etc., are signifiers of social standing.[25]

Be that as it may, memory and taste are closely related. It was the taste of a madeleine cake that sent Proust on his search for lost time. A forkful of Remy's signature dish did something similar to culinary critic Anton Ego in the Disney movie *Ratatouille*. The growing popularity of craft beers, artisan breads, small-batch spirits, organic fruit 'n' veg and comforting home cooking is testament to the importance of gustation, as is consumers' mounting distaste for processed, industrialized foods that megabrands like Kraft, Heinz and Campbell's made their own.[26] The Coca-Colas of this world, however, shouldn't be written off too quickly. As Jeremy Clarkson reminds us:

> In the early 1990s, Richard Branson was approached by a Canadian outfit that reckoned it had produced a drink that was even more zesty and refreshing that Coca-Cola. Now, you know and I know that this is impossible. On a holiday, or when you have a major league hangover, there is simply nothing to rival a cold can of Coke. The black doctor in the red ambulance is what I call it. Sadly, however, Branson didn't know this, so he invested a great deal of time, money and effort into launching Virgin Cola … And yet despite all this marketing push, it flopped.
>
> There are certain things in life – Google springs to mind here – that are nailed, things that are so good and so ingrained into the human psyche that nothing else will ever come close.[27]

Taste, nevertheless, remains the runt of the organoleptic litter. Of the five senses, it is the least widely exploited by brand managers bar those in the food and drink sectors. The trademarked taste of Colgate is an exception to the rule, Lindstrom says.[28] But if Steve Jobs' claim that the candy-coloured iMac was good enough to lick is any indication, can a Boots No 7 Shake be far away?

SLOGANS SELL

Ta Dah! is the current slogan for Boots No 7, the bestselling brand of cosmetics in Britain. As a slogan, it ticks all the brand boxes. Bar one. Yes, Ta Dah! is simple, memorable and effective. But it would work just as well with any transformational brand that delivers pleasant surprises to consumers, such as Argos, Apple, Amazon, Interflora, Domino's Pizza. Truly great slogans, we're told, include the brand name in the tagline: Coke is It; Virginia is for Lovers; Red Bull Gives You Wings; All the Way With LBJ; Happiness is a Cigar Called Hamlet; 100% New Zealand; Tetley Makes Teabags Makes Tea; Bisto Browns, Bisto Thickens, Bisto Seasons; The Future is Bright, the Future is Orange; There Are Some Things Money Can't Buy, For Everything

Else There's MasterCard.[29] This condition, clearly, isn't met by many of the most memorable commercial catchphrases: The Pause That Refreshes; Where's the Beef?; Impossible is Nothing; Exceedingly Good Cakes; We Try Harder; The Best a Man Can Get; Tell Them About the Honey, Mummy.

What we *can* say for certain is that the slogan is the epitome of the advertiser's art. At their best, they compress the entire brand – its ethos, its personality, its reason for being – into a one-liner that lives forever in consumer memory. When we hear the three little words Just Do It, the identity, logo and belief system of the brand spring instantly to mind. The same is true of Finger Lickin' Good, Have It Your Way, *Liberté Égalité Fraternité*, Don't Leave Home Without It, Believe In Better, Think Different, Wassup, Simples. As Helen Edwards points out, 'a great slogan is the jewel in the branding crown, a verbal gem that commands attention, captures light and refracts the lustre of the brand with dazzling intensity'.[30] And few slogans sparkle more brilliantly than Beanz Meanz Heinz, Got Milk?, J'Adore Dior, Should've Gone to Specsavers, Have a Break Have a Kit-Kat, The Milky Bars Are On Me, Heineken Refreshes the Parts Other Beers Can't Reach, Don't Forget the Fruit Gums Mum, and Ryanair's famously unforgettable, brook-no-argument tagline, No Fucking Refunds![31]

Moving swiftly on, there are as many slogans are there are logos and, as with emblems, many attempts have been made to make sense of the cacophony. Catchphrases, in the opinion of one academic authority, can be divided into fourteen different categories including metonymies, tautologies, parallelisms and linkages.[32] For present purposes, it is sufficient to note the seven basic types of tagline:

Poetic, where the slogan rhymes or makes use of recognized poetic devices like alliteration – Once You Pop You Can't Stop, Hey Mabel Black Label, Wonderbra for the Woman You Are, A Mars a Day Helps You Work Rest and Play, Oxo Gives a Meal Man-Appeal, If You Think You Know Spain Think Again, You Can't Fit Quicker than a Quik-Fit Fitter.

Prosaic, seemingly plain statements of fact, or honest promises, which are inarguable and, by implication, irrefutable – The World's Favourite Airline, The Ultimate Driving Machine, It Does Exactly What It Says on the Tin, Good Food Costs Less at Sainsbury's, Never Knowingly Undersold, M&Ms Melt in the Mouth, Not in the Hand.

Personal, catchphrases that collar the consumer and address them directly using the first person singular or plural – Because You're Worth It, I Like Ike, We're With the Woolwich, It Could Be You, I am an Iams Cat, You Know When You've Been Tango'd, Yes We Can, Let Your Fingers Do the Walking, Hey Whipple, Squeeze This!

Proverbial, taglines akin to ancient proverbs, sayings or kōan and are thus the repository of received wisdom – Every Little Helps, Diamonds Are Forever, It's Good to Talk, Time Flies Bulova Soars, When It Rains It Pours, Good Things Come to Those Who Wait, Things Go Better With Coke, *Vorsprung durch Technik*, Image is Nothing.

Pre-emptory, commands, imperatives, orders from on high, do as you're told and don't dare talk back to your betters – Just Do It, Think Small, Tell Sid, Keep Walking, Think Different, Do the Dew, Embrace the Pear, Call for a Carlsberg, Open Happiness, Come to Marlboro Country, Act Your Shoe Size Not Your Age.

Punderful, comprises plays on words, sometimes droll, often agonizing, arguably the epitome of sloganizing – Easy Daz It, Nothing Sucks Like an Electrolux, Think Outside the Bun, You Just Can't Help Acting on Impulse, Surely the Best Tactic (Tic-Tac), Just Like Mother Used to Heat (Campbell's Soup).

The seventh, and by far the biggest, category is *Painful*. The vast majority of catch-phrases are nondescript. They mean nothing. They are instantly forgettable. They are brand landfill. For every classic like Wassup? The Man Your Man Could Smell Like, Finger Lickin' Good or Lipsmackinthirstquenchinacetastin..., there are hundreds of Feel Betters, So Goods, Powers to You, Human Technology, Good Food Good Life and Driven By Passions (for BUPA, KFC, AXA Insurance, Nokia, Nestlé and Ford, in case you've forgotten).[33] Government departments, local councils, health authorities and tourist boards seem especially partial to banalities. This is because they get chosen by committee, whose members are reluctant to take risks.

The upshot is that slogans are falling out of favour. They are eschewed completely by some big brands, such as Google, Amazon and Starbucks (though this is changing). Tech brands in particular tend to be suspicious of anything that smacks of marketing and, as catchphrases are the acme of marketing, they bristle at anything with a tagline attached. I suspect that many netnocrats saw *Crazy People* back in the mid-1990s, a brilliantly funny spoof of advertising hyperbole, and they've been chary ever since:

- Volvo – Boxy But Good
- United Airlines – Most of Our Passengers Get There Alive
- New York City – Not as Filthy as You Think
- AT&T – We're Tired of Taking Your Crap
- Porsche – A Little Too Small to Get Laid In, But You Get Laid the Minute You Get Out.[34]

Ribaldry notwithstanding, a great slogan like They're Gr-r-reat! is a priceless branding asset that should only be changed, or abandoned, with gr-r-reat reluctance.[35] Classics like Don't Book It, Thomas Cook It continue to stick in consumers' minds long after they've been abandoned by the organizations concerned. They are branding earworms that refuse to go away. So much so that, if you test your grandparents with the following one-word question, which should be said with a rising intonation, they'll name the brand in one.[36] And that question is: *Chocolates?*

Nothing beats a good slogan, a snappy slogan, a sticky slogan when it comes to cementing brands into consumer consciousness and, moreover, bonding an organization. A memorable catchphrase fires up employees as well and makes them proud to be part of the brand. Ohhhh Yes.

NICE PACKAGE

Packaging is another potent component of branding. Although the package is less lauded than logos and slogans and brand names, it is impactful all the same. Whether it be Tiffany's beautiful blue boxes, Coca-Cola's classic contoured bottle, Jif's lemon-shaped juice dispenser, Lyle's sublime golden syrup tin, utterly unchanged since 1884, Toblerone's timeless triangular wrapper, which evokes jagged alpine peaks, Pringles' vacuum-packed cardboard cylinder, which once popped can't be stopped, or Toilet Duck's brilliantly biomorphic, U-necked container, which embodies the bleach brand's under-bowl promise, packaging can provide a powerful point of differentiation.[37]

Packaging's principal purpose, admittedly, is to protect and preserve the contents. Think of all those resealable plastic zips and flaps and lids and covers on brands of cheese, crackers, crisps, cereals, cooked meats, cartons of ice cream. However, they can be – and are – made to perform more than a protective function. Absolut owes much of its success to its innovative vodka bottle, subsequently the centrepiece of a legendary advertising campaign. Müller cornered the market in yogurt with its clever fruit-filled corners. After Eight mints are loved as much for their elegant individual wrappings – which conveniently remain in place when each delicious sliver is liberated – as they are for their exquisite taste. The pickled earthworm in authentic bottles of Mezcal tequila is just as appetizing, provided you're blind drunk at the time. Pez candy containers are so distinctive that they're bought and sold and traded by collectors (and inadvertently led to the creation of eBay). One of the joys of consumer society, as the 'unboxing' phenomenon indicates, is the experience of opening a newly purchased Apple product and removing it gently from its beautiful cardboard cocoon.[38] Jo Malone's beribboned personal care repair kits are equally exquisite, gorgeously erogenous.

Indeed, if ever proof were needed of packaging's importance, look no further than cigarettes and colognes. The tobacco companies have been up in arms of late, determined to resist the imposition of rules on plain packaging.[39] Ever since Australia introduced a 'ban on branding' in 2012 – by which they mean the look, the livery, the trade dress – Big Tobacco has been lobbying like crazy, threatening all sorts of legal challenges, raising the twin spectres of smuggling and counterfeiting, and presenting lots of scientific evidence that graphic design is no big deal when it comes to consumer choice. The very vehemence of their reaction is a sure sign that packaging is very important.

Perfume makers would surely agree. Because their beautiful bottles cost as much to develop as the fabulous fragrances do to create. Even the briefest of stops in Duty Free Shops provides a lesson in the art of packaging. Marc Jacobs' Daisy, Jean Paul Gaultier's Le Male and Ma Dame, Issey Miyake's minimalist masterpieces, Viktor & Rolf's remarkable Spicebomb, which looks like a hand grenade, and Chanel's magnificent modernist bottle for No 5, practically unchanged for the best part of a century, are monuments to the creative geniuses behind the brands.

There's more to packaging than bottles, boxes, tubs, tubes and tetrapaks, though. Packaging is best understood as a spectrum, an array that includes the primary container (carton, sachet, etc.), the protective wrapper (polythene, tissue paper), the shopping bag (Zara's are especially prized), the delivery lorries (e.g. Innocent Drinks' grass vans) and the retail stores/websites that sell the goodies. The stupendous flagship stores of Nike or Burberry or Louis Vuitton or Victoria's Secret are an increasingly important part of the package. They are the spectacular spaces where the full array of sensory branding can be unleashed.[40]

Even Victoria's Secret, however, must bow before the packaging tour de force that is Charmin's Potty Palooza. Also known as The Rolling Thrones, this comprises a massive mobile commode that tours the United States promoting Procter & Gamble's premier brand of toilet paper. Conley takes up the story …

> Complete with flushing porcelain toilets, hardwood floors and air conditioning, Potty Palooza gets little competition from the ranks of rented porta-potties lined up outside the concerts, sporting events and festivals it frequents. 'Guests' are offered a menu of toilet paper options that go beyond the standard white roll, with features that appeal to customers' sense of smell and touch. The high-end stalls have become so popular with visitors that many will walk half a mile and wait in a fifteen-minute line, passing vacant portable toilets along the way.[41]

What Conley *doesn't* mention is that Potty Palooza stalls are decorated in Charmin's proprietary shade of rich royal blue. Just as Sony used to advertise its Bravia televisions with the tagline Colour Like No Other, so too brands package themselves in signature shades of their chosen hue. Coca-Cola, as everyone knows, 'owns' red and white. Harrods is renowned for its dark green and gold livery. Selfridge's shopping bags are a striking shade of yellow. Jack Wills, the casualwear brand, is famous for its pink and blue candy-stripes. EasyJets are unmistakable thanks to their bright orange aircraft. Cadbury takes great pride in its imperial purple packaging and sued Nestlé for having the temerity to sell chocolate bars in its trademarked Pantone 2685C. Louboutin, the luxury shoe maker, likewise sued YSL for copying the China Red soles of its vertiginous stilettos. The Tour de France's famous yellow jersey is an echo of the event's first sponsor, a periodical printed on bright yellow paper. Diehard fans of Cardiff City football club are no less committed to the team's traditional blue kit. But, when new owner Vincent Tan changed it to red, in the belief that red sells better than blue, the supporters revolted en masse, continued to wear their old colours to home games and, after campaigning against the makeover, eventually got the Asian owner of the Bluebirds to see sense.[42]

The commercial use of colour is a fascinating subject. All sorts of dos and don'ts and old wives' tales and cultural taboos abound.[43] Gold, brand managers are told, stands for success, luxury, wealth, being number one. Green is fresh, natural, eco-friendly and Irish to be sure, to be sure. White is pure and innocent; black is elegant and mysterious; purple is rich, royal; orange and yellow denote discounts; brown is yuck, best avoided, the ugly twin brother of beige; red is the colour of passion, energy, danger; and pink is not just for little girls, Barbie fans and Juicy Couture onesies. Got that?

Since every culture sees colour differently, there are exceptions to every alleged rule. Little wonder many brand managers bring in colour consultants to help them solve their packaging problems. They tell us, for example, that up to 90% of consumer buying decisions are based primarily on the precise shade of the product or its packaging.[44] Brand naming consultants make broadly similar claims, mind you, as do logotype touts and sloganeers, those who sell the secrets of selling.

MASCOT MADNESS

Another thing Conley doesn't mention in his paean to Potty Palooza is that the facilities are supervised by Charmin's brand mascot, Leonard the Bear. As bears famously you-know-what in the woods, his presence might seem superfluous. However, mascots like Leonard have long been a key component of the branding mix. Tony the Tiger, Churchill the Bulldog, Charlie the Tuna, the Pillsbury Doughboy, the Guinness Toucan, the Playboy Bunny, the Linux Penguin, the Andrex Puppy, the Honey Monster, Mr Peanut, Mr Muscle, Bertie Bassett, Barry Scott, the Jolly Green Giant, the Go Compare Opera Singer, the Man from Del Monte and New Zealand's famous Four Square Guy are just a few of the more memorable brand mascots. They are known to millions and loved by millions more.[45]

Mascots not only burrow into consumers' affections but they can completely transform the sponsoring brand's fortunes. Consider Alexandr Orlov, the irritating meerkat mascot for Comparethemarket.com, who raised a run-of-the-mill price comparison website into one of the major players in a very competitive industry. The immortal Smash Martians similarly turned an unappetizing brand of instant mashed potato into the undisputed market leader thanks to their amusing alien escapades. Consider, conversely, the spokes-dromedary for Camel cigarettes, Smokin' Joe Camel, whose too cool for school attitude proved so popular with impressionable American teenagers that the Feds sanctioned his capital punishment. France's pneumatic Michelin Man may look more like a superhero nowadays than the bon viveur he began as, but in a world of identikit car tyres, Michelin remains the best known brand (Think Box 7).

THINK BOX 7

Nunc est Bibendum[46]

The Michelin Man – Bibendum – was conceived in 1894 when André and Edouard Michelin, the brothers behind the company, noticed how a display of rubber tyres looked a lot like a human torso. Later, in collaboration with graphic designer O'Galop, this tower of tyres was turned into a totemic mascot, albeit by accident. Touting for business, O'Galop showed the brothers a speculative sketch that had already been rejected by a brewery. It comprised a pot-bellied caricature of Gambrinus, the legendary king of Flanders who invented brewing, holding up a foaming flagon of beer while exclaiming in Latin, *Nunc est bibendum!* (now is the time to drink!).

Fortunately for O'Galop, André Michelin had previously used a similar expression at a civil engineering conference, when he claimed that his company's proprietary pneumatic tyre 'drinks up obstacles'. Inspired, O'Galop promptly redrew Gambrinus as a rotund tyre-man holding up a beer beaker filled with sharp nails, shards of glass and assorted road surface detritus. *Nunc est bibendum*, furthermore, was freely translated as 'the tyre that drinks up obstacles'. And in April 1898, the inaugural poster of the Michelin Man, later nicknamed Bibendum, duly appeared.

Once born, Bibendum didn't stand still. On the contrary, the chubby, cigar-smoking, lorgnette-wearing icon was soon exploited to the full. Facing fierce competition despite a rapidly growing market, the Michelin brothers sensibly refused to stint on brand building. O'Galop produced more than 300 separate designs, most featuring the rubber man in a host of poses, some satirical, some historical, some sporting, all brilliant, all boisterous, all completely over the top. Before long, Bibendum bestrode the globe, both literally and metaphorically, since the increasingly multinational company's mascot was often drawn at superhuman scale.

Many might imagine that there's nowhere to go after holding up the planet, Atlas-like. However, the mascot cannily reinvented himself as a public servant, the guardian angel of road users. He started producing much-admired guides to good food and lodgings, as well as the maps that helped travellers find their way to recommended waystations. When not working, what's more, Bibendum found time for the joys of family life. He got himself a wife, Mrs Michelin (who promoted air pumps), a bouncing baby boy, Bib (who was responsible for bicycle tyres) and an ever-faithful hound (who bounded along in Bibendum's pneumatic footsteps).

As the years rolled by, however, the Michelin Man gradually shed his adoring family and lost a fair amount of weight. In the aftermath of the First World War, motor car tyres became progressively wider – the so-called 'Comfort' tyre was introduced in 1923 – and, accordingly, Bibendum was drawn with fewer and fewer bands around the midriff. The upshot was a much slimmer, more youthful, reliably reassuring appearance, which the mascot retains to this day, despite numerous sales territory-necessitated adjustments. The sybaritic style of the early ads – a corpulent, drink-swilling, middle-aged man – has been superseded by an athletic, ever-youthful look, such as the famous face-forward, fist-pumping, 'Running Bib' designs of Walter Storozuk. More recently, he has been reimagined as a superhero. Is it a bird? Is it a plane? No, it's a tyre!

Thinking Outside the Think Box

Most brand mascots have a fascinating backstory. Select one of the following – Elsie the Cow, Smokie the Bear, Tony the Tiger, the Four Square Guy – and develop a biographical timeline, noting important departures along the way. Compare the latest version with the original. How does it differ?

Mascots can even work wonders in mature product categories, where market shares are practically set in stone. Take Cadbury's drumming gorilla.[47] As you may be aware, the drumstick-wielding silverback burst on to our screens in August 2007, when a ninety-second ad for Dairy Milk, Cadbury's signature chocolate bar, was first broadcast. It featured a glowering great ape sitting behind a drum-kit, preparing to play along with Phil Collins' 1981 number one, *In the Air Tonight*. Although the ad didn't depict the actual product – apart from a subtle hint of the company's purple livery – it sent sales into orbit. Dairy Milk's market share promptly increased by nine percentage points, which is a mind-boggling leap in a product category like confectionary. It boosted sales across the company's entire range for good measure, Curly Wurlys and Creme Eggs included. It also did much to restore Cadbury's corporate reputation, which had been damaged by contamination incidents and food hygiene scares at the firm's venerable factory in Bournville, Birmingham.

More than that, the drumming gorilla was a social media sensation. Within a week of its appearance, the great ape was viewed more than half a million times on YouTube. All sorts of parodies and spoofs popped up on the video sharing website and all kinds of tall tales bounced around the blogosphere, not least that Phil Collins himself was inside the monkey suit. The semi-retired rock star denied any involvement with a self-deprecating quip, 'The gorilla's a better drummer than me and he's got more hair!' But the very fact that Collins chose to comment added fuel to the branding flames and another decimal point or two to the gorilla's market share.[48]

Despite irrefutable evidence that mascots work, they are frowned upon by some. Whereas names and emblems get a lot of attention, mascots are generally regarded as gimmicky and childish, which they often are to some extent. Kids do indeed love them. However, they aren't confined to the breakfast cereal aisles of friendly neighbourhood supermarkets, nor the side-lines of sports stadiums, where they cavort and caper and keep kids happy while adults watch the match. On the contrary, a recent study of 1,200 brand mascots from the Aflac duck to the Investec zebra, revealed that they are found in every conceivable product category – cars, clothes, cosmetics, computers, credit cards, you name it.[49] More to the point, it showed that brand mascots generate visceral reactions from consumers of all ages. Kingsley, the scary, spiky, bright yellow mascot recently adopted by Partick Thistle F.C., is a perfect case in point, as is the cheeky monkey H'angus, who was voted Lord Mayor of Hartlepool in 2002 (and did a pretty good job by all accounts). Who, furthermore, can forget Cooly, the bovine mascot for the European Athletics Championship when it was held in Zurich in 2014? Cooly did the high jump, tried the pole vault, made a half-decent fist of the hurdles, tumbled into the water during an attempted steeplechase and, all things considered, gave Usain Bolt a run for his money.

SPECIAL OFFER

While you're getting your head round Usain's appearance in the European Championships, let me introduce a note of caution.[50] When studying branding it is easy to get caught up in the nuts and bolts of look and feel, the ins and outs of logos and liveries, the subtle connotations and denotations of brand names, the aesthetic appeal of the Helvetica font compared to the shortcomings of Comic Sans, the precise Pantone shade of the product's packaging and whether it can be trademarked or not, the benefits that humanoids bring as brand mascots compared to ungulates or amphibians, the ear-catching appeal of euphony versus the attention-grabbing clang of cacophony in successful advertising slogans.

Such things, important as they are, are less important at the end of the day than the *Offer*. That is, the actual products and services themselves. A brand's success or failure ultimately depends on the functions, the features, the price, the performance, the quality, the availability of the wares it offers to the consuming public. As Walker makes abundantly clear, 'If your airline's planes fall from the sky on a regular basis, that defines your brand, no matter how cutting-edge your social media strategy, award-winning your advertising, or appealing your logo may be.'[51] Several national airlines, beset by catastrophes, are terrible testament to this. As is BlackBerry, which despite its admirable brand name is a faller in the smartphone steeplechase and its brand equity has tumbled accordingly. Nokia's ringtone is undeniably unforgettable, but its once formidable phones are ancient history.

Now, this does not mean that the offered products or services are the be all and end all of branding. Red Bull, to cite but one celebrated instance, famously failed every look, taste and mouth-feel test known to man or beast. No other product had ever performed so badly. It was described by the testers as 'disgusting'. Yet the Red Bull brand not only triumphed in the only place that really matters, the marketplace, but it created a completely new category of beverages. It's a category that's full to the brim with Red Bull copycats – Monster, Rockstar, AMP and Full Throttle, for example – none of which are a patch on the original and best.

What it *does* mean, though, is that the offer is crucially important. There are lots of brands of hair straighteners on sale, but according to hair stylists of my acquaintance, none do the job as well as GHD. Ryanair treats its customers abominably from time to time and its advertising is crude and sexist. However it gets people to their destinations on schedule and offers the lowest fares bar none. Independent scientific tests show that Boots No 7 Protect and Perfect Intense Advanced Serum *really does* reduce the signs of ageing. Consumers, accordingly, queue round the block when it comes back into stock. Metro Bank delivers a level of customer service that far surpasses mainstream high street banks, who seem to care more about big bonuses for senior executives than hoi polloi punters who struggle with couldn't-care-less call centres and their infernal push-button menus.

Cillit Bang, similarly, is a barking mad brand name and Barry Scott its shouty spokesperson is the commercial equivalent of scraping fingernails down a blackboard. However, as the brand's superb product demonstration proves – a grubby penny becomes shiny after immersion in the goo – few products do a better job of cutting through bathroom grime. Decontamination experts use it to clean plutonium stains in decommissioned nuclear reactors, for goodness sake! 'Radioactivity levels have been significantly reduced following spray and wipedown with Cillit Bang', one says.[52] You can't buy brand endorsements like that.

By contrast, brands that fail to deliver the offer customers come to expect are heading for a fall. When Cadbury's new owner, Kraft, changed the consistency of the chocolate on Creme Eggs then added sultanas to Fruit & Nut, aficionados were affronted. When McVitie's reduced the fat content of its iconic digestives, biscuit lovers went ballistic (because the biccies disintegrated when dunked in a cup of tea). When big food companies downsized Roses chocolate boxes, Ritz cracker packets and bags of KP peanuts – while maintaining their prices – consumers noticed the difference and they weren't best pleased.[53] When Audi's cars started accelerating of their own accord, much to the alarm of their drivers, the brand's famous four-circle logo, legendary advertising tagline and memorable sonic mnemonic mattered not a jot. When massively successful sports brands suffer from a catastrophic loss of form, and the fans lose faith, only one thing is going to happen. Just ask Louis van Gaal. Or Stuart Lancaster, for that matter. When horsemeat is sold as beef by Tesco, when Colman's reduces the potency of its mustard, when Molton Brown alters the smell and consistency of its expensive shower gels, when Australia's favourite beer, Victoria Bitter, lowers its alcohol level to save a few cents on duty payments, when Coca-Cola changes its world famous formulation, as recounted in chapter 1, loyal customers won't stand for it!

Whatever else you read about branding, never forget that the offer – the core product or service itself – matters a very great deal. And if the offer goes awry, my friends, the only thing that can save the day is a persuasive brand story …

BRAND TASK

Get hold of a book of quotations – or go online – and pick a selection of memorable lines by famous poets. See if you can insert appropriate brand names, thereby turning them into useable taglines (e.g. I grow old, I grow old/Shall I wear the bottoms of my Wranglers rolled?). Then try inserting important poets' names into iconic advertising slogans (Just Donne It, Dante Leave Homer Without It, etc.). The funniest wins.

―――――――――――   **RECOMMENDED READINGS**   ―――――――――――

Rob Carney, *50 Best Logos Ever* (Future Publishing: Bath, 2013). Although it isn't the most comprehensive book on emblems, this text makes up in depth what it lacks in breadth. Carney asked a bunch of graphic designers to nominate their favourite logo and then explain why it's so good.

Satyendra Singh, 'Impact of Colour on Marketing', *European Journal of Marketing*, 44 (6), 2006, 783–789. The psychology of colour is a happy hunting ground for chancers and charlatans, who charge vast sums for their corporate services. This academic article takes a more sober approach to the subject.

Barbara J. Phillips, 'Defining Trade Characters and their Role in American Popular Culture', *Journal of Popular Culture*, 29 (4), 1994, 143–157. Barbara Phillips is the preeminent academic expert on brand mascots. She has written many, many papers on the subject, all of which are well worth reading.

Martin Lindstrom, *Brand Sense* (Kogan Page: London, 2005). Lindstrom's research is not to everyone's taste. Some scholars are sniffy about his work. However, he writes very well indeed. If you are going to read one book on organoleptics, make it this one. It's full of terrific brand yarns.

CHAPTER 4
BRANDS TELL STORIES

Overview

Stories are the Bitcoin of branding. A good story is worth its weight in gold. Like Playtex bras of old, stories lift and separate. This chapter tells the story of storytelling in branding, notes the significance of charisma and tradition, and identifies the elements of brand stories that most captivate contemporary consumers.

WHAT'S UP, WALT?

Walter Elias Disney (1901–1966) wasn't the most mild-mannered of men. Despite his avuncular public persona, and commendable desire to make Disneyland 'the happiest place on earth', Walt could be Grumpy at the best of times and Cruella de Vil at worst. If not quite Scar, Jafar and Shere Khan all rolled into one, he was closer to the Wicked Witch than he was Snow White.[1]

One day a nervous newspaper reporter approached Uncle Walt, hoping against hope he'd be in happy-go-lucky mood. 'What,' he asked Mickey's main man, 'is the secret of your brilliantly successful brand?' It was a reasonable question. Walt, by this stage, had made a string of superb animated movies from *Snow White and the Seven Dwarves* to *One Hundred and One Dalmatians*. He fronted a hugely successful television show, *The Wonderful World of Disney*, which garnered great viewing figures for NBC. And he owned the most supercalifragilisticexpialidocious amusement park on earth, complete with Cinderella's Castle, Mark Twain's Riverboat and multiple memorabilia merchants on Main Street USA.

The Disney brand was something to behold even back then and you might think that immodest mastermind behind the Magic Kingdom would be flattered by the reporter's obsequious question. But Uncle Walt bristled when he heard the bloodcurdling words 'what's the secret of your brand, Mr Disney?' Then he went completely bananas. His face turned red, his eyes bulged out and steam started coming out of his ears, just like in the cartoons.

Walt's fury, though, had nothing to do with revealing trade secrets. Unlike KFC or Coca-Cola, Disney didn't have a secret formula that had to be kept hidden, under lock and key, well away from prying eyes. Walt went nuts because he hated the word 'brand'.[2] As the reporter cowered in the corner, clutching his notebook, Walt let fly by way of reply. 'Branding is for cattle', he roared. 'Disney doesn't do branding', he added with a snarl. 'Disney tells stories', the great man hissed menacingly, 'and sells the tie-in merchandise.'

Now, it's no secret that Walter Elias Disney was a cross between Captain Hook and Lots-O'-Huggin Bear. Yet, innate irascibility aside, you might be wondering why he'd object so vehemently to the b-word. Part of the answer is that 'branding' has long been frowned upon in the cultural industries. And even today it's regarded either with a degree of discomfort or ice-cold anathema, as chapter 11 will explain.

The main reason Walt went ape, however, is because 'brand' was a buzz word – *the* buzz word in American business circles – back in his day. Although we're often told that the history of branding goes back to the dawn of civilization, with makers' marks on clay pots etc., the reality is that our understanding of branding – i.e. branding as we currently know it – dates from the 1950s (Think Box 8).

THINK BOX 8

The Story of the Study of Branding

Although many have written about the prehistory of branding, noting its antecedents like heraldry, watermarks and hallmarks. And although branding took off in the mid-19th century with the advent of mass production, mass consumption, mass communication and mass urbanization, the study of branding really only started in the early 1950s. It coincided with the postwar surge in television advertising and the birth of the baby boom generation. Several pioneering articles on brands and branding were published during this period and, in the decades that followed, ever more attention has been devoted to comprehending, conceptualizing and theorizing the subject.

According to Heding, Knudtzen and Bjerre[3], our understanding of branding has evolved through three main phases. The first was characterized by a focus on features, benefits and the communication of unique selling propositions (USPs). It was, in essence, company centric, principally concerned with the hands-on management of brands. How to do it and how best to go about it.

The second phase shifted the centre of branding attention from the company to the consumer. That is, the recipients of the marketing message rather than the senders. It was increasingly believed that, no matter what managers were trying to communicate about their brands, all that mattered was consumer reaction. Brands only really exist in consumers' minds.

The most recent phase regards brands as reeds in the wind of shifting socio-economic circumstances and the contradictions of contemporary consumer society. The brands that resolve these contradictions are those that rise above the rest, as Coca-Cola did in the turbulent 1960s with its Teach the World campaign and SUVs like Hummer did more recently in the post-9/11 world of existential anxiety.

These phases, it must be stressed, are not sequential. Although cultural approaches are in the driving seat right now, the consumer-centric and company-centric per-spectives still have many adherents. Heding et al.'s three schools of thought operate in parallel. The USP is still part of brand managers' lexicon and customer-focused concepts such as 'positioning' remain very much in fashion, not least because brand-ing ideas are being applied to ever more domains, from politics to places. There's room, it seems, for everyone. Branding is a house of many mansions. You pays your money and you takes your pick of paradigms, principles, practices.

Thinking Outside the Think Box

Heding et al.'s story of branding, like many stories, is an idealized, rags-to-riches nar-rative with a beginning, middle and end. It could be argued, though, that the reality of branding is closer to that depicted in *Game of Thrones*. Who are the Baratheons of branding, the Lannisters, the Starks? Where will it end?

The 1950s, of course, was the *Mad Men* era. It was the golden age of advertising. It saw the birth of our new brand world. One of the greatest of the real life Madison Avenue mad men was a suave English expat called David Ogilvy. After reading an article about branding in the *Harvard Business Review*, he immediately appropriated the magic word. It soon became his secret ingredient, the special sauce that helped his ad agency stand out from the make-a-bob mob on Madison Avenue.[4] He, more than anyone, turned it into the buzz word that Walt Disney abhorred.

Ogilvy was more than a smooth-talking showman, though. He was a brilliant copywriter with an unerring ability to weave intricate, merchandise-moving sto-ries around outstanding brands like Hathaway shirts, Schweppes tonic water and, not least, Rolls-Royce. 'At sixty miles an hour,' he wrote in perhaps his most potent ad, 'the loudest sound in this new Rolls-Royce comes from the electric clock.' He later revealed that, after reading the copy, the company's chief engi-neer shook his head sadly and sighed, 'It's time we did something about that damned clock.'

This statement about the engineer may or may not have been true.[5] But, embellished or otherwise, it exemplifies Ogilvy's brilliant ability to tell a terrific story. So much so, that he wrote several bestselling books full of fabulous brand yarns, not least a beautifully written autobiography which helped brand him as the foremost Mad Man of his era. It is entirely apt that the father of modern branding was a storyteller of the first water.

However, he wasn't as well-storied as Walt Disney. Whether it be the story of his multiple bankruptcies before *Steamboat Willie*, the all-or-nothing risk he took with *Snow White and the Seven Dwarves*, the out-and-out triumphs that were Disneyland and Walt Disney World, the studio's creative slump after his untimely death in 1966, its belated revival with blockbusters like *Lion King*, *Finding Nemo* and *Aladdin*, the bitter boardroom battles that damaged the brand at the beginning of the millennium, or the fable that Mickey's mentor is interred in a cryogenic capsule patiently waiting for medical science to get him back on his feet, Walt's multiple storylines may not be stranger than fiction, but they're fabulous all the same.[6]

The branded empire he presides over from his barometric casket currently includes movie studios and theme parks and cruise lines and television networks and retail stores and stage shows and social media and prodigious intellectual properties like Pixar, Marvel, *Star Wars* and *Frozen*. The last of these not only earned $1.3 billion at the worldwide box office, won two Academy Awards (for Best Animated Feature and Best Original Song), topped the Billboard charts with its triple-platinum-selling soundtrack for thirteen weeks, and sold so much ancillary merchandise that parents drew lots for the right to buy especially treasured tie-in items including limited edition Anna and Elsa dolls, but *Frozen* became a bona-fide cultural phenomenon. Consider this lovely little story, which was posted on a newspaper website in response to its columnist's claim that Frozen Fatigue was setting in:

> I was in K-Mart a couple of weeks ago with one of my two *Frozen*-obsessed daughters.
> *Let it Go* came on over the PA. Every girl in the store – dozens and dozens of them – as well as an awful lot of parents joined in. And everyone – all of the harassed shoppers and annoyed kids on a Saturday afternoon in a K-Mart in a mall – was happy.
> I'm a dyed-in-the-wool appalling music snob, and I should hate this sort of Dionesque warbling. But it's impossible not to like the effect of something like this. It's not often you see so many people cheered up by a song in a shop.[7]

BRANDS ARE STORIED!

If Walt Disney were alive today – and he may well be, come to think of it – his deep-frozen heart would surely be thawed by that uplifting anecdote. He might even be willing to concede that his brand done good. He'd no doubt add that you have to tell a tale to make the sale. But the gulf he envisaged between 'brand' and 'narrative' no longer exists. The two, in fact, are one. Brands are stories, according to many commentators. Branding, Twitchell tells us, 'is the application of a story to a product or service'.[8] A brand, Stern suggests, 'is a product or service with a story attached'.[9] The one thing all successful brands share, Tungate authoritatively states, 'is a great story'.[10] For John Williamson of the Wolff Olins consultancy, 'good brands are like novels you can't put down, they're the highest form of art and have to tell a fantastic story'.[11] Stanley Hainsworth, former creative director of Starbucks and Nike, concurs. When asked what is the most important thing to consider when creating a brand, he says, 'For me, it's all about having a story to tell.'[12] Tom Peters, the pugnacious uber-guru of business best practice, proclaims in his characteristically pithy manner, 'A brand is a story. Period.'[13]

The verdict, it seems, is in. 'Great brands are about smart and artful storytelling.'[14] Certainly, you don't have to look very hard to come across all sorts of intriguing brand narratives. These range from the shady stories of Bacardi, which allegedly involve bootlegging, the CIA, the Cosa Nostra and Chile's General Pinochet, through Gucci's over-the-top soap opera, which includes bitter family feuds, ferocious fisticuffs, and unsuccessful assassination attempts, via the philanthropic stories of Tata, the gigantic Indian conglomerate which is 66% owned by a charitable trust that gives generously to good causes across the subcontinent, to the legend of the IKEA flat-pack which was stumbled upon when an employee, Gillis Lundgren, cut the legs off a table to make it fit in the boot of his Volvo.

And if you think that's crazy, consider the wholly unfounded urban legends attached to prominent brands – Irn-Bru cures Ebola, Listerine is a carcinogen, Mountain Dew denudes sperm counts, Fanta was invented by the Nazis, Procter & Gamble are Satanists, Adidas stands for 'all day I dream about sex' – or indeed the all too true story about poor old Clarence Birdseye, who discovered the secret of flash-freezing fish during an expedition to the Arctic Circle in 1912. Then spent the next twenty years trying, trying, trying to break the pack ice of consumer resistance to frozen food.[15] He refused to let it go, akin to the kids in K-Mart.

Crazier still is the story behind Moleskine, the premium priced stationery brand, beloved by the creatives and hipsters among us.[16] According to the little booklet that comes with the legendary black notebook, the brand was used by esteemed artists and thinkers like Van Gogh, Pablo Picasso, Ernest Hemingway and Bruce Chatwin. The latter, writing in *Songlines*, describes his fondness for *carnets moleskine*, complete with end paper pouch and elastic band, which were sold by a specialist dealer in Paris. On hearing that the manufacturer is about to go bankrupt, Chatwin rushes to buy his much-loved moleskines in bulk. Only to discover that the maker has died and his heirs have sold the business. Shock. Horror. Tragedy. *Catastrophe!*

A decade or so later, a small Italian publisher came across Chatwin's *cri-de-coeur* and decided to bring back the moleskine, even though they had no connection whatso-ever to the original manufacturer. Modo & Modo outsourced production to China and marketed the repurposed product with aplomb to consumers who consider them-selves 'creative' or aspire to inclusion in the creative classes. The brand was acquired by venture capitalists in 2006 and subsequently listed on the stock market, where its shares were valued at €430 million. Some of the wannabe creatives who stump up for ultra-premium priced Moleskines may fear that the wool has been pulled over their eyes by clever marketing types. But, as it explains in the accompanying booklet:

> Today, Moleskine is synonymous with culture, imagination, memory, travel, and personal identity – in both the real world and the virtual world. It is a brand that identifies a family of notebooks, journals, diaries, and innovative city guides, adapted to various functions. With the diverse array of page formats, Moleskine notebooks are partners for the creative and imaginative professions of our time.

The real imagineers, my friends, are the storytelling brand managers at Moleskine.

STORIES, STORIES EVERYWHERE

Okay, so I've bought a Moleskine or two. Laugh if you like at my naivety. There's no fool like a sold fool. However, we're all suckers for stories. Humankind is a storytelling animal. We spend enormous amounts of time swapping stories. Telling jokes, trading gossip, spreading scuttlebutt, making excuses, writing blogs, forwarding emails, retweeting tweets, updating social media, whispering sweet nothings, engaging in banter, having a chin-wag, getting into arguments, listening to learned sermons, reading the daily newspapers and discussing the day with our partners after work are commonplace examples of common-or-garden storytelling.

Make no mistake, hard facts have their place. They are venerated by managers, heaven only knows. Spreadsheets are sacrosanct in corporate citadels, Amazon's apparently excepted.[17] However, as Collins correctly observes, 'We say we want information. But we don't experience the world through information. We experience the world through story.'[18] Who among us doesn't devote a lot of time to the invention of stories, not least at night when we dream sweet dreams or suffer recurring nightmares?

Still, the question has to be asked: Why do we do it? According to eminent scholars of narratology, stories help us make sense of this wildly unpredictable world and our painfully perilous existence. Hence the profusion of myths, legends, allegories and religious beliefs, which explain where we come from and where we're going to. Stories, we're also told, are social laboratories where the norms and customs of society are aired, transmitted and exposed to criticism. Stories enhance relationships, serve as a learning tool and help build an all-important sense of community. Stories help humans make sense of themselves. We weave our everyday experiences into life stories, which we strive to live by and, given the opportunity, recount to others. Storytelling, in the somewhat reductionist opinion of evolutionary psychologists, is nothing less than a survival mechanism.[19]

Storytelling is a selling mechanism, moreover. As Tom Peters points out, a good story has always been a good seller.[20] And you only have to look around for a few minutes to see that many, many, many brands are embracing the narrative imperative. Tiffany says that it's been celebrating the world's greatest love stories since 1837. Canon cameras, apparently, take more than mere pictures, they take stories. The Waldorf Astoria claims that 'stories begin here'. The iPad Air adds 'a stanza to the world's story'. Barclays issues a fairy story about banking, claiming that their brand makes dreams come true. Nationwide Building Society narrates a morality tale about its great British relaunch, concluding that it really is on the customer's side. Bulmers cider spins a yarn about the brand's unique taste, involving founders Percy and Fred and their put-upon pony called Tommy. Cono Sur wine urges consumers to live the stories that others only see in the movies. Israel's ministry of tourism claims that their county is a land of a million stories. Trollbeads bracelets assure buyers that every bead has a story and every story a bead. Land Rover relates thrilling tales about its Journey of Discovery from Britain to Beijing and invites adventurous owners to reciprocate. Dulux paint reminds home owners that life is a story which, with a covering of colour, will end happily ever after.

Look around for a few minutes more. What do you see? H&M launching an upscale sub-brand called & Other Stories; Molton Brown retailing a range of body washes based on literary classics like *Treasure Island, On the Road, Brave New World* and *The Four Musketeers*; John West boasting about 'the story on every can' that tells us when and where our sardines, tuna, mackerel and salmon were caught in a sustainable manner; and Kerrygold butter circulating a cute, child-friendly cartoon booklet about *City Sue the Cow*, a booklet not dissimilar to the ones previously circulated by Cheerios, Oreo, Froot Loops and Charmin bathroom tissue.[21]

As if that weren't enough to be getting along with, Berties shoe boxes come complete with a typewritten story (on the lid) about the birth of the brand in a remote Italian airport. Mimi Spencer's makeup bags contain a 'handwritten' note from the founder concerning best cosmetics practice. Full-scale biographies of much-loved brand mascots, including Aleksandr Orlov, PG Tips' Monkey and Ireland's own Mr Tayto, regularly top the bestsellers list (in the non-fiction category, naturally).[22] *The Lego Movie* storms the multiplexes to the tune of a $470 million worldwide gross (sales of the plastic bricks soar in addition). And Dustin Hoffman stars in a series of ads for Sky Atlantic, earnestly emoting 'Stories? We all spend our lives telling 'em. About this. About that. About people. But some – some stories are so good we wish they'd never end.'

There's no sign of them ending for branding. Audi, for instance, has recently retold Hans Christian Andersen's poignant fairytale *The Ugly Duckling*, where a much-derided, less than beautiful concept car of the 1920s turns into a drop-dead gorgeous, brilliant white A5. Louis Vuitton latterly blew its advertising budget on *L'Invitation au Voyage*, a fantastical flight in a hot air balloon from a vast empty square in central Paris to a masked ball in a packed palazzo in Venice. John Lewis goes for broke every

Christmas with big brand advertising epics involving imaginary penguins, love-struck snowmen, insomniac bears and a lonely old man on the moon. Levi Roots, the brains behind Reggae Reggae Sauce, not only tells the tale of his super-spicy condiments – a contestant on *Dragons' Den,* he sang his pitch to the panel and won them over – but also earns big bucks on the consultancy circuit telling the story behind the story of his super storied brand.

And, not to be outdone, Disney recently published a print ad promoting its storied theme parks with the wonderful words:

> We have always believed in the power of stories to fuel imagination. There is one story more magical than any other; a story that even Disney cannot create. A story of excitement, thrilled emotion, looks of amazement and shared memories. This is the story waiting for you to write with your kids at Disneyland Paris or Walt Disney World in Florida. This story starts the very moment you tell your children that you're all going to Disney. This moment is magical and so special, both for them and for you. This year, we're celebrating your story, paying tribute to our true heroes: your children. For the first time, they will be at the heart of the Park's magic. Your story begins at disneyparks.co.uk.

THE STORY STORY

Facts tell, stories sell. No doubt about it. But what's the story with stories? How come narrative's the bees' knees of branding nowadays? That's a good question. Some say it's human nature. Humans tell stories. Humans tell stories about the things that surround them. Consumers are surrounded by brands. Therefore, consumers tell stories about branding. End of story.

Others consider it, not as the workings of some deep-seated instinct, but as a sign of desperation. Goods and services are becoming increasingly indistinguishable. There are ever more almost identical products competing for increasingly choosy customers. Since the only thing that separates them is the story behind the brand – be it genuine or fabricated – the accompanying story gets told and retold and re-retold. End of story.

Yet others detect a bandwagon at work. If storytelling is seen to work for one brand, such as Comparethemarket.com, others embrace the idea and the bandwagon starts rolling. Momentum gathers. Specialist storytelling consultancies spring up, academic experts pile in as only they can, self-appointed experts in brand narratology emerge from the woodwork, and the idea accelerates ever faster. It's a freewheeling bandwagon, what's more, that's been rolling in many other domains besides branding – politics, medicine and jurisprudence among them.[23] When would-be Masterchefs boast about the stories they tell on their plates of food, it's fair to say that we live in a narrated age. It's a narrated age, yet other commentators contend, that owes much to latter-day technological developments, Web 2.0 in particular. Social media are story factories, story distributors, story portals, story vendors, story promoters, story resellers, story recyclers, story enforcers, story stores, story agora.

Regardless of the reasons, there's no doubt that brand narratives are big nowadays. And getting bigger as gurus like Tom Peters big stories up with erudite talk of myths, legends, epics, archetypes, symbology, spirituality and the Greco-Roman gods of the marketplace. In our overwhelmingly secular society, where scientific method is held in much higher esteem than the good book ...

> Just Do It becomes a profound philosophical statement. Brands step into the void created by the lack of an effective societal mythology. The human psyche is hungry for the order and meaning which myth provides. Brands are more than happy to offer up their own vision of how life should be lived. Our myths are increasingly created from what we buy. And what is sold to us.[24]

Whether consumers accept such claims or not, there's no doubt that stories abound in and around every element of the branding mix. Names, logos, slogans, mascots, packaging, products and organoleptics are narrative goldmines for the dream weavers of branding. To pluck a few examples at random:

Name

When it comes to naming, few names are more fascinating than Hush Puppies, the celebrated crepe-soled suede shoes that dominated the casual footwear market in the days before trainers were the comfy casuals of choice.[25] Legend has it that Jim Muir, the sales manager tasked with marketing the (unnamed) product, visited an old friend in rural Tennessee. Jim's pal owned several yappy dogs that wouldn't stop barking. To keep his pets quiet, he threw them little bits of fried corn meal, colloquially known as 'hush puppies'. Watching this, Jim put two and two together. Namely, that 'dogs' is a slang word for feet and that people with aching feet sometimes say 'my dogs are barking'. Hush Puppies was perfect for the product. A massive brand was born.

Logo

You've seen the Shell sign on innumerable petrol stations here, there and everywhere. But why, given the enormous variety of seashells in the world, choose a scallop as an emblem? What, indeed, do seashells – let alone scallops – have to do with oil wells, derricks, refineries and so forth? Well, apart from the fact that shells are one of the organic compounds that constitute fossil fuels, the name was adopted in 1894 because the oil tankers that transported the petroleum were all named after shells. The scallop came from the coat of arms of Shell's biggest customer in India, a certain Mister Graham. The Graham family had adopted St. James's shell after their ancestors made a pilgrimage to Santiago de Compostela in Spain. Throughout history, the scallop shell has served as an identity marker for pious people on pilgrimages.[26] Shell's pilgrim spirit, some allege, is sadly lacking nowadays on account of its eco-unfriendly derricks in the Arctic Circle. That's another story, though.

Slogan

In his brilliant book about the twenty best advertising campaigns of all time, Twitchell tells the story behind one of the most successful slogans of the 20th century, Clairol's 'Does She or Doesn't She?' Clairol was the first home hair colouring kit. It was a breakthrough product that transformed an expensive and elaborate multi-stage process into a simple, single-step, no-nonsense hair-care routine. Clairol had a problem, however. The only people who dyed their hair back then were glamorous Hollywood actresses, bottle blonde gold-diggers and what were euphemistically known as 'fast women'. The challenge of selling the unsellable was given to Shirley Pollykoff, a feisty young copywriter at Foote, Cone & Belding. Knowing that most women would 'rather die than admit they dye', she came up with the wonderfully interrogative tagline. With its slightly saucy connotations, 'Does She...' tapped into the racy reputation of hair colouring but also turned the slogan into a customer-attracting conundrum. Sales took off and, to this day, the hair colouring category is a massive money-spinner for the beauty industry. The products cost practically nothing to manufacture but the brands sell for a small fortune.[27]

Mascot

Although the Michelin Man is much better known, the most exquisite car-related mascot is Rolls-Royce's Spirit of Ecstasy. The diaphanously dressed female figurine, with arms outstretched, is almost as iconic as the luxury brand itself. She is inseparable from the Roller's allure. What many don't know, though, is that the 'silver lady' is a symbol of, and memorial to, a mad passionate love affair.[28] A century or so ago, a certain blue-blooded British aristocrat, Baron Montagu of Beaulieu, fell head-over-heels in love with his secretary, Eleanor Thornton. But rather than divorce his equally blue-blooded wife for a mere commoner – and the social ostracism that would surely follow – Montagu and his paramour conducted their affair in secret. The Baron commissioned a silver statue of Ms Thornton, which was mounted on the bonnet of his bespoke Rolls-Royce and subsequently served as the prototype for the Spirit of Ecstasy. Five years later, in December 1915, the love birds were on board a boat to India when it was torpedoed by a German U-boat south of Crete. Montagu of Beaulieu survived. Eleanor Thornton didn't, though she still lives on in spirit.

Package

There are so many incredible stories about packaging (such as the one attached to the Coca-Cola bottle, which was famously designed to be recognizable in the dark, and even when broken) that it's difficult to decide which one to tell. Let's go with Cohiba, the world-renowned cigars which symbolize Cuba in much the same way that Guinness embodies Ireland and Bentley Great Britain.[29] So much so, boxes of Cohiba are routinely given as official gifts by Cuban diplomats. Created in 1966, the packaging of the ultra-premium priced stogies – the limited edition Cohiba Behikes cost around £250 apiece – comprises a bright yellow livery on an embossed black-and-white background. That's distinctive enough, albeit nothing especially outlandish. The real kicker is that the packaging was designed by Fidel Castro himself. And, of course, the great man was often photographed puffing contentedly on his favourite brand. When the CIA mounted its farcical assassination attempt in the late 1960s, the infamous exploding cigars that didn't were none other than Cohibas. This might be misinformation, mind you.

Product

Another brand that's renowned for its packaging is Toblerone, not least on account of the rampant brown bear hidden in its muted Matterhorn graphic. There's a much-recycled urban legend, mentioned earlier, that the cardboard container of the triangular, chocolate-covered, honey and almond-flavoured product was inspired by the serrated shape of the Swiss Alps. Granted, the great confection carries coincidental connotations of Alpine peaks. Hence the fable. But the shape of the superlative chocolate bar was actually based upon an erotic dance routine from the Folies Bergère in Paris, whose saucy soubrettes ended their performances in the upskirt shape of a huge human pyramid. More intriguing than that – even more intriguing, if truth be told, than the secret knack of breaking apart the last two segments of an extra big bar – is the strange but true fact that the triangular design of the chocolate bar was patented. Not trademarked, patented. And the patent officer who granted the Toblerone patent was none other than Albert Einstein.[30] Suck on that Cohiba!

Organoleptics

Few smells are more familiar than Chanel No 5. Famously endorsed by Marilyn Monroe – and for men at a loss come Christmastime, a failsafe gift purchase for their long-suffering partners – Chanel No 5 was the very first synthetic perfume. Although all sorts of myths and legends surround the numeral (Coco's birthday? Her lucky number? The fifth sample out of eight?), it was her selling of the smell that really takes the branding garland.[31] Way back in 1921, Coco concentrated on the carriage trade and before her well-heeled clients arrived for their fittings, she'd surreptitiously spritz the changing rooms with the striking synthetic scent. When her customers enquired about the gorgeous aroma, Coco feigned indifference, saying it was nothing special, no big deal, just something she'd come across in Grasse. However, she just happened to have a few spare phials they could keep. And when they came back for more – and their friends did too – Coco 'reluctantly' agreed to make the fragrance commercially available. Supplies were strictly limited, she added conspiratorially. Meantime, her factory was working at full tilt, manufacturing the brand in bulk …

CHARISMA AND TRADITION ARE CRUCIAL

Coco's fables, of course, don't begin and end with olfaction. On the contrary, the brand she started is suffused with stories. From the contention that Coco spied for the Nazis, through her purported fling with the killer of Rasputin, past the strange unexplained intervention of Winston Churchill, who helped her escape the postwar purge of collaborators, to the maltreatment she meted out to many models, seamstresses, business partners, etc., Chanel swims in a sea of turbulent stories. All of them add to the mystique of her marvellous brand, as do Karl 'the Kaiser' Lagerfeld's latter-day exertions. These include the prodigiously expensive, narrative-led commercials starring Nicole Kidman, Brad Pitt, Gisele Bündchen et al., the totally over-the-top, money no object catwalk shows, such as the Chanel Airlines extravaganza in 2015, and his affronted reaction to the recent EC threat to No 5's special ingredients, which might necessitate a risky reformulation of Coco's magic potion.

Regardless of the legislative outcome, Chanel's multi-volume brand narrative rolls ever on. And we haven't even considered the Little Black Dress, the famous tailored jacket, the iconic two-tone shoes or the scandalous garçonne look of the 1920s. As the *Financial Times* acknowledges about the brand's imperishable appeal:

> What Chanel has that other fashion designers don't is as basic as the little black dress: a really fantastic narrative. And if history teaches us anything, it's that narratives – stories that can be passed on through generations – are what lasts. Especially narratives that contain love, sex, death, abandonment, jewels, Russian aristocrats, horses, feminism, drugs, Nazis – you name it, it's probably in there. As a result the mythology of Chanel has become larger than fashion … Like all mythological tales, it is open to endless reinterpretation.[32]

Whatever else is said about Coco, it can't be denied that she was unusually charismatic. Charisma is notoriously difficult to define, not unlike branding. But most authorities agree that it pertains to personal magnetism or charm.[33] It is an ineffable, indefinable quality that attracts or inspires adulation. It is a kind of special sparkle or divine talent that is given to some but not to others. Charisma, in short, is what Coco Chanel would presumably call *je ne sais quoi*.

Some brands have *je ne sais quoi* in abundance. According to Kevin Roberts, the worldwide CEO of Saatchi & Saatchi, these include Amazon, Apple, The Body Shop, CNN, Coca-Cola, Disney, Dyson, eBay, Google, Harley-Davidson, Italy, Lego, Levi's, McDonald's, Manchester United, Nelson Mandela, Nike, Nintendo, Nokia, Pampers, Red Cross, Swatch, Toyota, Vespa and Virgin. He terms them 'lovemarks' rather than trademarks and describes them as 'the charismatic brands that people love and fiercely protect, for keeps'.[34] Other commentators describe them as 'iconic' brands, 'legendary' brands, 'passion' brands, or 'cult' brands.[35] Whatever the terminology, they are charming, captivating, one-of-a-kind brands that consumers would be bereft without. Just like Chanel – and Chanel's greatest spokesperson, Marilyn Monroe – they have charisma to spare.

So where does this charisma come from? Some say it's inbuilt, a gift from the gods of branding and therefore beyond the reach of the majority. In reality, it's related to the multiplicity of stories that accumulate around charismatic brands, *à la* Chanel. As Hegarty rightly observes, 'a brand is an agglomeration of stories linked together by a vision'.[36]

Consider Guinness. The brand abounds in stories: stories of its founding, fables of its struggles, whispers of its ingredients, tall tales of its logo, shaggy dog stories of its advertising, legends of its involvement with – and the countless yarns recounted in – Irish theme pubs around the world, including the urban myth that the mighty brew is an aphrodisiac (in Nigeria it's colloquially known as 'a baby in a bottle'). True or not, all add to the beguiling beverage's allure.[37]

The Body Shop owes much of its (once formidable) charisma to the stirring accounts of Anita Roddick and her intrepid adventures while building an innovative, eco-friendly, socially-responsible brand of beauty products on ethical principles. Sustainable sourcing, recyclable containers, natural ingredients, no testing on animals and fair prices for third world suppliers. These are commonplaces of the personal care industry today. However, if it weren't for Anita's uncompromising attitude and her refusal to be browbeaten by naysayers – not to mention her unerring eye for a good story – the Body Shop brand would never have expanded beyond the back streets of Brighton, much less conquered the universe of cosmetics. Yes, her best-known story, the one about neighbouring funeral directors complaining bitterly about The Body Shop's brand name, may or may not have been true. I suspect not. But it's a fantastic bit of brand hokum, one that Roddick recounted repeatedly.[38]

Richard Branson likewise benefits from the multiplicity of (often contradictory) narratives that adhere to his charismatic brand.[39] The story of his failures at school, due to dyslexia. The story of his abject lack of business experience, hence the virginal brand name. The story of his titanic courtroom battles with big bad British Airways, where the underdog won hands down. The story of his long hair, shaggy beard, cheesy grin and casual attire that helps perpetuate the ageing hippie, anti-establishment, so not a capitalist, stickin' it to The Man myth. The story of his brilliant ability to seize every passing promotional opportunity – from the Sex

Pistols scandal to the conflagration on Necker Island – and turn it to his brand's advantage. The story of his larger-than-life escapades and near-death experiences in high altitude hot air balloons, super-duper speedboats racing across the Atlantic and the soon-to-be, maybe-next-year, almost-nearly-there space flights in Virgin Galactic is nothing less than the *Odyssey* of commercial life.[40] The fact that he has published six (yes, six) separate autobiographies tells us everything we need to know about Branson's narrative acumen. Love him or loathe him, Richard Branson's the John Grisham of branding.

It is this accumulation of lore – stories, rumours, allegations, insinuations, half-truths, little white lies – that sprinkles charismatic fairy dust on some brands but not on others: Virgin Atlantic rather than American Airlines; Body Shop instead of Boots; Guinness more so than Beamish; Chanel in lieu of Chloé; Nike above and beyond New Balance; Ben & Jerry's over Baskin-Robbins; Disney in preference to Centre Parcs; Apple as opposed to Asus; Red Bull, Harley, Selfridge's, Primark, Camper, Harry Potter and RMS *Titanic* rather than Dr Pepper, Honda, Debenhams, Matalan, Clarks, Artemis Fowl and RMS *Olympic* respectively.

This agglomeration of stories is partly a function of *tradition*. All other things being equal, the longer a brand has been around the more narrative wool it gathers along the way, the more yarns it spins, the more dreams it weaves, the more telling tales it cuts from the whole cloth. Many of our most loved brands have been available for a very long time and the very fact that our parents and grandparents once played with Duplo bricks, munched Kellogg's Frosties, sipped PG Tips tea, dunked McVitie's digestive biscuits, used Fairy Liquid to do the dishes, drove their Vauxhall past the Esso petrol station en route to Sainsbury's supermarket where they stocked up on Batchelors peas, Heinz beans, Hovis bread, Lurpack butter, Birdseye fish fingers and Mr Kipling's fruit fancies, means more than a little for many consumers. Levi's jeans are nowhere near as fashionable nowadays as, say, Made in Heaven, but the brand's still got heritage in spades. Liberty lacks the razzle-dazzle of Harvey Nichols but, as department stores go, it's a sleeping giant with lashings of lineage. Listerine mouthwash isn't short of competition, however the history of the brand is so bizarre that consumers can't help but be drawn to it. Named after Sir Joseph Lister, pioneer germ fighter, Listerine began as a powerful disinfectant. Derived from carbolic acid, it was used to swab out operating theatres before, during and after surgical procedures.[41] Thereafter, it was variously sold as an antiseptic, as an aftershave, as a hair restorer, as a cure for the common cold, as a treatment for acute athlete's foot, as a remedy for sexually transmitted diseases in general and gonorrhoea in particular. It's good to gargle.

Tradition isn't everything, admittedly. If it were we'd still be using Lycos not Google, MySpace not Facebook, Napster not Spotify, C&A not Next, Woolworths not Argos, Wimpy not McDonald's, Dillons not Amazon, the Co-op not Tesco, Skytrain not easyJet, Nokia not Samsung, Netscape not Explorer, MG Rover not BMW Mini, Triumph not Kawasaki, 4711 not CK1, and Britannica not Wikipedia.

What tradition provides, though, is the raw material for bedazzling brand stories. The challenge facing marketing managers is to mould that raw material into captivating narratives – the captivating narratives that can help raise charismatic brands above the rest. It is brand managers' ability to use the tools, techniques and tricks of the storytelling trade – surprise, suspense, cliff-hangers, happy endings and what have you – that keeps consumers transfixed, terrified, tormented, wondering what on earth will happen next.

TELLING COMPELLING TALES

What often happens next, in my experience, is that students struggle a wee bit with brand storytelling. Making the imaginative leap from brand-as-logo to brand-as-narrative is taxing enough. However, it's doubly taxing when grandiose words like myth, archetype, narratology, story arcs and so on are bandied about.[42] They all seem so *excessive* when we're talking about bags of crisps, bottles of water or bars of chocolate. On reading Holt's[43] claim that 'The product is simply a conduit through which consumers can experience the stories that the brand sells. When consumers sip a Coke, Corona or Snapple, they are imbibing the stories anchored in those drinks', their entirely understandable reaction tends to be: Huh?

In order to get over the huh hurdle, it's necessary to bear three things in mind. First, brand narratives, by and large, are closer to anecdotes than epics, more like Trivial Pursuit than *In Search of Lost Time*. We are not talking about the *Iliad* here, let alone *Beowulf*, though some are arguably in *Godfather* territory. Gucci's, for example. Bacardi's too. Virgin's as well.

Second, humankind has a natural flair for storytelling. It's no harder than learning to swim. True, only a select few are endowed with the yarn spinning abilities of J.K. Rowling or Stephen King or Steven Spielberg or James Cameron, never mind Walt Disney. However, we can hone what talents we have. Storytelling is a craft, a skill akin to pottery, painting, or playing a musical instrument. It's a craft that can be improved with graft, with practice, with persistence.[44]

Third, most stories contain five clearly identifiable elements which are readily interpretable in branding terms. These are *Character, Location, Action, Message* and *Plot*. When artfully combined, they CLAMP consumers tightly and keep hold of them thereafter.

The CLAMP model is briefly summarized in Think Box 9. But let's not get bogged down in the nuts and bolts of narration. There are lots of outstanding handbooks and academic articles on the subject.[45] It's sufficient to note that, from a branding perspective, the single most important component of CLAMP is the first one. Character, without question, is crucial. It's the characters more than anything that make narratives compelling and bring us back for more. People like Sherlock Holmes, Indiana Jones, James Bond, Bertie Wooster, Hannibal Lecter, Scarlett O'Hara, Lara Croft, Princess Leia, Lady Macbeth, Miss Marple, Lisbeth Sandler and suchlike remain in the memory long, long after we've forgotten the details of the stories that surround them. The frequency with which narratives are named after the principal character – *Cinderella, Lolita, David Copperfield, Don Quixote, King Lear, Jane Eyre, Huckleberry Finn, Madame Bovary, Moll Flanders, Anna Karenina,* etc. – is testament to the importance of the people who populate the stories we love.

THINK BOX 9

Clamping the Consumer

Character is king when it comes to telling stories that sell. The escapades of Sam Walton or Alan Sugar or Donald Trump or Oprah Winfrey or Howard Schultz or Mark Zuckerberg or Ingvar Kamprad or Michelle Mone or Simon Cowell are a crucial part of their products' appeal. The people behind the brands we love – and love to hate like *The X Factor* – are what keep customers coming back for more. If an authentic character figure doesn't exist, celebrities are a convenient standby. Their tendency to go off the rails, *à la* Lindsay Lohan, adds an additional frisson, furthermore.

Location is crucial for storytellers and much-loved by consumers (consider Middle Earth, Narnia, Westeros). So much so, many people want to live there. Iconic brands, Holt claims, create 'populist worlds', whether it be the Wonderful World of Disney, the not so wonderful world of *Grand Theft Auto*, the mythical Mexican beach that's associated with cool, refreshing Corona beer, or the high, wide and handsome mountain range of Marlboro Country where men are men and cigarettes are smoked with impunity.

Action is an essential aspect of storytelling. If nothing much is happening, people tend to lose interest, understandably enough. According to storytelling gurus like Zuckerman, *conflict* is the key to keeping consumers interested and getting them talking about the brand.[46] The head-to-head conflict – often decades long – between big belligerent brands is never less than fascinating. But making things happen, introducing new and improved products, mounting ad campaigns, tweaking the packaging, precipitating a price war, etc. are important activities too.

Message matters. The most meaningful brand stories are those that go beyond the basic message 'this brand is good for you, buy it'. They tap into something more profound, more meaningful for consumers. Just as works of fiction like *Uncle Tom's Cabin* can change the world, so too great brand stories, such as Dove's Campaign for Real Beauty, can make things happen. For the most part, brand messages are fairly straightforward – Coke refreshes, Tesco helps, Facebook connects, Amazon delivers, Olay rejuvenates – but a deeper level's possible as well.

Plot is prodigiously important, arguably second only to character. Ever since Aristotle, we've known that stories must have a beginning, middle and end. We also know that plots come in a limited number of forms including Overcoming the Monster, Rags to Riches, Comedy, Tragedy and Romance. These are clearly discernible in branding. Overcoming the Monster is very common, albeit the monsters tend to be headaches or cold sores or flyaway hair or household odours. Rags to Riches is integral to brands that claim to change lives (National Lottery, Nicorette, Weight Watchers). Comedy is common too (think of those wacky TV ads for brands of car insurance, household insurance, travel insurance), as is tragedy (cf. government information campaigns against speeding, smoking, drinking and driving). Romance goes without saying (especially on Valentine's Day).

Thinking Outside the Think Box

Are brand stories true stories? Should they be true stories? Not a single word of Hollister's backstory is true. Does this matter? What do we do with Harry Potter or Sherlock Holmes, since the brand is built on a fictional figure? Are embellishments permissible? Where do we draw the line on them?

All impactful stories have heroes or heroines and the same is true of brands. Brands frequently present themselves in an heroic light – Guitar Hero, Guinness, Starbucks, Solpadeine, Mr Muscle, North Face, Nike – or they are fronted by larger-than-life figures, such as Donald Trump, Martha Stewart, Oprah Winfrey, Ronald McDonald, the Michelin Man, Rupert Murdoch, Vijay Mallya, Jack Ma, Wang Jianlin, the late great Steve Jobs, David Ogilvy back in the day, Don King in his preposterous pomp.

In addition to hero figures, of course, narratives are ordinarily peopled with plenty of secondary characters. Traditionally termed 'stock characters', these include the trusty companion or sidekick (Dr Watson), the sage or mentor (Obi-Wan Kenobi), the outlaw or rebel (Jack Sparrow) and the trickster or comic foil (Donkey in *Shrek*). Many, many brands present themselves to consumers as one of these stock types. The trusty sidekick or boon companion is especially common, since most brands want to be dependable friends – Budweiser, Facebook, Boots, LinkedIn, Weight Watchers, MasterCard, most financial service companies. The sage or wise one is not unusual either (BBC, *The Economist*, McKinsey), nor is the outlaw (Jack Daniels, Pirate Bay, *Grand Theft Auto*), ditto the trickster (Pot Noodle, M&Ms, Specsavers, Paddy Power). There are lots and lots of additional character types, such as the unattainable beauty (Ferrari, Barbie, *Cosmo*, *Men's Health*) and the wizard or magician (Disney, Sony, Simon Cowell, Oil of Olay), which can be embraced as brands see fit.

The power of a strong brand character is perhaps best illustrated by the Most Interesting Man in the World. A charismatic character created for the Mexican beer brand Dos Equis, the Most Interesting Man in the World is a bearded, tuxedo-wearing, supremely self-confident alpha male, who makes Ethan Hunt look like a limp wimp. In a series of TV commercials, he performs all sorts of incredible feats including cliff diving in Acapulco, catching a giant marlin, parallel parking a train, slamming a revolving door, releasing a trapped grizzly bear, splashing down in a space capsule, finding the fountain of youth yet refusing to drink and stitching up his own wounded shoulder in hospital, without recourse to anaesthetic. MIMW's a septuagenarian man's man whose 'blood smells like cologne'; who is 'allowed to touch the paintings in museums', who 'once had an awkward moment just to see how it feels'; who finds that people 'hang on his every word, even the prepositions'; who appreciates that the police 'often question him just because they find him interesting'; who is so admired by great white sharks that 'they have a week dedicated to him'; and whose personality is 'so magnetic he can't carry credit cards'. MIMW not only encourages drinkers to 'Stay Thirsty, My Friends', but he openly acknowledges that 'I don't always drink beer. But when I do, I prefer Dos Equis.' Little wonder that, after his arrival, the brand's sales soared by 17% in a steadily declining market.[47]

If you give your brand character, it'll live happily ever after. Just ask Walt.

BRAND TASK

The ten components of branding are Names, Emblems, Organoleptics, Slogans, Packaging, Mascots, Offers, Narratives, Charisma and Tradition. When their capital letters are rearranged, they spell out COMPONENTS. Using the COMPONENTS framework, evaluate a brand of your choice. Award marks out of ten for each individual element. Then do likewise with your chosen brand's closest competitor. Evaluate how they compare on each component. What are their relative strengths and weaknesses? Should your brand strive to match its rival on every element or build on the dimensions where it's ahead?

RECOMMENDED READINGS

Douglas B. Holt, *How Brands Become Icons* (Harvard Business Review Press: Boston, 2004). Doug Holt had a dazzling academic career – Stanford, Chicago, Harvard, Oxford – but he gave it up to test his ideas in the real world of brands and branding. This book is his masterpiece. Albeit written for managers, it can be read by students with profit.

Robert V. Kozinets et al., 'Themed Flagship Brand Stores in the New Millennium: Theory, Practice, Prospects', *Journal of Retailing*, 78 (1), 2002, 17–29. Kozinets and his colleagues have published numerous articles on flagship stores, all stuffed with stupendous brand stories. This paper is perhaps his most expansive.

Anthony Patterson et al., 'How to Create an Influential Anthropomorphic Mascot', *Journal of Marketing Management*, 29 (1–2), 2013, 69–85. Few stories are more fun-filled than that of Aleksandr Orlov, the meerkat mascot from Comparethemarket.com. Patterson and his compatriots tell Aleksandr's stirring tale with considerable aplomb.

James B. Twitchell, *Twenty Ads That Shook the World* (Three Rivers Press: New York, 2000). A Professor of English Literature, Twitchell has written several books about American consumer society. They're all worth reading, but this one is especially good because it recounts the stories behind many much-admired brands, including Marlboro, Coke and Clairol.

PART II
COMMANDMENTS

CHAPTER 5

BRANDS ARE LIVING THINGS

Overview

A pint of Guinness is an inanimate object. But the brand claims to be 'alive inside'. This assumption may seem ridiculous, but it is an assumption made by many brand managers. They regard their brands as living things – as do consumers – and do so for very good reasons. Humans personify the things around them, brands included. This chapter dissects the anatomy of living, breathing brands.

IT'S A BRAND!

There's a telling moment in the 2015 movie *Steve Jobs*. It comes just before the launch of Apple's breakthrough computer, the Macintosh. Extolling the machine's virtues to a female employee, Jobs doesn't talk about its CPU or GUI or innovative operating system. He talks, rather, about the computer's cute face, its friendly disposition, its attractive physical features. He treats the plastic contraption as a living thing. It's a belief that's reinforced during the official launch of the Macintosh, where the machine performs a short stand-up comedy routine in a robotic monotone then thanks its father, Steve Jobs, for bringing this baby into being.[1] Papa Jobs is so touched by the computer's kind words – and the audience's enraptured reaction – that he almost bursts into tears on stage. Bearing in mind that Jobs was one of the meanest mothers in the IT industry, that's some achievement by an inanimate object.

Jobs' belief that Apple is a living, breathing brand never wavered. It's a belief made manifest in the iMac, the great man's candy-coloured comeback product, who greeted new users with the cheery word 'welcome', as do iPads and iPhones to this day. It's a belief that's embodied in Siri, the brand's ask-me-anything digital assistant, and the Watch, which keeps an 'i' on our daily activities like an anxious mother hen. It's a belief that makes its presence felt through the power light on Apple laptops, which waxes and wanes when asleep, as if it were breathing gently. It's a belief that's repeated again and again in Apple's advertising, from the legendary *1984* commercial, where a lone female (symbolizing the mighty Mac) strikes a devastating blow against Big Brother (symbolizing the then magisterial IBM), to the equally classic Think Different campaign (which unashamedly claimed affinity with radical rule breakers like Albert Einstein, Muhammad Ali, Amelia Earhart, Maria Callas, Mahatma Gandhi and more).[2]

It's a belief that's perhaps best illustrated in the celebrated I'm a Mac/I'm a PC advertising campaign.[3] In the ads, PC is an uptight, know-it-all, suit-and-tie wearing Bill Gates clone. Mac is casually dressed, easy going, somewhat geeky, vaguely Steve Jobs-ish. They stand side by side against a plain white background. 'Hello, I'm a Mac', the casual guy says. 'And I'm a PC', the suit informs us. After the introductions, which remain the same throughout the entire campaign, they proceed to compare their respective features and benefits. Every infuriating thing about Microsoft – slow, ugly, clunky, crash prone, virus ridden, ubiquitous – is contrasted with Apple's attractiveness, adaptability, amiability and aesthetic appeal. Mac comes across as a nice guy. PC, if not quite pomposity incarnate, is a fool is uncool clothing. The campaign, comprising 66 separate spots, ran for four years between 2006 and 2010. It won all sorts of awards and generated numerous online spoofs, which reinforced the Apple-knows-best message of the original.

BRAND EMBODIMENT

The notion that brands are animate things with motor skills and minds of their own isn't confined to the 'Crazy Ones' of Silicon Valley. Spend a few hours watching commercial television and, as Think Box 10 indicates, you'll conclude that most brand managers share Steve's sentiments about sentience.

─────────────── THINK BOX 10 ───────────────

Anthropomorphic Advertising

A silver Citroën C4 sits alone in an empty rooftop car park. Dance music starts up from nowhere. The car rises of its own volition and reassembles itself as a giant

Transformer, complete with bright red baleful eyes and singularly aggressive wing mirrors. It launches into an elaborate dance routine, shimmying, sashaying and shaking its booty – boot, rather – on the rooftop car park dance floor. When the music stops, our strutting saloon sinks to the ground and rapidly rearranges itself, as if nothing had happened. 'The Citroën C4,' a voiceover announces, 'Alive With Technology'.

The rhythmic drumbeat pounds and hammers, steadily increasing in intensity. White-suited figures soar upwards in ever mounting numbers. They bounce off massive vibrating trampolines, thrumming, tumbling, twisting and turning as they go. The helmeted homunculi seem to be incarcerated in a vast dark cavern. They surge and swirl and swivel, hundreds of them. Thousands. All dressed identically in sleek, figure-hugging uniforms. All hurtling upwards with reflective visors firmly in place. The camera pulls back to reveal a settling pint of Guinness. 'It's Alive Inside', the strapline informs us.

Fleetwood Mac's *Don't Stop* starts up against the backdrop of an ordinary suburban house. The toys within perk up, rise up and march outside in formation. Books, beds, sofas, sideboards, pots, pans, crockery, cutlery, clothes, cabinets all make their way toward the front garden, as do the toaster, cooker, fridge, kettle, telly and analogous electrical equipment, once they manage to untangle and unplug themselves. The hapless husband, sitting relaxing in his favourite armchair, is swept along in this tide of possessions. So too is the teenage son, still asleep in his pit. Already outside, their Canon SLR masterminds the operation, adjusts itself on a tripod and takes a group photograph for the record. A record that'll be forwarded to the family's friendly neighbourhood household insurer, John Lewis.

The screen fills with black and white images of old technologies, scrolling right to left. First generation televisions, ancient electric fans, huge top-loader washing machines, piston-pumping steam trains appear and disappear with rapidity. A voiceover intones 'There are machines that want to do things for us. Machines that can make things for us. Machines that can see right through us.' Monochrome shots of X-rays, eye-tests, brain scans, eerie androids, malevolent dolls and disembodied mechanical legs arrive and depart. The voiceover continues, 'And machines that want to be us, want to replace us. But they are not us.' The images change to colour as the camera pans over the sleek exterior of a gleaming automobile. 'There is one machine that makes us greater. A machine so instinctive, so seductive, it's as alive as we are.' The luxurious interior occupies centre screen, as the authoritative voice goes on, 'It doesn't click or buzz.' A finger pushes an ignition button. The car emits a thrilling deep-throated growl. 'It roars.' The ad ends on a full-frontal shot of the monster. 'Jaguar', he says as the screen goes black. Words appear. 'How Alive Are You?'

Thinking Outside the Think Box

Monitor the commercials during an average evening's television viewing. Note those that use personification in some shape or form. What proportion, roughly, of the evening's ads are anthropomorphic? Do the same for your favourite glossy magazine. How do they compare? Account for the difference, if you can.

Such ads – and there are many just like them[4] – raise an interesting existential question. Are brands living things? Are they, in the words of the Jaguar commercial, as alive as we are? The obvious answer to this question is, 'No, of course not!' Brands are inert products, inanimate objects, lifeless devices. Motor cars are lumps of metal, pieces of plastic, bundles of glass, rubber, fabric, leather, trim. They are not alive and kicking, except when they're portrayed that way by advertising agencies and marketing departments. When confronted with dancing coffee beans, love-struck mobile phones, amorous chocolate bars, grumpy vacuum cleaners, malevolent bathroom bacteria, yodelling credit cards and friendly pro-biotic yogurts, we're not expected to take them seriously. Their aliveness is metaphorical rather than literal. Isn't it?

Some brands *really are* alive. As noted in chapter 1, we routinely talk about celebrity brands, the Brads, the Oprahs, the Tigers, the Rihannas, the Gwyneths, the Kanyes, the Jay-Zs, the Kims of this world. Politicians, preachers, physicians, models, authors, artists, architects, academics, journalists, businesspeople, scientists, television personalities and so forth are often described as brands these days. And they are treated as such by their managers, agents, representatives, spokespersons and sycophantic entourages. Everyone, according to the BYOB (Be Your Own Brand) paradigm, can be a brand of sorts. Granted, there was a wonderful moment in series six of *The Apprentice*, when one of the contestants claimed to be a 'brand' and was ripped to shreds by a hit man from human resources. But the idea that people can be brands is widely accepted and pretty much incontestable.[5]

It is equally incontestable that some consumers treat goods and services as living things. More than a few 'ordinary people' consider brands to be alive, sentient, animated.[6] I have personally interviewed thousands of shoppers down the years and, without any encouragement on my part, they personify products, services, brands. Consumers often talk about Galaxy or Thornton or Kinder chocolate bars calling out to them ('eat me, eat me') or Paul Smith suits whispering seductively as they walk by ('buy me, buy me') or stunningly beautiful Jimmy Choo shoes in shop windows that make them go weak at the knees then fall head over heels in mad passionate love ('I must have them, I must have them').[7]

Set against this, Tesco's shopping trolleys are sometimes seen as bad tempered brutes who do everything in their power to make life difficult for consumers. Many have minds of their own. Malevolent minds. And it's not just trolleys. Barcode scanners are no less sentient, as are cashpoints, petrol pumps, traffic lights and the like.

You may scoff. But I'm not the only one to have found this. Lindstrom, for instance, tells us about a fanatical Gucci enthusiast who has the brand name tattooed on his neck, barcode included. The bloke genuinely believes that the Gucci brand is a person, a friend he can relate to, a family member rather than a range of expensive luxury goods. Lindstrom likewise reports the results of fMRI studies of consumers' brains. These show that when consumers look at images of Mini Coopers, the regions of their brains that respond to faces light up like beacons. The appeal of the Mini, he concludes, isn't in its engine or airbags or stylish interior but its adorable baby face.

'It was a gleaming little person, Bambi on four wheels, or Pikachu with an exhaust pipe. You just wanted to pinch its little fat metallic cheeks, then drive it away.'[8]

SELLING SENTIENCE

Lindstrom, of course, is a prominent brand consultant and consultants are renowned for attention-grabbing gimmicks (such as fMRI scans) designed to sell their expensive services to companies with more dollars than sense. Thus they pontificate about brand DNA, viral branding, brand gyms, brand ecosystems, brand symbiosis, guerrilla brands, purple cow brands, living the brand and suchlike, all of which assume sentience of one kind or another.

Yet even the most sober-sided scholars say brands are alive inside. The marketing magus Philip Kotler contends that powerful brands 'have learned how to make their brand live in the customers' minds'.[9] Mike Beverland tells managers to 'imbue their brands with warts and all humanity'.[10] Nick Kendall posits that *'the* critical question for the 21st century … is how to bring the brand alive'.[11] For Graham Hales, 'a brand is a living business asset, brought to life across all touchpoints'.[12] Prominent ad man Dan Wieden declares that 'if a brand isn't human, it isn't worth shit'.[13] Paul Feldwick prefers to put things more poetically:

> Buildings age and become dilapidated.
> Machines wear out.
> People die.
> But what live on are the brands.[14]

Let me be clear here. Despite the claims of brands like GE, which purports 'to bring good things to life', please bear in mind that we're talking metaphorically. I'm not suggesting that Guinness is *literally* alive inside (Think Box 11 below). I'm not hypothesizing that branding is a bit like *Toy Story, Night at the Museum* or the *Nutcracker Suite*, where brands come to life in the supermarket after hours when the customers have gone home.[15]

What I *am* saying is that it's useful to treat brands *as if* they are living things. Because humanizing a brand increases its consumer appeal. Why that's the case, I'll explain shortly. For the meantime it's sufficient to note that treating brands as living, breathing entities is a sensible and successful marketing strategy. It's a sensible and successful strategy that is systematically employed by numerous brand managers and comes highly recommended by expensive management consultants. It works. It's tried and tested. It unfailingly gets – as Schultz and Schultz remind us – 'to the heart of the brand'.[16]

In this regard, it is no accident that many brands have hearts as logos: Hartley's jam, Walls ice cream, DFS furniture, Müller yogurt, Quaker oats, Paper Mate pens, Pampers nappies, Thomas Cook, Southwest Airlines, Cow & Gate, Diane von Furstenberg, Divine chocolate, LV car insurance, Argos's Heart of Home range, the Eurovision Song Contest and the 'Heart of Asia' itself, Taiwan. Heart-shaped logos like Nestlé's may be cheesy but the perennial popularity of Valentine's Day – not to mention red heart emojis – demonstrate that humankind can't get enough of heart-shaped symbols. The iconic I♥NY emblem is the most copied work of visual identity in the world. Designed by Milton Glazer way back in 1977, I♥NY is the Energizer bunny of logos. It just keeps going and going and going.[17]

DO BRANDS HAVE NINE LIVES?

That's a good question. CAT, the construction equipment to clothing brand, is likely to answer in the affirmative, since it's been successfully reanimated on several occasions. But for most brands the honest answer is 'nobody knows'. What is known, though, is that the living breathing brand has nine main features: *name, face, voice, gender, age, offspring, physique, personality* and *relationships*. Or as an Irish poet once put it:

> Names and Faces, the sound of a Voice.
> Gender and Age and Offspring rejoice.
> Physique, Personality, there isn't a choice.
> Relationships, tho', are the key to Rolls-Royce.[18]

Name

As noted in chapter 2, brands are often named after their founder or founders: Rolls and Royce, Ben and Jerry, Barnum and Bailey, Procter and Gamble, Dolce and Gabbana, Gilchrist and Holmes, Baylis and Harding, Toni and Guy. On one level, eponyms denote ownership and the attendant property rights and responsibilities.[19] On another level, eponymous brand names carry connotations of 'the personal touch'. They help humanize brands, insofar as consumers feel they are dealing with an identifiable individual rather than an anonymous corporation.[20] Yes, the founders may be long dead or have very little to do with the organization in its current form. Karen Millen, famously, founded the fashion house that bears her name. However, she no longer works there and can't set up a new and improved KM, because she's lost legal title to the name. Her own name. Much the same thing happened to Jil Sander, Sonia Rykiel, Chantal Thomass and the McDonald brothers, Dick and Maurice, who founded the burger behemoth but had nothing to do with the restaurant chain we know and love today. Ryanair, likewise, has long since flown the nest of its founder, Tony Ryan, who's been replaced in consumers' minds by Michael O'Leary.

Yet for all that, there's something more human about eponymous brands. Even though many of Viktor & Rolf's fashionable outfits are made in far eastern factories, the name on the label implies that the maestros are making them to order in their Amsterdam atelier. Diners at Gordon Ramsay's global brand of franchised restaurants, 42 strong at the last count, probably wonder if they'll have a personal encounter with the irascible chef or overhear him effing and blinding in the kitchen.[21] The chances of that are slim – albeit the hope remains – since Gordon's principal contribution to his chain consists of promotional activities, menu development and receiving an appropriate portion of the franchisee's profits. His name is the sizzle that sells the steaks. But Gordon isn't doing the cooking.

Face

Faces, arguably more than anything else, bring brands to life. Most brands nowadays are blessed with kissers and countenances of one kind or another. Sometimes the face of the brand is a famous person, such as George Clooney (Nespresso), Jennifer Aniston (SmartWater), Keira Knightley (Chanel) or Gary Lineker (Walkers Crisps). Sometimes they are the owners or chief executive of the company, larger than life figures like Larry Ellison (Oracle), Jack Ma (Alibaba), Michelle Mone (Ultimo) and Sheryl Sandberg (Facebook). Sometimes they are jobbing actors – or, on occasion, genuine employees – who become intimately associated with the brand in consumers' eyes. Celebrated examples include Howard Brown (Halifax), David Leisure (Isuzu), Darrell Winfield (Marlboro), Lynda Bellingham (Oxo), Maureen Lipman (BT) and John Hewer (Birdseye).

The brand's face, furthermore, doesn't have to belong to a person, let alone a real one. Cartoon mascots and cute critters akin to Felix the Cat, Bertie Bassett, Cap'n Crunch, the Dulux Sheepdog, the Budweiser Clydesdales, the Taco Bell Chihuahua and the PG Tips Chimps can do the job just as well, if not better, than their human counterparts. As a rule, they are much cheaper, less temperamental and a better long-term bet than unreliable actors or celebrities who are prone to go loco and do collateral damage to the brand. Uncle Ben has never been caught in flagrante with Aunt Jemima, nor is the Pillsbury Doughboy the Michelin Man's secret lovechild. And even if they were, brand managers have a failsafe fallback: the smiley-faced logo. There's nothing like a smile to make a brand welcome. Just ask LG or Pepsi or Amazon or Argos or Kraft or Danone or Prudential insurance or Innocent drinks or Thomson holidays or Simple cosmetics or Henry Hoover or, indeed, every ad you'll ever see for a wrist watch. Almost without exception, the hands on the watch's face are set at ten past ten or ten to two. That is, in the smiley-face position. You'll be hard pushed to find a watch ad where the hands are positioned at frowny-face twenty past eight or twenty to four.[22]

Perhaps the most brilliant use of a familiar face, however, was Coca-Cola's conscription of Santa Claus back in the 1930s. As McCracken observes, Coca-Cola all but invented the modern conception of Christmas.[23] The red and white outfit that Santa traditionally wears is Coca-Cola's livery. Prior to Coke's Santa-centred advertising campaign, the great man was usually depicted wearing a green get-up and tended to be tall, skinny, somewhat gawky. The fat, friendly, cherubic, white-bearded Santa Claus in his bright red outfit we owe entirely to Coca-Cola's hugely expensive, high-risk advertising campaign mounted at the height of the Great Depression. It was a bet-the-brand gamble that paid off big time. Because Coke now 'owns' Christmas to all intents and purposes. For many consumers, the Christmas season doesn't begin until 'Holidays Are Coming' is broadcast.

Voice

Holidays Are Coming is a classic jingle, a jingle that sticks in the memory forever, much like Try a Taste of Martini or I'm a Cadbury's Fruit & Nut Case or For Hands That Do Dishes Can Feel Soft as Your Face, With Mild Green Fairy Liquid. Jingles, admittedly, are out of fashion these days.[24] Brands believe that entire anthems, such as those associated with major movie franchises of the Star Wars, James Bond, Indiana Jones kind, pack an emotional punch that the classic catchy jingle lacks.

Be that as it may, establishing a distinctive voice for a brand – be it musical or spoken – is becoming ever more important. Just as humankind speaks in tongues, not to mention Received Pronunciation and regional accents, brands can say a lot about themselves by the tone of voice they adopt. Innocent Drinks is renowned for its felicitous verbal flourishes, though some find them too twee for words (especially after the brand was bought by Coca-Cola's branding machine). The resonant voiceovers that accompany Honda's ongoing advertising campaigns also help differentiate the brand from its automotive competitors, each with their simple, almost indistinguishable, three-note sonic logos. BrewDog, the belligerent Scottish brand of head-banging beer, is partial to the verbals as well. 'We hate Carling' its bars bellow in in-your-face fashion.[25]

The growing ascendency of verbal identity – the voice of the brand – is partly a consequence of the visual overkill noted in chapter 3. But it can't be separated from the rise of social media, where pithy texts are as significant as eye-catching images. The two-way conversations that brands strike up with today's connected customers necessitate the adoption of an appropriate tone of voice. Choosing and maintaining that tone of voice – jocular, affable, bantering, authoritative, profane, erogenous – is considered crucial, as is consistency across diverse channels of communication. The rise of celebrity bloggers, whose social media presence many brands crave, owes much to their idiosyncratic voices. The Internet of Things, where Bosch washing machines speak to Smeg fridges and Bose Bluetooth speakers are on AppChat with Dr Dre earphones, is another context where voice is increasingly salient. It's important in storytelling too.

Verbal identity may not have surpassed visual identity in the great branding scheme of things. But its voice is becoming ever more insistent and ever more difficult to ignore.[26]

Gender

It may be politically incorrect to point this out, but brands are gendered for the most part.[27] Think Dove deodorant versus Lynx. Think Diet Coke versus Coke Zero. Think Special K versus Shredded Wheat. Think Topshop versus Topman. Think *Cosmo* versus *GQ*. Think Fiat 500 versus Ford Mondeo. Consider also McCoy's allegedly man-sized crisps (with ridges!). Consider Yorkie chunky chocolate bars, which boast they're 'not for girls'. Consider Gillette Fusion Proglide, which is nothing less than 'the best a man can get'. Consider Wing Co malted milk drink, which claims to be the 'manly chocolate milk for men, with added man'. Consider the seemingly dead and almost buried man-brand, Old Spice, which enjoyed a major injection of marketing mojo with the much-admired ad campaign 'Smell Like a Man, Man'.

Now, this does not mean that brands are exclusively one gender or another. On the contrary, most brands go to great lengths to emphasize their bisexual credentials. It's daft to do otherwise because appealing to a single gender cuts off half the potential market. That's why there's a Dove for Men range and female-friendly forms of Lynx. That's why Gillette sells male and female Fusion razors, with the latter proving particularly lucrative.[28] That's why Jean-Paul Gaultier markets male and female-shaped bottles of his signature scent, as do all the perfume brands. That's why Lego unleashed a little girl-oriented range of its iconic building blocks – called Lego Friends – despite many complaints about gender stereotyping. That's why Harley-Davidson has been making huge efforts to cultivate female fans of its quintessentially masculine brand, even to the extent of establishing women-only chapters of the Harley Owners Group (including the incomparable Dykes on Bikes).

It's undeniable, moreover, that certain celebrated brands have undergone the commercial equivalent of gender reassignment surgery. Right Guard began as a female-focused antiperspirant – it also boasted the very first aerosol container – but became increasingly masculine through time. Doc Martens kicked off as mucho macho working boots, though they're pretty much pan-sexual nowadays, as are the female-to-start fast fashion chains Fat Face and River Island. Marlboro, meanwhile, is the manliest brand on earth. However, it started as a distaff-side cigarette back in the 1930s and, after a landmark advertising intervention by Leo Burnett, Marlboro was reinvented as the brand for rugged he-men. Smoked, seemingly, by rough-necked cowpokes who slept standing up, drank red-eye whisky in fly-blown saloons and wrestled grizzly bears in their spare time, the Marlboro Man soon became an American icon. The only remaining link to the brand's original gender is its bright red livery, a faint echo of the scarlet filter that once disguised unsightly lipstick traces.[29]

Yet for all the cross-dressing, trans-gendering and a-sexual androgyny it's a fact that many brands are targeted at, or associated with, one gender or the other.[30] Hermès handbags, Manolo stilettos and New Balance sports bras don't have more than a few male enthusiasts. Bluebeard, Bull Dog and King of Shaves are overwhelmingly man-brands, whereas Always and Bodyform aren't. The battle between the sexes is still ongoing, furthermore, as Porsche drivers' infuriated reaction to the female-friendly Cayenne shows. The SUV sold like Bud on Super Bowl Sunday, though.[31]

When it comes to gender-based branding, however, Japan stands head and shoulders above the rest. DoCoMo specializes in small and stylish mobile phones which fit more easily into a woman's hand and handbag. WiLL is no less ahead of the curve. Also Japanese, it partners with a number of prominent brands to provide products that are specifically suited to women.[32]

Age Rage

Another unavoidable fact about branding life is age. Some brands are young, youthful and full of get-up-and-go, having undergone massive growth spurts. Twitter, Tumblr, Spotify, Pinterest, BuzzFeed and Flickr among them. Not one of these brands existed a decade ago. Yet now, along with Uber, Instagram and Airbnb, they are some of the best known and most acclaimed brands on earth. Other brands, by contrast, are golden oldies. They've been around for a long, long time and are trusted, much-loved, cared about because of that. Pears soap dates from 1807. Evian has been flowing since 1826. Burberry was born in 1856. Heinz is 146 years young. Colgate made its debut in 1873. Quaker is pushing 140. Kellogg's is getting on for 120. Goodyear is still good to go at 117.

Old or young, one thing they all share is birthdays. As with consumers, brands celebrate their birthdays like there's no tomorrow. Wikipedia is making a fuss of its fifteenth as I write and easyJet is doing likewise with its fortieth. John Lewis beats them both, having made a huge fuss about its 150th only last year. By the time you read this Kraft will be going wild and crazy about its centenary, as will Converse All-Star sneakers, as will Vans footwear with its fiftieth. Meanwhile Arthur's Day, an annual event established by Guinness in 2009 to mark the 250th anniversary of the brand's foundation, soon turned into a secular day of obligation, until the whole event went pear shaped (Think Box 11).[33]

THINK BOX 11

My Goodness, My Guinness

Few brands have employed personification more astutely – or more consistently – than Guinness. From the name of the product, through the signature on the label, to the manifold biographies of the founder, Arthur Guinness's presence is apparent in every bottle, can and keg.

From the award-winning 'Noitulove' ad, which depicts human evolution in reverse, through the famous 'Darwin' poster of 1985, which shows the slow but steady ascent of brand, to the smiling faces on the pints in early Gilroy illustrations, the stout's corporeality is constantly emphasized.

From the action hero embodiment of the brand in Nigeria (Michael Power), through its association with supreme sporting achievement (such as Five Nations rugby and Gaelic games), to the muscular draymen, brawny lumberjacks and iron girder-carrying construction workers of the classic 'Guinness For Strength' posters, the product's larger than life personality is incessantly articulated.

From the totemic Guinness Storehouse, which recreates the black magic nectar in brick and mortar and imagination, through the Man With a Guinness ads of the 1980s (starring Rutger Hauer), to the belief in parts of Africa that Guinness is good for procreation (a 'baby in a bottle', no less), the entire history of the iconic Irish brand is incarnation incarnate.

However, the apotheosis of Guinness's personification dates from 2009, when the 250th birthday of King Arthur was celebrated. In addition to limited edition birthday brews, a world-spanning party was thrown for 'Arthur's Day'. At one minute to six p.m. (i.e. 1759), the assembled party-goers raised a glass of the holy water 'To Arthur!' So successful was the inaugural event that Arthur's Day became an annual celebration. It was held every 22 September, with Guinness footing the bill for the music, the mayhem, the parties, the craic in Dublin, Cork, Galway, Belfast and scores of Irish theme pubs from Kathmandu to Kinshasa.

Arthur's Day, it's fair to say, was fast becoming a secular day of obligation. Until several right-on rock stars started complaining about 'over-commercialization'. Instead of moaning about The Man, as per normal, they took their ire out on The Man in Black. However, as the event depended on their support – and as relation-ship between commerce and culture has always been fraught (see chapter 11) – the birthday parties petered out. The pint pot is empty for now. But Guinness won't give up without a fight. The brand is Made of More.

Thinking Outside the Think Box

Grab a pint of Guinness. Drink it, if you can. What do you think of the brand? What kind of person is it? It's colloquially known as 'the blonde in a black dress'. How do you feel about that? Are you tempted to start a relationship with him/her and, if so, what kind of relationship?

Akin to humankind, moreover, we can identify a Brand Life Cycle (BLC). New brands are born every day, notwithstanding enormous mortality rates. Brands grow and develop, some more rapidly than others. Brands gradually mature and get on a bit, though most try to remain youthful with periodic marketing makeovers. Yet for all that, they eventually die and end up in the branding boneyard. Just think of all the ostensibly healthy brands that perished – or had near-death experiences – during the recent economic recession: Blockbuster, Woolworths, Habitat, MFI, HMV, Zavvi, Alexon, Aquascutum, Peacocks, Phones4U and many more. Only a few years ago Alta Vista, Netscape, Napster, MySpace, Pressplay and Friends Reunited were the poster children of e-branding. Where are they now? Does Bebo still exist? Or AOL for that matter? Digg anyone?

Whatever way you look at it, the BLC is often nasty, brutish and short. Many newbies die young as a result of terrible brand traffic accidents. Sunny Delight was a feisty fruit drink launched by P&G in 1998. Positioned as a healthy alternative to fizzy drinks like Fanta and Club Orange, Sunny D took off like a fruit-fuelled rocket. Competitively priced and displayed in supermarket chill cabinets, alongside yogurt, milk and similar perishables, it was exactly what worried parents wanted. Sunny D, clearly, was much better for their children than fructose-filled alternatives. Kids loved it too. They lapped up P&G's bright orange nectar like you wouldn't believe.

Ere long, however, parents noticed that there was more sugar in Sunny Delight than the stuff it was supposed to replace. They realized that the golden gloop was far less healthy than the allegedly unhealthy alternatives. It dawned on them that there was absolutely no need for the chill cabinet pretence, because Sunny D's shelf-life was more like a half-life.

And then things really kicked off. An innocent child in North-East England chugged several large bottles of P&G's addictive brew. A few hours later, she turned bright orange and was rushed to A&E. The brand imploded then and there. It was withdrawn from sale, radically reformulated, then relaunched to understandable consumer indifference. But to all intents and purposes, Sunny D is dead and buried. How art the mighty fallen.[34]

Offspring

Few things in branding are certain. But one thing comes pretty close: brands breed. Successful parent brands have lots and lots of offspring. The preferred term for this procreation process is 'extension'. Branding experts expound at length about brand extensions, brand stretch, brand elasticity, sub-brands, sub-sub-brands, stand-alone brands and so on. However, a better way of thinking about it is in terms of brand 'families' or 'clans'.

The BBC is a classic example. Its big bouncing brand family includes TV channels 1, 2, 3, 4 and CBBC, Radios 1, 2, 3, 4 and 5 Live, the one and only World Service, the BBC website, the BBC iPlayer, BBC Books, BBCStore.com, several BBC orchestras and BBC Worldwide, the commercial arm that does lucrative licensing deals. Sony's sprogs include Sony PlayStation, Sony Bravia, Sony Pictures, Sony Music, Sony Computers, Sony Financial and Sony Mobile (formerly Sony Ericsson). Google has recently sorted out its hitherto uncertain family circumstances under the auspices of its all-grown-up parent brand, Alphabet. Apple's website, what's more, introduces us to its happy-clappy family of brands – the iPod, the iPad, the iPhone, the Watch, the App Store and more besides – much to the irritation of certain opinionated commentators:

> I got an e-mail last week from Apple ... and in the subject line it said: 'Meet the new iPod family'. And I thought to myself: 'Oh sod off, you grasping enormous American computing supergiant ... with your frankly vomit-inducing attempts to sound folksy and local and homespun by describing your new range of stupid little gadgets ... as if it were a FAMILY! It's not a family. It's just bloody not. It's some flat bits of metal with tinny music coming out ... It's the same old iPod Touch, iPod Nano and iPod Shuffle with some startling new differences from the old models, visible only to intergalactic Chinese-American supernerds though a microscope, that Apple thinks, for no reason I can see, are best marketed by being presented as a family.[35]

At the opposite end of the scale from clamouring brand clans like Kellogg's – with its Corn Flakes, Bran Flakes, Rice Krispies, Coco Pops, Crunchy Nuts, Froot Loops, Frosties, Ricicles, Special K and what have you – are lively little brands like Victorinox, which is best known for the Swiss Army Knife. For decades and decades, it focused on building better penknives, with ever more attachments and gizmos. Ten years or so ago, the company woke up to the fact that it owned one of the most distinctive brands around, with a logo and livery that just about everyone knows and trusts. Therefore it started a family and Victorinox now sells watches, torches, tools, luggage, fragrances and foodstuffs, such as Swiss milk chocolate, as well as a redoubtable range of kitchen equipment.

That said, some brands aren't breeders. They are exceptions to the rule. They choose to remain childless. There is one brand name and one brand name only: IKEA, HSBC, Starbucks, McDonald's, Amazon, eBay, Shell, Accenture. Sure, they may have multiple outlets with national variations. But, to all intents and purposes, they're singleton brands with a singular identity, as indeed are most small- and medium-sized enterprises. In my own neck of the woods there's no shortage of SME 'celibates' such as Send My Bag, a discount delivery service for students' suitcases, such as Consarc, an architectural practice specializing in historic building restorations, such as Abbey, an indigenous car and home insurance agency, such as Appletree Press, the small but beautifully formed publisher of books about the Emerald Isle. There's plenty in your locality as well.

Physique

Just as family size varies, so too brands' physiques differ widely. As with humankind, brands come in all shapes and sizes. Some are absolutely gigantic, built like South African rugby players on growth hormones. Walmart, the biggest retail brand in the world, boasts 9,000 stores, 2 million employees and a $500 billion turnover. With half a million employees, Samsung isn't just the most ginormous tech company on the planet, well ahead of Apple (100,000) and IBM (380,000), but it has massive branded interests in insurance, construction, shipbuilding, aerospace, theme parks, advertising agencies and enjoys annual revenues of $300 billion. Facebook, by contrast, is one of today's biggest brands bar none – in terms of name recognition – yet it employs fewer than 10,000 people worldwide. Twitter's even tinier at 4,000 or so. Uber doesn't employ anybody, though the jury is out on that one.

At the opposite end of the scale are teeny-weeny brands with puny physiques. They are the jockeys, the gymnasts the bantamweight boxers of branding compared to GE's cruiserweights, IBM's true-blue line backers or McDonald's muscular front-row forwards. Herat is a tiny ice cream brand in Afghanistan, whose vanilla wafer sandwiches and almond-coated mini-magnums are popular with treat-needing customers from Khost to Nuristan. Miss Patisserie, based in Cardiff, is a petite maker of bath bombs in the small but beautifully formed shape of cookies, cupcakes and similar comestibles. WOW Air, out of Reykjavik, is trying to break into the lucrative low-cost airline business. With four aircraft and 23 destinations, however, it'll be a while before WOW bulks up enough to beat the behemoths of the sector.[36]

Brands, then, can be big like AXA or small like Abbey, huge like HDR Architecture or compact like Consarc. And while most brands, be they giants or gnats, are lean and mean – they have to be, because kill or be killed competition is constant – it's not unusual to hear talk about 'ailing' brands, 'weak' brands and 'tired' brands, alongside those that are 'robust' or 'strong' or 'muscular'. It's also not unusual for middle-aged brands to let themselves go. Dell computers was buff when Michael Dell built the machines to order in his university halls of residence. His brand kicked butt at the height of the laptop boom, largely on account of its just-in-time web-based logistics and distribution. But when the main man retired early after making his millions, the brand became morbidly obese and missed the smartphone-led changes that were transforming the market. Michael came out of retirement and is trying to shed the corporate pounds by returning Dell to its fighting weight. But it's an uphill struggle. The old saying, A Moment on the Lips, A Lifetime on the Hips, applies to branding as well.

The same concerns are currently being expressed about BMW's Mini. When the iconic brand was relaunched at the start of the millennium with the marvellous Mini One, it took everyone's breath away and sold like crazy (to the tune of 300,000 units per year). Since then the range has ballooned to include a Clubman estate, a four-seat convertible, a two-seater roadster, a 4x4 called the Countryman and the portly Paceman, a mini monster that competes with the 'baby' Range Rover Evoque. On top of that, the models themselves have mushroomed. The Countryman is colloquially known as the Mini Fatso and when it came out in the States, the *Wall Street Journal* wrote a memo to BMW with the subject line 'what part of Mini did you not grasp?' The Mini Cooper S, on its relaunch in 2013, was described as 'Like a Tardis in reverse. It grows ever bigger on the outside yet is still a squeeze on the inside ... If she continues on like this, she'll be bigger than a double-decker bus.' A Mini minibus is on the cards, mind you, as is a Mini pickup truck, as is a Mini scooter. As the *Sunday Times* despairs, 'A car that made its name as a single model has had so many nips, tucks and tweaks that, like an ageing Hollywood starlet, it has almost forgotten what it looks like or stands for'.[37]

Personality

Still, the Mini's got personality to spare and personality is yet another thing that living, breathing brands share with humanity. Some, like Virgin, are extrovert. Some, like Muji, are introverts. Some are sporty, such as Fred Perry. Some are serious, akin to Vision Express. Some are playful, Pot Noodle for starters. Some are socially responsible, Greenpeace springs to mind. Some are seriously sexy, *à la* Victoria's Secret. Some are sad and frumpy, much like Mothercare. Some are edgy (Adidas), some are irritating (gocompare.com), some are snooty (Farrow & Ball), some are creepy (American Apparel), some are nerdish (*World of Warcraft*), some are down-to-earth (*The Sun*), some are too twee (Cath Kidston), too smug (Innocent Drinks), too crass (FCUK apparel), too wacky (Johnny Loves Rosie jewellery), too offbeat (Synge and Byrne restaurant), too cool for school (Citizens of Humanity jeans).

Whatever form it takes, acquiring a personality is paramount. The belief that a brand should possess a distinctive personality – one which appeals to as many consumers as possible or, alternatively, the discerning few with suitably deep pockets – is as close to a golden rule as it gets in the branding business. According to one authority:

> A distinguishing personality can offer the single most important reason why one brand will be chosen over another, particularly as the product and service features of competing brands grow more similar. The personality gives the consumer something to relate to that can be more vivid than the perceived positioning, more alive than the physical attributes of the product, more complete than whatever is conveyed by the brand name alone. It can be the difference that tips the customer toward trial, or the one factor that subconsciously binds the user to the brand and prevents switching to a competitor.
>
> The personality is, in some ways, much more real than the other aspects of a brand because it is the outstretched hand that touches the customer as an individual.[38]

This sounds a lot of hot air. But a moment's reflection reveals that the basic idea makes a lot of sense. Detailed research into the personalities of brands – the so-called Big Five personality traits of openness, conscientiousness, extraversion, agreeableness and neuroticism – indicates that consumers readily attribute personalities to brands.[39] As consumers, we gravitate toward the kinds of brands we're comfortable with, brands that reflect our own personalities. And the brands absorb and transmit those personalities in turn (just as they do with gender).

Personalities, of course, aren't fixed. Dull and boring brands are often given personality transplants. Old Spice was famously transformed from a sad and lonely old man's brand, as unfashionable as you can imagine, to a seriously cool man brand thanks to an award-winning advertising campaign, 'The Man Your Man Could Smell Like'.[40] Lucozade, likewise, metamorphosed from a kind, caring, medicinal brand – traditionally, you brought a bottle of Lucozade to someone in hospital, along with a bunch of grapes – into a supercharged energy drink that enhanced sporting performance. Despite the rise of Red Bull, Powerade, Monster and more, Lucozade remains the bestselling brand in that particular category.

Some personality transplants are more successful than others, admittedly. For decades, Ovaltine malted milk has been trying to get away from its cosy, comforting, dressing-gown-and-bedroom-slippers image. To no avail. But if Old Spice can do it, nothing is impossible. Except, perhaps, changing Ryanair's personality. The brand is widely regarded as rude, crude, brash, bullying and downright nasty on occasion. But that doesn't make Ryanair a bad brand. On the contrary, Ryanair is a very distinctive, brilliantly successful brand, because it doesn't sugar-coat the offer. Ryanair promises to get passengers to their destinations on schedule and at the lowest possible price. That's the deal and every customer knows it. If anyone wants fancy service, special treatment, in-flight snacks, or wishes to bring mounds of extra luggage, then they'd best fly with someone else. Or expect to pay a sizeable surcharge for the add-ons.[41]

That said, Ryanair is in the process of changing its tune. It is trying to become more amenable, more helpful, less abrasive, less loathsome than before. And it seems to be working. Profits are up since the makeover from hell. Whether it lasts remains to be seen. As long as Michael O'Leary is lurking in the background, belligerence won't be far away. The bullying of suppliers, travel agents, airport operators, airline manufacturers and industry regulators hasn't stopped, that's for sure. These days, the flight attendants smile when you come on board but many suspect that they're grinning through gritted teeth and itching to charge £1 for every visit to the on-board bathroom.

Relationships

The very fact that we keep travelling with Ryanair, despite our secret conviction that they'd replace the seats with spikes if they could, perfectly illustrates the final parallel with living things. Specifically, that we have relationships with brands in much the same way as we do with the people around us. On the face of it, the idea that we have 'relationships' with brands seems somewhat fanciful. But if you think about TV commercials that refer to 'Your Toyota', 'Your Marks & Spencer', 'That's My Ariel, What's Yours?', 'It's Not Terry's Chocolate Orange, It's My Chocolate Orange' or the personalized packaging of Nutella and Coca-Cola, where consumers' names are printed on the labels, it's clear that brand–consumer relationships are often implied and imputed. Fosters, for instance, recently relaunched its iconic Australian brew under a

'Raised in Friendship' banner and held off growing competition from imported beers as a result.[42]

This notion that we have personal relationships with brands has been studied in detail by Susan Fournier.[43] For her sins, Susan spent several years studying three American consumers, Jean, Karen and Vicki. She itemized the brands they interacted with and systematically examined the role of these brands in their lives. After gathering and analysing more than one hundred stories about her informants' brand-related beliefs and behaviours, Susan identified fifteen different kinds of consumer–brand relationship. Just as relationships with friends, neighbours, workmates and relatives often vary quite considerably, the same is true of brands. We are close friends with some brands and casual acquaintances with others. We have short-lived infatuations, mad passionate affairs and committed lifelong partnerships. Love-hate relationships aren't unusual either. We are prepared to ditch or divorce brands that have let us down one time too many.

In my own case, the most important brand in my life – my best buddy brand – is Nike. As an ageing jogger who goes out running six days a week, I depend on my Nike Pegasus training shoes. I've no doubt that there are lots of better shoes out there and I'm well aware of Nike's disreputable business practices. But the Nike brand of training shoes has kept me reasonably free from injury for the best part of 30 years. Most of my kit is Nike as a consequence. Not all of it. I'm not a Nike or nothing kind of guy. But 70–80% of it is, for sure. And under no circumstances whatsoever would I buy anything by Adidas.[44]

Call me crazy if you wish. However, I reckon many of you have an equivalent to my Nike. Perhaps it's Facebook. Perhaps it's your iPhone. Perhaps it's GHD hair straighteners. Perhaps it's the new and improved Sunny D. But here's a simple test if you own or drive a car. Does your car have a nickname? And, if so, why? It's just a lump of steel, glass, plastic, fabric and rubber, after all. It's not a living thing. Yet lots and lots of people act *as if* their cars are alive and kicking. Studies show that more than 40% of British drivers give their cars nicknames, the most popular being Betty, Bertie and Bob.[45]

As a rule, we give nicknames to things we care for or have relationships with. And when you stop and think of how many brands have been given nicknames of one kind or another, it's apparent that there's something to this 'relationships' malarkey. Thus consumers talk about a Bud for Budweiser, a Beemer for BMW, a Mac, a Jag, a Coke, a Chevy, Harvey Nicks, Marks & Sparks, Stoli, Bolly, Mother's Little Helper (Valium) and the Blonde in the Black Dress (Guinness). Stella Artois, conversely, is colloquially known as 'wife-beater'. BlackBerry in its prime was called the Crackberry. IKEA sells a self-assembly shelving unit known within the company as the 'divorce-maker'. McDonald's, meanwhile, is variously known as Mickey Ds, Mackey Ds, McDicks or Maccas, depending on the nationality of the speaker.

Think too of the frequency with which people name their children after brands. These include Chloe, Mercedes, Tiffany, Armani, Apple, Infiniti, Celica, Canon, Chanel, Cartier, Versace, Maybelline, Timberland, Wrigley, Hummer and, believe it or not, Nutella.[46]

REASONS WHY

Names notwithstanding, there's no doubt that the personification of brands is pretty much ubiquitous. Brands may not be living things – celebrities, etc. excepted – but it's sensible to treat them as such. There are three main reasons for this.[47]

The first of these is because it works. Marketers have discovered that celebrity endorsers, cartoon mascots and suchlike – the 'faces' of the brand – help move the merchandise. It really does work, as the 'Duchess of Cambridge Effect' on the sales of dress designers, maternity wear, children's clothing and baby buggies bears witness. Michelle Obama has had a similar effect on the sales of J. Crew, a brand she has worn since college. Aflac was an anonymous car insurance company until it adopted a duck as a mascot. The quacking brand hasn't looked back.[48]

The second reason is legal precedent. Ever since the company acts of the mid-19th century, which ruled that joint stock companies are artificial persons charged with the same rights and responsibilities as real people, the belief that businesses are living things has been enshrined in law. This belief has been repeatedly reinforced by statutes emanating from the US Supreme Court (and its EC equivalents), such as the recent decision that companies are entitled to freedom of speech and have the right to make unlimited financial contributions to political parties (as per any private person). It is little wonder that managers ordinarily regard their organizations as living things. The language of management is full of personifications and anthropomorphisms – problem children, cash cows, hidden hands, long tails, fail whales, weasel words, cubicle monkeys, 800 lb gorillas and the ever-present elephant in the room. It's perfectly natural to apply this line of thinking to marketing and branding. All the talk of personalities, relationships, life cycles, brand DNA, touchpoints, brand soul and so forth, ultimately stems from personification's enshrinement in law.

The third reason, and perhaps the most profound, pertains to personification. History shows that humankind is predisposed to personify. That is to say, we tend to treat animals, vegetables and minerals – all the things that surround us – as living things. From the cave paintings of Neolithic hunter-gatherers, via the unforgettable beast fables of Aesop, through the fantastic fairy stories of Hans Christian Andersen, to the cartoon capers of the indefatigable Bugs Bunny, we impute human characteristics to non-human things. Poets talk of weeping willows, babbling brooks, dancing daffodils, whistling winds, smiling sunbeams. We see a man in the moon, armies in the clouds, the face of Jesus in pepperoni pizzas and laugh at cats that look like Hitler. The names we give to sports teams – the Ospreys, the Wallabies, the Glasgow Warriors, the Dallas Cowboys, the Sydney Swans – and the prodigious personifications of nation-states, such as Uncle Sam, John Bull, Mother Russia and Marianne, the enchanting embodiment of France, are examples of this personifying propensity.

Humanity's anthropomorphic instinct has generated much debate.[49] It is variously seen as a childhood trait (since kids are especially fond of cuddly cartoon critters) and a deep-seated evolutionary instrument (a primal urge that helps ensure human survival and reproduction). However, the reasons for it are less important than the fact that it happens, that it's innate, that it can help sell the brands of beer or boats or bath salts or breakfast cereals that managers are responsible for.

The secret of success, in short, is to humanize the brand. And while this is easier to do when the products are animate – that is, they move rather than remain static, as in the case of cars, fizzy drinks or computer consoles like Wii – never forget that 'A brand is a fragile living thing. It needs to be cultivated, nurtured and cared for. Otherwise it will wither and die.'[50]

BRAND TASK

Identify your 'best buddy' brand. Dissect its anatomy then write an obituary. Describe your relationship with the dear departed. Do the same for a brand you've ditched or divorced or would like to see dead. What have you got against it? Is there any way back for the brand you've abandoned so cruelly?

RECOMMENDED READINGS

Stuart Guthrie, *Faces in the Clouds* (Oxford: Oxford University Press, 1993). This is the seminal text on anthropomorphism. Although it claims to be a theory of religion, it reads more like a compelling cultural history. Everything you need to know is here.

Stephen Brown, 'It's Alive Inside', *Irish Marketing Review*, 21 (1–2), 2012, 3–11. Apologies for foisting one of my own papers on you. But it focuses on Guinness as an exemplar of personification and few brands do it better. Ignore the matrix, BTW, it's rubbish.

Susan Fournier, 'Consumers and their Brands: Developing Relationship Theory in Consumer Research', *Journal of Consumer Research*, 24 (March), 1998, 343–373. Susan is a super-star of consumer research and this is her signature article. Academic articles can be a bit dry and dusty. This one's an exception to the rule.

Jennifer Aaker, 'Dimensions of Brand Personality', *Journal of Marketing Research*, 34 (August), 1997, 347–356. This influential, if controversial, quantitative study identifies five brand personality types, similar to the Big Five found by human personality testers, though their names and nature are different.

CHAPTER 6
CONSUMERS BEWARE

Overview

Brands live on a diet of consumers. And they must watch what they eat. Studying the customer – understanding his or her habits, motives, foibles – is of paramount importance if brands are to survive in a cruel, competitive world. This chapter identifies six major influences on consumer behaviour and shows how these can be manipulated by canny brand managers.

YOU ARE WHAT YOU EAT

If brands are living things, the following questions must be asked. What keeps them alive? What do they live on? What do brands eat to remain hale and hearty? The answer, in all three cases, is simplicity itself. Consumers. Brands consume consumers. Without a steady diet of consumers – consumers with money to spend – brands curl up and die. Consumers may adore IKEA's quirky adverts, such as the one where empty T-shirts take wing, or imitate the 'Tasty' tagline of Müller's Germanic bear shilling Rice, Rice, Baby. But unless consumers buy, buy and buy again, brands die, die, die another day.

Brands need customers. Brands feed on customers. And some brands are very choosy, very picky eaters with very special dietary requirements. Rolls-Royce, for example, preys on affluent middle-aged men, Fortune 500 company directors and obscenely wealthy plutocrats with money to burn. The Montblanc brand of expensive pens, the Chopard brand of precision timepieces, the Noma brand of Danish fine dining are equally choosy about whose pockets they pick, wrists they wrap and taste buds they tantalize. McDonald's, Matalan, Marlboro and Microsoft, meanwhile, are omnivores. They eat anything and everything and, indeed, must consume consumers voraciously in order to keep on keeping on.

Some brands, to put it another way, are a bit like lions or camels. They need one big meal, or drink, and can then survive quite happily until the next big feed or binge drinking session. Other brands are more like bull elephants or blue whales. They have huge appetites, massive metabolic rates, which require constant replenishment. Most brands are somewhere in the middle. But all rely on a diet of consumers.

The consumer is central to brand survival and the marketing ecosystem more generally. In order to eat out on consumers – to sink our fangs into their swollen pocketbooks, so to speak – we must understand their habits, their habitat and what makes them tick. The customer is one of the foremost concerns of brand and marketing managers. Most spend massive amounts of time and energy tracking customers, contemplating customers, thinking about ways to capture customers and adapting their brands to customers' changing behaviours. True, few managers are prepared to admit that customers are their prey. Instead, they talk about serving the customer, delivering customer satisfaction, enhancing the customer experience, etc. They portray themselves as helpers not hunters.

At the same time, it's important to understand that the ultimate purpose of branding is to sell stuff. That stuff may be a product, a service, a cause, an idea, a lifestyle – a lifestyle that is healthy, fulfilling, uplifting, frugal even – but it's stuff that can only be sold if the buyers' needs, wants, desires and behaviours are understood by the brand doing the selling. As Wally Olins, the so-called 'father of branding', astutely observed:

> We should remain quite clear that what marketing, branding and all the rest of it are about is persuading, seducing and attempting to manipulate people into buying products and services.[1]

No matter what you read elsewhere about brands and branding, never forget this fact: Brands that sell, survive; those that don't, won't. Consumers are food, fuel, forage for brands and, without a reliable supply of customer fodder, brands starve. Malnutrition, moreover, is especially common in times of famine – like the lean years since the last financial crisis – when the customer harvest is less bountiful than normal.

CONSUMERS ARE CANNY

Some readers may be unsettled by such statements. Those who've swallowed the 'customer-is-king' ideology that's reiterated in most marketing textbooks, might even be aghast. But before you burn me at the stake, dear reader, we need to clarify a few things.[2] First, the customer-is-king cliché is itself a selling device. It pays to present ourselves as servants rather than masters. No customer wants to be told that our intention is to rip the wallet out of their chest and feast on its plastic contents. So we sugar-coat our venial intentions. Even the most egregious payday loan providers – those who charge eye-watering rates of interest for their parasitical services – burnish their embezzling brands with warm and fuzzy, caring-sharing, oh-so-solicitous, we're-here-to-help hogwash. I could name names, but you know the wongaful people I'm referring to.[3]

Second, consumers are clever. They know they are prey, for the most part.[4] They know how to avoid capture, outwit predators and defend themselves. Sixty years ago, at the very height of the Mad Men era, when television advertising was regarded as a miracle marketing device, a sagacious advertising executive stated that 'too much advertising is produced on the principle that it is like shooting fish in a barrel; unfortunately, the fish are learning to swim faster and developing armour plate'.[5] Or, as an exasperated executive put it rather more recently, 'consumers are like roaches. We spray them with marketing and for a time it works. Then inevitably they develop an immunity, a resistance.'[6] Even more so than in the 1950s fish barrel, 21st century consumers are marketing savvy. Having been exposed to advertising since birth, they are brand literate. They are wise to marketer's wiles. They can second-guess sales pitches. They are fluent in ad speak, mall talk, product patter. And they know how to escape from the yawning jaws of customer-chomping carnivores.

Third, today's consumers do more than flee from brands' fangs. They are more than capable of turning the tables. They routinely do things with brands that are beyond managers' comprehension. When Adidas became the brand of choice by rap band Run DMC, their energy, their enthusiasm, their uninvited endorsement via the hit song *My Adidas*, left executives of the sports colossus at a loss. They didn't know how to react. Should they strive to stamp it out, the way Burberry did when chavs embraced its signature check? Should they ignore the fact that their clean-living brand had been hijacked by an outlaw-orientated subculture? Or should they embrace the rappers' 'bad' behaviour and exploit a marketplace opportunity that had suddenly opened up before them? Concluding that the last of these would give their brand an 'edge' that it hitherto lacked, they ran with Run DMC and never looked back.

Coca-Cola likewise didn't know how to respond when word got round about the Mentos manoeuvre. As everyone now knows, when a Mentos mint is dropped into a bottle of Diet Coke, a volcanic eruption ensues. A spout of soda gouts out of the bottle and shoots up into the stratosphere. When a pair of pranksters performed a Diet Coke homage to the Bellagio Casino's fountains – and posted it on YouTube, much to Coca-Cola's dismay – they tried to stop the show in its tracks. Mentos, by contrast, recognized a publicity coup when they saw one and they supplied free mints to the mischief makers. Eighteen million YouTube views later, the Coke-Mentos show is still worth watching.[7]

When Warner Brothers acquired the Harry Potter brand, they couldn't begin to comprehend what consumers were doing with their intellectual property.[8] The tribute websites, the pornographic fan fiction, the exponents of 'wizard rock' music, the rise of quidditch as a university team sport, had major IP implications. However, their rabid response – sending cease and desist letters to tiny tots and tweenagers – triggered an immediate consumer backlash and WB quickly retreated with its reputation between its legs. Heaven only knows what they made of this confession from another, rather older fan of the boy wizard brand:

> All the Harry Potter novels have provided many a laugh for me but some have spilled over into my social life. After a crowd of my mates and I went to watch the first movie, it is not uncommon for the following phrase to be shouted out randomly on a night out. 'You're a wizard, Harry!' may seem a bit strange to onlookers, but believe me it is bound to have us in stitches. And of course it is a lot funnier when you are drunk![9]

RESEARCH IS UNRELIABLE

On top of consumers' marketing nous, there's a fourth factor that hammers brand managers: the imperfect tools and techniques marketers use to understand and anticipate consumer behaviour. Consumer research isn't all it's cracked up to be. Its record is patchy. There are many infamous examples of false positives, where the research recommended a course of action, which when followed, had catastrophic outcomes.[10] The New Coke brand debacle described in chapter 1 was based on a massive programme of detailed consumer research. The Edsel imbroglio outlined in chapter 2 was also predicated on a prodigious amount of pre-launch research. A massive study of consumer behaviour by McDonald's 'proved' that the world was gagging for an adult-orientated gourmet burger. But when Mickey/Mackey/Macca D's added the new and improved Arch Deluxe to its menu, consumers responded with the apt if unwelcome words, Ain't Lovin It.[11]

False negatives are frequent too. That is, when the research rejects a course of action, which when ignored, turns out to be a winner anyway. Red Bull, as noted earlier, was systematically studied before it was launched and the results were wholly negative. But Dietrich Mateschitz ignored the naysayers and his brand took wing. Apple's iconic *1984* advert was hated by every single person in every single focus group in every single pre-test.[12] However Jobs went with it regardless and his brand's reputation as a Think Different renegade is intact to this day. Cadbury's drumming gorilla got the thumbs down when it was market researched beforehand. The newly appointed brand manager overruled the findings – a make-or-break career decision if ever there was one – and was rewarded with a breakout campaign that added substantially to the brand's market share.[13]

Failures of this magnitude have tainted consumer research in certain people's eyes. When you read around the subject, you'll come across many condemnations of the research process. Steve Jobs once said that if Henry Ford had asked his customers what they wanted, they'd have wanted faster horses. Charles Saatchi, the advertising guru, claimed he placed as much faith in market research as he did in long range weather forecasts. Howard Schultz used to dismiss research with the words: 'If, before Starbucks, I'd gone to a group of consumers and asked them if I should sell a $4 cup of coffee, when it cost a buck or so elsewhere, what would they have told me? Get the heck out of here!'[14]

Comments like these, needless to say, have prompted vigorous counterarguments. The research that failed was flawed, some say. The research that failed is ancient history, others retort, adding that they have a super-duper new method that's the magic bullet everyone's been waiting for. The basic problem, yet others like Olins proclaim, is that research is reliable when enquiring about the here and now (what brand of car do you drive, deodorant you use, smartphone you own?) but unreliable when dealing with the future (would you buy this brand of gourmet hamburger if it were available, what about an Apple iCar or Apple bottled water?).[15] Drink Different.

These pro- and anti- arguments obscure the fact that brand managers' understanding of consumers is often flawed, frequently faulty and never future-proofed. It's not negligible, nevertheless. They might not know everything there is to know about consumers, but they know an awful lot more than before. Managers are not operating in a state of complete ignorance. Thanks to Robert B. Cialdini, a social psychologist who has written the seminal text on the art of persuasion, most managers are familiar with the mainsprings of consumer behaviour. Namely, *reciprocity*, *scarcity*, *consistency*, *authority*, *enchantment* and *sharing*.[16]

MAINSPRINGS OF CONSUMPTION

Reciprocity

Reciprocity refers to give and take. Tit for tat. You scratch my back, I'll scratch yours. When we are given something, we feel obliged to settle the debt. If we are indebted to someone, it nags away at us until we are quits. Brand managers are aware of this. That is why they shower their customers with free gifts, free samples, free vouchers, free trials, free downloads, free test drives, free check-ups, free squirts of perfume in department stores, free mints at the end of a meal, free promotional codes for astute online operations like BooHoo.com. However, there's no such thing as a free lunch, not when marketers are doing the cooking. The beneficiary always feels indebted to their benefactor. Consumers pay the brand back with their custom.

This obligation, it must be stressed, is an extremely powerful consumer motivator. As Cialdini makes clear:

Because there is a general distaste for those who take and make no effort to give in return, we will often go to great lengths to avoid being considered a moocher, ingrate or freeloader. It is to those lengths that we will often be taken and, in the process, be 'taken' by individuals who stand to gain from our indebtedness.[17]

So compelling is reciprocity, indeed, there's an inbuilt tendency to overcompensate. That is, to respond with a larger favour than we received in order to get it off our conscience. Reciprocity is also integral to the negotiation process, where one party makes a 'concession' and the other is obliged to do likewise. Worse, it often foments resentment from recipients who aren't in a position to repay.[18] Charitable donations can upset those who receive them – even among the homeless or famine-ravaged nations – not because they are ungrateful, but because they can't settle the debt. The free gift compounds their misery.

Be that as it may, gift giving is one of the most fascinating forms of consumer behaviour (Think Box 12). It is hard to overstate the importance of gift exchange for brand managers. Annual occasions like Christmas, Easter, Valentine's, Thanksgiving, Halloween, not to mention birthdays and anniversaries and the so-called 'Hallmark Days' devoted to Mothers, Fathers, Grandparents, etc., are veritable orgies of gift giving, as are intermittent special occasions like weddings, engagements, graduations, christenings, confirmations, 21st birthdays, baby showers and high school proms.

THINK BOX 12

You Shouldn't Have!

The psychology of gift giving is fascinating. Who among us hasn't bought an inappropriate present for someone, or been embarrassed by an excessively generous gift that puts our own tatty token to shame? Everyone has a horror story. Here's mine.

A few years ago I bought the absolutely perfect gift for Linda, my long-suffering wife. Now Linda is very handy. She's brilliant at DIY, building repairs and doing all the little jobs around the house that lazy gits like me never quite manage to tackle. Hence, I thought I'd show my heartfelt appreciation by buying her a stepladder for Christmas. Yes, a stepladder.

Before you say anything, I'll have you know that this was no ordinary stepladder. It was the Lotus Elan of stepladders, the Louis Vuitton of stepladders, the Louboutin stilettos of stepladders. It was made of anodized aluminium. It came with non-slip steps. It had all sorts of special features. It was the bees' knees of stepladders. I wrapped it up in beautiful marbled Christmas paper, what is more, and placed it tenderly under our bauble-decked, tinsel-swaddled, star-surmounted Christmas tree. Where, I have to admit, it looked a wee bit like an Ancient Egyptian mummy in its alabaster sarcophagus.

Well, on Christmas Day we did our traditional ritual thing. All our extended family of aunts, uncles, nieces, nephews, etc. gather round the tree and we open the presents in turn, oohing and aaahing and clapping as each perfectly-chosen gift is unwrapped.

Well, when Linda unwrapped her stepladder, there was total silence, dead silence, sepulchral silence. A howling wind picked up from nowhere. A bell tolled mournfully in the distance. As I recall, a ball of tumbleweed rolled across the floor in front of me.

It took me months, months of flowers, chocolates, cards and the like to repair the damage. To this very day, whenever we do our Christmas thing, someone will always say, 'Do you remember the year with the ladder?' And everybody laughs at sad old Stephen's gift-giving mortification.[19]

Thinking Outside the Think Box

What is the worst present you have received? What is the worst present you have given? How come so many people are happy to receive hard cash as a gift, yet remain reluctant to give hard cash as a gift? What's going on with gift vouchers, since they too are made of paper, just like banknotes?

When, what's more, you add in benefactions from beyond the grave (bequests), the donations made to charities (shops, sponsorships, telethons, etc.), the tips left for service workers who diligently do consumers' bidding (in taxi cabs, hairdressers, restaurants and more), and the little rewards we give ourselves after a hard day at uni (self-gifts), it's easy to infer that gifts make the branding world go round.[20] And in certain respects they do, not least in cultures like China or Japan, where the gift economy is vast, where gifts are given and received on every imaginable social occasion and very strict etiquette applies.[21] Gifting is the gift that keeps on giving to brand and marketing managers. Many brands depend almost entirely on the Christmas gift-giving season for their annual profit, when approximately 80% of Tiffany's or Toys R Us's turnover transpires.

Cialdini's insights are reinforced by recent work in behavioural economics. After a series of laboratory experiments, Ariely found that the word FREE is a gift, a magic word that draws consumers like nothing else:

What is it about FREE that is so enticing? Why do we have an irrational urge to jump for a FREE item, even when it's not what we really want? I believe the answer is this. Most transactions have an upside and a downside, but when something is FREE we forget the downside. FREE gives us such an emotional charge that we perceive what is being offered as immensely more valuable than it really is ... If you are in business and understand that, you can do some marvellous things. Want to draw a crowd? Make something FREE. Want to sell more products? Make part of the purchase FREE.[22]

Free is the most powerful word in marketing's vocabulary. Second only to sex. Never use the two in combination, by the way, because 'free sex' can trigger a stampede ...

Scarcity

Dash if you must, dear reader, but before you go read *Yes*, Cialdini's co-authored primer on the science of persuasion.[23] In it, he tells of how a tiny change to a shopping channel's sales pitch made a massive difference to consumer response. Instead of saying 'Ring now, our operators are waiting for your call', the smiling salesperson said 'If our lines are busy, call back'. By implanting the idea that the phones are ringing off the hook as consumers scramble for the desirable merchandise, others rush to buy before it is too late. Human psychology, he reflects, is such that when things aren't available, we want them all the more. By deliberately limiting production, luxury brands like Lamborghini and Louis Vuitton increase demand and maintain their massive profit margins. The Hermès Birkin handbag not only boasts a two-year waiting list, there's a waiting list for the waiting list. Many expensive brands of bespoke cosmetics and hand-crafted Swiss watches (such as Floris and Hublot respectively), operate on the same principle. We are all familiar, furthermore, with the strategic stock shortages perpetrated by toy shops come Christmastime and which drive parents frantic trying to get the must-have toy of the moment, otherwise their kids will make their lives miseries. Here's how it works:

> They start prior to Christmas with attractive TV ads for certain special toys. The kids, naturally, want what they see and extract Christmas promises for these items from their parents ... They *undersupply* the stores with the toys they've gotten the parents to promise. Most parents find those toys sold out and are forced to substitute other toys of equal value. The toy manufacturers, of course, make a point of supplying the stores with plenty of these substitutes. Then, after Christmas, the companies start running the ads again for the other, special toys. That juices up the kids to want those toys more than ever. They go running to their parents whining, 'You promised, you promised' and the adults go trudging off to the store ...[24]

As consumers ourselves, we have all felt the full force of the scarcity effect. We know only too well that it triggers the gotta-have-it, gotta-get-it, gotta-gotta-gotta urge. Consider closing-down sales. Consider limited editions. Consider everything-must-go stock clearances. Consider rock-bottom-never-to-be-repeated price deals. Consider canny 'only five items left in stock' statements by online emporia. Consider farewell tours by antiquated rock bands like The Rolling Stones or Meatloaf, both of whom have been doing 'last chance to see' tours for years. And although these things can turn into a bit of a joke – the DFS furniture sale, for example – when it works, it really works. Just think of the consumer pandemonium every November when H&M, the fast fashion brand, releases its capsule collection by leading designers including Karl Lagerfeld, Stella McCartney, Alexander Wang, Isabel Marant. The queues stretch down the street and the range sells out in no time. IKEA does something similar with its extra special deals during new store openings, which have led to punch-ups in the car parks as bargain-hunting consumers fight over the offers. If you can get customers fighting over your brand, you must be doing something right. Fisticuffs are not unknown on Black Friday either, when many retailers mark the start of the Christmas shopping season with deeper than deep discounts that drive deal-prone customers to duke it out over bargain basement brands.[25]

Scarcity sells in two main ways: restricting the amount of merchandise that's available and restricting the time that it's available for. The luxury goods business is based on the former, as exclusive limited editions of deluxe brands like Cartier, Prada, Manolo Blanick, Patek Philippe and Moët & Chandon attest. The latter is exemplified by 'flash sales', 'weekend specials', 'boiler room' scams and, of course, 'happy hours', that timeless tavern standby when drinks are cheap, time is tight and drinkers tighter still. Cadbury's Creme Eggs, which used to be sold 'when in season', is another illustration of the same principle, as is Snapchat, the social media site where images evaporate after six seconds, as is Krispy Kreme's famous flashing sign – Hot Donuts Now! – which is illuminated when a fresh batch of the sugar-rush specials is available. The most impressive results, though, occur when the two tactics are combined: limited goods, limited time. The frantic consumer behaviour in H&M, the consumer fistfights on Black Friday, the moment of Chinese madness that is Singles Day (11 November) and the going-going-gone excitement of eBay or fine art auctions, where fanatical collectors bid, bid, bid for one-of-a-kind treasures, are the epitome of Cialdini's scarcity principle.[26]

Collecting, ironically, is a commonplace consumer activity that's almost as ubiquitous as gift giving. Many collections begin with a gift. But soon take on a life of their own. As TV programmes like the *Antiques Road Show* amply demonstrate, the urge to gather, to assemble, to arrange and to curate precious possessions is immensely powerful and incredibly widespread.[27] Anything and everything it's possible to imagine – beermats, teapots, teddy bears, toby jugs, Barbie dolls, Beanie Babies, advertising signs, airline sick bags – is collected by someone or other. And brands that build collectability into their offer, such as Swatch watches, Waterford crystal, Pandora bracelets, Moshi Monsters, Transylvanian Families, My Little Pony and the one and only Hello Kitty are laughing all the way to the brand bank. The same principle applies to Air Miles and loyalty cards and Facebook friends and Twitter followers. Collect, collect, collect. Collections mean cash for companies like Mattel, which owns the mega-successful American Girl brand.[28] This comprises a chain of vast flagship stores selling extremely expensive dolls, all with their bespoke outfits and backstories and birthdays and associated merchandise and beauty parlours (where consumers can get their doll's hair done) and in-store restaurants (where the dolls are taken for a slap-up meal) and in-store theatres (where the dolls and their owners can catch a show).

Consistency

Consistency is a polite word for inertia and habit. Humankind is a creature of habit. Once consumers settle into a routine, they are inclined to stick with it, whether it's the weekly trip to the supermarket, where they often navigate the store in exactly the same sequence on every occasion, or their tendency to stick with the same brand of high street bank, insurance agency, ISP, mobile phone network, no matter how indifferent the service becomes.[29]

Consistency, it must be stressed, is not another word for laziness. There are often very good reasons for staying put. It means we don't have to make lots of time-consuming choices, much less learn new mobile phone menus or laptop operating systems or word processing software or e-tailer checkout procedures. The QWERTY keyboard is a classic case in point, which survives despite its demonstrable inefficiencies and notwithstanding numerous attempts to replace it. In keeping with Zipf's 'principle of least effort', most consumers are too busy to make incessant decisions, unnecessary changes or alter established routines.[30] Consistency, in short, is a shortcut, a time saver.

The habit habit, however, is very important from a marketing perspective, because people tend to stick with the brand they're with. And that's wonderful for the manager of the brand they're with. But not so good for managers trying to get consumers to switch to *their* brand. Inertia is a big issue for brands, albeit one with pros and cons. On a positive note, it enables managers to categorize consumers and make confident predictions about each segment's behaviour. If you read around the textbooks, or simply keep an eye on the trade press, you'll come across countless classifications of consumer 'types'. The venerable social class dichotomy ABC1/C2DE is probably the best known. But hardly a week goes by without the identification, and naming, of some new consumer type – chavs, dinkies, yuppies, hipsters, slummy mummies, soccer moms, metrosexuals, mamils and more.[31] Lynx once produced a series of ads depicting different types of girlfriend – party girl, brainy girl, flirty girl, sporty girl and high maintenance girl – which brilliantly spoofed the whole consumer categorization process. The labels are handy, and fun to think about, but they are convenient caricatures at best and dehumanizing distinctions at worst.[32] They're widely used, though.

Consumers' consistency-driven predictability also forms the basis of loyalty card promotions, such as the frighteningly accurate Clubcard Rewards produced by Tesco, as well as the cookie-enabled advertising we're exposed to while browsing the web. They know who we are. They know what we want. They also form the basis of the feted Ehrenberg–Bass models of consumer behaviour. Based upon mountains of barcode scanner data across a vast range of product categories including toothpaste, detergent, shampoo, coffee, cat food, computers and financial services, these studies allege that there are several 'laws' of branding, such as the Pareto Law (more than half a brand's sales come from 20% of customers), the Natural Monopoly Law (the greater a brand's market share, the more casual buyers it attracts), the Double Jeopardy Law (the smaller a brand's market share, the less loyal its consumers) and the Retention Double Jeopardy Law (when brands lose buyers, that loss is proportional to a brand's market share).[33]

A rather less formal law related to consumer consistency is 'rituals bring rewards'. Ritual behaviour is a human universal, whether it's praying before going to bed, saying grace before breaking bread, shouting 'cheers' before imbibing a brewski or, like many superstitious sports stars, putting on their kit in the same sequence before taking to the field of play.[34] Many brands have rituals attached and once consumers get attached to them too, loyalty increases exponentially. Shaking the sludgy Orangina bottle, popping the top of a packet of Pringles, observing the nine-step pour of Stella Artois lager, slicing the foil of Kit-Kat with a fingernail (then snapping off the fingers in sequence), removing the gherkin before eating a Big Mac. Maybe that's just me ...

Ritual actions like these add to a brand's appeal and should be cultivated in much the same way as glasses of Sambuca are lit before drinking, tequila is swallowed in a salt, shot, suck, shiver sequence, and original Levi's 501 jeans are shrunk-to-fit (in a bath of cold water).[35] Concocting consumer rituals can cause problems, however. When the TV ads for Tango, a fluorescent orange soft drink, depicted a strange orange humanoid boxing the ears of unsuspecting bystanders, it was copied by boisterous schoolboys throughout Britain and led to perforated eardrums up and down the country. When Doritos attached a Russian Roulette ritual to a new brand of chips – some of which were ferociously hot, twenty times more intense than jalapeño – some asthmatic consumers who participated in the take-it-in-turns ritual ended up in hospital and the brand was banned in several places. In keeping with the scarcity principle, however, bans aren't necessarily bad for business. They increase demand by leaps and bounds. Bans build brands.

What *is* bad for brands is when managers assume that consistency is consistent, that customer loyalty is unshakable, reliable, guaranteed. The very process of identifying consumer 'types' can blind managers to the diversity that exists among their clientele and the fact that some customers are more likely to switch than others.[36] Studies of innovations show that consumers differ in their appetite for adventure. Some are early adopters. Others follow the leaders. Yet others are laggards. The same consumers, what is more, can lead and lag simultaneously in different areas of their lifestyle.

Authority

Consumers, then, are inconsistent in their consistency. Consistency shouldn't be confused with obduracy, though. It's just that some consumers are reluctant to shift themselves. One way in which change can be accelerated is through authority. Consumer behaviour is swayed by authority figures, important people, role models, significant others. In the past this tended to be royalty or highly respected pillars of the community. Just think of the royal warrants that used to adorn the exteriors of aristocratic retail stores like Harrods or Fortnum & Mason.[37] However, the same principle applies to other esteemed individuals including priests and preachers. In the 19th century, when society was much more religious than today, many brands employed ministers as ambassadors and spokespersons. Nowadays, of course, con-sumers not only have their doubts about clergymen but they look up to film stars, fashion models, television personalities, stand-up comedians, celebrity sportspeople, high-profile businesspeople and authorities on consumer behaviour like Cialdini. Angela Jolie's double mastectomy, for instance, inspired many at-risk women to con-sider the drastic procedure and support the third sector brands that surround it. The annual Movember campaign, when prominent sportsmen grow moustaches to raise awareness of testicular cancer, is another worthy illustration of authority in action.

In this regard, it is no accident that we often see dentists in ads for Sensodyne toothpaste, since they are authority figures in the dental sphere, or find veterinarians endorsing proprietary brands of dog food, because they are presumed to know what's best for our pets.[38] Never forget, furthermore, that the top-selling brands in a cat-egory, be it Intel or IBM or McDonald's or McKinsey, have authority too. Consumers are drawn by the fact that the brand draws other consumers, more consumers than any other brand. It follows that McDonald's must be the best. The proof of the pud-ding is in the eating. The compilers of music, book and computer game charts, where bestselling brands sell more by dint of the fact that they're bestsellers, make the most of the authority principle.

It further follows that by far the most important authority figures are other people. Consumers often take their cue from the consumers around them. Although we like to think of ourselves as free spirits, as independent decision takers, as people who don't follow fads, who do our own thing, who do things differently, the reality is that humankind is a herd animal.[39] We follow the crowd. We gravitate toward the latest fashions, or trendy nightclubs or must-see movies. We stand in line with all the others to get the latest iPhone or *Grand Theft Auto* or tickets to see that way-cool rock band that everybody's talking about. If everyone's wearing loom bands or play-ing *Candy Crush Saga* or watching the latest viral video on YouTube – or, if you're slow on the uptake like me, doing it Gangnam style – we all do it too then burst into contagious laughter as we do so. This doesn't mean that consumers are sheep who follow the leader unthinkingly, but merely that consumers are influenced by consumers like themselves:

> That's what brands play on. It's part of our nature to want to be accepted. Yet, at the same time, we have this desire to feel like we're different from everyone else – which is the complete opposite of that yearning for acceptance but is nonetheless relevant. I remember being in London in the 1970s and first seeing punks in Trafalgar Square. They had their hair 'Mohawked' up, and they wore jackets covered in safety pins. I couldn't help but imagine them at home, preparing themselves to go out, in order to look very different from anyone in their household or in their neighbourhood. But once they were out, they looked exactly like everyone else in Trafalgar Square. No matter how hard we try to look different, we almost always still look like someone. Once a lot of people get access into an exclusive club, the original members get turned off and leave to find another smaller, more exclusive club to join.[40]

This desire to be part of a club, one of the cognoscenti, is exemplified by the recent rapid rise of brand communities. Whereas traditional communities organized themselves around the church, the village, the school, the factory or the social club, contemporary communities are increasingly found around brands. Enthusiastic owners of Lambretta motor scooters may have more in common with other Lambretta owners than they do with their next door neighbours. And they hook up, usually through a combination of social media and formally affiliated or semi-official owners' groups. Also known as consumer tribes, such associations are especially prevalent around iconic or cult brands like *Star Trek*, Vespa, *Twilight*, Hello Kitty, *Hunger Games* and Quisp breakfast cereal (Think Box 13).

THINK BOX 13

Cereal Killers

Made by Quaker Oats from sweetened corn, Quisp is a flying saucer-shaped breakfast cereal. It was introduced in 1965 and soon commanded a sizeable market share among sugar rush-seeking youngsters. With its endearing backstory of an abandoned alien who wished to return to Planet Q, Quisp's sales rose, if not like a rocket, then slowly, steadily, successfully.[41]

The product peaked in 1972, when Quaker pitted Quisp against Quake, a sibling cereal. One brand would be cut from the company's roster, the other given a stay of execution. Everything depended on the outcome of a consumer plebiscite. Fearful that their favourite alien was about to be axed, cereal lovers voted in their thousands. Quisp carried the day and Quake was banished to the brand boondocks. It was a pyrrhic victory, though, because Quisp too was withdrawn from national distribution in 1977, when the kids who grew up with it grew out of it.

The dead and buried brand remained interred for the best part of 20 years. Until such times as Quisp kids had their own kids to feed and started wondering whatever happened to the sugary cereal that nourished them morning, noon and night. An online community of Quisp lovers sprang up and started exchanging stories of their Quisp-addled childhoods. The community pressurized Quaker into re-releasing the product, which was all decked out in a bright new, cartoon-encrusted box, courtesy of *South Park* supremoes Trey Parker and Matt Stone. Happy days …

Except that the re-released product wasn't up to scratch. As far as the Quisp community was concerned, the new cereal was an imposter, an alien comestible in a cartoon alien's body. It was a premium-priced rip-off to boot.

Formerly united in their adoration of Quisp as was, the community descended into faction fighting depending on their attitude to the imposter brand. Some hated the new formulation; others were just happy to see it back; and yet others engaged

(Continued)

(Continued)

in extended debate – complete with forensic photos of cereal grain evidence – about the comeback product's provenance.

Regardless of such differences in opinion, the Quisp buffs were as one in their anti-marketing attitude. Not only did Quaker's mendacious marketers get them hooked as children – only to peremptorily remove their desperately-needed, sugar-suffused narcotic – but the product pushers brought it back in a different, less refined form.

Quaker couldn't win. Despite responding to the community's calls in a customer-responsive manner, they were lambasted unmercifully for doing so. Cereal killers, some called them. More than a few were even less complimentary and hurled their slurs from the cyber rooftops. I bet Quaker wish they hadn't bothered.

Thinking Outside the Think Box

When casting for her stage show *Harry Potter and the Cursed Child*, J.K. Rowling gave the role of Hermione to a black actress, Noma Dumezweni. She defended her laudable yet controversial decision by stating that the books never specified Hermione's ethnicity. However, the Harry Potter brand community promptly pointed out that the books do, in fact, mention Hermione's 'pale white face'. Who's right and who's wrong here? Is the brand owner's decision final? Always?

There are numerous studies of brand communities, all well worth reading.[42] I myself spent several years studying the consumer tribe surrounding Harry Potter. You won't be surprised to hear that most community members are fanatical, almost to the point of obsession. It is exemplified by the restroom of Nicholson's restaurant in Edinburgh (now known as The Elephant House), where J.K. Rowling wrote the first book while she was a poverty-stricken single parent on unemployment benefit. The toilet walls are covered in graffiti written by fans from all over the world. Dumbledore's Army, one says, Still Recruiting …

Harry's brand fans, like those of Justin Bieber, One Direction, Taylor Swift, Lady Gaga and the Fiat 500 for that matter, are more than mere enthusiasts. They are true believers. They spend vast amounts of time discussing the brand, interacting with fellow brand fans and, as often as not, getting themselves tattooed with the logo, just like the Gucci guy in chapter 5. They come together on web forums and chat rooms. They organize brandfests – such as the communal motor bike rides of Vespa owners or off-road weekends for Range Rover drivers – and they turn up at the factory in droves when the company celebrates its birthday with special anniversary events.[43]

Now, from a branding perspective, the existence of a consumer tribe is brilliant. Not only do they buy the brand, they buy into everything the brand stands for. They promote it to other people, moreover. For free. They act as unpaid, self-appointed brand ambassadors. The downside, though, is that the membership often feels quite proprietorial about 'their' brand. If the brand owner makes changes that tribe doesn't like, the community cognoscenti are very quick to make their feelings known. A study of the *Star Wars* community revealed that fans had few nice things to say about George Lucas and some of the brand-damaging decisions he'd taken along the way.[44] From a brand manager's standpoint, the tribe can be a double-edged sword. Devotees sing the brand's praises to anyone who'll listen. But they assume brand owners march to their tune. They're the brand management equivalent of pester power.

Enchantment

Few would deny that Harry Potter is an enchanting brand. *Twilight* too. *Star Wars* as well. According to Cialdini, consumers are enchanted by enchantment. True, he prefers to call it 'likability'. But the word 'like' lacks magic these days. In a world of supercharged superlatives, where managers no longer aspire to satisfying customers, but delighting them, enthralling them, enrapturing them, 'like' means average at best inadequate at worst. Like's been commodified by Facebook.

Irrespective of the terminology, enchantment is important. Because we buy the brands we like. We buy from beguiling people. We buy from places we admire. We buy brand stories that enchant us. It's as simple as that. Salesmen and women the world over know that openness, amiability, enthusiasm and a modicum of personal charm are crucial when getting hard-working people to part with their hard-earned cash.[45] Their sales training programmes are specifically designed to take advantage of this fact of marketing life.

Enchantment doesn't just come from personal charm, toothsome smiles and a stock of funny stories. Consumers admire people who are physically attractive. Would it were otherwise, but good lookers do better in all walks of life, brand management included. We are equally drawn to people who are similar to ourselves. That's why salespersons mirror our posture and body language, while nodding and grinning all the while. That's why they miraculously share our interests like golf, gardening, hang-gliding, global warming, taking care of gingivitis-afflicted grandparents or whatever it happens to be.

Enchantment, in short, pays dividends. Consumers fall truly, madly, deeply in love with good-looking products, with handsome brands, with simply gorgeous Jimmy Choo shoes.[46] Consumers likewise find it hard to resist the blandishments of brand name politicians who can get away with just about anything on account of their prodigious personal charm, their possession of the common touch, the twinkle in their eye. Bill Clinton, Boris Johnson, Tony Blair (pre-Iraq), Narendra Modi and Aung San Suu Kyi all have it, as did Ronald Reagan, Margaret Thatcher and Nelson Mandela in their day. Donald Trump has too much, perhaps, as did Sarah Palin before him.

And then of course there's flattery. Flattery always helps when it comes to selling stuff.[47] We appreciate people who flatter us with lines like 'suits you, sir', 'you have wonderful taste', 'you look fantastic in that!' We say we have no time for flatterers, lickspittles, ass kissers, sycophants. And of course we don't. At the end of the day, however, we believe what they say. Because that's what we believe too.

Flattery works. But of course you wonderful, outstanding, super-intelligent students know that already. Though if you still harbour doubts, have a close look at the mirrors in the changing rooms of your favourite fashion store. Ever so slightly concave, they are expressly designed to flatter the customer. As is the dress size deflation – where size 10 today was 14 twenty years ago – that's perpetrated by certain retail chains to make consumers think they're more svelte than they are. Reflect also on the motivational mirrors in IKEA superstores. These are mirrors that light up with 'handwritten' messages for the person they're reflecting including 'You Look Fabulous Today'; 'Wow, Have You Been Working Out?'; and 'Darling, Your Dress Looks Amazing!' Harry Potter's Mirror of Erised has nothing on IKEA.

Enchanting antics like IKEA's mirror, or the flagrant flattery of Because You're Worth It, are a bit of bare-faced branding fun. However, many journalists, sociologists, cultural commentators and concerned citizens are deeply alarmed by marketers' customer-captivating capabilities.[48] They regard capitalism in general and branding in particular as a den of iniquity, where high-powered techniques of persuasion and compliance are employed to dazzle, then dupe, hapless customers. Brands stand accused of selling consumers stuff they don't need, such as personal protection insurance, or tempting susceptible people to spend money they don't have on gambling websites like William Hill's. With some justification, it has to be said. The less said about junk food and sugary drinks the better.

The perception that consumers are victimized and exploited by mendacious marketers goes back a long way. However it came to a head in the late 1950s when a book called *The Hidden Persuaders* was published. Written by crusading journalist Vance Packard, it comprised a whistleblowing expose of the tricks of the trade.[49] A massive American bestseller, it triggered a moral panic, near enough, when people discovered that marketers were manipulating consumers' minds through 'subliminal' advertising. These are secret commercial messages embedded in movies and adverts. Unbeknownst to consumers, they surreptitiously shape their buying behaviours. According to some batty observers, Robert Wilson Key among them, sneaky marketers insert the word SEX into their communications and consumers inadvertently rise to the bait. Mr Key is famous for seeing the word SEX everywhere he looks. Ice cubes in drinks are his favourite hobby horse, though he doesn't stop there. Hell no. For years, Key has been something of a standing joke in marketing circles – advertisers periodically spoof the sexy subliminal ice cubes scenario – but more recent evidence suggests that subconscious processes are very influential in purchasing situations and that consumers can be primed to act in ways they wouldn't otherwise countenance.[50] Enchanting stuff.

You may sneer, but before you skip ahead to the next chapter, reflect for a moment on the sheer enchantment of Hello Kitty. Forty something years ago, a young designer Yuko Shimizu came up with six sketches for Sanrio, a Japanese character goods company. One of them, a cute cat with wide eyes, no mouth and a bow tie was sufficiently captivating to go into production. The Hello Kitty character was imprinted on stationery, handkerchiefs and aprons to start with. By the turn of the millennium, this had risen to 6,000 Hello Kitty items, bestsellers one and all.[51] Such was the demand that Sanrio awarded licences to other eager organizations, which promptly produced 16,000 additional lines and sold them in forty separate countries. When research subsequently revealed that fully one-third of Hello Kitty customers were adults – not just the young girls Sanrio had assumed – the brand went stratospheric with ranges of lingerie and jewellery and credit cards and coffee makers, to say nothing of bicycles, computers, mobile phones, golf bags and diamond-encrusted wristwatches costing $30,000. If that's not consumer enchantment, I don't know what is.

Sharing

When Robert Cialdini was doing the research that became his bestselling book – a brilliant mixture of experiments, anecdotes and participant observation – there was no internet, no email, no search engines, no social media. Although he updated his work on several occasions and took technological developments into account, the 'weapons of influence' Cialdini identified in the first edition remain unchanged more than 30 years on.

Perhaps he's reluctant to change a winning formula – or maybe it's his consistency principle at work – but the rise of Facebook, Google, YouTube, Flickr, Pinterest, Spotify, AppChat and suchlike have thrown up another fundamental of consumer behaviour. Sharing. Whether it's file sharing, slide sharing, car sharing, or sharing our thoughts via blogs, tweets, chat rooms and other social media, the proffering imperative is everywhere apparent in today's hyper-connected consumer society.[52] We share jokes, stories, diets, recipes, ideas, opinions, music, gifs, fashion tips, fitness regimes, restaurant reviews, medical regimens, DIY challenges, childrearing dilemmas and photographs beyond number. We not only share with the world at large, we do so without reward other than the satisfaction of assisting, amusing or enlightening other people. Sure, kudos come from the esteem of 'followers' and so forth. And it is true that Google, Facebook, Instagram, Spotify and similar sites are required to earn their keep through advertising. But the basic idea of sharing with anyone and everyone – for free! – remains gratifyingly intact.

Take Wikipedia. From humble beginnings at the start of the millennium, January 2001 to be precise, Wikipedia has grown into a vast repository of information.[53] It is a repository used by 500 million people per month, on average. It is a repository of 37 million articles in 250 different languages, from Cornish to Corsican, Cebuano to Chichewa. It's a repository that was disparaged to start with, on account of its 'inaccuracies' and has got caught up in numerous controversies since. But the service is available to all for free. The contributors are anonymous and go unremunerated. Almost unbelievably, there is no advertising on the site. Anyone can contribute and millions do. For no reward other than the joy of sharing. Granted, contributors' expertise is acknowledged within the Wikipedia community, through the award of honorary 'barnstars'. However, these hardly compensate for the effort that goes into building the brand, a brand that's Number One in its category, a brand that killed off richly resourced competitors like Britannica and Encarta, a brand that is one of the five most visited websites in the world, after Google, Microsoft, Facebook and Yahoo!, a brand that's free at the point of sale and that, as a charitable foundation, doesn't make a brass farthing in revenue.

Sharing overlaps to some extent with reciprocity. You give me the gift of your playlist, I rate your exquisite taste in return. Reciprocity, nevertheless, is predicated on give and take, whereas sharing presupposes that it is better to give than to receive. The model is the family, where share-and-share-alike tends to prevail. Family members typically share the pets, the phone, the fridge, the cooker, the utilities, without any careful accounting of who owes what to whom. It's a model that prevails in many brand communities, such as Vespa's, where advice, guidance and assistance with tricky restoration jobs are expected and freely given. It's a model, moreover, that goes back to the dawn of time when tribal societies hunted in packs and shared the spoils one and all. It's a model, some commentators believe, that can change today's cruel, capitalistic world for the better. It's a primal form of consumer behaviour that many brands misunderstand and misinterpret. When Facebook uses our personal data for money-making ends, many people get upset. When celebrity vloggers use their YouTube channels to flog goods and services, consumers feel exploited. When financial institutions purport to be our friends – family members, near enough – then turn nasty when we have a temporary cash flow problem, our loathing increases immeasurably. Sharing is caring and all too often supposedly caring sharing brands couldn't care less about their customers.

CARESS THE CONSUMER

Happy as I am to share these thoughts with you, hoping you'll reciprocate by buying my books, it's necessary to stress that Cialdini's principles of consumer behaviour are neither universally applicable, nor are they immutable. They vary from time to time, place to place, person to person, segment to segment. They aren't clear-cut either. They intermingle and meld and mutate. Clarins cosmetics gives ample samples, sells limited editions, boasts celebrity spokespeople and its in-store demonstrators both flatter their customers and recommend makeup routines that should be adhered to consistently.

Yet for all the creative variations on customer capturing, there's one thing that can be said for certain about Reciprocity, Scarcity, Consistency, Authority, Enchantment and Sharing. Their capital letters, when rearranged, spell CARESS. Not only is this easy to remember, but brand managers can't go far wrong if they adopt caress as their watchword.

BRAND TASK

Reflect on your daily rituals (in the bathroom, bedroom, boardroom or whatever). Reflect on the brands involved. Reflect on how well ritual is used by brands like the British royal family. Reflect on the 'unboxing' phenomenon where brands are unwrapped in a ritualistic manner on YouTube. Then select a brand that's part of your wash-rinse-repeat routine and think of ways to increase its ritualistic appeal. Share your reflections.

RECOMMENDED READINGS

Robert B. Cialdini, *Influence: The Psychology of Persuasion* (HarperBusiness: New York, 2007). Cialdini's book is a must-read classic. *Yes*, his co-authored primer is worth reading too. You'll notice that his categories are slightly different from mine. I'm not convinced by his distinction between authority and social proof. But don't let that put you off.

Dennis W. Rook, 'The Ritual Dimension of Consumer Behavior', *Journal of Consumer Research*, 12 (December), 1985, 251–264. This is an oldie but a goodie, arguably the seminal statement on consumer rituals. Dennis is charm personified and this award-winning article is Dennis at his most charming.

Russell W. Belk, 'Sharing', *Journal of Consumer Research*, 36 (February), 2010, 715–734. Russ is the most well-read academic in the universe. His articles can be a bit overwhelming at times. But this one, on the rise of sharing in contemporary consumer society, is worth sticking with.

Bernard Cova, Robert Kozinets and Avi Shankar (eds.), *Consumer Tribes* (Routledge: London, 2007). This is an important edited collection on brand communities, ranging from Hummer to Warhammer. You don't need to read it all to get a feel for tribal branding. Dip in and out as you see fit.

CHAPTER 7
BRAND MANAGEMENT

Overview

Outstanding brands are the sacred vessels of consumer society. They are venerated, worshiped, idolized, sanctified. And brand managers are the high priests of this secular belief system. The religion of branding has its rites, observances and sacraments. This chapter sets out the ten commandments of brand management.

HOLY MOLY

What is the world's greatest brand? That's a hard question to answer. However, it's a question John Hegarty tackled twenty-five years ago, when the branding concept was beginning to burgeon. Although you might not know his name, you'd recognize John Hegarty if you saw him. He pops up on every TV programme about branding, advertising, marketing and popular culture. A stalwart of Saatchi & Saatchi when it was Britain's foremost ad agency – and a founder of stellar hot-shop Bartle Bogle Hegarty – he was the person behind some of the most successful brand building campaigns in British history. These include those for Audi, Boddingtons, Häagen-Dazs and, most famously, Levi Strauss. If anyone was in a position to identify the world's greatest brand back then, that person was John Hegarty.

According to the ad man's own account, he was asked the 'Greatest Brand' question at an American marketing conference, where most of the other speakers played safe.[1] They singled out Coca-Cola (the original and best), Marlboro (the brand with personality to die for), the VW Beetle (subject of the best ever advertising campaign) and Nike (the ass-kicking new kid on the block), whereas our plucky Brit begged to differ. He suggested – to the shock and awe of his audience – that the world's greatest brand was the Catholic Church. It had the world's best logo, a simple wooden cross. Its slogans were superlative: Seek and Ye Shall Find; Do As You Would Be Done By; Our Father, Who Art in Heaven. It was the first truly global brand, selling successfully in all five continents. It offered seven day opening at its monumental flagship stores, which were situated in prime locations. It had built a committed brand community before brand communities were invented. Best of all, it sold intangible beliefs rather than physical products. 'The oldest brand in the world', he concluded …

> … is actually the most modern. Nearly 2,000 years after its founding, it's still going strong. It's suffered competitive pressure – the Lutherans, Protestants, Episcopalians and Calvinists did their best to offer an alternative – but none of them matched the power and longevity of that 'first in market' position the Church adopted. Whatever your beliefs, you had to admire the innovation and commitment to brand building as demonstrated by this formidable institution.[2]

EVANGELICAL BRANDING

A quarter of a century on from Hegarty's provocative presentation, his arguments would unsettle few branding experts. Regarding religious beliefs as 'brands' is standard practice. Many, in fact, might be inclined to add that the Catholic Church's new CEO, Pope Francis, is restoring the fortunes of a badly damaged brand, one that lost much of its lustre during a series of reputation-ruining scandals. They might also be inclined to observe that, in today's largely secular society, brands have become a surrogate religion.[3] Iconic brands akin to Hermès, Hennessey, Harley-Davidson and Hello Kitty aren't short of worshippers, true believers who go out of their way to convert the multitudes. Having studied more than a few of these, including the *Star Wars*, *Harry Potter* and *Da Vinci Code* communities, I'm familiar with the fervour of some brands' disciples. And I'm not the only one. As an informant once made clear to me:

> I like to think I have managed to remain neutral about Harry Potter, but because I am not a devout fan this can be very testing. It's a bit like Christianity. Harry Potter lovers feel they must spread the message of the 'good book'. They automatically make a dash for non-believers with the aim of saving them from their non-Harry Potter ways.[4]

Fool that I am, furthermore, I once wrote a light-hearted article about Harry Potter's most dedicated devotees – those who wait in line for hours outside the Orlando branch of Ollivanders magic wand shop, then spend vast sums of money on what are, let's be blunt, varnished twigs in a box – and my in-box swiftly filled with curses, death threats and burn-in-hell blasphemies from the boy wizard's zealots.[5]

On a more positive note, Harry Potter's ability to instil that kind of blind loyalty is a model of branding best practice. It is a model that many brands aspire to nowadays and that many academic authorities have explored. Apple, for instance, has been subject to considerable spiritual speculation, up to and including impertinent parodies of the King James Bible:

> In the beginning (of the Information Age) was the void. And the void was digital. But lo, there came upon the land, the shadow of Steven Jobs (and Stephen Wozniak). And Steven (Stephen) said, 'Let there be Apple'. And there was Apple. And Steven (Stephen) beheld Apple. And it was good. And Apple begat Macintosh. And it was good. And soon upon the land there began to appear, The Cult of Macintosh. For they had tasted of Apple. And it was good.[6]

Consider also these episcopal comments on Apple's celestial store in the Big Apple:

> As you enter, you are faced with a stunning but simple glass staircase. On the first floor there are side chapels dedicated to the worship of digital photography, MP3s, and sleek laptops. Upstairs is the confessional – the Apple bar – where past mistakes are corrected and absolved on software misuse and hardware abuse. Worshippers' doubts are heard and some truths and answers are given here too. Along the galleries are the ecclesiastical libraries of software, and the sacred texts – the manuals and user guides. And everywhere, ministering quietly and reverentially, are the black clad acolytes, always on hand to explain the doctrine of loading software or give instruction on downloading music. At the top of the stairs you enter an inner sanctum. Congregants quietly gather there on slick pews facing a pulpit to the left of a giant flat screen exploding with colour and life. The pastor of the day (the sermons are advertised on hand-outs given to you as you leave the store) will preach on the doctrine of OS X, the uses of Adobe Photoshop, the salvation of FinalCut. Off to the right of the entrance is the altar, the last drop for a member's hour of supplication. A long smooth plinth of light coloured wood, cash registers accept offerings from the dedicated, mediated by the smiling deacons.[7]

Even Apple's ignominious failures, most notably the Newton handheld device, have been given the brand-as-religion treatment.[8] Whatever else is said about the i-conic brand, it's not short of militant missionaries.

HEAVEN CAN'T WAIT

Fun as it is to make 'fancy-that' comparisons between outstanding brands and organized religions, the analogy is more than a joke. Given that most brands in most categories are fairly nondescript, there's much to be said for spiritual approaches to brand management (Think Box 14). Managers are ministers of sorts. They believe in the brands they serve. They possess 'Brand Bibles' and consult them religiously.

They deliver salvation to consumers, in theory at any rate. They may lack the cassocks, surplices and dog collars traditionally associated with the clergy, but many are evangelicals when it comes to branding. Praise the Lord and Pass the Loyalty Card.

THINK BOX 14

Holy Water?[9]

Situated in the depths of the Irish countryside, Slaughterhouse Farm has been in Paul Piper's family for generations. Although their land, on the lower slopes of Mount Slemish, isn't the most fertile in County Antrim, the Pipers somehow managed to build a solid agricultural business around barley, beef, lamb and a little bit of rural tourism. A local legend – invented by Paul's great-great-grandfather, Peter – that St. Patrick quenched his thirst from the nearby spring in Quare Quarry, attracts a trickle of visitors from all parts, usually around Eastertime.

For years, Paul has joked about getting into the bottled water business. With an outstanding source of supply on the premises, the Pipers have been sitting on an aqueous goldmine for ages. True, tests suggest that their spring water contains numerous impurities. But only healthful ones like potassium, magnesium, silica, sulphate and zinc. The basalt in Slemish's famous volcanic plug not only serves as a natural filter and a source of invigorating minerals, it imparts a very distinctive flavour to the Slaughter water. Unfortunately, it reminds many drinkers of ammonia. 'Tastes like piss', some say, though Paul often wonders how they could possibly know that.

Luckily, the impurities are easily removed and, with the aid of a small, second-hand bottling machine, Paul sells Slaughter Water to tourists in his farm shop alongside fresh vegetables, cured meats, St. Patrick T-shirts and so on. When they ask about the name, often with a worried look on their faces, he laughingly explains that 'slaughter' is an Anglo-Norman mutilation of an old Irish word 'slachmhar', meaning neat, tidy and in good condition. The water is especially good, he goes on with a wink, when added to locally-distilled poteen, though he can't guarantee that they'll be in good condition afterwards. Slaughter Water also helps with the hangover to come ...

Never more than a side-line – the bottles are recycled, the packaging is haphazard, the name and story are the selling points – Slaughter Water took on new significance when the weather went wild in 2015 and wreaked havoc on the Pipers' core agricultural operation. So Peter, thinking strategically, decided to seek salvation in his water supply.

After consultations with a friend of a friend, who worked in the branding business, Peter was advised to abandon 'Slaughter', since the word carried unsavoury connotations, and reposition the product as a spiritual water predicated on the St Patrick connection. However the owner of Slaughterhouse Farm isn't convinced.

Thinking Outside the Think Box

Should Peter follow his friend of a friend's advice? Or is sticking with Slaughter Water a better, if offbeat, branding bet? How can he make best use of the St. Patrick connection and spirituality more generally? Is he wise to enter the bottled water market at all?

Everlasting life is every brand's aspiration. In order to achieve it, however, managers must be familiar with the Ten Commandments of Branding. These comprise the creed of contemporary brand management. Read them. Learn them. Act upon them. Otherwise eternal damnation ensues. Or a lifetime in brand limbo at least.

FIRST COMMANDMENT: THOU SHALT NOT FAIL

Books about branding, marketing and business more generally present an idealized picture. The case studies, the concepts, the bullet-pointed lists of dos and don'ts are Photoshopped representations of reality. The same is true of rigorously researched academic articles, the carefully structured narratives of which camouflage the messiness of the research process. There's no intent to mislead, rest assured. The cropping and filtering and retouching is perfectly in order. They help make the picture more striking, more memorable, more instructive. However, it's easy to get the wrong impression, to assume that all brands are as successful as vaunted exemplars like Armani, Bulgari, Chobani, Disney, eBay, etc.

If only. Would it were otherwise, but the reality of business life is that most start-ups stop, most companies collapse, most innovations implode, most mergers misfire, most R&D founders, most forecasts flub, most new products flatline, most advertising campaigns are ineffective, most killer apps die an agonizing death, most star CEOs turn out to be black holes, most brands either buckle or are a bust or have a backstory full of botches, blunders, clangers and catastrophes.[10]

The first rule of branding, then, is to survive. As the great marketing guru Ted Levitt once quipped, 'the business of business is to remain in business'.[11] And despite what it says in the textbooks, that's much easier said than done. Failure is the norm. You only have to watch a few episodes of *Dragons' Den* – sensationalized though they are – to realize that Reggae Reggae sauces are few and far between. Notwithstanding all the hype surrounding Kickstarter, the crowd-funded source of peer2peer venture capital, most of the proposals don't get enough financial pledges to make them viable. More than a few get nothing at all.[12] Research repeatedly shows that between 80% and 90% of new business ventures fail.[13] Most brands are stillborn. They don't last long enough to become the living, breathing, consumer-consuming brands encountered in chapters 5 and 6. The brand that has benefitted most from Kickstarter is Kickstarter. The brands that benefit most from *Dragons' Den* are the brands run by the dragons themselves.

I'm conscious of course that this reality check is disheartening. No true believer likes to hear that perdition not paradise is their likely fate. On reading the names of once brave brands that fell by the wayside – Moonshine Aftershave, Oasis Deodorant, Sudden Soda, Panda Punch, Tingle Pants, Skunk Guard, Climax Ginger Ale, Hagar the Horrible Cola, Puss 'n' Boots Cat Food – one can't help but be reminded of war graves, Remembrance Sunday and the poignant poppy display at the Tower of London.[14] The good news, though, is that failure assails even the biggest brands in the world. Remember Google Glasses? Remember Apple Maps? Remember Unilever's Persil Power? Remember Amazon's Fire Phone? Remember Disney's *John Carter*? Remember the WiiU handset? Remember Microsoft 8, the operating system that no one could? Remember the Airbus A380, the superjumbo jet that was supposed to revolutionize the airline industry (but is still struggling to reach cruising altitude)? Remember Li-Nang, the cheap and cheerful Chinese sportswear brand that dominated the market with 8,000 retail stores from Guangzhou in the south to Changchun in the north, then tried to compete with premium-priced sportswear brands like Adidas? All fell by the wayside.[15]

The other piece of good news is that there are degrees of failure. None of the brands just mentioned went belly-up because of their marketing mishaps. Sunny Delight died but P&G didn't lose much sleep. Google's glasses shattered but its driverless cars are coming ever closer. The Edsel famously flopped but Ford is still ticking over. *John Carter* tanked but Disney bounced back with *Frozen*.

Others are less fortunate. When Gerald Ratner, the boss of a cut-price chain of jewellery stores, made a frivolous remark about his company's 'crap' products, the brand was tainted for ever and ever, amen. When the lauded e-tailer Boo.com went live, everyone thought a new Amazon had arrived. But it was soon engulfed in a rainforest of failure thanks to its sluggish website, appalling logistics and ill-thought-through returns policy. Arthur Andersen was once one of the highest of high-flying firms of accountants. But when Enron crashed and burned, the Andersen brand burned as well, because it had been fiddling the books all the while. Thus did a hero become Nero.[16]

A spectrum of failure can be discerned. At one extreme there are simple slip-ups, such as Penguin Books' botched attempt to reorganize its logistics, which left brand name authors out of pocket. At the other extreme brands can succumb after an epic fail, as Dasani water demonstrably did in the United Kingdom.[17] Most fails are either stumbles, such as Virgin's God-awful cola, or slumps, where a brand loses the lustre it once enjoyed and never really recovers. The Body Shop's halo slipped badly when Anita Roddick was accused of being a gimlet-eyed businessperson who 'built an entire enterprise on a lie'.[18] Her brand, however, is still in business. At present, it possesses 2,500 retail stores worldwide.

SECOND COMMANDMENT: THOU SHALT GET LUCKY

The Body Shop escaped eternal damnation. Its deeply unpleasant backstory, involving intellectual property theft, barefaced fibs about its eco-friendliness and failure to practise what it preached on fair trade, should have consigned the sinner to the flames. But Roddick's brand got lucky. The same is true of Alibaba, the Chinese e-tailing titan, which took off during a SARS outbreak when western buyers were unwilling to travel to the PRC and ordered online instead. It's no less true of Highland Spring, the sparkling Scottish water, which came on-stream at the very moment when market leader Perrier was withdrawn from sale because of a benzene contamination scare. In a similar stroke of good fortune, Paul Smith found a lucky charm that had fallen off someone's bracelet and thought to himself, 'that would make a great button for a shirt'. Thirty thousand shirts later, the fashion brand founder still counts his blessings. Chance really can be a fine thing.

Luck, however, is four-letter word in business and management circles. Managers like to think that they're in control, call the shots, make things happen and, with the aid of powerful computer algorithms, predict the short- and medium-term future. Academics and educators are especially prone to this kind of thinking, since their careers are built, by and large, on rigorous analytic methods, models, mind-sets. The honest truth, though, is that luck, chance, serendipity, happenstance, good fortune and so forth play a big part in business and branding both.[19]

Kellogg's Corn Flakes, Dom Pérignon champagne, 3-M's Post-it Notes, Nike's waffle sole, Lindt milk chocolate and the once imperious Sony Walkman are just a few of the blockbuster brands that came about by happy accident. Procter & Gamble is renowned as the most rigorous brand builder bar none. Yet the history of the company reveals that everything from Ivory soap and Tide detergent to Pampers nappies and Pantene Pro V were a consequence of chance. McDonald's mighty fast food empire was likewise founded on a whim when Ray Kroc, a milkshake machine salesman, was sufficiently intrigued to make a trip to San Bernardino where the McDonald brothers' burger bar was selling shakes hand over fist. Pfizer was searching for an angina alleviant when it discovered the ithyphallic side-effects of Viagra and thereby earned the undying gratitude of erectile tribulation sufferers.[20]

And if that lot is insufficient to convince you of serendipity's unpredictable importance, take a look at Apple. Now everyone knows that it was Steve Jobs' reluctant visit to Xerox's PARC facility in 1979 that inspired his 'invention' of the GUI, drop-down menu and mouse-manoeuvred point-and-click procedure. What is less well known is that he wanted to withdraw the classic *1984* commercial from its pre-booked slot during the Super Bowl. He was unable to do so and the ad ran despite Steve's misgivings. It was the most fortuitous branding decision he ever made because Apple's rebellious image was established by Ridley Scott's superb commercial, a counter-cultural image it has exploited ever since. Luck moves in mysterious ways.

Luck doesn't last, though, as the cautionary tale of FCUK attests. Formerly known as French Connection, Stephen Marks' formulaic fashion retailer was going nowhere fast. Despite the owner's best efforts, it was firmly stuck in midmarket mediocrity. Enter an enterprising ad man, who'd been called in to sprinkle some marketing magic dust on the bland brand. Purely by chance, he noticed that the abbreviation FCUK (short for French Connection United Kingdom) was in widespread use throughout the organization (on its internal documents, memos, faxes and so forth). Recognizing a lucky break when he saw one, he seized upon this almost offensive acronym and turned it into one of the most provocative, high-profile advertising campaigns of the 1990s. Plastered across enormous billboards, the deathless words 'FCUK Fashion' stopped traffic, caused outrage and generated enormous sales for next to nothing. The brand was instantly transformed from a minnow to a monster:

> Beginning as it intended to go on, French Connection quickly squeezed every conceivable variation out of its unforgettable acronym. FCUK me, FCUK fear, FCUK off, FCUK FM, FCUK Santa and so forth all had their moment in the fcukin sun. The unspeakable initials were plastered on everything from FCUK deodorant and FCUK lingerie to the company's flagship store, 'the biggest FCUK in the world'. Sales space doubled, turnover burgeoned, America was invaded and everyone wanted a slice of the FCUK action, even Boots the Chemist, which stocked the complete FCUK range. Heaven only knows what Jesse Boot, the company's Puritan founder would've made of it. Fcukin hell. Hell indeed was where FCUK finished up. In classic Icarus brand fashion, the company crashed and burned in five short years. A joke can only be told so many times and FCUK wore out its welcome faster than most. By 2004, it was well and truly fcuked.[21]

FCUK lucked out. Ditto the Aflac duck, the Michelin Man, the Marlboro Man, Aleksandr Orlov and many other much-loved brand mascots, all of whom came from serendipitous strokes of good fortune, as did Velcro, Teflon, Kevlar, NutraSweet, Minoxidil, Penicillin and Louboutin's legendary red-soled stilettos, which were the result of an accidental spillage of China Red nail varnish. As John Lewis, the founder of the eponymous department stores, once observed, 'It would surely be manifestly absurd to suggest that mere luck is not a very great factor in the making of enormous fortunes.'[22] Or, as Daft Punk put it more succinctly, you got to get lucky.

THIRD COMMANDMENT: THOU SHALT NEVER GIVE UP

Another brand that got a lucky break is Scrabble. The legendary board game broke through in 1950, when the president of Macy's department store played it on holiday. He enjoyed scrabbling so much that, on his return to work, he commanded branch managers to carry the brand. Within five years Scrabble was selling 4 million sets per annum. For twenty years prior to that, mind you, Alfredo Butt had been trying to get people interested in the word game that he'd invented at the height of the Great Depression. Although the unemployed architect's idea was turned down by every board game maker, Parker Brothers included, he refused to give up and eventually got lucky.[23]

Perseverance in the face of failure may not be the secret of branding success, but it is a quality that all great brand owners and managers possess in abundance. Clarence Birdseye, as noted earlier, struggled for decades to sell the idea of frozen food. Colonel Sanders failed as a soldier, salesman, lawyer and, believe it or not, freelance gynaecologist before he came up with the idea of franchising fried chicken. Ruth Handler, the brains behind Barbie, was denounced as a pornographer by her peers, toy stores refused to handle her busty creation and even the employees at Mattel rebelled before the brand started selling like hot cakes. Hot buns, I should say.

Henry Ford furthermore was a complete failure for much of his early career. From 1899 (when he set up the Detroit Automobile Company) to 1908 (when he finally hit pay dirt with the Model T), every single car 'Crazy Henry' invented failed to set the world on fire (an electric one included). More recently, Sir James Dyson spent ten years developing his innovative vacuum cleaner. Five thousand plus prototypes were tested to destruction. He faced ridicule, experienced rejection and toiled away with very few resources. However, he won through in the end when his range of bagless cleaners not only transformed the market but remain the bestselling brand in Britain, despite an ultra-premium price point.

Chance and persistence are interrelated. Those who try hardest for longest make their own luck. As Gary Player, the multiple major-winning golfer, is reputed to have said: 'The more I practice the luckier I become.' Nowhere is this better illustrated than in the legendary 1990s advertising campaign that transformed Levi's jeans from a once-fashionable label utterly out of touch with the youth market into a super-cool icon of contemporary style with brand cachet to burn. John Hegarty – he of the Catholic Church contention – had just left Saatchi & Saatchi to set up his own agency. As a tiny hot shop start-up, Bartle Bogle Hegarty had nothing going for it except the partners' reputations. That got them added to the short list of major agencies pitching for Levi's lucrative account. All of the others had resources to spare. BBH didn't even have their own offices. They hadn't a hope. They were there to make up the numbers. Embarrassingly, their seat-of-the-pants presentation was made in an empty boardroom, with bare walls, no desks and a bunch of brand new office chairs, just delivered from Italy:

> The big day arrived and about eight people from Levi Strauss turned up, stepping over half-completed office walls smelling of wet paint.
>
> Lee Smith was one of the group. Lee was the head of Levi Strauss Europe. In the end he was the person who had to approve the appointment of the agency. Lee was about 6 feet 4 inches tall, suntanned and Californian. He looked as though he jogged every day and had a handshake that could crack a bag of walnuts. He'd flown over

from San Francisco for the pitches. As soon as I saw him I thought, 'It's all over. He's never going to buy an upstart new agency, without walls in their office. Not a chance. He's too corporate.'[24]

But BBH gave it their all. They told the Levi's people the unvarnished truth about their uncool brand. They gave it to them straight. Their once brilliant brand was a bust:

> When the presentation finally finished Robin Dow, who was the President of Levi Strauss in the UK, turned to Lee and said, 'You've not said anything. Is there anything you'd like to say?' Lee leaned back in one of our incredibly stylish Italian chairs and said, 'There's only one thing I want to say'. We all waited with bated breath. This was the moment he was going to say 'You must be joking. These people haven't got any staff, they've hardly started their company and haven't even got an office.'
> He didn't. He said, 'You know, these are the most comfortable chairs I've ever sat in.' We had won the account.[25]

The ability to find positives in negatives is an attribute of never-say-die brands. Bailey's Irish Cream, far from being based on an ancient Hibernian recipe, as many imagine, was invented in the mid-1970s, as a means of using up surplus stock of Irish whiskey and milk. Burt's Bees, the massive lip balm brand, resulted from a glut of honey on the Dexter, Maine, farm of former bohemian Burt Shavitz. Rather than sell off the golden gloop for a song, Burt and his partner Roxanne Quimby put on their thinking caps, came up all sorts of possible uses, including furniture polish and hand lotion, then knocked on doors until the elixir was sold at a profit.[26] When the VW Beetle was launched in the United States, the tiny, underpowered, fin-free car brand was the antithesis of everything 1950s automobile buyers had come to expect. Coming so soon after the Second World War, what's more, the American public's perception of Hitler's people's car was wholly negative. If ever a brand was certain to be strangled at birth, and simply not worth the effort, it was the VW Beetle. Yet by treating the car's shortcomings as reasons to buy – Think Small – and by constantly repeating the message through a brilliantly innovative advertising campaign, Doyle Dane Bernbach created a brand icon and transformed the US advertising industry into the bargain.[27]

FOURTH COMMANDMENT: THOU SHALT BE DIFFERENT

Being different is what branding is all about. Difference is its most central tenet, enshrined in law, and integral to the definitions included in chapter 1. Every able-bodied manager strives to differentiate his or her brand from the competition and, if asked, could count the ways in which theirs is the best. In this regard, renowned branding gurus like Kevin Keller make a key distinction between POPs and PODs.[28]

POP stands for points of parity. What it means is that a wannabe brand has to match the offer of all the others in its category. POD refers to points of difference. These are what lift and separate a would-be brand from the rest. A brand isn't a brand unless it's got a POD or two to its name.

The problem nowadays, though, is that PODs are increasingly difficult to tell apart. In category after category, be it bottled water, battery chargers, baby-grows, backpacks, bicycles, beauty creams, barbeque grills, beard trimmers, or blockbuster movies, what once were PODs are POPs offered by all. Go into any electrical store and, although the choice of cookers, fridges, televisions, washing machines, microwave ovens, tumble driers, sound systems, satnavs and so on is never less than vast, the products themselves are practically impossible to tell apart.[29] There are plenty of variations. But no variety. You have to be a real connoisseur of the category to appreciate the differences that brands brag about so blithely.

As Youngme Moon explains, category after category suffers from heterogeneous homogeneity.[30] Yes, there are differences between individual brands of laptop, airline, detergent, dishwasher, e-reader, DVD player, 4G provider, utility supplier, insurance agent, music streaming service and so on. However, the differences are so microscopic only the brand managers responsible can recognize them. For the rest of us, they're all the same. With the noteworthy exception of those few that aren't. Real difference is rare, but it does exist. Google's uncluttered homepage was a WTF revelation when the brand first appeared. Established web search sites, such as Excite, AOL and Yahoo!, were cluttered, confusing and clunky by comparison. The Wii radically rewrote the rules of the computer console handset back in 2006, when it blew Xbox and PlayStation out of the water. The first low-cost airlines, such as easyJet and Southwest, completely transformed the air travel experience. Innocent Drinks and Benefit Cosmetics were unlike anything else in the fruit smoothies and personal care sectors respectively, not least on account of their clever packaging and cute positioning. Heston Blumenthal's culinary creations may be a bit bonkers – Snail Porridge in particular – but there's no denying that his delirious dishes are deliciously different.[31]

Points of difference are quickly denuded through competitive pressures, though. These days, brand managers must aspire to POWs. Points of Wow! That is, breath-taking, bedazzling, stunning, staggering, simply stupendous branding achievements that boggle the mind and beggar belief.[32] Red Bull Stratos, Felix Baumgartner's supersonic skyfall in 2012, is a POW and a half, as are Olympic Games opening ceremonies, as is Fondazione Prada, a totally over-the-top exhibition experience in Milan, as is the Guggenheim Bilbao, which rebranded a declining industrial city in one fell swoop, as is the world's biggest shopping mall, the New Century Global Centre in Chengdu, as are Sony's truly stunning series of television ads for the Bravia, starting with *Balls*, as is the annual Neiman Marcus catalogue, which naturally includes his-and-her snowmobiles (diamond encrusted, doubtless), as was the gull-winged DeLorean back in the day, as are Japanese department stores every day of the year, as are the fabulous dancing fountains at the Bellagio casino complex in Las Vegas.

POWs don't have to be expensive, BTW. Zappos shifted the paradigm of online shoe selling with its nothing-is-too-much-trouble customer service. The Ice Bucket Challenge cost buttons, yet it raised $100 million for motor neurone disease. New Zealand Air's innovative flight safety videos, such as the legendary *Lord of the Rings* spoof, were made for a song and, more importantly, appreciated by millions. Yeo Valley yogurt raised its profile, and substantially increased market share, through a single parody ad (featuring a boy band of rapping dairy farmers) that was broadcast during the finals of *X Factor*. As Sir John Hegarty adroitly puts it, 'I'd rather be noticed once than missed a dozen times.'[33]

FIFTH COMMANDMENT: THOU SHALT GET THY STORY STRAIGHT

In chapter 4 we noted the importance of storytelling. Storytelling, in truth, has become a bit of a buzz word. In certain respects it's a 21st century synonym for strategy. Strategic planning used to be a pretty big preoccupation for brand managers. Rigid, formal, rigorously quantified exercises that took a long time to prepare, strategic plans were taken very, very seriously.[34] They contained confident predictions that were considered sacrosanct within organizations. All manner of proprietary models were developed to improve these prognostications – including the Boston Consulting Group's much-imitated matrix and Michael Porter's famous five forces framework – and many management consultancies enriched themselves during the great strategy boom of the 1980s and 1990s.

However, the bloom has since faded from the strategy rose, partly on account of the speed of change in today's hyper-connected world, where iPOW brands pop up from nowhere determined to overthrow conventional wisdom, and partly because of the great economic crash, which even the most far-sighted strategists on Wall Street failed to anticipate. The old testamental beliefs about strategy – this is the word of God, written on tables of stone – have been shattered. The title of a recent book on the subject, *Your Strategy Needs a Strategy*, says it all.[35]

None of this means that strategy is passé. The word may be tainted but the planning process – deciding what a brand stands for and where it wants to be – is as important as ever. The most successful strategists these days are storytellers akin to Mauborgne and Kim, who tell and sell a spellbinding tale involving inviting Blue Oceans where buoyant brands swim and splash to their hearts' content.[36] The problem with many contemporary brands, however, is that they are confused about which story to tell. They try to be all things to all people, telling meandering shaggy dog stories, rather than tightly plotted yarns that keep customers captivated and coming back for more. They are closer to James Joyce than E.L James, not so much Edgar Wallace as David Foster Wallace.

Bushmills Whiskey is fairly typical in this regard. The oldest distillery in the British Isles, it has illustrious heritage to spare. Once visited by Peter the Great – the father of Russia, the founder of St Petersburg, the most enlightened monarch of his day, a man who considered Bushmills' ambrosial nectar to be the best in Europe – the ancient Irish brand isn't short of storytelling raw material. Yet it has consistently underperformed in the key North American market, despite steady growth in the brown spirits category. Back in 1989, Bushmills was neck and neck with Jameson, Ireland's bestselling whiskey. But its US market share has since fallen from 22 to 8%. This disconcerting decline has been laid at the door of Diageo, the parent company, where Johnnie Walker is cock of the whisky walk and Scotch is held in higher esteem than Irish. But Bushmills' seeming inability to tell a convincing tale – a story that's different from the standard whiskey narrative of authenticity and ingredients – is partly responsible for its plight.[37]

Twitter is another case in point. Although the tech titan has been prodigiously successful – 300 million weekly active users, 500 million daily tweets, annual revenues of $1.4 billion – the brand is not as successful as it could, and should, be. According to the *Financial Times*, Twitter is 'the startup that never grew up'.[38] And as far as Facebook's founder Mark Zuckerberg is concerned, 'It's as if they drove a clown car into a goldmine and fell in.' Zuckerberg would say that, of course, since dissing rivals is the norm among nerds. However, the difficulties new users experience with Twitter's interface, the constant chopping and changing in the corporation's C-suite, and the lack of consensus about what the brand is, or what it wants to be, suggest that the plot has been lost. When CEO Jack Dorsey invited users to describe the site in three words, he reinforced 'the sense that the people running Twitter had trouble defining the social network themselves'. In the opinion of the brand's new CFO, Anthony Noto, 'The number one reason people don't use Twitter is because they don't understand why people should use Twitter.'[39] Is it 'a media platform', 'a democratic community', 'a free-speech sanctuary', 'trolling with brevity', 'broadcasting for introverts', 'time absorbing hell' or 'better than Facebook'? Who knows? Twitter doesn't.

SIXTH COMMANDMENT: THOU SHALT NOT WORSHIP CUSTOMERS

The basic problem with most brand strategists turned storytellers is that, despite their best efforts, they don't CLAMP consumers. They need to get a grip. They need to get a grip by letting go. They need to eschew the holy writ of marketing and embrace the idolatrous. They need to recognize that the most important lesson to be extracted from Twitter's tangle, its three-word trip-up, is that customer consecration is a mistake. Dorsey's act of customer engagement, inclusion, participation, co-creation – whatever you want to call it – only added to the confusion and exacerbated the brand's existential angst.

As noted in the previous chapter, there's a widespread belief within marketing that the customer is not just king but the king of kings, all-seeing, all-knowing, all-powerful, all-important. This belief is reinforced by branding experts when they contend, as many do, that brands only really exist in consumers' minds. This fatuous notion is further re-reinforced by the recent, web-fuelled rise of co-creation, crowdsourcing, user-generated content, etc., where brands approach consumers for suggestions on the best way forward. Unilever, P&G, Chevrolet, Honda, Nestlé and PepsiCo's Walkers Crisps, to name but a few, have swallowed the co-creation Kool-Aid and brought 'prosumers' on board as fully-fledged partners in the brand building business.[40] Wikipedia, Linux, Firefox, YouTube and Android, what's more, have been loudly lauded as exemplary instances of user-generated open-source branding. The wisdom of the consumer crowd, we're told, is much greater than that found in the Blofeld-like lairs of old-school brand managers.

The basic problem, though, is that consumers don't know best. Research repeatedly shows that, marketing savvy though they often are, consumers tend to think in conventional terms. In terms of what they already know. Audi's iconic strapline, *Vorsprung durch Technik*, was extensively market researched and the carmakers were very strongly advised not to use it ('nobody in Britain understands German!'). The revival of Levi's 501s was almost abandoned after focus groups couldn't get their heads round the brand's button fly ('zip fasteners are readily available').[41] The proposed relaunch of *Dr Who* was likewise researched by the BBC and it got the thumbs down from children and adults alike ('a niche show for sad, sci-fi followers'). The commissioning editor buried the research report and a huge, ratings-busting brand regenerated.

Now, this does *not* mean that consumers should be ignored. It does *not* mean that Unilever, P&G, Guinness, Sony, Adobe, Chevrolet, Gap and so forth were wrong-headed when they co-created, crowdsourced, conducted consumer research or whatever. It does *not* mean that Jack Dorsey was a duffus when he invited his followers to define Twitter in three choice words, like Listening to Customers. There is a crucial difference between listening to customers – attending to them, considering their suggestions, getting informative feedback – and worshipping customers, working on the assumption that the customer knows best. By all means include customers in the conversation but their words, no matter how eloquently phrased, should never be regarded as gospel. As one cynic observed about crowdsourcing, 'if you wouldn't ask just about anyone to get involved in building a high speed train, why trust anonymous third parties with marketing activity?'[42] The market itself is a crowd, remember, with lots of brands jostling for attention. In such circumstances, it takes a single-minded POWer brand to stand out from the crowd and single-minded POWer brands are often the product of single minds like Jobs or Branson or Roddick or Zuckerberg.

When it comes to open-source branding, what's more, even the most evangelical exponents of this over-praised approach have been forced to recant their customer-is-all credo. Wikipedia's open edit system, where anyone can make changes to existing articles, has often degenerated into a fractious free-for-all as contributors fight over the content of particularly contentious articles.[43] The infighting over Gdansk/Danzig become so serious that Wikicops, so to speak, were appointed to keep the peace. With extreme prejudice. Certain parts of the site are off limits to all but the most senior administrators. The wisdom of the crowd is one thing. The warring of the crowd is something else again. Customers should be listened to not given a licence to kill the offspring of brand managers.

THINK BOX 15

Seventh Commandment: Thou Must Keep a Secret

Mysteries move merchandise. Fact. Consider the secret recipes that help sell all sorts of comestibles including KFC, Heinz Ketchup, Kellogg's Frosties, Mrs Field's Cookies, Caramilk, Nutella, Big Macs and, the ambassador's choice, Ferrero Rocher. Consider the secret ingredients in beverages such as Coca-Cola, Courvoisier, Benedictine and Red Bull, the last of which includes macerated bull's testicles. Allegedly. Consider the secret menus in Mickey D's, Burger King, Subway, Chipotle, In-N-Out Burger and Starbucks, which includes 'babyccinos', specifically formulated for kiddie coffee consumers. Consider the cosmetics industry (secret of youthfulness), the proprietary medicine business (secret of healthfulness) and the tourist trade (secret hideaways a speciality).

Consider also blockbuster movies with their staggeringly expensive teaser trailers (wanna know what happens next?) and no-budget indie films which urge reviewers not to reveal the secret (or issue a spoiler alert at the very least). Consider the secret Cinema brand, where movie-goers don't know what they'll be seeing till they get there only to find themselves involved in an immersive, film-themed experience. Consider Secret Sales, which offers 'designer labels' in two- to four-day bargain bonanzas for fashion cognoscenti only. Consider JAR, the world's most elusive jewellery designer based in Paris, who makes the Scarlet Pimpernel look like a shameless show-off.

While you're at it, consider Victoria's Secret, the secret of which is that there's no secret. Everyone knows that sex sells. And seriously sexy sells even better.

Once you've recovered, consider Kinder Eggs, Tiger Balm, Listerine, WD40, Google's secret algorithm or the one and only Robert Galbraith, aka J.K. Rowling.

As Hannah et al. show, the simple fact of the matter is that secrecy is marketing's secret weapon.[44] Always has been. Always will be. It's important, though, that brand managers spill the fact that a secret exists. And shill the fact that they've spilled the fact that there's a secret. Keep that to yourself, BTW. It's our little secret.

(Continued)

EIGHTH COMMANDMENT: THOU SHALT TO THINE OWN SELF BE TRUE

It is of course difficult to resist consumer pressure. The lines of customer communication are so open these days that their voices are unavoidable and can't be cancelled with corporate earphones. The ideology of consumer orientation is so deeply engrained in branding's belief system, what's more, that ignoring customer input is considered preposterous, perverse to the point of lunacy. Yet many brilliantly successful brands adopt a like-it-or-lump-it attitude. They refuse to pander to customers. They take a take-it-or-leave-it position. They know they're not for everyone. They are proud of the fact that they alienate some consumers, divide opinion and generate more than a modicum of hostility.

Marmite is arguably the most extreme manifestation of this, with its adore it/abhor it advertising, its website, which is divided into love-Marmite/hate-Marmite sections, its bestselling board game, Love It or Hate It, and its large-format brand book, half of which sings Marmite's praises while the remainder revels in the consumer revulsion that the spreadable yeast extract stimulates. The brand name indeed has entered the vernacular for someone or something that divides consumer opinion. Russell Brand is a Marmite celebrity. Kanye West is a Marmite musician. Ed Sheeran is a Marmite singer-songwriter (and is proud of the fact).[45] Stewart Lee is a Marmite stand-up comedian. Piers Morgan is a Marmite television personality. Red Bull is a Marmite beverage, so is Guinness. The Prius is a Marmite automobile, so is the Hummer. Crocs are Marmite footwear, so are Uggs, Scholls and Birkenstocks. Tesco is a Marmite supermarket, so is McDonald's for anti-fast food fundamentalists and Starbucks for coffee connoisseurs. Marmite, in short, is shorthand for schismatic branding.

Marmite may be an outstanding exemplar of the my-way-or-the-highway school of brand management. But it isn't the only one. Pot Noodle takes pride in its standing as the junkiest of junk foods from the junk food farm. A Bathing Ape is a Japanese brand of T-shirts that not only plays hard to get but is practically impossible to find and will only sell to those consumers it deems suitable. Lululemon, likewise, is not reluctant to lambast cruiser weight customers who aren't the right shape for its super-stylish sports gear. Its brand name, bizarrely, includes three l's to make it unpronounceable by Japanese nationals. Huh?

Much the same is true of Hollister, which sells a way-cool So-Cal lifestyle to impressionable teenagers. Provided they're petite enough to fit into the restricted range of styles that the brand-for-beautiful-people makes available. The kids' parents are unwelcome too. Hence the dimly lit, nightclub-like interiors, the blaring indie music, the overpowering smell of seriously sexy scent and the extra-lengthy queues at the changing rooms and checkouts. Parents'd pay anything just to get the hell out of there.

Kerching!

According to Moon, this take-a-stand stance began with Benetton back in the 1990s.[46] A vibrant brand of Italian casual apparel, its United Colours poster campaign comprised a series of provocative images – a collage of condoms, the aftermath of a car bomb, a nun kissing a priest, a dying AIDS victim surrounded by his grieving family, a new-born baby complete with uncut umbilical cord – which aspired 'to raise awareness' of serious social issues. The brand, unsurprisingly, was accused of hideously exploitative behaviour. However its determination to take a stand on undeniably unpopular issues paid dividends. Heretical brands are heavenly for the chosen few, albeit Benetton ended up in hell when its luck ran out in FCUK fashion.[47]

NINTH COMMANDMENT: THOU SHALT SERVE A HIGHER PURPOSE

As the mainstream reaction to badass brands like Benetton illustrates, many consumers are more than a little cynical when corporations attach themselves to 'issues' or 'ideas' that are 'bigger than the bottom line'. If Ryanair started campaigning on conservation or environmental protection, most of its passengers might smell a rat. Or the stench of a PR stunt at least. Yet, in a world of increasingly identical goods and services, many, many brands are 'getting soul' in order to rise above the rest. These include good living brands like Ben & Jerry's, Innocent Drinks, Boost Bottled Water and TOMS shoes (which donates footwear to the unshod in destitute nations), to say nothing of Children in Need, the Salvation Army, Amnesty International and the Rainforest Alliance.

Unilever is also doing good deeds. In addition to its Sustainable Living Plan, which aims to improve the health and wellbeing of 1 billion people worldwide, a benevolent member of its brand family, Dove, masterminded the brilliantly successful Campaign for Real Beauty. This did much to improve self-esteem among women around the world. Fair Trade, with its yin-yang yellow-and-blue logo is likewise committed to the betterment of often grievously exploited agricultural producers in emerging economies. Fair trade is only fair, they maintain, and big name brands who sign up to Fair Trade's credo are allowed to place the iconic emblem on their packaging and promotional material. The BMW Mini, meanwhile, captivated the American market with a campaign that condemned – in a good-natured way – the gas guzzling gigantism that had spawned massive SUVs, hog-the-road Hummers and a widespread sense among consumers that, when it comes to automobiles, bigger is better big time. 'Let's sip,' Mini said, 'not guzzle.'[48]

Now, this is all very worthy. Admirable even. Acting the Good Samaritan is seriously good for business. But it also invites close scrutiny. Fair Trade has been accused of 'being a do-gooders badge that fails those it was set up to support'.[49] Unilever's commitment to women's issues has been derided because a delinquent member of its diverse brand family, Lynx (aka Axe), is irredeemably sexist. American Apparel was lauded for its eschewal of far eastern sweatshops and praised for paying fair wages to its all-American workforce.[50] More than a few of the latter, however, turned out to be illegal immigrants. BP claimed it was committed to renewable energy sources. Proudly proclaiming that BP stood for Beyond Petroleum, it changed its logo to a ripening flower in eco-friendly green. Then there was a fatal explosion at Texas City Refinery, caused by poor maintenance, swiftly followed by the infamous Gulf oil spill at Deepwater Horizon.[51] When subsequent investigations revealed that BP was aware of the dangers beforehand, the brand's reputation plunged so precipitously that it seriously contemplated a name change to Amoco.

It's clear, then, that if brands purport to be holier than thou, someone is certain to scrutinize their holy-roller credentials and publish the results on social media. Nike, Nestlé, Starbucks, Walmart, Coca-Cola and UK charities, such as Oxfam, Macmillan and the British Red Cross, have been exposed as egregiously hypocritical brands. Tesco too is detested for its two-faced behaviour, whispering Every Little Helps to customers while crucifying its suppliers with ruinous demands. Like-it-or-lump-it brands like Ryanair are at least open and honest about their profit-making orientation – 'maximizing shareholder value' is the preferred euphemism – and there's nothing wrong with that. Strange as it seems, they garner consumer respect for their candour:

> Ryanair is the unashamed villain of the corporate world. Other companies probably do worse things but Ryanair is the only one that delights in stepping into the public eye wearing an opera cloak and laughing maniacally ... This approach is unusual and refreshing. Most companies persist in trying to persuade us that they're nice and care about charitable causes, the obesity epidemic, equipment for schools and the environment. But these are publically traded corporate entities, so they're incapable of caring – they're merely trying to make money for their shareholders and believe that this affectation of human feelings will help them do so.[52]

Alan Sugar, similarly, once bragged that he'd sell mass-produced nuclear weapons if he could turn a decent profit on them. Whatever else is said about him, you can't deny that this gives a whole new meaning to 'You're Fired!'

TENTH COMMANDMENT: THOU SHALT NOT WORSHIP FALSE IDOLS

The problem with spiritual branding – or corporate social responsibility, if you prefer – is not the hideous hypocrisy of, say, high street bank brands telling consumers how much they care for their welfare. (Do they really imagine that their nefarious behaviours have been forgotten or forgiven?) The real problem is that, instead of being true to themselves, they've fallen for the latest management fad. There's an enormous industry devoted to 'thought leadership', to formulating tools and techniques and theories and tablets of stone that save management sinners.

The thought leadership industry began with Tom Peters' classic co-authored text, *In Search of Excellence*. Based on an empirical study of 43 (originally 62) high-performing American organizations (including NCR, Wang and Xerox), and published at a time when Japanese brands like Honda and Toyota were making significant inroads into the US marketplace, his eight rules of excellence became the management mantras of their day: Stick to the Knitting; Productivity Through People; Close to the Customer, etc.

There have been many management mantras since Tom Peters' most excellent heyday. The new product category he created was, like all new product categories, soon filled to the brim with competing brands. These idea brands are trademarked for the most part and sold with a degree of ruthless efficiency – via books, seminars, websites, consultancy gigs – that'd put Costco to shame. Jim Collins' *Good to Great*, Gary Hamel's *Leading the Revolution*, Nordström and Ridderstrale's *Funky Business* and *Funky Business Forever* are just some of the better known brands in what is a vast, highly competitive and utterly unregulated market. Business isn't getting any easier, after all, and sellers of catechisms, indulgences and holy writs have a ready market among C-suite sinners keen to follow the gurus' straight-and-narrow testaments, especially those whose profits have been backsliding.

Although many cynics rightly disdain such hellfire-and-brimstone, three-steps-to-heaven, snake-oil-suffused sermonizing – most of Peters' excellent exemplars went belly up, Collins' great group didn't do so good after his parables about their prowess appeared, and one of Hamel's foremost role models was none other than Enron – the reality is that much-hyped ideas like re-engineering, relationship marketing, crowdsourcing and so on do indeed work for the early adopters. However, when everyone is swimming in a blue ocean or orbiting a giant hairball or wondering who moved the cheese (don't ask) or is *au fait* with the iceberg model of branding or, for that matter, has embraced the marketing concept of customer orientation, then the advantages are cancelled out. That's the problem facing marketing at the minute. The marketing concept has been too successful. We live in a world where marketing is ubiquitous, where every executive is familiar with marketing principles, where every degree programme contains the same core modules, where every textbook writer parrots the parrots that parroted previously.

What, then, is the secret of success when the secret of success is known to all? Ah, that would be telling. It's a secret. Nothing less than the secret seventh commandment on page 135 (Think Box 15).

BRAND TASK

Formed in Paris in 1833, the St Vincent de Paul Society (SVP) is an international Christian voluntary organization dedicated to defeating poverty and disadvantage. Neither discriminatory nor judgemental, SVP helps the homeless, single-parent families, asylum seekers and socially isolated individuals. The causes it champions, however, are less high-profile than those pertaining to, say, animal welfare, environmental protection, political oppression or infectious disease. Come up with a POW to put SVP on the map. Big up the brand.

RECOMMENDED READINGS

Russell W. Belk and Gülnur Tumbat, 'The Cult of Macintosh', *Consumption, Markets and Culture*, 8 (3), 2005, 205–217. Many books and articles examine the brand-as-religion/shopping-mall-as-cathedral analogy. This adaptation of the idea to Apple is as good as it gets.

Sir John Hegarty, *Hegarty on Advertising: Turning Intelligence into Magic* (Thames & Hudson: London, 2011). Hegarty's book's here not solely on account of his Catholic Church contribution or the wry yarn about the Levi Strauss account. It's just a great read, as is his companion book on creativity.

Youngme Moon, *Different: Escaping the Competitive Herd* (Crown: New York, 2011). Moon's book follows in the footsteps of fellow Harvard professor Ted Levitt, who claimed that everything can be differentiated. She fills out his insight with lots of readable stories concerning iconic brands, from IKEA to Hollister.

David Hannah et al., 'It's a Secret: Marketing Value and the Denial of Availability', *Business Horizons*, 57 (1), 2014, 49–59. Wanna know a secret? I once wrote some stuff on secrecy. Keep it to yourself. Not least because this article is better than anything written by me. Don't let on to my publisher.

Overview

Driven by the demands of the stock market and managers' towering ambitions, brands are inclined to expand to infinity and beyond. Much like the universe itself. This expansion process may be planned or opportunistic or a bit of both. But it transpires in eleven main ways. This chapter identifies the whys and wherefores of brand expansion from product-led development to platform-based enlargement.

ONCE UPON A TYRONE

Back when I was footloose and fancy free, I spent a fair amount of time in international markets. My university used to do consultancy work for local entrepreneurs, would-be exporters who wanted to conquer the world. Assisted by groups of postgraduate students, we travelled hither and yon – France, Germany, Belgium, Holland, Brazil, Indonesia, Thailand, China, Canada, the United States – investigating potential markets for drainage pipes, dairy products, double glazing, aircraft seats, hair-care requisites and, of all things, five-bar farm gates. Happy days.

The consultancy gig I remember most vividly involved a crystal-ware producer which wanted to expand into Japan. Tyrone Crystal manufactured mouth-blown, hand-cut, full-lead crystal, not dissimilar to that made famous by Waterford Glass. And the omens for Tyrone Crystal were good. Encouraged by JETRO, on account of Japan's massive trade surplus with the west back then, many European luxury goods makers had entered the Japanese market with their upscale offers. Japan's prodigious gift economy also boded well for our client, since crystal glassware is often given as a gift. Tyrone's packaging was somewhat worrying, though. The crystal pieces were swaddled in tissue paper and individually packed in dark green-and-gold cardboard tubes, with a plastic peel-back lid at either end. Don't get me wrong, the packaging was very attractive in a Pringles-meets-Harrods kind of way. But we worried that it might not be up to exacting Japanese standards.

Anyway, we spent two weeks in Japan, scrutinizing the crystal-ware market.[1] We interviewed department store buyers, talked to industry representatives, met with JETRO officials, touched base with Irish and British diplomats, and generally tramped from store to store studying layouts, displays, price points, competing products, shopper behaviour and so on. It was a real eye-opener, the commercial counterpart of culture shock. Everyone *hated* the products. Our full-lead crystal was instantly dismissed as rough, crude, rustic and utterly unsuited to Japanese tastes, aesthetics, lifestyles. What we regarded as the winsome charm of our mouth-blown, hand-cut Irish glassware, with its cording, abrasions, air bubbles and analogous indicators of 'authenticity', was considered unacceptable on account of poor quality control and slapdash production methods. Tyrone Crystal, in short, cut no ice in Japan. With one notable exception. Everyone *loved* the packaging. The dark green and gold livery bespoke timeless elegance. The peel-back lids, with a little bit of delicious vacuum-packed resistance, were a big hit. The logo, a stylized representation of an ancient Irish castle keep, hit the heritage spot. However, the products themselves were substandard.

So, we flew back to Ireland with our findings. We were tempted to tell Tyrone's top management team that 'we have some good news and some bad news'. Bad news: smash the glassware. Good news: sell the packaging. Instead, we recommended that they develop a range of lighter, rather more delicate crystal pieces for the Japanese market. Which they did. And it proved surprisingly successful. So much so, Tyrone then launched the range in the domestic market, where it sold quite well to younger Irish consumers who weren't keen on the traditional, Waterford-oid styles that older generations admired.

The moral of my story is that Tyrone Crystal's brand expanded. But not in the way its managers anticipated. What we also failed to anticipate was the emergence of 'the brand'. Back then, brands were considered a sub-component of Product, one of marketing's 4Ps alongside Price, Place and Promotion.[2] At no stage during our TC consultancy gig did anyone say anything about 'brands' or 'branding'. We talked, rather, about products, ranges, lines, sets, markets, packages and craftsmanship.

The entire exercise, in fact, could quite easily be encapsulated in Ansoff's ancient 2×2 product–market matrix, which explains corporate expansion in terms of existing and new products alongside existing and new markets.[3] Tyrone Crystal started out thinking about existing products in new markets but ended up selling new products in existing markets. Brands didn't enter into the equation. Linguistically, at least.

THE BIG BRAND THEORY

Branding's Big Bang, ironically, coincided with our abortive attempt to export Tyrone Crystal. The late 1980s/early 1990s was a time when branding burgeoned in Britain. This was largely on account of PM Margaret Thatcher's privatization programme, when former state assets entered private ownership. It also saw the first appearance of brand equity on corporate balance sheets. In 1989, the London Stock Exchange accepted the concept of brand valuation and allowed the inclusion of intangible assets during takeovers.[4] A period of merger mania ensued and the practice burgeoned thereafter. The contemporaneous collapse of communism, which opened up vast new markets for western goods; the rise of the internet, with its abundance of i-brands; and the convergence of world economies, under the auspices of free trade agreements, added further fuel to branding's Big Bang.

As with its counterpart in the physical sciences, branding has been expanding ever since. Although marketing cosmologists continue to debate the origins of the brandiverse – the singularity is variously identified as Bass's trademarked red triangle and Josiah Wedgwood's jasperware in the 17th century[5] – no one doubts the Big Brand Theory's plausibility. The only debate is whether it will end with Google gobbling up the globe while mouthing its brand mantra 'Don't Be Evil' or Facebook removing its Zuckerbergian mask to reveal an alien life form within. The invasion of the brand snatchers is upon us.

For the meantime, it is sufficient to note that branding is expanding at warp speed. This expansion, moreover, operates in several spheres simultaneously. The first of these is sectoral. As noted in chapter 1, the b-word is applied to anything and everything these days, from heaven-sent religious denominations, through supernova sports people, to stars of stage and screen, not least celebrity cosmologists like brand Brian Cox, brand Stephen Hawking and brand Sheldon Cooper.

The second sphere is discursive. There is an enormous amount of brand talk, brand chatter, brand blether nowadays – in blogs, on websites, and via social media, to say nothing of newspapers, magazine articles, television channels, radio stations and good old-fashioned books. Remember those? Diverse academic disciplines have turned their tools, techniques, theories and all-round intellectual firepower on the subject and provided ample food for branding thought, furthermore.

However, the third and most important sphere is organizational. Branding is no longer a subsidiary element of one of the four Ps.[6] It has swallowed the marketing department. It has devoured HRM (internal branding), accounts (brand valuation), legal (IP is all), strategy (brand storytelling) and even the MD (brand Branson come on down). Branding lives in a corner office on the C-suite, like Audrey II in *Little Shop of Horrors*. Feed me. Feed me. Twiglets, if you have them.

Little wonder many wonder whether branding's expansion is a good thing. Little wonder many wonder where it's headed. If, as a consequence of the Brand Me movement, every single person on the planet is a brand, along with their grumpy cats and doleful dogs, what's left for branding to colonize? What will be the new bottled water? Fresh air? Probably.[7]

Sometimes described as 'brand creep', this process of relentless expansion, if not exactly creepy, is unsettling for some. It is unsettling for established frameworks as well. Marketing's mnemonics and matrices, such as the 4Ps and Ansoff's product–market model of brand expansion, predate branding's Big Bang. We need to expand our understanding of branding in order to understand the expanded branded universe.

GROWTH IS GOOD

Let's begin with the basics. Why, at an organizational level, does brand expansion occur? The simple answer is that it's a natural law, not unlike the Big Bang Theory. Just as work expands to fill the time available, according to Parkinson's Law, so too brands expand until something stops them. If we accept that brands are living things, they will multiply until they fill their ecological niche. Overpopulation, competition and depleted resources will eventually take their toll.

There's more to it than Marketing Malthusianism, however, because brand expansion is precipitated by pressure groups such as the stock market, merchant banks and venture capitalists, which insist on ever-increasing returns from the organization. Otherwise the funds they need to thrive will shrink and the brand will wither and die.

Nor should we forget brand managers' competitive instincts. They want to win. They aim to be the biggest and best. They hope to overthrow the market leader. They're tasked with growing the brands they're responsible for. It's a job requirement. Expansion is expected. It comes with the territory.[8] Salaries are often tied to performance, as are promotions, as are senior executives' share options, pensions, golden parachutes, etc. Expansion, in such circumstances, is inevitable. And when new market opportunities open up as a result of technological developments (e-cigarettes, for instance) or legislative change (the decriminalization of marijuana, say), brands blossom like bluebells in spring, tra la la.

Regardless of the reasons, brand expansion is a fact of life. Tarry for a few minutes in the toilet tissue aisle of a typical Sainsbury's supermarket and the outcomes of brand expansion are all too apparent. In the authoritative words of the *Financial Times*:

> When I was a child there were two sorts of lavatory paper: hard and soft. Each sort was available in little folded sheets or on a roll. In those days consumers had a real choice, and as far as I was concerned, my parents – who bought the hard sheets – always made the wrong one.
>
> Things are not so straightforward now. On the shelves of our local Sainsbury's, loo paper takes up a whole aisle, occupying as much shelf space as the entire contents of the grocer's shop from which my mother used to buy the offending Izal. There

is Soft, Super Soft, Quilted, Double Velvet, and Softer & Thicker. There is Economy, Medicated, Recycled, Soft Recycled, Recycled From 100 Per Cent Low Grade Waste, and something called Greencare. Most of these come in a variety of pastel shades: mint green, honeysuckle, snowdrop white, peach and rose pink. Some have patterns on them and are called things like 'bouquet,' and 'chantilly.' In addition, there are wet wipes and a new product offering 'advanced personal hygiene.'

If this is choice, I don't want it.[9]

What Lucy Kellaway doesn't say is that every single brand of toilet tissue – Andrex, Cushelle, Velvet, Asda's own label, Lidl's cheap sheets – is offering the same intra-category choice. She was also writing before the advent of Bum Fresh and omits to mention the excretory Elysium that is nappies.[10] The recent rapid rise of pull-ups, nappies for older youngsters entering the traumatic toilet training years, have expanded the nappy market immeasurably.

ALL THE WAY UP TO ELEVEN

Above and beyond the rationale for expansion is the pragmatics of how to do it. In what ways are brands expanded? What forms do they take? Well, the answer is that brands expand in eleven main ways. These ways, however, combine and intermingle in forty million different forms (which is more than enough for practical management purposes).[11] Fortunately for students facing examinations, all eleven begin with the letter P.

Product

Stretching the product or service is the principal way in which brands are extended. As noted in chapter 4, brands breed like billy-o. So much so that brand stretch often becomes overstretch and an elastic limit is reached. Ferrari, for example, has opened forty retail stores around the world selling watches, laptops, apparel, accessories, et al., as well as a dedicated theme park in Abu-Dhabi. And now that the brand is listed on the stock market, plans are on hand to expand even further, possibly into the SUV segment hated by petrol-heads.[12] The upshot is that Ferrari products are more available than ever before, arguably to the detriment of the iconic brand's allure.

That said, product expansion typically transpires in three ways:

Addition, where the volume of production of existing products is increased thereby making them more available. Many luxury goods brands have gone down this road in recent years including top-end automakers like Bentley, Jaguar, Lamborghini, Land Rover and Rolls-Royce. The first of these, for instance, has increased production from approximately 4,000 to 12,000 units per year and hopes to sell 20,000 p.a. by 2020.

Augmentation, where the product itself bulks up through feature inflation, the provision of ever more bells and whistles. The specs of laptop computers (faster chips, additional memory, brighter screens), smartphones (which typically combine the functions of camera, MP3 player, gaming console, personal organizer) and, lest we forget, razor blades (lubricant strips, vibrating heads, flexball joints, extra blades) are increasing all the time

Proliferation, where the range of products is increased. Thus Coca-Cola begat Diet Coke which begat Coke Zero and Coke Life and any number of other Cokettes, including Cherry Coke, Vanilla Coke, Caffeine-Free Coke and Diet Coke Plus. Colgate, similarly, sells all sorts of variations on its venerable toothpaste, as does Head & Shoulders shampoo. The manifold formulations of Ariel soap powders, Kit-Kat chocolate bars, Olay brand cosmetics, Reggae Reggae sauces, Moleskine notebooks and the *Freakonomics* phenomenon are testament to the more more more mind-set of brand expansion:

> *Freakonomics*, which began life as a book, has turned into a brand. There is the Freakonomics movie, the Freakonomics radio show, the Freakonomics blog. You can hire the Freakonomics guys for business consultancy, for conferences, for after-dinner speaking (maybe for weddings and bar mitzvahs too).[13]

Price

Pricing is another important aspect of brand bloat. Brands typically command a price premium over commodities. One of the timeless rules of brand management is to resist discounting at all costs, because it devalues the brand and risks reducing it to commodity status. That rule, however, is less applicable in a world where everything is regarded as a brand, even the deepest of deep discounters like Ryanair and Poundland. These days, cutting prices expands the brand. Just ask Lidl or Aldi or IKEA or Matalan or Groupon or JD Sports. Free is no barrier to branding either, as Twitter and Instagram and Deezer and Dropbox demonstrate. On the contrary, 'free' is the killer app of 21st century branding. Or i-branding at any rate.

Price's place in brand expansion is important in other ways. One of the most frequent ways brands expand is by moving up and down the price point spectrum. Many luxury labels, for example, expand by developing diffusion or bridge ranges, which are cheaper than the main line.[14] These reach down to less affluent consumer segments, some of whom will trade up to pricier items as their disposable income permits. Armani's Emporio, Versace's Versus, Donna Karan's DKNY, Tiffany's T range and the Mercedes A series are exemplary examples of expanding down, as are GE's and Unilever's recent experiments in 'frugal innovation', as is Elon Musk's SpaceX, which offers a cheap and cheerful means of launching satellites into earth orbit.[15] In a similar vein, Procter & Gamble now offers 'low end extensions' of its mid-tier brands like Tide detergent and Flash floor cleaner.

The reverse process operates too, inasmuch as bargain basement brands often expand by edging up into higher price brackets.[16] Supermarket own-label products typify this upward marketing mobility. They began as cheap and nasty generic products, down-market equivalents of 'proper' brands of cornflakes, crisps and cola, but subsequently matched and eventually surpassed their better known rivals (e.g. Tesco's Finest, Asda's Chosen by You, Sainsbury's Taste the Difference). Fast fashion brands like Zara, H&M and Topshop are likewise expanding up to the lower reaches of luxury labels' down-ward drift, as are 'masstige' minded mainstream stores like M&S.[17] Pure Gym and Gym Group are flexing their cut-price muscles, furthermore, while kicking sand in the faces of LA Fitness and Fitness First. EasyJet too escaped the race to the bottom of low-cost airlines by introducing flexible ticketing, seat selection, priority boarding, all of which appeal to businesspeople and those who prefer to avoid the first-come-first-served seat-grabbing passenger scrum that used to prevail.

Promotion

Augmenting the offer is all fine and dandy. Covering the price point continuum is a smart move for ambitious brands. But unless potential buyers are made aware of the enhancements, extensions, extrapolations – that is, the additional choice or better value they're being offered by caring, sharing corporations – the distended brand will shrivel and dwindle and disintegrate. When every brand is stretching itself, something's got to give. And it's those who promote themselves assiduously that catapult forward while other elastic brands snap. Fortunately, the promotional vehicles available to expanding brands are themselves expanding rapidly. The prolif-eration of television channels, radio stations, periodicals, magazines, websites, blogs, vlogs, Vimeo, YouTube, telemarketing, direct mail, spamarama and social media is something to behold. As is the ever-growing number of ambient and outdoor adver-tising opportunities including hoardings, billboards, vending machines, bus shelters, sales receipts, shopping trolleys, toilet seats, urinals, sandy beaches, park benches, manhole covers, delivery vehicles, baggage carousels, supermarket checkout belts and even people's faces.[18] In addition to outdoor, which now extends to airships and thunderstorms, there's product placement in movies, TV shows, video games, pop songs, paintings, novels and, it is rumoured, student textbooks about Brands & Branding.[19] Not all of them, unfortunately …

While I'm waiting for Veuve Clicquot to call, it's necessary to acknowledge that, when it comes to promoting brands, there are three main media options: *paid*, any advertising or publicity or promotion that costs money; *owned*, corporate websites, blogs, in-house magazines-cum-catalogues like Acne's, Asos's or Jack Wills'; and *earned*, social media mentions, sharings, retweets, likes and similar brand amplifiers.[20] Expanding the conversation around the expanded brand is challenging, admittedly. However, it's here that jaw-dropping POWmotions come into their own. For all the talk about digital advertising's takeover, awe-inducing ads akin to Apple's *1984*, Levi's *Laundrette*, BA's *Face*, Honda's *Cog*, Sony's *Balls*, Dove's *Evolution*, Chanel's *The Film*, Coke's *Happiness Factory*, Cadbury's *Drumming Gorilla*, Hovis's *Boy on a Bike* and Hamlet's imperishable *Photo-booth* are hard to beat when it comes to magnifying a brand's buzz, reach, impact, equity. And, if ad-blocking apps become as ubiquitous as some doom-mongers predict, innovative promotional activities will prove ever more necessary for ever more brands.[21]

Place

Place has long been the problem child of marketing. For decades it was very much the fourth out of 4Ps, the runt of the litter. No more. Just as branding is expanding out of the marketing department and absorbing organizations as a whole, so too place is increasingly first among equals. Far from being destroyed by the internet, which many believed would be the death knell for distance, cyberspace is a happy hunting ground for burgeoning brands.[22] The global reach of Amazon or Alibaba or Airbnb attests to the primacy of place. It has never been easier for small brands, such as Chain Reaction, a Northern Irish online bicycle store, to expand thanks to the tools and templates of e-commerce (Think Box 16). The biggest brands in the world these days are emplaced – iPlaced rather – and place branding is perhaps the most rapidly growing specialism. Towns, cities, regions, countries and continents are getting the branding treatment as never before, as are specific sites like Uluru, Machu Picchu, Burj Khalifa, Hadrian's Wall and the Petronas Towers.[23] True, place branding can be tricky, largely because a plethora of opinionated interested parties, including local councils, concerned citizens, tourist boards, inward investment bodies, etc., participate in place branding decisions.[24] But place branding's ever-accelerating expansion is incontestable.

THINK BOX 16

All the Way Up to Chain Reaction

If ever an illustration were needed of the brand-expanding power of the internet, there's no need to look any further than Chain Reaction. Born in the tiny village of Ballynure, County Antrim, CRC started as a strictly local bicycle repair business. However, with the aid of a £1,500 bank loan, the Watson family expanded their firm into small-scale retailing. Ballynure Bicycles' first retail sale was a chain link, which went for all of eleven pence (all the way up to eleven pence, as it were).

In 1989, the business relocated to the nearby town of Ballyclare and changed its name to Chain Reaction. Catering for hard-core cyclists, with specialist brands like

GT, Marin, Proflex and Cannnondale, CRC steadily built its reputation as the place to go for top gear. The shop quickly became a hang-out for cycling cognoscenti and, consequently, keen riders came from far and wide to see what was in stock and enjoy the craic with fellow bike fans. A family-run business, CRC acquired an extended family of enthusiasts – a proto brand community – by accident.

The next obvious step was mail order and, after placing small ads in specialist cycling magazines, business picked up for the Watsons' one-stop shop in a one-horse town. Such was the interest, that the owners had difficulty keeping up with the demand:

> We were staggering down Ballyclare Main Street towards the Post Office at closing time with our arms full of parcels. We knew there had to be a better way.[25]

Something had to be done. So the company expanded by contraction. CRC abandoned the retail store side of things and pinned their hopes on mail order. They acquired a spacious warehouse, which allowed them to stock a wider range of bike brands and put important processes in place (racking, packing, tracking, billing, etc.). These helped CRC cope with accelerating demand. Computerized stock control came next, swiftly followed by bulk buying, bigger adverts and, eventually, the registration of CRC's domain name in 1999.

There are plenty of bicycle websites and there were even at the turn of the millennium. From the outset, however, CRC kept its system simple and was absolutely transparent about stock levels. Unlike rival websites, which listed items that weren't in stock, CRC operated on an honesty-is-the-best-policy principle. If an item wasn't in stock, they said so.

Things 'went crazy' thereafter and they've stayed crazy despite attempts by Amazon, Halfords and Marathon to muscle in on the market. Much of this growth has been fuelled by the cycling boom, the latter-day plague of MAMILs (Middle-aged Men in Lycra). But Chain Reaction's commitment to its brand community through team sponsorships, CRC race meetings, powerful social media presence and a recently opened flagship store in Belfast suggests that it'll still be selling all the way up to eleven chain links for some time to come.

Thinking Outside the Think Box

After decades of focusing on clicks not bricks, Chain Reaction has opened a retail store. Just as many real-world retail brands have struggled with online operations, so too online retailers can find it hard to get real. Read up on others' experiences and identify the retail pitfalls that Chain Reaction faces.

This space race, what is more, hasn't diminished brands' expansion using more conventional means. The growth and spread of Starbucks (23,000 outlets in sixty-five countries), Subway (45,000 and counting), Specsavers (looking good with 1,700), 7-Eleven (open all hours in one hundred nations), Santander (which reigns from

Spain with 15,000 branches) and Stanford University (meeting nerds' needs in twelve overseas locations from Berlin to Beijing) are models of old-school Ansoffian expansion. Primark is expanding into the United States as I write. J Crew is coming across the Atlantic, all brands blazing. Shanghai Tang, a Chinese luxury label, is opening doors within the fastness of western fashion.[26] Shoprite is setting standards in fourteen African countries, including twenty-two supermarkets in Zambia alone. Dunnes Stores, an Irish clone of Marks & Spencer (the early years), is eyeing opportunities in Great Britain now that BHS is a bust and M&S is more vulnerable than before. Many successful online brands, such as Priceline, Bonobos, Screwfix and Kiddicare, are expanding from clicks-and-order to bricks-and-mortar. The online offers of traditional retail stores, such as Selfridges, House of Fraser, Asda and Next, are second to none. Even the most i-phobic luxury brands now recognize – thanks to the pioneering endeavours of Net-a-Porter, Matches, Farfetch and Yoxx – that bedazzling flagship stores can be built on the world wide web as well.

Purchase

Expanding the brand by accretion is a time-tested tactic, as Mars, Lynx, Dettol, Lemsip, Fairy Liquid and many familiar household names are testament. However, it tends to be a slow and stately process. Gillette introduced its Blue Blade razor in 1930, which was followed forty years later by the first twin blade, Trac II, which was superseded after eighteen years by Sensor, which gave way to the Mach 3 within a decade.[27] Expansion is much more speedily achieved by purchasing existing brands, be they complementary brands, competitive brands or contrasting brands that deliver diversification opportunities into different categories, sectors, industries. It was acquisitions, indeed, that triggered the branding bonanza of the late 20th century and sent the b-word into orbit. Reckitt & Coleman's acquisition of Airwick, Grand Metropolitan's purchase of Smirnoff, Cadbury's takeover of Schweppes, Ladbrokes' absorption of Hilton and Rank Hovis McDougall's brand-bolstered defence against Goodman Fielder Wattie's takeover bid, brought branding's value to everyone's attention, not least the financial community.[28] Purchase has been the most popular form of brand expansion ever since. Hardly a week goes by without acquisition activity. Heinz recently bought Kraft. Poundland made 99p Stores an offer it couldn't refuse. Ladbrokes has taken a punt on Coral. BT and EE are tying the knot. Aer Lingus has flown into the arms of AIG. Vue cinemas is casting a cold eye over Odeon. AB InBev, the biggest brewing brand in the world, has swallowed SAB Miller, the monster brewer behind Peroni, Grolsch and Corona. A snip at $71 billion.

M&A activity famously waxes and wanes in regular cycles. At present, a particularly noteworthy trend is the purchase of western brands by corporations in emerging economies. China is a prodigious commercial powerhouse but with the noteworthy exception of Huawei, Alibaba and Haier it thus far lacks the brand smarts that built the Marlboros, the McDonaldses, the MasterCards, the Mercedeses, the Microsofts, the Mitsubishis, the Manolo Blahniks of this world. Purchase, therefore, is the preferred option. Bright Food recently gobbled up Weetabix, SAIC swallowed MG motors, Sanpower devoured Hamleys and House of Fraser, and of course Lenovo has taken several significant bites out of Big Blue. Indian titans like Tata, Brazilian behemoths like 3G Capital and hungry Turkish corporations like Yildiz are also tucking into yummy European brands.[29]

Purchase, without doubt, represents the fast track to brand expansion. Consider Premier Foods. In a few short years, it acquired a host of golden-oldie brands including Birds, Ambrosia and Angel Delight. Premier then pounced on Rank Hovis McDougall, home of Hovis, Bisto and Mr Kipling among others. That's some brand portfolio. The only problem with portfolios and purchase-propelled expansion more generally is coordinating and integrating the acquisitions. Should they all be branded under a single name like Tata or Virgin or Ford, where the acquisitions essentially exist as sub-brands? Or should the brands retain their individual identities under a separate entity like Diageo, whose portfolio includes Guinness, Gordon's, Johnnie Walker, Captain Morgan and Bailey's Irish Cream, all of which compete independently? LVMH likewise owns a stable of free-standing luxury brands, such as Fendi, Pucci, Givenchy and Berluti. At the opposite end of the spectrum, AG Barr, best known for Irn-Bru (itself available in several variants), also possesses the Strathmore water, Rubicon fruit juice and Funkin cocktail mixer stand-alone brands (Think Box 17).

THINK BOX 17

Hugo, We Have a Problem

In my experience, the thing that most confuses students about branding is 'the Hugo Boss problem'. That is, the relationship between lines, ranges, sub-brands, brands and even bigger entities known as parent brands, umbrella brands, corporate brands, master brands, megabrands and more besides. The brand hierarchy – which in Hugo Boss's case comprises Boss Black, Boss Orange, Boss Selection, Boss Green, Hugo, and all sorts of HB ancillaries – is not clear-cut. Although brand managers may be clear in their own minds about how the bits fit together, the nature of the arrangement is unclear to customers. Individual brand managers, moreover, are inclined to use the terminology of 'master', 'range' and 'sub-' in different ways, which further adds to the confusion. As Ries and Ries recount, quoting a spokesperson for Ford:

> Ford is not our brand. Our brands are Aspire, Contour, Crown Victoria, Escort, Mustang, Probe, Taurus, and Thunderbird. 'What's a Ford then?' 'A Ford is a megabrand.'[30]

(Continued)

(Continued)

Numerous authorities have tried to make sense of all this and they've used different metaphors to clarify matters. Some talk of brand portfolios, using the 'property'
premise we noted in chapter 1. Others add to that with figurative buildings, most
notably the 'branded house' and 'house of brands' arrangements.[31] Yet others talk of
'brand families' with parent brands and their various offspring (an extension of the
'living thing' idea in chapter 4).

I myself make do with 'living arrangements', which blends the building and family
approaches. I distinguish between 'nuclear families' that live under the same roof
and share the same name (Kellogg's Corn Flakes, Kellogg's Bran Flakes, Kellogg's
Special K, etc.) and 'student flats' or 'halls of residence', where a group of unrelated
individuals live together, eat together and benefit from each other's company (such
as the Smirnoff, Guinness, Bailey's, Johnnie Walker inhabitants of Diageo's branded
bonded warehouse). As with families in the real world, there are all sorts of variations on these arrangements (Nestlé brands like Shreddies, Coffee-Mate and Milky
Bar appear to be independent entities, but closer inspection reveals that they sport
the Nestlé logo).

However, we need a better way of conceptualizing such matters, a way that
everyone can buy into. Cosmology is a possibility. The astronomical hierarchy from
stars to quasars, supergiants to white dwarfs, is surely applicable to branding: plan-
ets, moons, comets, asteroids, galaxies, nebulae, black holes (like Hugo Boss). It's
all there, ready and waiting for someone to make a name for themselves. Is there a
Hawking in the house of brands? Or should that be branded house?

Thinking Outside the Think Box

Take Tata. Map out its brand architecture. What sort of house does it occupy? Do the
same for BMW, Google, Kering and Haier. How do their living arrangements compare
with Tata and each other?

Past

If integrating acquisitions is problematic, it often has a hidden benefit. Even if the
purchased properties are integrated under a single brand banner – e.g. Tesco's acquisition of 800 T&S convenience stores, which became Tesco Express – the abandoned
brand names can always be reactivated. HSBC's rumoured revival of Midland Bank
is a case in point, as is J.J. Abrams' reboot of Disney's *Star Wars* franchise. One of the
most popular paths to expansion is reaching back into the past. Although marketing is ordinarily associated with a 'new and improved' worldview – bigger, better,
more features, added ingredients, etc. – the recent rise of retrobranding reveals that
the past is profitable too. The relaunch of the Volkswagen Beetle in 1998 triggered

a tsunami of retroautos including the BMW Mini, the Chrysler PT Cruiser, the new Ford T-Bird, the Fiat 500, the Citroën DS, the Vauxhall Viva, the Jaguar E-Type, the Mazda MX-5, and even Morgan's Three-Wheeler of 2011, a throwback to the British brand's beginnings as a four-seat, three-wheel cyclecar.

And it's not just the motor industry. Every big name sports brand sells a range of heritage sneakers, such as Adidas Originals and Nike Sweet Classic. Every famous fashion brand has riffled through its archive and is selling suitably updated versions of its signature originals (Raf Simons' inaugural collection reinvented Dior's New Look, for instance). Every fast-moving consumer good with history on its side, such as Kellogg's, Tetley's and 7 Up, has variously disinterred old logos, reanimated abandoned taglines, resuscitated half-forgotten mascots, rereleased special editions in the original packaging or, in the case of Cadbury's Milk Tray, launched a nationwide search for a he-man to replace the he-man who secretly delivered a box of chocolates to his loved one, despite obstacles aplenty. And All Because the Lady Loves Milk Tray.[32]

According to Reynolds, a prominent commentator on popular culture, the world has gone loco for retro. Although, he observes, retro is most prevalent in music and pornography ...

> ... there's also retro toys (crazes for everything from the View-Master to the Blythe Doll of the early seventies) and retrogaming (playing and collecting old-school computer, video and arcade games from the eighties). There's retro food (sandwich chain Pret A Manger offers 'Retro Prawn on Artisan', a sort of poshed-up sandwich version of that seventies fave the Prawn Cocktail) and there's also retro interior design, retro candy, retro ring-tones, retro travel and retro architecture. You even get retro-style commercials on television now and then, like the one for Heinz Baked Beans that mega-mixes snippets from vintage UK ads from the sixties, seventies and eighties, capped off with the imperishable slogan Beans Meanz Heinz.[33]

Even the highest of high-tech brands go back to the future on occasion. None more so than Apple. For all its alleged cutting-edge credentials, the incumbent of Infinite Loop, Cupertino, has consistently expanded the brand by pillaging the past. Whether it be the Art Decoish iPods, the *Star Trek*ish iPads, the Sixties psychedelic iMacs, the legendary TV ad *1984*, which evoked George Orwell's 1940s vision of the future, or indeed the 'Think Different' campaign featuring monochrome images of venerable iconoclasts like John Lennon, Maria Callas and Thomas Edison (while cocking a snoot at 'Think', IBM's iconic Watson-era slogan), Apple echoes as much as it anticipates. The merest glance at the icons on iOS8 – steampunk Settings, Notes *à la* Filofax, FaceTime's anachronistic rostrum camera, Safari's ye olde magnetic compass – reveals that Apple takes its cue from days of yore. The same is true of the new Watch, which looks like the timepiece of a 1970s porn star.[34]

Periodicity

Retromarketing may be a passing management fad, ebbing and flowing like merger and acquisition activity. Periodicity, nevertheless, is a significant form of brand expansion. Perhaps its most high-profile expression is the pop-up phenomenon. Comme des Garçons, the Japanese apparel brand, kicked off the craze with its pop-up stores in insalubrious locations like abandoned factories and warehouses. However, the idea proved so popular with consumers that pop-ups are now an important part of the branding landscape. Nightclubs, cinemas, hotels, pubs, clinics, coffee shops, nail bars, you name it. Even top-tier restaurants like Copenhagen's four-Michelin-starred Noma are getting in on the pop-up act, as are art galleries, museums, music festivals and, annoyingly, online advertisers.

Be that as it may, many major multinational brands, including Chanel, Target, Levi Strauss, Doc Martens, Marc Jacobs, Louis Vuitton, Selfridges, Samsung and our old friend Marmite, whose pop-up stores sell Marmite chocolate, Marmite deodorant and Marmite body wash, have eagerly grasped the pop-up nettle. The trend, clearly, owes a lot to the availability of ample empty retail space, a consequence of the economic recession and online's onslaught. Yet it represents a fantastic opportunity for neophyte brands, which can test the water for a short period of time and discover if their brand idea is scalable. Innocent Drinks famously began at a rock music festival, when the founders made smoothies for three days and invited customers to throw their empties into one of two bins. One for those who thought they shouldn't give up the day job, the other for those who believed they should sell the smoothies full-time.[35]

Pop-ups, of course, are not new. Periodic marketplaces, carnivals, fairs, fetes, fiestas and so forth have been around since the dawn of time. Pop-ups, in fact, are the primal form of marketing activity. It was the intermittent markets of the Middle East that stimulated the emergence of urban life and civilization. Mobile shops, farmers' markets, ice cream vans, Avon ladies, itinerant door-to-door salesmen are part and parcel of periodicity's long history. They tap into the scarcity factor noted in chapter 6. Get them while they're hot! Or cold in the case of ice cream.

Periodicity, however, isn't confined to Debenhams' pop-up concessions come Christmastime or the application of fast fashion principles to cosmetics by Italian brand Kiko or, for that matter, the blink-and-you'll-miss-them benisons of Snapchat. It is evident in guerrilla and ambush marketing escapades, where renegade brands hijack or gate-crash events sponsored by bigger, better-funded brands during the Olympics, the World Cup, the Super Bowl or other high-profile occasions.[36] Thus the biggest success of Super Bowl XLVII, when a power cut in the stadium plunged the contest into darkness, was not the brands who'd paid vast sums of money to advertise during breaks in play. It was Oreo cookies, which tweeted a spur of the moment message – You Can Still Dunk in the Dark – and boosted their biscuit brand thereby.

Periodicity is also evident in brands' burning desire to associate themselves with special occasions like Christmas (Coke), Valentine's (Hallmark), Halloween (M&Ms and candy makers more generally), Red Nose Day (Comic Relief), No Shopping Day (Adbusters), Singles Day in China (Alibaba) or, for that matter, expand into different times of the day such as breakfast, lunch and dinner.[37] McDonald's for example, has been building up its breakfast menu. Pret a Manger is offering evening meals. Starbucks sells alcohol and serves as a surrogate pub by night. Wetherspoons, meanwhile, is going after breakfast in a big way and cutting the price of its Lavazza filter coffee to 99p, with free refills. 'It's possible', the brand's MD says, 'we'll be selling more coffee than beer in fifteen years.' How long, some wonder, before IKEA opens a flat-pack nightclub?

Partnership

If IKEA *were* to open a nightclub, they would likely do so with the aid of the Ministry of Sound or Cirque du Soleil. Brand partnerships of one kind or another are commonplace. Getting into bed with another brand is a popular way of satisfying both parties. It is much less fractious, not to say far less expensive, than merger and acquisition. Partnerships come in many shapes and forms, mind you. Sometimes, as with Sony and Ericsson, it involves the creation of a combined corporate entity. Sometimes, as with Intel and Dell, it's a case of co-branding, where two brands benefit from their joint venture. Sometimes, as with Duracell and Gillette Fusion, it's a collaboration involving two separate brands from the same corporate stable, Procter & Gamble. Sometimes, as in the case of Kellogg's Pop Tarts and Smucker's jam, it's a mutually beneficial melding of ingredients. Sometimes, as with Hershey and Ferrero, it's a back-office bond where warehouses and delivery vehicles are shared. Sometimes, as with the classic packet of Persil soap powder in Hotpoint washing machines, it's a cross-category combo of complementary products.

And oft-times it's sponsorships, such as Barclays' association with the English Premiership; dealership networks, where local garages align with multinational carmakers; voluntary groups, like SPAR's alliance of independent supermarkets and forecourt stores; endorsements, along the lines of Fair Trade's stamp of approval on Cadbury's chocolate brands; and, of course, consumer created combinations, whereby Red Bull and Jägermeister equals jagerbomb mayhem. All are excellent examples of expanded brand partnerships. Ditto brands like Groupon, where consumers club together to negotiate better deals for all, and department store brands like John Lewis, which is a partnership of all 90,000 employees.

Perhaps the most high-profile modes of partnership are franchising and licensing. The former involves a mutually beneficial partnership between the franchisor, the owner of a branded business format, and the franchisee, an independent business entity that operates one or more outlets of the franchise in a specified geographical area for a specified period of time.[38] In return for upfront fees and an agreed proportion of total turnover, the franchisee is supported by the franchisor. This support usually includes training, administration, advertising, promotion, fitting out, stock control systems, partly-prepared ingredients and, not least, membership of an established brand family, such as Domino's, Dunkin' Donuts, Baskin-Robbins, 7-Eleven or Hertz. The franchisor, conversely, can rapidly expand their proprietary brand at comparatively low cost, since the franchisee is paying for the privilege of partnership.

Licensing is similar, except that it tends to be intangible intellectual properties – the brand name, the logo, the trademarks, et al. – that are leased out to the licensee by the licensor.[39] The rights to Mickey Mouse, Peppa Pig, The Simpsons, SpongeBob SquarePants and innumerable others, from university colleges and dead celebrities to the ubiquitous bright yellow smiley-faced symbol, are managed by large licensing companies like Iconix and RVH. This is an extremely lucrative business, since the manufacturers of the licensed memorabilia – coffee mugs featuring Snoopy, Kermit, Charlie Brown, the colour-coded M&Ms characters, or whatever – bear most of the financial risk. That said, if too many richly remunerative deals are signed by the licensor, the brand can be undermined through overexposure. Pierre Cardin was once a desirable luxury brand. However, it licensed its good name to so many suppliers, including toothpastes and toilet-brushes, that its once formidable cachet was irreparably damaged. Gucci and Burberry and Calvin Klein and Tommy Hilfiger almost went the same way, but came to their senses before licensiousness took its mortal toll.

Platform

If licensing is a long-established expansion strategy, albeit one that has burgeoned during the post-1990 branding boom, platforms are the new kid on the block.[40] They are a creature of cyberspace. They comprise enormous brand expansion engines that know no bounds, operate on a principle of limitlessness and seem intent on ruling the universe. The so-called Gang of Four – Google, Amazon, Apple and Facebook (GAAF) – are the preeminent platforms on our planet. Much has been written about GAAF's ruthlessness, voraciousness, arrogance and decidedly cavalier attitude to consumers' private information. Much has also been written about GAAF's expansion through conventional means including product development (Google's Android, Glasses, Fiber and so forth), purchasing activities (Facebook's acquisition of Instagram, WhatsApp, etc.), place-based developments (Apple's superlative retail stores) and of course price-related prestidigitation (Amazon Prime, which reinforced the fact that free really is a four-letter f-word).

However, the real genius of GAAF's platforms is that they are open to others, third party providers, app developers, branded content creators and assorted small fry e-tailers, who not only sell their wares through, say, Amazon Marketplace or Apple's

App Store, but make use of the prodigious platform's back office for billing, fulfilment, web services, data storage and, where needed, same-day delivery. Clearly, there's an element of coercive lock-in here, as there is for consumers of the branded platform's products. But the reach that Apple's App Store gives ambitious brands is truly remarkable, even when Tim Cook's 30% slice of every sale is taken into account. It's much more than branding's equivalent of the Hadron Collider, accelerating wannabe brands to infinity and beyond. It's a veritable brand nebula, the ever-expanding birthplace of stellar sellers.

Amazon, most agree, is the mothership of brand platforms. It's an enterprising holodeck that's light years away from Cadabra, the discount book business Bezos built. There's no shortage of corporate Klingons though, rapidly expanding platforms on the frontiers of the GAAF federation. Perhaps the most important of these is Alibaba.[41] The brainchild of Jack Ma, a former schoolteacher from a remote Chinese province, Alibaba began as the B2B equivalent of eBay. Albeit with the added attraction of instant messaging, which facilitated the relationship building that is integral to Chinese commercial life. Not content, however, with providing a shop window on the online world for millions of Chinese wholesalers and manufacturers, Jack Ma's platform progressively added whole new planks, such as 1688.com, a wholesale site for domestic trade; Taobo.com, a Chinese consumer-to-consumer site that's a cross between eBay and Amazon Marketplace; T-mall, an upmarket site for established brands, including famous foreign brands like Gap, Levi's, Adidas and Ray-Ban; Juhuasan, a consumer group buying facility akin to Groupon; and AliPay, the Chinese equivalent of PayPal, with a popular mobile feature AliPayWallet. Of late, a collaborative logistics consortium, China Smart Logistics Networking, has been added, as have Alibaba Pictures (television and movie production), Alibaba Cloud (computer power and storage), AliMama (Big Data analytics), Youku Tudou (the closest China comes to YouTube), the *South China Post* (in an oriental echo of Jeff Bezos) and a Gaongquan football team, Evergrand. Ever-grand indeed could be Alibaba's watchword, going forward. A future first among equals, Ali Baba and the Gang of Four sounds good to me. Sounds ominous, I should say.

Parlance

In his biography of the Alibaba brand Erisman makes an interesting observation.[42] Whereas in the west, he says, Alibaba is often described as 'the Amazon of China', 'the Google of China', 'the eBay of China' or 'the PayPal of China', that's not true of the developing world. Many e-commerce ventures in emerging economies describe themselves, not as the Amazon or eBay of India (FlipKart), Indonesia (Tokopedia), or Nigeria (Konga.com), but the Alibaba of their homeland.

When a brand name is used as an exemplar, as the epitome, as shorthand for an entire class or category of commercial activity, it has attained the pinnacle, the zenith, the acme of expansion. Being part of the vernacular is as good as it gets. And why? Because consumers routinely use brand names as verbs, nouns, adjectives, gerunds, superlatives, punctuation marks, all of which speak volumes about their place in people's consciousness ('the most valuable piece of real estate in the world', remember). When we do an online search, we Google. When we video chat, we Skype. When we vacuum clean our carpets, rugs and wooden floors, we Hoover. When we photocopy a document in America, we Xerox. When we send stuff to colleagues by overnight delivery, we Fedex. Even though our chosen carrier may be UPS or TNT, we still call it Fedexing, just as we're Googling when we're using Yahoo!, Ask Jeeves or Bing. No one Bings, let alone Yahoos. Linguistically at least.

Not every manager, admittedly, is happy with this idiomatic use of brand names. Being described as the New Coke of nappies, the Edsel of electric cars, the Marmite of maternity wear, the Woolworths of wellington boots, the *Titanic* of political parties, the *Hindenburg* of haemorrhoid creams, isn't necessarily what the brand managers of Huggies, Nissan Leaf, Mothercare, Hunter, New Labour and Preparation H want to hear, especially the last of these. Brand-based nomenclature is almost as popular among critically minded academics, who employ terms like McDonaldization, Disneyfication and Coca-Colonization to describe the degenerate state of contemporary consumer society. Even that, though, is as nothing compared to what poor old Kool-Aid has had to suffer. Once a much-loved brand of powdered drink mix – which came in the six classic flavours of cherry, grape, orange, raspberry, strawberry and lemon-lime – Kool-Aid was permanently tainted by the 1978 Jonestown massacre, when 900 members of a religious cult committed communal suicide by drinking glasses of the beverage laced with cyanide.[43] The event is immortalized in the American expression 'Drinking the Kool-Aid', meaning disastrous self-delusion.

That said, most shorthand uses of brand names come in the form of comparisons, and, more often than not, superlatives. Managers frequently describe their brands as the Rolls-Royce of such-and-such or so-and-so, meaning the best of the best, a cut above the rest. Ambitious entrepreneurs aspire to be the Amazon of pharmaceuticals, the Cadillac of snowmobiles, the Apple of angioplasty, the Google of gastroenterology, the Chanel of colostomy bags, the Ferrari of stairlifts, the Zara of zimmer frames, the Uber of dieticians, personal trainers, window cleaners, rat catchers, etc. What brand wouldn't want to be part of the argot, the patois, the vernacular, nothing less than a figure of speech? It means that they own the category. They are its embodiment. Theirs in the brand that comes to mind when we write with a ballpoint pen (Biro) or on an adhesive notepad (Post-it) or choose to relax in a hot tub (Jacuzzi) after a hard day's work.

It's unwise to relax too soon, however. Once brand names become verbs, or colloquialisms of any kind, there's a very real danger of 'genericide'. When a brand name becomes generic – that is, used as the default term for an entire category rather than a specific product within that category – the name can lose the legal protection it previously enjoyed.[44] Rollerblade, NutraSweet, Muzak, Klaxon, Zipper, Styrofoam,

Bubblewrap, Novocaine, Plexiglas, Frisbee, Popsicle and Onesie – yes, Onesie – are all brand names assassinated by the spectre of genericide. Potential loss of a trademark is a high price to pay for top-of-the-mind consumer recall. The funny thing, though, is that contemporary platform-based brands don't seem particularly bothered by this prospect. The promotional benefits that their brand gains though idiomatic expansion – its popularity as parlance – far exceeds the (fairly low) risk of losing its intellectual property. Legally, one of the best defences against genericide is, of all things, brand expansion.[45] Apple's extended family of products and services bearing its brand name, paradoxically enough, reduces the risk of ruination. Google can rest easy for now.

Paradox

The paradoxes of brand expansion go far beyond genericide. One of the best ways of expanding a brand, strange though it seems, is by contraction. Massive brand conglomerates like Unilever and Procter & Gamble are showing that slimming down, and shedding some of the brands they've built and bought over the years, is beneficial for all concerned. The former, for instance, has recently divested one hundred major brands, many of them to Coty. The latter has dispensed with Ragu, Bertolli, Peperami and SlimFast. Sony has got shot of its Vaio laptops. General Electric, similarly, said farewell to financial services. And eBay has recently abandoned its old friend PayPal.

A smaller brand portfolio isn't necessarily a worse one. On the contrary, it concentrates corporate resources on a limited number of 'master' or 'power' brands rather than spreading things too thinly across myriad brand demands.[46] And it's not just portfolios. The same principle applies to individual brands, sub-brands, ranges and lines. When P&G reduced its distended Head & Shoulders family from twenty-six variants to a paltry fifteen, total sales rose by 10%. When beleaguered Japan Airlines slashed routes, shed staff and cut overheads, turnover took off again. When Heinz closed factories and eliminated product ranges deemed excess to requirement, its sales soared by 35%. When, in a much-cited experiment by behavioural economists Iyengar and Lepper, twenty-four separate flavours of the same brand of jam were put on display, only 3% of consumers made a purchase. However, when the choice was cut to six flavours, some 30% of consumers splashed out. It seems that when there's too much to choose from people can be paralysed by choice.[47] They can't decide. So they decide not to bother. We have all stood behind undecided consumers in an ice cream shop as they hum and ha and struggle to take their pick from the gorgeous array of gelati. 'Get a move on!' we are tempted to shout, though they don't thank you for it (as my broken nose bears witness).

Many brands have learned this less-is-more lesson, often the hard way. A case in point is Marks & Spencer, which went brand crazy several years back. They birthed sub-brand after sub-brand across both their male and female apparel departments – Indigo, Portfolio, Autograph, Autograph Plus, Per Una, to name but a few – and left loyal consumers nonplussed as a result. Most, I imagine, pined for the good old days when M&S had one label and one label only, St Michael. Marks finally came to its senses, slimmed down its sub-brands and, although their clothing sales aren't out of the woods, they're heading in the right direction. Premier Foods, the Hovis to Ambrosia brand combine, is currently decluttering its congested portfolio and investing in selected power brands like Mr Kipling and Oxo. It was only a few years back, furthermore, that Howard Schultz came out of early retirement to revive the Starbucks brand, which had become bloated and directionless since his departure. He immediately shuttered several hundred outlets and the brand bounced back, leaner, meaner and more profitable.

As Robertson recounts in detail, the same streamlining strategy was adopted by Lego in 2004, after a decade in which the venerable brick brand expanded far too far in far too many categories and completely lost its way.[48] After appointing a new CEO, Jorgen Vig Knudstorp, its 'back to the brick' campaign involved selling off the theme parks, closing the retail stores, reducing the product range by 30%, focusing on its core assets (the timeless Duplo and Lego bricks) and core customers (children aged five to nine). Sales swiftly surged by 12% and they've increased ever since, not least when the mega-successful *Lego Movie* demonstrated that everything is awesome with Denmark's greatest brand.

For some brands at least, less spells success. IKEA among them. According to Moon, Sweden's superbrand marched to total global domination on the back of its ruthlessly edited offer, which contrasted markedly with traditional furniture stores. The latter, she says, typically offered wide product ranges in a multiplicity of styles and with sufficient sales assistants to help customers decide, as well as home deliveries. IKEA, by contrast, made do with minimal variety in four basic styles, a complete lack of in-store assistance and, not only expected shoppers to transport their purchases, but assemble them as well.[49] In-N-Out Burger, she further notes, is less-means-more writ large. The California-based eatery doesn't bother with salads, desserts or Happy Meal-style children's specials, let alone the have-it-your-way options of Burger King. In-N-Out's menu consists of six items and six items only.[50] Unlike its larger rivals, however, every single order is made from scratch, using fresh not frozen ingredients. And while service takes that little bit longer, the resultant burger is well worth the wait. No wonder, then, that when an In-N-Out popped up in a North London suburb (for all of three hours in April 2012), meat patty mayhem immediately ensued. You don't get that at McDonald's.

Never forget, though, that the vast majority of brands – even the biggest – began as niche players, selling a very narrow range of products. Coco Chanel was a milliner. Ralph Lauren started off selling ties. Paul Smith was a shirt specialist. Zegna built its brand on bolts of cloth. Tesco commenced with a market stall in London, as did M&S in Leeds. Samsung sprang from an unpropitious background in noodles and dried seaweed. Sony's founder, Akio Morito, started the ball rolling with an iffy electric rice cooker. HP, Apple, Amazon and Google all began in a garage (not the same garage, admittedly). Mickey D's was once a one-horse carry-out in San Bernardino, serving 5-cent burgers and milkshakes. Brands, by and large, expand as much as they can, until they are constrained by extraneous circumstances, including their own overindulgence.

BRAND TASK

'Jumping the Shark' is a term that's sometimes used when a brand expands too far. It refers to an infamous episode of the hit sitcom *Happy Days*, when the situation became too preposterous to be funny. Red Nose Day, some say, has gone the same way (donations fell to £78 million in 2015 from £100 million in 2013). Do you agree? What can be done to restore Comic Relief's fortunes? Taking the brand off air is not an option, nor is dropping its signature red nose.

RECOMMENDED READINGS

Jim Bell and Stephen Brown, 'Tyrone Crystal: Striking Out in Japan', *Irish Marketing Review*, 4 (2), 1989, 23–32. If you're keen to read the full story of my Japanese adventure, all the gory details are recounted in this little article. It's a bit dated, not least because Tyrone Crystal is no longer in business. Not. My. Fault. Honest. How dare you infer otherwise!

Wilson Bastos and Sidney J. Levy, 'A History of the Concept of Branding: Practice and Theory', *Journal of Historical Research in Marketing*, 4 (3), 2012, 347–368. Sid Levy is a pioneer of branding. He formulated the brand concept back in the 1950s. This article bills itself as an historical overview, but it also contends that branding is overtaking marketing in corporate esteem.

Simon Reynolds, *Retromania: Pop Culture's Addiction to Its Own Past* (Faber & Faber: London, 2011). Although this book isn't specifically about branding – or marketing, for that matter – it's still an illuminating exercise that's well worth reading. The timeline alone is a tour de force.

Bernard Cova, 'Re-branding Brand Genericide', *Business Horizons*, 57 (3), 2014, 359–369. Genericide has long been regarded as the branding equivalent of Ebola, a fatal affliction. However, this terrific article knocks that notion on the head and helps us better understand why great brands like Google are blasé about the Big G.

PART III
CONSTRAINTS

CHAPTER 9
THE BRAND STOPS HERE

Overview

Branding is a battlefield. No quarter is given. No mercy is expected. Most inter-brand battles are short-lived, little more than skirmishes. But some are closer to vendettas, wars of attrition with no prospect of peace. Unless legislators or other interested parties intervene. This chapter considers the many and varied constraints on brand expansion, including those that are brands' own doing.

ONCE UPON A BRAND

There's a true story about Jeff Bezos, the ebullient boss of Amazon. Back in the early days of the brand, when the organization was operating out of dilapidated premises in Seattle's inner city, Jeff used to call All Hands meetings. Short for All Hands on Deck, these get-togethers gave him an opportunity to update employees on the brand's performance. If not quite a workers' council, it was as close to democracy as cut-throat dotcoms dare. Inevitably, the AH meetings became increasingly ceremonial through time. A stage was set up and tastefully dressed with an artificial fireplace, a pair of old-fashioned wing-backed chairs, an ornate claw-footed coffee table and an amiable interlocutor, who threw predictable questions at Amazon's head honcho.[1]

The ritualistic qualities of Jeff's 'fireside chats' extended to the Q&A segment when anyone and everyone had a chance to grill the great man. At some point in the proceedings, someone or other would always ask Bezos the same question: 'In a fight between a silverback gorilla and a grizzly bear, who would win?' Jeff's answer was always the same: 'It depends on the terrain'. Although this exchange was, presumably, a light-hearted interlude that helped bond an upstart organization, Jeff's 'gorilla and grizzly thing' soon loomed large in the psyche of Amazon's over-eager, over-worked, over-imaginative employees. According to Daisey's account of Amazon's early days, employees debated the conundrum incessantly, wondering what, exactly, Bezos was getting at and whether the animal encounter was an allegory, a metaphor, a paradox or pertaining to retailing, where Amazon was taking aim at Walmart. Maybe, Daisey concludes after consuming several cups of extra-strong Starbucks coffee:

> ... the answer has nothing to do with the question – that it's a trick. It's not about comparing paw strength and jaw size but location and positioning. Or maybe it means that all that matters is what arena we're dealing with – the landscape defines the battle, like a Sun Tzu kind of thing only with bears and gorillas. So if one of the bears has a slingshot, for example, then that is one tough bear because he has these ranged attacks, so you think he's going to bite you but instead he chucks a rock at your head, and you're a gorilla and you're like 'Shit!' because it's outside your paradigm. This crazy fucking bear is fucking with you from a distance and you're like 'Damn!' because you know that this is how people are going to take care of business, you know, on the web, because we need to be the armed bears. Bears with guns, the bears who come equipped, or we'll end up being the gorillas who get their asses kicked.[2]

Apart from the fact that it's very funny, as is the eye-opening book it comes from, Daisey's account of the Bezos All Hands ritual is important for a couple of reasons. First, it illustrates the anthropomorphic essence of business life, the brand as living thing considered in chapter 5. Second, and more pertinently for present purposes, it raises the spectre of competition. Branding is a brutally competitive business. Brand managers battle for every percentile of market share.[3] Woody Allen once said that the only certain things in life are death and taxes. But that's not the case in branding. Brand death can be avoided for a very long time. Veuve Clicquot is 245 years old, remember, Wedgwood china is 256 and, as everyone knows, brands like Amazon, Topshop and Vodafone evade taxes as a matter of course. What can't be circumvented, however, is competition. Competition is the single biggest constraint on brands. The inexorable brand expansion process is curbed by competition more than anything else. For the most part, brands plot their way through the minefields of business life, not by consumers' expressed desires, but by what their competitors are doing, planning, scheming.[4]

This battle-hardened mind-set is made manifest on brand managers' bookshelves. As the continuing popularity of texts like Sun Tsu's *Art of War*, von Clausewitz's *On War* and Roberts' *Leadership Secrets of Attila the Hun* clearly shows, managers in general and brand managers in particular tend to see the world through a militaristic lens.[5] The language of warfare – fighting for market share, targeting consumers, flanking attacks, brand grenades, who dares wins and what have you – is endemic. Real-world training regimens, such as paintballing sessions for the sales force, are no less martial, as are the stars, medals and decorations doled out to high-achieving employees. From the five-star fast food servers in Mickey D's to the barnstars worn by Wikipedians who have contributed articles above and beyond the call of duty, branding is war by another name. It is a never-ending world war of all against all. No quarter. No mercy. No surrender. May the best brand win.[6]

Clearly, there's an element of bluster, sabre rattling and gunboat diplomacy about all of this. Belligerent brands' commanders in chief, such as Michael O'Leary and Richard Branson, have been known to don fatigues and steel helmets and drive tanks on to the lawns of their principal rivals.[7] Ryanair's Rommel even composed a marching song for the occasion: 'I've been told and it's no lie/easyJet's fares are way too high'. Larry Ellison, the chief executive of software systems giant Oracle, once bought a Russian MIG fighter to strafe Microsoft's redoubt in Redmond, Washington.[8] I suspect, furthermore, that the popularity of brand names making use of military rank – Captain Morgan, Cpt'n Crunch, WingCo Malted Milk, General Electric, General Foods, General Mills, General Motors and the legendary Private Label, represent brand managers' getting in touch with their inner Field Marshall.[9] It may not be full metal jacket. But it's definitely full of something.

BATTLE WARY

It's easy to mock brand managers' pretensions, especially when it comes to brands' increasing tendency to see themselves as nation states, complete with a diplomatic corps of ambassadors, representatives, satraps and so on. At the same time, there's something genuinely thrilling when great brands go to war. Visa versus MasterCard, Levi's versus Lee, Tesco versus Sainsbury's, McDonald's versus Burger King, Starbucks versus Costa, Cadbury versus Mars, Ariel versus Persil, Ford versus GM, Bud versus Miller, Barbie versus Bratz, PlayStation versus Xbox, Pixar versus DreamWorks, BBC versus ITV, CIA versus KGB, Oxford versus Cambridge, Harvard versus Yale, Marvel versus DC comics, *Batman versus Superman*.[10]

These battles, let's be clear here, are enthralling for onlookers. They raise consumer interest in both parties. They're also energizing for employees who are forced to raise their standards in order to see off the antagonist. Brand battles, indeed, are akin to spectator sports, not least Super Bowl Sunday, where America's biggest brands battle with their biggest rivals in ad breaks before, during and after the big game.[11]

There's a crucial difference between sporting contests and brand hostilities, however. The former tend to be time-bound, whereas the latter can go on for generations, as in the classic case of Coke versus Pepsi. It's a fact, furthermore, that the no-holds-barred rivalry between Nike and Adidas has lasted longer than the rivalry between legendary sports stars such as Coe and Ovett, Ali and Frazier, Proust and Senna, Federer and Nadal, Navratilova and Evert, Brady and Manning.[12] Of late, admittedly, Nike has pulled ahead in every continent except Europe, notwithstanding its dubious human rights record. The BRICs economies in particular – Brazil, Russia, India, China – are becoming outposts of Nike's great brand empire on which the swoosh never sets. Adidas was slow out of the blocks with fitness apps like Nike+ and its unwillingness to lay siege to the stupendous brand citadels called Niketown means that Just Do It has Impossible Is Nothing on the ropes. True to its slogan, though, Adidas is taking the battle to Nike with plans to grow its brand from 6% to 12% of the massive US market. If the Spartans could win at Thermopylae, Adidas must surely stand a chance in Tuscaloosa. Time will tell.[13]

The stakes, then, are high for Adidas and Nike alike. But they are bantamweights compared to the heavyweights – the sumo wrestlers, frankly – that are Airbus and Boeing. As symbolic representatives of Europe and America respectively, they are the nearest things to warring nation states that capitalism has to offer. For decades, the battler from Seattle ruled the skies with its 727, 737, and subsequent 747. However, from the A320 onwards, the tiddler from Toulouse gradually caught up thanks to its innovative use of the fly-by-wire system and lightweight composite materials in construction. Currently, the market share split is about 50/50, albeit both are gambling heavily on the next generation of aircraft. Namely, Airbus's much-delayed double-decker A380 and Boeing's bothersome battery-equipped 787. The gloves are off in what *Forbes* describes as a battle between the McCoys and Hatfields of aviation.[14]

The diamante gloves are also off in Paris, as are the watered silk shorts, artificial fur singlets and crushed velvet jockstraps. YSL and Dior, one a kick-boxer for Kering, the other LVMH's veteran cage-fighter, have been spitting and snarling and sticking their tongues out at each other for the past few seasons. Both brands stumbled in the aftermath of John Galliano's defenestration and Stefano Pilate's decision to move on to challenges new. Their replacements Raf Simons and Hedi Slimane have much to prove in the catfight that's haute couture. And what better way to do so than by a catwalk-off, *à la* Derek and Hansel in *Zoolander*. The former's ahead on points, at present, because the latter's decision to change the brand's name from YSL to St Laurent Paris antagonized many old-fashioned fashionistas. Slimane's clashed with the editor of *WWD*, what's more. Belligerence is one thing, but fighting on several fronts simultaneously is never less than foolhardy.[15]

YOU TALKIN' TO ME?

For all we know, though, the Dior/YSL smack-down may have been an attempt to attract media attention. Just as professional boxers trade insults before the bout in order to drum up custom, so too brand rivalries benefit both parties. Both parties know that only too well and act accordingly. Play acting, trash talking, trouble making and shit stirring are par for the course.

Braggadocio notwithstanding, there are two things we *do* know about battling brands. First, history is written by the winners. Wikipedia's defeat of Britannica,

Netflix's demolition of Blockbuster, Facebook's decimation of MySpace, Alibaba's destruction of eBay's Chinese operation all seem obvious in retrospect. But the victor wasn't apparent at the time and their triumph had as much to do with the incumbent's fatal mistakes as the usurper's natural nous. Britannica had ample opportunities to kill Wikipedia in its cradle, as did Encarta. Blockbuster's in-store promotions had Netflix on the ropes, ready to throw in the towel before it fatally changed tack. MySpace expanded too quickly, couldn't service the demand, and Facebook benefitted from its failings. eBay's refusal to adapt its gladiatorial auction model to collaborative Chinese norms was its undoing when Alibaba avoided the bidder-versus-bidder scenario with relationship-led arrangements.

The second thing, again exemplified by all five of the foregoing, is that the small guy won.[16] David defeated Goliath. Frodo felled Sauron. Harry vanquished Voldemort. It's the size disparity as much as anything else – the asymmetry of the contest – that's especially exciting for onlookers. When Miller and Budweiser, Tesco and Sainsbury's, Sony and Samsung, or Dior and YSL duke it out, they're fairly evenly matched. But when a minnow like Virgin takes on a monster like British Airways, when bad grrrl Bratz tangles with queen bitch Barbie, when a nobody called Xiaomi challenges iPhone to a duel, when the itsy-bitsy Body Shop confronts L'Oréal's evil empire, when an angel fish like Hilden brewery faces off against the great black shark that is Guinness, when a Daniel like the Mini enters the lion's den of the American motor car market, where SUVs snarl and Hummers are ready to rumble, the world holds its breath in anticipation.

Even in defeat, however, the challenger wins. Because the half-pint brand's reputation is enhanced by the encounter. In branding at least, challengers are champions. Unsurprisingly, then, the notion of 'challenger' brands has attracted a lot of attention in recent years.[17] So much so, it has become a bit of a cliché. Just about every brand claims to be a challenger of one sort or another, even the market leaders. It's possible, nevertheless, to identify four basic types of challenger brand: *underdogs, usurpers, disruptors* and *defenders*.

Underdogs ...

... go head-to-head with the top dogs, usually with a product or service that is similar to, but slightly different from, the incumbent. It may be cheaper, it may be faster, it may be smaller, it may be more user-friendly, it may represent better value for money, it may offer superior after-sales service. Whatever. Avis is the archetypal challenger, determined to 'try harder' in the car hire business than Hertz, the top dog. Norwegian Air Shuttle is flexing its muscles for the no-holds-barred battle that is low-cost aviation, where easyJet and Ryanair rule the roost.[18] Metro Bank is a post-crash alternative to the Big Four bank brands, offering improved personal service, extended opening hours and none of the mis-selling that previously poisoned the well. Pepsi is yet another perpetual underdog, a brand that mounted the 'Pepsi Challenge' against

Coke for decades, a challenge it won hands down on taste and precipitated king cola's catastrophic change in formulation. Few brands in fact have faced more challengers than Coke. These include Virgin (Britain), Mecca (Middle East), Jolly (Denmark), Two Guys (Germany) and Thums Up (India).[19] Coke's still standing, though. For all its faults, Coca-Cola is the All Blacks of branding. 'Holidays are Coming' is its haka.

Usurpers ...

... are the classic challenger brands identified by Adam Morgan, whose book *Eating the Big Fish* started the fad for small fry brands.[20] They differ from underdogs insofar as usurpers unsettle an entire category. As noted in chapter 8, these are brands akin to IKEA and Google and Wii and Pixar and Snapple and Hollister and Innocent Drinks and Ben & Jerry and Whole Foods Market and Cirque du Soleil and In-N-Out Burger and BrewDog, the belligerent Scottish craft beer. These are the POWer brands that overthrow the conventions of the category and reset its competitive compass. 7 Up challenged the conventions of the American soda market with its lemon-lime flavour, boldly selling itself as the un-cola. Amazon likewise claimed to be an un-bookstore back in the days when Jeff was hosting All Hands events and silver-back gorillas stalked the mean streets of Seattle. Aldi is cutting a swathe through the great British grocery market, as is Lidl, and the incumbents are struggling to respond, Morrisons and Asda especially. Huawei, the Chinese telecoms corporation, has recently announced plans to usurp the servers, storage and data-dredging equipment market, which is currently dominated by 'bloated' brands like IBM, Cisco and HP. Few put it past it.

Disrupters

If there is one word that eclipses 'challenger' in brand managers' lexicon – and even eclipses 'storytelling' in the empyrean – that word is 'disruption'. Disrupters are usurpers on steroid sandwiches, washed down with a crate of Red Bull Turbo Boost. Disrupters lay waste to entire industries. Or alter them irrevocably ever after. The brainchild of Clayton Christensen, Harvard Business School's superstar professor, disruptive innovations are often ugly duckling operations.[21] They are cheap. They are nasty. They are disparaged by incumbents and dismissed as a standing joke. But the ugly duckling becomes a golden eagle and the smug swans suffer the consequences as gales of creative destruction sweep across their breeding grounds. Wikipedia obliterated the old rules of the encyclopaedia business. Napster did much the same to the music industry. Samsung's smartphone consigned handset makers like LG, HTC and Nokia to oblivion. Uber is threatening to do likewise to taxi services worldwide. Ditto Airbnb in accommodation. Google's AdSense undermined *Mad Men*-esque advertising agencies and its driverless cars may do the same to diehards in Detroit. Kodak was once one of the greatest brands in the world, regularly ranked among the top four. Blindsided by digital photography, it's confined to the history books instead of standing on the commanding heights of today's selfiescape. Kodak, ironically, invented the technology that destroyed it.

Defenders

As the name implies, defenders are brands that stand against the above UDUs, usurpers, disrupters, underdogs. Also known as 'fighting brands', these are the aggressive offspring of big successful brands that enjoy healthy profit margins and wish to avoid a price war with publicity-seeking upstarts.[22] Rather than descend to the level of the new arrival, thereby legitimizing its challenge, the incumbent remains above the fray and lets fighting brands do the dirty work. Strategically, this stance makes sense. Occupying the Goliath role in any conflict is always best avoided, because it forfeits public sympathy. Everybody loves the scrappy street urchin, the Rocky Balboas of branding. So threatened brands spawn street urchins of their own. Marlboro launched a fighter brand called Bond Street to battle steeply discounted Russian substitutes. Budweiser brought out a cheap and cheerful beer called Busch Bavarian when cut-price competitors came too close for comfort. British Airways birthed Go! when easyJet and Ryanair said No! to the old airline order. Qantas did something similar with Jetstar when Virgin Blue set out to shake up Australian aviation. The Celeron chip was Intel's response to AMD's encroachment while keeping Pentium pristine. Saturn was a highly successful fighting brand for General Motors. Now defunct, it disrupted the disrupters for the best part of a quarter century. Although it never made any money, Saturn helped circle the wagons around Chevrolet, Pontiac and Buick while fending off Toyota, Honda and so forth.

Defenders excepted, the distinctions between UDUs are not clear-cut. What category does Glasgow's challenge to Edinburgh's Scottish hegemony – with its famous Miles Better branding campaign – fall into? Is Camper a usurper of the footwear market on account of its environmentally-friendly, anti-fashion-forward wares, or is the brand just a self-publicizing clever clogs? Does Uber really deserve its current standing as Silicon Valley's Disrupter of the Year? Some commentators have their doubts:

> The real lesson of Uber ... is that it's time to discard the rose-tinted spectacles with which we have hitherto viewed these Silicon Valley outfits. For too long they have been allowed to trade fraudulently on the afterglow of the hippie libertarianism that supposedly infected the early days of the personal computer industry. The billionaire geeks who currently run the giant internet companies may look and talk like a new species of entrepreneur but it would be more prudent to view them as John D. Rockefellers in hoodies. And the economic philosophy that's embedded in this new digital capitalism is neoliberalism red in tooth and claw.[23]

PESTLE POWER

Regardless of its degree of disruptiveness, Uber exemplifies the dog-eat-dog character of inter-brand competition. It is ruthless. It is relentless. It is ruinous. It isn't the
only constraint on brand expansion, however. The notion that branding is akin to
a duel between two evenly (or unevenly) matched competitors is incorrect. *Kung Fu
Panda* is a better benchmark, inasmuch as brands are surrounded by constraints, only
some of which are the competition. Contextual constraints are equally significant,
if less evident at first glance. Summarized under the PEST acronym – subsequently
expanded to PESTLE – these comprise the uncontrollable or situational forces that
affect a brand's room to manoeuvre.

Political

Political forces comprise the many and varied governmental influences on brands'
freedom of expression, execution, extension. The Russian government, for instance, is
currently cracking down on drunkenness and public displays of inebriation. Carlsberg
is feeling the branding consequences, because Russia is one of the beverage's biggest
export markets. The sanctions imposed on Russia by western nations – in the aftermath of its intervention in the Ukraine – and Putin's tit-for-tat response are adversely
affecting many luxury brands, holiday resorts and auction houses, to say nothing of
food producers.[24] Foreign food brands have been bulldozed by Russian border guards,
much to the dismay of Putin's poorest people. Forced to watch good food going to
waste, in order to teach the EC a lesson, they are understandably upset by the sight.[25]
But consumer desire and brand strategies count for next to nothing when power politics is being played.

Economic

Economic forces are even more impactful on brands' ambitions. The recent economic
recession has been a boon for pound shops and payday loan providers and cut-price
grocery retailers – way to go, Netto! – but brutal for 'squeezed middle' brands which
can't compete with the rock bottom prices of the discounters and lack the cachet that
cushions top-tier luxury labels. Thus midmarket car brands *à la* Peugeot, Renault,
Fiat, Opel and Vauxhall have been shedding market share.[26] Factory closures (Opel,
Fiat), ruinous discounting (Renault) and brand death (Saab) are not uncommon.
Meanwhile German luxury marques are doing exceedingly well (as was Volkswagen
until its emissions were exposed as hot air). However, it's the bargain basement cars
like Dacia, Proton, Suzuki and SsangYong that are really making the most of the
downturn. The only surprise is that they haven't relaunched the Lada. Where's the
Wartburg when you need one? Trabant too.

Social

Social forces range from basic demographic trends, where a bigger population means greater demand, to the seemingly inexplicable rise and fall of fashions and fads like loom bands, Beanie Babies, Angry Birds and hoverboards. Until comparatively recently, the Chinese market, with its fast-growing population, faster growing economy and, not least, socially mandated ethos of liberal gift giving, has been a Shangri-La for western sellers.[27] Nowadays, the ostentatious display of big brand names is frowned upon in an increasingly sophisticated, somewhat sated consumer society. China's gift-giving propensity has also fallen off a cliff, partly on account of a government crackdown on graft, and growing consumer awareness that luxury western labels have been padding their prices for years. As a consequence, Burberry, Bentley, Gucci, Chanel and even the mighty Louis Vuitton are getting the cold shoulder from Chinese shoppers.[28] The country's worrisome economic slowdown, which accelerated to a veritable slump in 2015, is likewise likely to affect consumer confidence and social propriety for the foreseeable future.

Technological

Technological forces have done more to shape the 21st century brandscape – and contemporary consumer behaviour – than almost anything else. The BuzzFeeds, AppChats, Pinterests, Snapchats, Instagrams, Bitcoins and Dropboxes of this world didn't exist a decade ago. At most, they were gleams in the eye of ambitious Silicon Valley start-ups, as were drones, 3D printers, ad-blocking apps and video streaming services. A decade ago, indeed, Blockbuster and Netflix were in a fight to the finish over DVD rentals, YouTube had only just been launched, and its founders (Chad Hurley, Steve Chen and Jawed Karim) were openly acknowledging that their video sharing website was inspired by Hot or Not, the online dating service. Online dating has likewise come a long way since then. Just ask the aspiring adulterers exposed by the infamous 2015 hack of Ashley Madison. Tinder, Tickr, Grindr, Happn, Bumble, Whim and market leader Match.com are just a few of the brands that show there's plenty of fish in the sea.[29] And if they don't work there's always PlentyofFish.com. Speed dating seems sluggish by comparison. Eyes meeting across a crowded room is antediluvian. Personal ads of the WLTM, GSOH variety are positively prehistoric.

Legislative

Legislative forces are the bedrock of branding. If it weren't for the landmark trademark legislation of the 19th century, branding as we know it wouldn't exist.[30] Legislation can constrain brands too, be it Britain's 'living wage' debate or the proposed/imposed levies on fast food, fizzy drinks, sugary cereals, alcoholic beverages and plastic carrier bags. The EU's geographical indications regulations are equally impactful, since they afford a degree of protection to 'traditional' brands of Cornish pasties, Roquefort cheese, Waterford blaa, Herefordshire cider, etc. from the full force of competition (while penalizing those less geographically blessed).[31] In India, leaded fuel was abolished in 2000 yet heavy metals still leach into the rivers, the soil, the aquifers and the food chain. This is largely due to lead paint's continuing popularity, reckless electrical equipment recycling and excessive use of pesticides in the agricultural sector. However, it was Nestlé that paid the price when its Maggi brand noodles were banned by Indian food safety authorities on account of their lead levels, which exceeded permissible limits.[32] Unilever, PepsiCo, GlaxoSmithKline and Japan's Nippon Foods are also under investigation. They're hardly the worst offenders on the subcontinent but their brands are radioactive right now in Indian consumer consciousness.

Environmental

Environmental forces refers to both the foregoing 'uncontrollable' factors and the rather more familiar environmental issues like global warming, CO^2 emissions, oil spillages, GM foods, famine, fracking, desertification, deforestation, strip-mining, nuclear power proliferation and so on. Contemporary brands, it's fair to say, are acutely conscious of these concerns and, Ryanair possibly excepted, pay at least lip service to the sustainability agenda. They can't do otherwise because social media's rent-a-mob mentality keeps all but the most egregious offenders in line.[33] Thus, despite a litany of contamination incidents, groundwater quarrels and food additive imbroglios, Coca-Cola proudly boasts of its commitment to the welfare of Canada's polar bears. The brand's Arctic Home campaign, run in conjunction with the WWF, commenced in 2011, generated $2 million in donations during its first year and has since been rolled out across seventeen European countries, where Coke is committed to matching all donations up to €1 million.[34] Although some cynics see this as unconscionable corporate exploitation of the increasingly endangered animal, whose habitat is shrinking by the season, the rescued polar bears aren't complaining too loudly.

PESTLE comprises a combination of constraints that few brands can withstand. As with aikido, though, the strength of an opponent can be used against it. The uncontrollables are not as uncontrollable as textbooks suggest. Uber, Airbnb, Axiom and WeWork's rise is attributable, at least in part, to their circumvention of the legislation that shackles established brands of taxis, hotels, legal services and office space provision. Amazon's ability to offer sizeable discounts in its early days depended heavily on the location of its distribution centres, which avoided US states with crippling sales taxes. Volkswagen showed what can be done when official emission controls are not to a brand's liking, albeit the consequences of circumvention proved catastrophic. Google may not spend much on advertising itself as such, but Alphabet's outlay on Washington lobbyists – who are paid to control the controllers of the uncontrollables – speaks volumes. The mills of politics often grind slow. With the aid of appropriate lubricants, however, they can be made to speed up or slow down as necessary. In Britain's House of Lords at least, dough means slow.

CORPORATE CONSTRAINTS

Tooth and nail competition, combined with the vagaries of the macromarketing environment, are constraints enough for even the most ambitious brands. However barriers to expansion don't stop there. Some of the biggest impediments brands face are internal to themselves. Brands can be their own worst enemies, shackling themselves at every turn, doing the competition's job for free.

Gerald Ratner, as noted earlier, ruined a thriving jewellery business with a single ill-timed remark and, while he has since made a living recounting his fall from grace on the conference circuit, that isn't much consolation to the thousands of hard-working employees whose livelihoods were affected by Gerald's behaviour.

Benetton's march to gory glory with its controversial United Colours campaign came to a sudden calamitous stop when it featured photographs of prisoners on Death Row. The parents of one of the prisoner's victims were deeply upset by the photo-shoot and they protested outside a nearby Benetton store.[35] Local TV stations picked up on their story and before long it became a national scandal. The ire of Middle America descended on the Benetton brand – just like New Coke, only angrier – and its seemingly unstoppable advance suddenly stopped. There. And. Then.

American Apparel, once the coolest fashion brand on the high street, is in a comparable position right now. This is largely on account of the unsavoury actions of its CEO, Dov Chaney, whose priapic shenanigans – it is alleged in *The Guardian* – included sexting sales associates, jailbait advertising campaigns and 'masturbating eight times in the presence of a female journalist'.[36]

Sod's Law, the belief that 'if things can go wrong, they will', self-evidently operates in the branding sphere. Just ask FIFA. Or Persil Power if you prefer.[37] For present purposes it is sufficient to note the four most significant corporate constraints: namely, *Resource* constraints, *Imitative* constraints, *Organizational* constraints and the constraints that come from *Tradition*.

Resource

The vast majority of brands operate with strictly limited resources, start-ups in particular. They don't have deep pockets. They can't afford expensive advertising. Their human resources are often limited too, as are their channels of distribution, as is their credit worthiness, as are their production facilities, as is their networking nous. Their reputation is non-existent, what's more. Their R&D is negligible, needless to say. Their negotiating position is pitiful, as are their chances of success.

The funny thing, though, is that this very lack of resources can be their greatest asset.[38] Studies repeatedly show that unlimited resources are troublesome. More isn't always better, as the Boo.com debacle bears abysmal witness.[39] Ask yourself, would more people use Twitter if the word limit for tweets were extended to 1,400 characters or 14,000 for that matter? The opposite is more likely, because it is the concision that appeals to consumers in the first place.

Google's legendary homepage, the majestic minimalism of which swept rivals aside, wasn't a statement of aesthetic intent. Brin and Page were not (and are not) aesthetes. The homepage was minimalist because Larry Page lacked the coding skills to produce anything more elaborate.

Southwest Airlines' celebrated ten-minute turnaround time – the breakthrough idea that pretty much inaugurated the low-cost airline industry – came about because Southwest was forced to sell one of its planes. Desperate to keep its routes, the management had to find a way to service four destinations with three aircraft.

Super Mario, arguably the most celebrated character in the world's best-known video game, likewise owes everything to technical constraints. Mario is as colourful as he is:

> ... because of the challenges of eight-bit technology. To compensate for poor pix-ilation definition, designer Shigeru Miyamoto gave the character a large nose to emphasise his humanity, a moustache to obviate the need for a mouth and facial expressions, overalls to make it easier to see his arms in relation to his body, and a cap to free him from the problems of animating hair.[40]

Absence of resources forces brand impresarios to be more imaginative, to throw cre-ativity at the problem rather than cash. David Ogilvy, the original Mad Man, relished the limitations imposed by his big brand clients, because it gave him 'the freedom of a tight brief'. When it comes to working creatively without resources, however, Ogilvy was an amateur compared to his contemporary Howard Gossage, some of whose greatest hits are summarized in Think Box 18.

THINK BOX 18

The Age of Gossage, the Sage

Madison Avenue is the Olympus of branding. And the golden age of the avenue – its Arcadian epoch – can be confidently dated to the 1950s. Branding burgeoned during the *Mad Men* era. It was a time before time when the gods of advertising strutted their stuff, stalked the sidewalks and called the shots on the spots that punctuated the programmes of the Big Three TV networks.

The Zeus of this Olympus was Rosser Reeves, the kingpin of the Ted Bates agency. Renowned for his unremitting, no-nonsense, hammer-it-home messages for

Anacin, Alka-Seltzer and M&Ms, Reeves battered television viewers into submission. He invented the Unique Selling Proposition and sold the idea so relentlessly that it remains one of marketing's most famous concepts, alongside the 4Ps.

Hera, the powerful mother goddess of Olympus, was the imperious David Ogilvy whose powers of persuasion were second to none. The brother-in-law of Rosser Reeves, Ogilvy was as opinionated as Hera herself and had more self-regard than Narcissus. However, he was a brilliant Mad Man whose golden rules of copywriting are employed by many to this day.

The advertising equivalent of Hermes – the trickster god of the marketplace – was the one and only Bill Bernbach. A branding nonpareil, who put VW on the map, coined We Try Harder for Avis and initiated advertising's 'creative revolution', Bernbach believed that making mock moved merchandise. He had no time for 'technicians'. He maintained that advertising was the art – not a science – of persuasion.

However, our Apollo, the seer god and one of Olympus's most important deities, was Howard Gossage. An erudite man who came to advertising late in life, Gossage eschewed television for good old-fashioned print. However, he invented what we today call 'social media' and 'co-creation'. His campaigns were designed to engage consumers in conversation. Yes, he used coupons and competitions and various cut-out-and-keep devices to generate consumer response. Respond they did, though. In their thousands.

Gossage's single greatest campaign was for *Scientific American*, a campaign that invited consumers to devise the ultimate paper plane. The contest comprised four categories: duration aloft, distance flown, aerobatics and aesthetics. Two prizes were awarded, a Silver Leonardo for amateurs and a Titanium Leonardo for professionals. The response – back in the days before social media, remember – was staggering. Eleven thousand entries from twenty-eight different countries, plus oodles of free publicity from newspapers, magazines and TV programmes, made it one of the biggest ever bangs-per-buck campaigns in branding history.

Better still, creatively at least, was Gossage's work for the Whiskey Distillers of Ireland. The campaign only ever ran in the *New Yorker*. However, it began with arguably the most eye-catching, head-scratching, one-word headlines of all time: Flahoolick. The word, Gossage claimed, was an Irish term meaning open-handed, generous, expansive, etc. And the body copy listed the kinds of things that qualify as flahoolick, Irish whiskey included. It also gave examples of unflahoolick including tea bags (then regarded as the work of the devil). The subsequent ads expatiated on flahoolickness and, at one stage, incorporated coupons for a free Flahoolick badge, shipped all the way from Dublin.

New Yorker readers loved it, even the ad that stopped in mid-sentence, having run out of space. When one of the weekly ads failed to appear, scores of readers wrote in asking about its absence. The Apollo of advertising's next ad replied: 'Well bless your

(Continued)

(Continued)

heart, if we published every week it would have us out on the street, advertising is that expensive. But thoughtfulness costs nothing at all.'[41]

Now, that's what I call conversing with customers, treating them as acquaintances, as accomplices, as equals who are as fallible as ourselves.

Thinking Outside the Think Box

Twitter is contemplating cutting restrictions on tweets. No longer confined to 140 characters, they can be up to 10,000 characters long. Do you think this is a good idea? Some see it as a sign of desperation. Others contend that long-form writing is making a comeback. Consider Twitter's dilemma. Identify the advantages and disadvantages of both options. What would you do if you were Dorsey?

Imitation

Is the bane of branding. Following the leader, matching the competition, keeping pace with the latest developments in the category is a one-way ticket to me-too, middle-of-the-road mediocrity. Despite all the talk of cut-throat competition, battling underdogs, disruptive innovations, POWer plays and suchlike, the day-to-day reality of business life involves emulating the competition not eviscerating it. Follow the leader perpetuates the status quo and limits a brand's ability to expand.

Stasis is further perpetuated by brand managers' reliance on consumer research. As Bill Bernbach (Think Box 18) rightly observed, consumers tend to talk in terms of the familiar, what already exists, the offerings of other brands ('work that researches well is predicated on what has gone before; anything different, or out of the ordinary, will test badly, for the very reason that it is different').[42]

Unsurprisingly, then, when Westin Hotels introduced its Heavenly Bed – a marvel of mattress technology, the Dreamliner of divans – every other hotel chain followed suit. Hilton hit back with its Serenity Bed. Marriott did its bit for somnolence with Revive, and Hyatt raised the roof with its Great Bed. Radisson, naturally, refused to take these developments lying down, so it came up with a Sleep Number, Crowne Plaza went one better with a Sleep Advantage programme. And Premier Inns piled in with its aptly named Hypnos mattress.[43]

The same is true of almost any sector you can imagine. Costa, Starbucks and Café Nero slug it out incessantly, monitoring and matching each other's moves, as do McDonald's and Burger King, easyJet and Ryanair, Primark and Topshop, Apple and Samsung. But they're involved in a zero-sum game. Blinded by the battle, their vision is constrained. Failure to keep up can be, and often is, fatal. But blind brands shouldn't follow blind brands blithely.

Organization

Although branding has come a long way in recent years, it is still seen by many as something that belongs to the marketing department. Logos and slogans and liveries are all too often regarded as set dressing, as fluff and puff and stuff and nonsense.[44] We here in human resources, R&D, production, sales, finance and so forth don't need to bother with such trivialities. The logocops in the marketing department'll keep us right and complain bitterly if we fail to treat their 'brand guidelines handbook' as gospel and recite it from memory.

Marketers are no less culpable in this regard, since they often act as if branding 'belongs' to them rather than the organization as a whole. Organizations are irredeemably political institutions where internecine warfare is the norm. Branding often gets caught up in intra-management power plays, especially when 'ridiculous' amounts of money are spent on rebranding exercises or refreshing the logo or changing the brand name from, say, University of Ulster to, whoop de doo, Ulster University. As the business grows and the brand expands, this compartmentalized, departmentalized mind-set becomes ever more marked.[45] Cliques appear. Silos rise. Necessary knowledge isn't shared. The sunset of Sony, one of the most outstanding brands of the 20th century, is almost entirely due to faction fighting. Microsoft as well. Toshiba also. When Netflix appeared on the scene, Blockbuster was beset by battles between its staff officers at corporate headquarters (who wanted to develop an online presence) and the franchisees on the front line (who remained committed to DVD rental). They couldn't have made it easier for the resource-less upstart.

Organizations, of course, are aware of this issue and many strive to avoid silo thinking through staff rotation on a project by project basis (Apple), architectural arrangements which force specialists to interact rather than remain physically separate (Pixar), all-in boot camps for new employees before they're dispersed to different departments (Facebook) and internal branding programmes, where employees are exhorted to 'live the brand'. Given that consumers' experience of a brand is greatly shaped by the employees they encounter – especially so in the service sector – internal branding's importance cannot be overstated. In the sagacious words of Nicholas Ind:

> It is employees who interact with the outside world and converse with external stakeholders. It is employees who share knowledge with each other and create the experiences (sometimes with consumers) that generate value. It is employees who help to drive the customer loyalty that strengthens the brand and secures future cash flows.[46]

Tradition

Even the most effective internal branding exercises, unfortunately, can founder on the reefs of tradition. Just as consumers are often set in their ways – as per the consistency trait identified by Cialdini[47] – so too brands can get stuck in a rut. Resistance to new ideas (not invented here), reluctance to change things that are working well (don't rock the boat) and recalcitrance in the face of hard facts (marketing myopia) are ties that bind even the most progressive brands. Research shows that disruptive innovations succeed, not because the innovators' offers are so much better than existing products, but because the incumbents refused to recognize the threat they posed. The 'that won't affect us' assumption, the 'we tried that and it didn't work' syndrome, the 'we've always done it this way' statement, the 'change would upset our customers' contention are standard rhetorical reactions that can, and do, prove fatal.

The fashion industry, for example, is famous for its fixation on the new, the latest, the next big thing, which changes by the season. Yet almost to a brand, they resisted online shopping, arguing that fashion-conscious customers would never buy apparel without feeling the material, trying it on, checking how the garment looks in natural light. And when that assumption was disproved by brands like Zappos (which sells shoes through the mail), Asos (which retails fast fashion items online) and Net-a-Porter (which specializes in luxury brand overstocks), they still refused to face the facts of fashion branding. Dolce & Gabbana, unforgivably, lost the D&G domain name because of its dotcom dithering (then refused to buy it from the enterprising site squatters, thereby compounding the problem).[48] Hermès, furthermore, was such a slowcoach when it came to e-commerce that a clever middleman called Michael Tonello built a multi-million dollar business buying Hermès handbags from stores all over Europe, one or two at a time. After adding a hefty mark-up, he sold them on to fanatical fashionistas through a wild and crazy channel of distribution called eBay. The book describing his adventures, *Bringing Home the Birkin*, is well worth reading, if only to better understand how tradition can blind even the most bedazzling brands (Think Box 19).

THINK BOX 19

Bringing Home the Brandungsroman

These days, every luxury brand in the world has a super-slick website, an awesome, super-deluxe, i-Purchase operation. But it wasn't always thus. For a brief interval in the early years of the millennium, an opportunity opened up for web-savvy secondary sellers. These were entrepreneurial individuals who bought in store then sold online to far-flung consumers with money to spend and ready access to the 'information superhighway', as it was then known.

One such canny customer was Michael Tonello. An affluent American trust-fund type, he moved on a whim from Rhode Island to Barcelona. However, the job he'd moved for fell through and, in an attempt to earn a crust, Tonello started auctioning his old stuff on eBay. Back then, eBay was in its pomp as the coolest website on the planet. Hence he had no trouble selling his luxury label cast-offs – bespoke Ralph Lauren scarves, exquisite Pringles sweaters and suchlike – for a tidy sum.

Michael's overflowing wardrobes soon emptied. Before long, he was reduced to auctioning an old Hermès silk scarf that he'd bought in a moment of madness and worn once.

eBay went bananas for his black and gold collector's item. The bidding took off. He realized a very handsome profit. More than that, Tonello realized that this was a potentially lucrative business opportunity. So Michael decided to buy up Hermès silk scarves from its network of European stores then sell said items to Hermès enthusiasts in the States.

Business was good. Many treasured scarves that had sold out in North America were still knocking around Hermès' network of outlets in Spain, France and Italy. Michael went on road trips with his 'shopping lists' and, from someone who knew absolutely nothing about the Hermès brand, he soon became a connoisseur, an e-tail-preneur of the first water.

Inevitably, the Birkin raised its croc-skin head. US collectors were desperate for the Hermès holy-of-holies, the ultimate 'it' bag that cost anything between $7,000 and $100,000, depending on the material. Birkins were ultra-exclusive bags that couldn't be bought for love nor money. There was, allegedly, a two-year waiting list and a waiting list for the waiting list.

When in Madrid one day, Michael asked for a Birkin. He was rebuffed. He was rebuffed in every store he tried and, in several cases, threatened with ejection from the premises for having the temerity to ask about the bag's availability.

Then, purely by chance, our hero stumbled on the secret formula that opened the Birkin bat cave. He realized that if he purchased $1,000 worth of scarves and assorted accessories – the table stake, so to speak – his subsequent request for a Birkin would be granted. The mistake he'd been making was to ask for a Birkin first, only to be told that the store didn't stock them. However, when he ponied up the price of entry, an entire world of Birkins opened up for him. Using the formula, Michael bought Birkins by the dozen. He toured the network of European stores, picking up a handbag or two at a time. Then selling the 'unobtainable' leather treasures to American aficionados, who couldn't believe their luck. They paid top dollar for Tonello's sourcing expertise.

It couldn't last. But while it did, it was wonderful. Michael's book about his Hermès escapades, *Bringing Home the Birkin*, recounts his rollicking, laugh-out-loud adventures in detail.[49] I won't tell you how it ends. Suffice it to say that the denouement involves a Birkin bag-napping incident on the streets of Gay Paree. Track down a copy on eBay and read about them for yourself.

There's a long-standing literary genre called *bildungsroman*. Bildungsromans are coming-of-age stories such as *David Copperfield*, *Tom Brown's Schooldays*, *Catcher in the Rye* and Goethe's *Sorrows of Young Werther*. Typically, these recount the growth and development of a young, often naïve person as they learn about life and encounter hard knocks along the way. Tonello's text is the branding equivalent, the world's original and best brandungsroman. Enjoy.

Thinking Outside the Think Box

Birkin bags aren't just arm candy or receptacles for knick-knacks. They are investments. Recent reports reveal that they have performed better, between 1980 and 2005, than the stock market. This is due, analysts say, to the Birkin's restricted availability. The above, however, suggest that it's the impression of unavailability instead of actual unavailability that's key. Do you agree? What are the branding implications?

CONGENITAL CONSTRAINTS

If the limits to brand expansion were a function of corporate myopia, environmental flux and competitive pressures, it might be possible to develop a predictive model which, with suitable calibration and empirical testing, is capable of calculating the effective extent of brand expansion. However, there are all sorts of miscellaneous occurrences that can knock individual brands for six or throw a spanner in the works. Just as the best laid military strategies never survive contact with the enemy, so too brand building strategies go awry very easily. As Tolstoy almost said, 'happy brand families are all alike, every unhappy brand family is unhappy in its own way'. This so-called Anna Karenina Principle has been applied to business situations – by the founder of PayPal, Peter Thiel – where it refers to idiosyncratic issues that can prove fatal for a brand. These potential pitfalls are many and varied. They include bad luck, bad weather, bad timing, bad tempers, bad moods, bad behaviour among investors, stockbrokers, stakeholders, etc.[50] However a trio of craters filled with corporate quicksand are especially worthy of note: *celebrities*, *countries* and *consumers*.

Celebrities

Consumer behaviour, as noted in chapter 6, is influenced by authority figures of various sorts. In the past, regal, religious and military figures were brands' spokespersons of choice. These days, it's sports stars, movie stars, pop stars and TV stars, as well as the new breed of celebrity vloggers like Zoella and Tanya Burr, whose engaging interactions with brands are part of their consumer appeal.[51]

Although celebrities are badges of brand pride, worn proudly like military and campaign medals of yore, they can be branding booby traps too. They often explode without warning and do serious collateral damage to the sponsoring brands. The revelations about Lance Armstrong's drug taking damaged Nike's brand equity, as did the Oscar Pistorius imbroglio, as did Tiger Woods' infamous indiscretions. Martha Stewart, Nigella Lawson, Gordon Ramsey, George Michael, Charlie Sheen, Tom Cruise, Dov Chaney, Bill Cosby, Vijay Mallya and Lindsay Lohan, to name but a few, have all suffered high-profile implosions, which adversely affect their partner and personal brands alike. Justin Bieber's growing pains, Mel Gibson's bigoted outbursts and Scarlett Johansson's SodaStream slip-up during the Super Bowl are just a few of branding's Anna Karenina moments. The former face of Dior, Sharon Stone once made impolitic remarks about Mongolia, which came at a time when LVMH was expanding into China, and her brand ambassadorship was revoked on the spot. One Direction's decision to break up, Rihanna's couldn't care less attitude to the press gang and Lady Gaga's underwhelming third album must have had their PR people running for cover, spinning all the while.

Countries

Country of origin is a formidable branding attribution. The advent of globalization, Olins observes, has precipitated a countervailing tendency toward localization.[52] Few global brands fail to proclaim their national or regional loyalties. Most, in truth, are mercenaries, inasmuch as their wares are often designed in one place, assembled elsewhere and sold from somewhere else again. At one stage, for instance, Aston Martin was owned by a Kuwaiti consortium, managed by a German chief executive and manufactured much of its true-blue British brand in Austria.

Be that as it may, Made in Italy, Made in Ireland, Made in Germany, Made in Japan, or wherever remain meaningful marketing markers. Brands benefit from the associations, assumptions and stereotypes consumers attach to the countries concerned. Germany's perceived prowess in chemical engineering throws an aura around the country's pharmaceutical brands, Bayer especially. Made in Italy is a boon for Italian fashion brands or indeed pretend Italian brands like India's Bammbino or Ireland's Remus Uomo. Japan's proficiency in tech is so esteemed that Dixons' own brand was called Matsui, in the hope that Japan's reputation would rub off on a (nondescript) British product. Vodka is so strongly associated with Russia that, even at the height of the Cold War, American vodka brands were routinely given fake Russian identities (e.g. Crown Russe).

The other side of this coin, of course, is that national stereotypes can adversely affect brands from the non-stereotypical sectors. German fashion is not highly esteemed, Hugo Boss, Jil Sander and Karl Lagerfeld notwithstanding. Italian engineering isn't exactly covered in glory, despite Vespa and Maserati's best efforts. Russian pharmaceuticals are not highly prized, truth serums and steroidal sports supplements possibly excepted. Scottish whisky may be beloved worldwide. But Scottish cuisine fires few gastronauts' imaginations, apart from those with a deep-fried Mars bar fixation. Or should that be death wish? There is no doubt, moreover, that China is a manufacturer of unrivalled versatility. However, Chinese brands don't really cut the mustard with western consumers right now. Hence the arch reminder on Apple's iProducts: Designed in California. Assembled in China.

Consumers

For all the talk of strategies, feints, enfilades, pincer movements and mercenaries that come with the business-as-warfare metaphor, branding success ultimately boils down to one thing above all others. The consumer. Consumers are the shock troops of capitalism. They can carry a brand to everlasting glory or they can mutiny, turn tail and desert in their droves. When consumers retreat in disorder or panic, no amount of exhortation by the brand commander-in-chief will make a blind bit of difference. Granted, there are several reasons why consumers recoil, conscientiously object, or resist conscription in the first place.

Sometimes they simply dislike the brand, often for no rational reason. I loathe Richard Branson, for example, and avoid his brands if humanly possible. Ditto Peter Jones, the smug git off *Dragons' Den*. Ditto James Dyson, he of the overpriced vacuum cleaners. Ditto Donald Trump, despite his presidential campaign catchphrase, 'We Shall Overcomb'.

Sometimes the consumer beats a retreat because the brand becomes too popular, excessively ubiquitous, and the cachet it once enjoyed is denuded. Tommy Hilfiger, Calvin Klein, Crocs, Starbucks and *Angry Birds* have been down that road already. Ugg boots, by contrast, are so far out of fashion that they're back in again.

Sometimes, moreover, consumer retribution is a factor. When a brand steps out of line by, say, awarding itself untoward rewards, maltreating its downtrodden employees, failing to live up to its high-falutin ideals or simply failing to deliver the requisite standard of customer service (as United Airlines once did to Dave Carroll), they live to regret it. According to Iezzi's account of the Carroll case:

> United Airlines passenger and musician Dave Carroll complained that his Taylor guitar was wilfully destroyed by the airline's baggage handlers during a flight in 2008. After United repeatedly declined to compensate him for the damage, he wrote a wonderfully catchy song decrying the airline's customer service and made an entertaining music video featuring his band, his guitar and some actors playing some comically callous United staff and posted it to YouTube. Ten days after it launched, the video was viewed by 3.2 million people and elicited 14,000 comments. It has since been viewed nearly 9 million times. In the aftermath of the video's explosion on the web, United's stock price sank more than 10 percent. Did one man's opinion, expressed engagingly and distributed for free to millions of people wipe $180 million off the airline's market cap? We may never know. But we do know that 9 million people have a worse impression of United than they did before (if such a thing is possible). And all the lovely, lyrical advertising in the world isn't going to change that.[53]

When good brands go AWOL, consumers exact retribution on the deserter. Betrayal is a capital offence. As is brand misbehaviour.

BRAND TASK

Cannibalization is a perennial problem for ambitious brands. Also known as dilution, it refers to a situation where additional products or services or branches can undermine existing products, services or branches. There are benefits from doing so, though. With reference to a brand from one of the following categories – smartphones, motor cars, fast food – make a case for cannibalism.

RECOMMENDED READINGS

Adam Morgan, *Eating the Big Fish* (Wiley: Chichester, 1999). Morgan's book, its updates and offspring, started the fad for fiery, feisty, small-fry brands. It's worth reading, as is Morgan's more recent excursus *A Beautiful Constraint*.

Jill Lepore, 'The Disruption Machine', *The New Yorker*, June 23, 2014, www.newyorker.com. Disruption is one of the world's biggest buzz words right now. This article disrupts the disruptors by showing that Christensen's inaugural study was flawed. Lepore's piece caused an uproar, needless to say.

Mark Ritson, 'Should You Launch a Fighter Brand?' *Harvard Business Review*, 87 (10), 2009, 86–94. Mark Ritson is the Al Murray of marketing, its resident pub landlord. An esteemed academic, he writes a column in *Marketing Week* that's never less than provocative. These are his characteristically belligerent thoughts on fighting brands. Sparks fly.

Michael Tonello, *Bringing Home the Birkin* (HarperCollins: New York, 2008). Try to track this book down on eBay or Amazon Marketplace. It's a terrific read that offers fascinating insights into the weird and wonderful world of Hermès, its collectors, gatekeepers and imperishable allure. If you don't laugh out loud on occasion, you shouldn't be studying branding.

CHAPTER 10
THE DARK SIDE OF
THE BRAND

Overview

Brand managers talk a good game. Their sole concern is customer satisfaction and delight. They are faithful retainers who do our bidding for paltry reward. The reality is very different. Branding can be a very dirty business. This chapter sheds light on the dark side of brands and branding. However, it notes that consumers aren't angels either, anti-capitalist consumers included. Humankind gets the brands it deserves.

A CAUTIONARY TALE

The only son of a coal miner in South Wales, Alun Richards is a serial entrepreneur. Determined to be a millionaire by the age of thirty, he earned his stripes selling solid-state traction batteries – for milk-floats, fork-lifts, golf-buggies, coal-mine machinery, etc. – though he was equally adept with life insurance, real estate, used cars, time shares. By the age of thirty-five he lived in a big house on Beach Road, Penarth, complete with BMW 5-series Alpine, bespoke Bang & Olufsen television, top-of-the line Linn Sondek sound system, and walk-in wardrobes full of Prada, Paul Smith, Ralph Lauren, Hugo Boss. He also owned a luxurious holiday home in the Dordogne and spent several weeks every winter powder skiing in Klosters.

Rather than rest on his laurels, however, Alun went for the big kill. Traction batteries had come a long way since he'd been flogging them to milk-float fleets. So, with the assistance of his acquaintances in the industry – and a generous grant from the Welsh Development Agency – he built a state-of-the-art battery factory in a former mining valley. Oakvale they called themselves. Their innovative product held charges longer, was more environmentally friendly and cheaper to run than those based on conventional technologies. With its striking transparent casing – which made it easier to monitor and replenish battery acid levels in each cell – the Oakvale brand represented the biggest breakthrough in the battery business since the Energizer Bunny. Alun sank everything he had into the start-up and, as Chief Marketing Officer, his job was the build the brand into a market leader, then conquer the traction battery universe.

At first, things went well for Oakvale. Reception was positive, trials went smoothly, contracts were negotiated and sales rose swiftly. Before long, however, the scuttle-butt turned nasty. The word on the shop floor was that the Oakvale battery was unreliable, unstable and liable to explode. None of this was true but the rumours, started and spread by the competition, were difficult to dispel. Every impassioned denial only made matters worse, because traction battery buyers worked on a no-smoke-without-fire principle. The damage was done. Sales slumped. Suppliers balked. Creditors circled. Backers backed out. Oakvale was undone by the dirty tricks departments of incumbent brands. Oakvale's batteries may or may not have exploded, but the brand most definitely did.[1]

DISHING THE DIRT

Alun Richards' experience is not unusual. Dirty tricks and dark ops are par for the course. In a world where kill-or-be-killed competition is the norm, people are going to cheat, chisel and connive to keep the show on the road and the wolf from the door. We may be appalled when we read that Larry Ellison, former CEO of leading software brand Oracle, once said he'd happily stick a hose pipe in the mouth of a drowning adversary.[2] Or that Thomas Edison, the greatest inventor of all time, went out of his way to knobble Nikola Tesla, his foremost opponent. However, this no-holds-barred attitude, if not the norm, is fairly widespread among battling brand managers. The 'dirty tricks' that Richard Branson endured when challenging BA ended up in the courts. The 'blade wars' between Gillette and Wilkinson led to industrial espionage on an industrial scale. Netflix employees joined online discussion groups and posted unpleasant anonymous messages that denigrated their competitors. Alibaba's main Chinese rival, Qihoo, gave users free anti-virus software, which when installed treated the Alibaba site as malware and blocked user access.[3] The 'chocolate wars' between Cadbury, Kraft and co. got so bitter that Cadbury's stellar reputation as one of the most ethical brands on the planet, founded by puritans, was irredeemably tainted (Think Box 20). The Italian wine industry has been beset of late by wanton acts of vandalism, where the storage facilities of leading brands like Brunelli are being attacked at night by adversaries with a grudge (and a selection of sledgehammers).[4]

The shenanigans on TripAdvisor.com, where competing restaurants, hotels, bars and night clubs not only big themselves up through fake five-star reviews but dish the dirt on their dank, dirty, dreary, doleful rivals, almost beggar belief.

THINK BOX 20

Compromising Cadbury

Cadbury is one of many brands built by the Quaker community in Britain. Committed by their religious beliefs to plain dealing, total integrity, absolute honesty and worker welfare, the Quaker community founded Boots the Chemist, Barclays bank, Lloyds bank, Rowntree's confectionary, Fry's chocolate, Clark's footwear, K Shoes, Bryant and May matches, Huntley and Palmer biscuits and many more besides.

Founded in 1831, Cadbury was one of many chocolatiers back then and a fairly small one at that. At a time of widespread food adulteration, however, Cadbury made its reputation on the purity of its products. This positioning was disadvantageous initially because it meant that Cadbury's prices were higher than most. But when the Adulteration of Food Acts were introduced in 1872 and 1875, the purity of Cadbury's products gave it an edge that competitor brands lacked. Sales took off and, driven by Great Britain's rising affluence and growing population numbers, demand increased rapidly. Especially so after the 1905 introduction of Cadbury's Dairy Milk, whose smoothness, creaminess and melt-in-the-mouth quality represented a giant leap in taste sensation. Sales surged, and surged again on account of the First World War, which effectively killed off the foreign competition (due to import restrictions). Cadbury also sold huge quantities to the military, since chocolate formed part of soldiers' daily rations.

Come the 1920s, Cadbury dominated the moulded chocolate business in Britain and, with the added advantage of modern factory premises in the Bournville sub-urb of Birmingham, was able to massively increase output at ever-lower costs. This ensured that prices steadily dropped and the market rapidly expanded as more and more ordinary people found they could afford Cadbury's chocolate. Once the preserve of the rich, chocolate became an everyday treat. Heavy advertising, incessant promotion, widespread distribution and ubiquitous availability ensured that the 'glass and a half' message got through to everyone. Understandably, Cadbury expanded its brand portfolio – Milk Tray, Whole Nut, Fruit & Nut, Creme Eggs, Flake – and foreign operations began in Australia, New Zealand, Canada, South Africa and Ireland, some more successfully than others. The logo was also changed in 1921 to the cursive script – the Cadbury's signature – that consumers know and love. The livery likewise changed from lilac to the imperial purple that is indelibly associated with the brand.

Although Cadbury's fortunes waxed and waned in the decades since its golden age – not least a failed attempt to crack the American market during the 1950s – its

(Continued)

(Continued)

brilliantly innovative advertising and steady additions to the product portfolio, including Wispa, Twirl and Chocolate Eclairs, have consistently held the brand in the highest esteem. The quality of its products, the dedication of its workforce and its unwavering commitment to corporate social responsibility ensured that few brands were more admired than Birmingham's finest.

Until it was acquired by Kraft in January 2010. Then things went to hell in a handcart. Factories were closed willy-nilly, agreements with employees were dishonoured, time-tested recipes were altered to accommodate cheaper ingredients and turbo-charged American capitalism replaced the benign Quaker traditions that built the brand. Or so the story goes.

The reality, however, is that Cadbury compromised their Quaker principles at every stage of the brand's evolution. From the very first advertising campaigns of the 1880s, via several unseemly episodes of industrial espionage, to trash-talking attacks on its early European rivals, Cadbury has always been prepared to set aside its holy-roller principles when competition was at its fiercest and failure seemed certain. The Kraft takeover was not a fall from grace. Grace left the building some time beforehand.[5]

Thinking Outside the Think Box

Cadbury's Creme Eggs were once a special treat. They were sold when 'in season'. Once they were gone, they were gone. These days, there's a glut of them. Changes to the recipe, year-round availability and the rise of competing products have denuded Creme Eggs' cachet. How would you recapture their allure? Is restricting supply sufficient?

Esteemed academics are almost as bad. Some have been known to post one-star reviews of the books of their peers, while praising their own published writings as works of genius. Still, not to worry. There are digital click farms for hire in emerging economies like Bangladesh, where Facebook likes, YouTube views and five-star reviews can be purchased in bulk.[6] If a rival ridicules your brand, swamp the one-star reviews with several hundred five-stars, thereby restoring your unsullied reputation. Mind you, if your rivals then reply with bulk bought negative comments, everyone's back where they started and somewhat the worse for wear.

Although, as previously noted, almost everyone has a soft spot for underdog brands who are forced to fight dirty to defeat the big bad incumbents, the basic problem is that it doesn't stop there. Underhand tactics are endemic throughout business and, while this might be pardonable if it were only combatants who suffered, consumers get caught up in it too. Customers are affected by brands' devil-take-the-hindmost mind-set. Nowhere more so than in the recent great recession when bank brands'

unconscionable behaviour destroyed the pensions, the livelihoods, the employment prospects of millions of people. Have the banks learned their lesson? Are they
ashamed of themselves? Token apologies aside, are they contrite? Not if the LIBOR
rigging activities by Barclays are any indication. Not if the self-enriching ruses of
Goldman Sachs (and similar merchant banks) are typical. Not if the revelations about
Santander's involvement in money laundering for Mexican drug cartels (while boasting about its ethical standards) are in any way representative. Not if the activities of
RBS's insolvency department (small businesses were denied loans by one arm of the
bank and, when they went bust, their assets were expropriated by another) passes for
an honest day's work at head office.[7]

And it's not just the banks. Hardly a day goes by without allegations of big brands'
misbehaviour.

- IKEA, for instance, has been accused of using slave labour, which was employed in Poland
(and Cuba) during the communist epoch.[8] Volkswagen once did something similar, when
Ferdinand Porsche pulled the strings of the brand. The latter-day emissions scandal pales
by comparison.
- W.H. Smith's airport shops insist on seeing passengers' boarding cards. Passengers
assume it's a security measure, and comply. But the practice has nothing to do with
security. It helps Smiths avoid VAT. They charge premium prices in their hospital outlets, furthermore, where visitors and patients have no real retail alternative.[9]
- In a devastating critique by *The New York Times*, Amazon is accused of exploiting its
employees, failing in its duty of corporate care and running a ruthless, up-or-out regime
of social Darwinism that's not only red in tooth and claw but brutal to boot. Bezos vehemently denies the accusations. His bear and gorilla aren't available for comment.[10]
- Shell ignores the protests of concerned environmentalists and drills in Alaska's
Chukchi Sea, despite an 75% chance of serious oil spills in one of the few pristine
parts of the planet that remain untouched by human brand. The lessons of Deepwater
Horizon have yet to be taken on board by the barons of Big Oil.[11]
- Olympus, the venerable camera brand, has been charged with making 'unjustified payments' to assorted financial advisors, as well as third parties involved in a series of
strange corporate acquisitions (small brands with no obvious link to the Japanese
giant's core camera business). Some see the long arm of the Yakuza at work.[12]
- Alibaba's senior sales team has been indicted on charges of criminal fraud when
shady suppliers have been knowingly signed up by the platform and 2,300 store
fronts fraudulently awarded its prestigious 'Gold Supplier' accolade. And they have
the gall to complain about Qihoo.[13]
- Three years after the Rana Plaza disaster, when 1,134 Bangladeshi factory workers died in a ramshackle building producing clothes for scores of western brands
including Primark, Zara and C&A, many have yet to contribute to the compensa-
tion fund. Fast fashion firms are still selling £4 T-shirts, £8 jeans and £10 sweaters,
though.[14]
- The Italian government, critics contend, is fomenting gambling addiction among its
citizens. Strapped for cash during the financial crisis, the government legalized lottos,
unleashed scratch cards and let online betting run wild. Gaming brands like Lotteria

Italia are raking it in, as is the state thanks to its 50% slice of the action. But vulnerable punters are paying the price.[15]

- Addyi, a brand new pharmaceutical brand, goes on sale for a condition – female sexual dysfunction – whose existence is debatable at best. However, the potential profits from a 'female Viagra' are too vast to forgo.[16] If it works, presumably, there's bound to be a knock-on demand for Viagra Turbo, then Addyi Extra, then Viagra Maximum Thrust, then Addyi Yippee! Watch this space.

To be sure, stories such as these are the stock-in-trade of tabloid newspapers, which use unscrupulous shock-horror tactics to sell their own media brands. Bad news is good for newspapers. And if bad news has to be manufactured for the good of the brand, so be it. Even if that news bears no relation to the truth and the newspaper brand's behaviour – phone hacking, for instance – is just as bad as the behaviour it condemns. Representative or not, the incessant drip, drip, drip of shady stories reinforces consumer perceptions that corporations in general and big name brands in particular are lying, thieving, conniving, scheming scumbags. The entire marketing system, for some consumers, is a poisonous nest of vipers. As an analysis of disreputable 'dark marketing' practices points out:

> The arms trade, the drugs trade, the sex trade, the sale of body parts, blood diamonds, surrogate children and counterfeit goods, the funeral industry, the gaming industry, the human trafficking industry, the private security industry and aspects of the fashion industry, all fall under dark marketing's ignoble auspices. So vast, in fact, is its remit, that marketing could be considered a dark practice, full stop.[17]

BAD TO THE BONE

Make no mistake, many of these charges are valid. There is no shortage of unprincipled practice in branding. The last-brand-standing ethos of the capitalist system brings out the worst in people. Although, in my experience, most marketing managers genuinely care for their customers and want to do what's best for them, for their community, for conservation, for sustainability, for the greater good, the nature of the beast gets the better of them. As with elite athletes, it's hard to compete when you're clean and drug cheats escape censure. Granted, the cheats don't see themselves as cheats. Some consider the above dirty tricks to be the equivalent of gamesmanship in sport. That is, of ungentlemanly conduct in tennis, of sledging in cricket, of diving in football, of faking injuries in rugby, of pre-bout trash talking by heavyweight boxers, of the psychological mind games that are used to unsettle opponents. Steve Jobs never apologized for the fact that he stole Xerox's ideas – the mouse, the drop-down menu, the graphical user interface – when developing the Macintosh. Boots made no bones about the fact that its Natural Collection was a rip-off of The Body Shop, whose sales plummeted when Jesse's descendants stole their thunder. Tommy

Hilfiger openly acknowledged that everything he knew about fashion he 'learned' from Ralph Lauren, albeit Ralph's preppy look was appropriated, in turn, from the English upper crust. Tom Peters, the great management guru mentioned earlier, showed no contrition after confessing that his *Excellence* findings were fudged. P.T. Barnum, the greatest marketing man of the 19th century, repeatedly boasted of his ability to hoodwink, bamboozle and generally pull the wool over the eyes of his sheepish customers.

Barnum's heirs are all around, as are Peters', Tommy's, Jesse's and Steve's. According to *The Economist*, the vast majority of disruptive innovations involve illegal activities of one kind or another, law-breaking that is justified with spurious claims about 'setting information free' or by asserting that 'vested interests' are out to stifle competition.[18] Some have complained that Uber breaks certain regulations that apply to conventional taxi firms; others contend that people letting accommodation on Airbnb are running unlicensed hotels, which don't meet requisite health and safety standards; Prosper, the successful peer-to-peer lending platform, purportedly avoids the financial authority oversight that constrains conventional lenders. SpaceX, Elon Musk confesses, flouted every city ordinance when setting up its first rocket factory. YouTube ignored the laws of copyright in its salad days. Pirate Bay streamed pop songs with impunity until Swedish authorities clamped down on the matelots. IBM's founders were jailed for blatant commercial conspiracy before the brand broke out of office supplies and into big blue computers. Henry Ford and his fellow carmakers had to battle against 'rules of the road' which were designed with the horse and cart in mind.

THE ANTI-BRANDING BACKLASH

Freedom fighters brands may be – or believe themselves to be – but many people regard capitalism as a voracious 'vampire squid'.[19] And with good reason. The consumer fightback began around the turn of the millennium, when campaigning journalist Naomi Klein published a coruscating attack on the misbehaviour of big brands like Nike, Starbucks and McDonald's. Her book, *No Logo*, became the bible of consumer activists worldwide.[20] A spate of anti-capitalist street protests in Seattle, Genoa, Barcelona, Prague, Cancún, Porte Alegre, London and several other cities rapidly descended into rioting. Photographs of activists storming Starbucks, trashing Niketown and dismantling McDonald's were splashed across the world's glossy magazines. Although shocked readers noted that many of the Nike ninjas were wearing Air Max sneakers while they desecrated Mammon's temple, the Rubicon of branding had been crossed.

The 'Battle of Seattle' has since evolved into a war of attrition on corporate malfeasance. From the culture jamming jamboree after the dotcom crash, through the Occupy movement that rose in response to the great banking crisis, via the activities of Uncut and Anonymous, who protest against the tax minimization activities of

Google, Vodafone, Topshop, etc., to the one-man crusade pursued by Reverend Billy (who sings the praises of Buy Nothing Day), the No Logo generation is both brand conscious and brand conscientious. They fight fire with fire, PR with PR.

Although activists' concerns are a legitimate and necessary corrective to warp-speed capitalism, two things must be borne in mind. First, the Nologoistas are brands too. Uncut, Occupy and Reverend Billy employ the tools and techniques of branding to stand out from the crowd of anti-capitalist organizations. The Guy Fawkes masks worn by Anonymous are logos looking right at ya. The slogans they plaster on banners – Capitalism Isn't Working, We Are The 99%, Trade Not Aid – are brand tag-lines by another name. Their astute use of celebrity endorsement, such as Charlotte Church trilling protest songs outside the offices of Shell, are borrowed from the Louis Vuitton playbook. Russell Brand is the Richard Branson of Occupy and Naomi Klein is the Coco Chanel of counter-revolutionary chic. Her heartfelt defence of the brand she created seems a bit rich, especially as it appeared when a new, updated edition of her book was about to be published. You gotta move the merchandise, Naomi. Sell, sell, sell that anti-brand brand of yours!

> The offers for *No Logo* spin-off projects (feature film, TV series, clothing line ...) were rejected. So were the ones from the megabrands and cutting-edge advertising agencies that wanted me to give them seminars on why they were so hated (there was a career to be made, I was learning, in being a kind of anti-corporate dominatrix, making overpaid executives feel good by telling them what bad, brand brands they were).[21]

In fairness to the activists, they have their hearts in the right place. Not so for many consumers, our second caveat. Although more than a few brands get up to disreputable practices in pursuit of market leadership, consumers can be pretty disreputable too. Despite marketing's credo that the customer is king, much consumer behaviour is less than regal. As Mitchell and Chan show, consumers fiddle their taxes, inflate insurance claims, return outfits for full refunds (after wearing them on a night out), do runners from restaurants (when emboldened by drink), say nothing when given too much change at a convenience store (by mistake) and conveniently forget to mention their motor car's mechanical defects (when selling it to a sucker).[22] Consumers drop litter, jaywalk with impunity, exceed the speed limit, ride bicycles on the footpath, keep phones on in the theatre, park in spaces for the differently abled and assume that the rules of good behaviour apply to everyone but themselves.

But you're not like that, are you? No, of course not. You're as law abiding as the day is long. Truthful too. You wouldn't dream of buying something that fell off the back of a lorry. You wouldn't dream of downloading music or movies illegally from the internet, because it deprives the straightened entertainment industry of its revenue streams. You wouldn't dream of buying counterfeit goods – not even on holiday – because you know that fakes damage the brand equity of caring, sharing, customer-orientated corporations like LVMH and provide a front for nefarious criminal gangs in Italy, Russia and South America.[23]

SHADES OF GREY

For those of us who live on Planet Earth, the oft-repeated assertions that big bad brands are exploiting chaste and credulous consumers do not withstand close scrutiny. One is as bad as the other. We get the brands we deserve. Most people try to live their lives in a decent, law-abiding, good-neighbourly manner. Most brands do their best for customers in an honest, transparent, mutually beneficial way. It's in everyone's interest to cooperate, but things can get complicated at times.

Take brand extensions. When a luxury brand allows its logo to be slapped on anything and everything – be it Montblanc perfume, Harley-Davidson deodorant or Hello Kitty boxer shorts[24] – and then charges premium prices for wares that are bog-standard at best or substandard at worst, can we really castigate consumers who choose to buy fakes? The brands, after all, are counterfeiting themselves with their egregious licensing agreements. Big brands who appropriate street fashion for their latest collection, or employ cool hunters to find out what's happenin' in the 'hood, are stealing ideas from consumers then selling them back at ridiculously inflated prices. Crowdsourcing, similarly, is a form of cyber slave labour, since contributors are paid a pittance for their intellectual property. When Burberry sells 'Britishness' (after peremptorily closing its UK factories), then complains bitterly about chavs tarnishing its reputation, is that right and proper? If critical consumers help keep greedy bastard brands in check, so much the better for everyone.[25]

Conversely, consider the curious case of shoplifting. According to the mass media, shoplifting is unconscionable. It's theft pure and simple. It means higher prices for all and sundry, because security measures have to be installed, and store detectives employed, at enormous expense. It's got to be stamped out! Shoplifters will be prosecuted! Flog them, hang them, force them to watch Go Compare commercials until they beg for mercy!

THINK BOX 21

Rebranding Barbarity

In November 2014, the infamous sign on the gates of Dachau concentration camp, *Arbeit Macht Frei*, was stolen. An even more notorious example of the same National Socialist sentiment – *Work Sets You Free* – was purloined from the entrance to Auschwitz concentration camp five years earlier. In both cases, the miscreants were quickly tracked down and prosecuted for their unconscionable hate crimes. For many appalled commentators, the thievery was symptomatic of the rising tide of neo-Nazism, anti-Semitism and right-wing intolerance that is disfiguring Western European society.

(Continued)

(Continued)

It is also, albeit rather less obviously, indicative of the mounting branding problems that face the managers of 'dark tourism' attractions, like Sachsenhausen, Mauthausen and many more.[26] The camps attract millions of visitors every year and tell the story of the Holocaust in a respectful, regretful, reverential manner.

Their customers are changing, however. Those with a direct connection to the awful events have largely passed away and many of their descendants have died out as well. Contemporary visitors, for the most part, have no personal recollection of the original events, or the liberation of the camps, or the appalled societal reaction to the horrors perpetrated some seventy years ago by the National Socialists. For some consumers at least, Auschwitz is just part of the holiday package, a stop-off on their city-break getaway, one among many 'dark tourist' destinations, sites of murder and mayhem that sell illicit thrills.[27]

When the marketplace changes, rebranding comes into its own. Names are changed, logos are tweaked, slogans are scrapped and repositioning takes place. But how do you rebrand a concentration camp without egregiously offending opinionated stakeholders? Any misstep is likely to generate negative headlines worldwide and damage the attraction's carefully curated reputation.

Thinking Outside the Think Box

What would you do in the site manager's shoes? Should you do nothing? What about making incremental changes on the fly? Are you willing to embrace wholesale change, since visitor numbers are sure to rise after the ensuing controversy? Consider the strengths and weaknesses of each course of action.

Now, I am not condoning criminal activity in any way, shape or form (Think Box 21). Nor do I deny that gangs of professional shoplifters, those who steal goods to order, are a major headache for retail brands. However, shoplifting is more complicated than the lock-them-up brigade contends.[28] Apart from the fact that most 'shrinkage' is attributable to brands' own employees and the fact that many shoplifters – such as preteen girls, little old ladies and light-fingered celebrities – are motivated by the thrill of transgression, by the need for attention, by the pressures of fame rather than anything remotely criminal, retailers are partly responsible for the perpetration of kleptomania. Faced with the tantalizing displays, the tempting products, the sybaritic atmospherics, the beguiling advertising campaigns, the persuasive sales assistants, the now-or-never price reductions, the buy-one-get-one-free promotions and the general air of self-indulgent permissiveness – customer-is-king, you-can-have-it-all, because-you're-worth-it – it is hardly surprising that some consumers succumb. The really surprising thing is that shoplifting isn't more prevalent than it is. The retail system is arranged to arouse the avaricious urge. It unleashes the buy-buy-buy beast within. Shoplifting comes with the shopkeeping territory. Marketing means misconduct:

> Consumer misbehaviour is an ineradicable component of consumption culture itself ... Following the strategic doctrine embodied in the 'marketing concept', the marketer genuinely tries to reach out to and to please consumers by such means as alluring displays, proliferation of product choices, easy access to credit, self-service and ceaseless coddling in an open and friendly atmosphere. These practices have become widespread precisely because of their appeal to consumers. At the same time, however, they have also encouraged misbehaviour. Further, these links are continually reinforced by the marketing efforts that encourage the culture of consumption.[29]

To reiterate, I am not endorsing unlawful activity. I'm saying there's more to it than thievery. The rise of the self-service checkout has been accompanied by an increase in shoplifting. But this has been triggered as much by the frustrations of checking out while disembodied voices intone about unexpected items in the bagging area, as it is by consumers' larcenous inclinations. When brand managers pontificate about customer misbehaviour, it's worth remembering that Coco Chanel spied for the Gestapo during the Second World War, that Hugo Boss supplied uniforms to the SS, that KFC's Colonel Sanders was convicted of manslaughter, that Nestlé behaved abominably when selling baby milk in Africa, that Coca-Cola usurped water supplies throughout drought-ridden rural India, that Martha Stewart, America's domestic goddess, was sent to jail for insider trading, that the Enron scandal was perpetrated by alumni of America's premier business school, that Fred the Shred Goodwin, of RBS financial services infamy, was knighted by a grateful British nation, that the Gucci family feud ended up with hit men and assassination attempts, and that J. Bruce Ismay, the managing director of the White Star Line, decided against additional lifeboats for the *Titanic*, because they would spoil the look of the promenade deck.

THE IMAGE/IDENTITY DICHOTOMY

In light of the foregoing, it is tempting to respond with Shakespeare's choice words 'a plague on both your houses'. On the one hand, we have brands that misbehave in the most monstrous ways, while claiming that 'the competition made me do it'.[30] On the other hand, we have conniving and chiselling consumers, who cheat and lie and take liberties with the truth. Then complain long and loud about 'their rights'.

What we're really dealing with here is the classic marketing distinction between identity and image.[31] A brand's identity is what it believes about itself and how it presents that self to the consumer. Image refers to the way in which a brand's identity is perceived by its consumers. Ideally, identity and image align, what you see is what you get. In reality, the two can diverge quite markedly. McDonald's regards itself as friendly, family-orientated and unfailingly fun-filled. Numerous consumers, though, see it as a malign pusher of high-fat junk food that's doing untold damage to our increasingly obese children. Coca-Cola is in the same ambivalent boat. Disney ditto. Nike likewise.

This image/identity dichotomy doesn't only apply to brands. It's equally true of consumers. That is to say, within branding the prevailing image of 'the customer' is that they're the king, the queen, the judge, the jury whose word is law and who must be satisfied, delighted, obeyed. According to the textbooks that is. Yet consumers' true identity – as opposed to the ideology – is rather more complex. They're cantankerous, demanding, unpleasant, untruthful and often get things wrong. Many are more trouble than they're worth. Pandering to their peremptory demands can knock a brand off course. Certain consumers *shouldn't* be given what they want, because it can denude brand equity and lead to the ludicrous licensing agreements that undermine a brand's appeal. Calvin Klein is an infamous case in point. And Calvin's not alone:

> Some companies run out of ideas and are forced to trade in on their brand name, selling T-shirts to pad the bottom line. Others cut corners, slapping their brand on cheaper and cheaper products, selling little more than the name until the equity of the name is compromised. Levi jeans, Elizabeth Arden, Tommy Hilfiger – all have launched low-cost lines at Wal-Mart in recent years. Famous designers like Isaac Mizrahi, Todd Oldham and Oscar de la Renta are producing clothes for Target and Dillard's. Some call this diluting the brand – others prefer 'design slumming'.[32]

Another key thing to consider is that brand misbehaviour comes in a variety of forms, some more unpleasant than others. The degree of darkness varies. Most would agree, for example, that there is a world of difference between the darkness of Halloween – where all manner of brands pile into the demand for scary masks, spooky costumes, crazy candy, fearsome fireworks, prodigious pumpkins and frighteningly fattening party foods[33] – and the deep darkness that inheres in the blood diamonds business or the people trafficking business or the endangered species business or indeed the arms trade, where legacy brands like BAE Systems sell high-tech weaponry to repressive regimes around the world and are rewarded with Queen's Awards to Industry. What, moreover, are we to make of the fact that Tide, P&G's premier brand of detergent, is used as a surrogate currency by crack cocaine dealers in American inner cities?[34]

DARKNESS FALLS

Rather than attempt to encapsulate consumers' concerns, it's better to recognize that a broad spectrum of 'dark branding' exists. The components of this continuum can be difficult to discern, because they merge into one another imperceptibly. It is possible, nevertheless, to identify five gradations of dark branding: *light dark, slight dark, quite dark, night dark* and *fright dark*:

Light Dark

Darkish branding is commonplace in popular culture. The books and movies in the *Harry Potter* franchise, for example, are filled with all sorts of dreek and drear experiences including death, destruction, dementors, dark marks and more. The attendant tie-in merchandise, theme park rides and spin-off stage shows likewise ramp up the wickedness factor, since scary sells well and seriously scary sells even better. Scary sells best, though, when it's sold as being 'too scary for children'. Such warnings encourage the under-aged, as *Harry Potter*'s brand handlers presumably appreciate. Still, it's only a fairy story, a fictional fantasy of sorts, and therefore it's all right. The horrors aren't real. The darkness is light.

The same is true of so-bad-it's-good branding. Think Marmite's I Hate Marmite stance. Think Persil detergent's Dirt is Good campaign. Think of the tongue-in-cheek irreverence of the Amsterdam hostel Hans Brinker, which claims to be The Worst Hotel in the World, nothing less than 'the proudly sagging underbelly of the hotel industry'.[35] Its website is a cyber-catastrophe, full of broken links and obstacles to easy booking. The brochure claims that it's 'close to the best hospitals in Amsterdam'. Its flyers are printed on the 'cheapest paper money can buy'. The atmosphere and ambiance 'helps improve residents' immune systems'. It's advertising campaign comprises before check-in and after check-out photographs of satisfied guests, the former fresh-faced and rosy-cheeked, the latter gaunt, harrowed, dishevelled, unwell. However, as the budget hotel's high occupancy rate attests, light dark is right on the money.

Slight Dark

Slight dark is exemplified by the Black Spot sneakers debacle. As outlined above, the anti-capitalist protest movement that flourished in the aftermath of the Battle in Seattle loudly denounced the iniquity of big brands. A glossy magazine called *Adbusters* was one of the movement's foremost flag-bearers. Each issue parroted, parodied and punctured the expensive advertising campaigns of miscreant global brands. Just Sew It, one ad said, a reference to Nike's sweatshop soiled sneakers. Joe Chemo, another announced, complete with an illustration of Camel cigarette's mascot undergoing treatment for lung cancer. Obsession, a third decried, accompanied by a picture perfect portrait of a muscular young man staring disconsolately into his CK underwear.

Emboldened by the success of this (often brilliant) investigative journalism, *Adbusters* released its own range of 'unbranded' sneakers called Black Spot. However, their black spot looked like any other logo and, as many critics pointed out, *Adbusters'* expensive sneakers were no different from Nike's, except that the lifestyle they sold was radical chic rather than athletic achievement. Although *Adbusters'* intentions were good, they had become what they condemned. As Nietzsche once observed, 'if you stare long enough into the abyss, the abyss stares into you'. Or, in the words of branding guru Sean Adams:

> I remember sitting in a conference watching a presentation by the folks at *Adbusters* when they proposed a Buy Nothing Day – a day where people choose not to buy anything. But if you go to the organisation's website, you can buy T-shirts and *Adbusters* subscriptions. That doesn't sound right to me. They're branding themselves using the very tenets of branding that they disdain.[36]

Quite Dark

Anti-capitalism may have inadvertently overstretched itself with Black Spot, but compared to the dark marketers at the pharmaceutical giant Merck, who enthusiastically sold the Vioxx brand of anti-arthritis medicine despite its known side effects, *Adbusters* is a veritable Mother Teresa.[37] The pharmaceutical sector, which is worth approximately $700 billion per annum, brings enormous health and welfare benefits. The haleness, heartiness, sprightliness and general quality of life enjoyed by those who receive the sector's benefactions are evident.

Equally evidently, Big Pharma is characterized by unethical sales tactics and decidedly dubious marketing strategies. These include inexcusable profiteering, especially among impoverished sufferers in the developing world who can't afford to pay for treatment; shameless astroturfing, where the understandable concerns of, say, breast cancer sufferers are callously co-opted for companies' commercial ends; barefaced hypocrisy, where excessive profits are justified by allegedly enormous R&D costs, even though Big Pharma's marketing spend far exceeds its investment in new product development; calculated committee cozening, where supposedly independent medical regulators are pressurized into (for instance) lowering the official threshold of 'hypertension', thereby vastly increasing the market for ACE inhibitors; sneaky patent prolongation, where highly profitable brands are tweaked slightly or reformulated a tad, which extends their protection and guarantees hefty margins going forward; devious double-detailing, where vast sales forces use every trick in the boiler-room book – such as free gifts a-go-go – to bend physicians to the pharmaceutical industry's will; and, not least, disingenuously identifying debatable medical conditions which they then proceed to cure, often with minor reformulations of existing drugs. Restless Leg Syndrome, Social Anxiety Syndrome and Female Sexual Dysfunction are notable examples of the industry's 'make the ills, sell the pills' mind-set. When all sorts of spurious research, statistical chicanery and data dredging are added to the mix, the quite darkness of the pharmaceutical industry is incontestable.[38]

Night Dark

For all its well-documented faults, Big Pharma's allopathic achievements can reason-ably be regarded as extenuating circumstances, a moral counterbalance to its quite dark marketing practices. The same cannot be said for masters of night dark market-ing, not least the Ku Klux Klan.[39] Although the Klan is nowadays regarded as the last redoubt of reactionaries, rednecks, racists and right-wing buffoons with more preju-dice than sense, it wasn't always thus. On the contrary, the KKK was an enormously powerful and hugely popular organization during the 1920s, when an estimated 15% of the eligible US population were fully paid up members or affiliates. The organi-zation may have commenced as a post-Civil War protest movement in the former confederacy, but the second wave Klan was a nationwide organization, with overseas affiliates in addition. This surge in popularity was largely attributable to rising immi-gration and the anti-outsider sentiments that immigration engendered among White Anglo-Saxon Protestants, who saw their Caucasian culture being diluted by Irish, Italian and Polish Roman Catholics, as well as Ashkenazi Jews from Eastern Europe.

More pertinently perhaps, the Klan's astounding growth during the Jazz Age was due to highly effective marketing practices. These included its nothing if not distinctive branding activities (white livery, striking logo, proprietary salute), its headline-grabbing publicity stunts (burning crosses, torch-lit processions, gigan-tic rallies called klonklaves), its eye-catching advertising campaigns (including the widely circulated poster of an 'heroic' Klansman on a rearing steed), its supremely professional sales force (who perfected multi-level marketing long before the Avon lady), its canny exploitation of the value chain (robes and regalia were manufactured in-house and sold at huge mark-ups), its absolute commitment to corporate social responsibility (charitable works for the local community, including generous dona-tions during church services) and, above all, its brand savvy leadership.[40] Most of the organization's managerial cadre, not least the Imperial Wizard Colonel 'Doc' Simmons (a lapsed lingerie salesman), were converts to cutting-edge marketing methods and kept up with the latest branding thinking. All things considered, the then unstoppa-ble rise of the KKK is less ludicrous than it seems in retrospect. The picture presented in the Coen Brothers' movie *O Brother Where Art Thou?* (Klan as standing joke) is hard to reconcile with the organization that proudly paraded down Pennsylvania Avenue in 1925 and numbered American presidents among its membership.[41]

Fright Dark

Most neutral observers would agree that, notwithstanding its branding acuity, the Klan is an affront to civilization. But at least it's ancient history. The same can't be said for some of the heinous things that go on beneath the placid waters of everyday e-commerce, as well as high street shopping for certain family-friendly, fast-moving food brands.

Reflect, for example, on the dirty denizens of the dark net, such as Silk Road dotcom. Aptly described as 'a parallel universe, a universe where eBay had been taken over by international drug cartels and Amazon offers a choice of books, DVDs and hallucinogens', Silk Road sells every illegal substance known to humankind.[42] Its categories include cannabis, dissociatives, ecstasy, opioids, prescription, psychedelics, stimulants and precursors. It comes complete with star ratings from satisfied customers, detailed reviews of the merchandise and, presumably, there's a click farm somewhere faking good reviews of the platform's bad-to-the-bone brands. The Walter White of the operation, who at least deserves some credit for Silk Road's fantastic brand name, is called Dread Pirate Roberts. Or he was when the FBI shut down his operation in November 2013 and arrested the brand's founder, a Texan physics graduate called Ross Ulbricht.[43]

Worse still, if only because of its ubiquity, is the barefaced scandal surrounding Italian olive oil. Olive oil is something most of us give little or no thought to as we fill our trolleys on a Friday night or Saturday afternoon. Yet, according to Mueller's disturbing exposé, all sorts of adulteration, decontamination and deodorization – not to mention scrubbing, flavouring and colouring – goes on in order to turn seed oil, rape oil, palm oil, hazelnut oil, vegetable oil and oil chemically extracted from the stones, skins and twigs of olives' solid waste into 'extra virgin' olive oil.[44] Much of this is a pale imitation of the real thing and some of it, allegedly, is unfit for consumption. The profits in olive oil crime are comparable to cocaine trafficking, with none of the risks. The Bertolli brand in Renton's view – and his alone, your honour – 'provides a good tour of the rottenness of the trade'. As he recounts in *The Observer*:

> The Bertollis were bankers and traders who never actually owned an olive tree, despite the bucolic Tuscan scenes depicted on their labels. They got rich on the back of an incomprehensible twist in European law that, until 2001, allowed any olive oil bottled in Italy to be sold as an Italian olive oil, which, absurdly, is what we all pay most for. In fact, even now 80% of the oil Bertolli uses comes from Spain, North Africa and the Middle East. It is still flogged in bottles with 'Lucca' and 'Passione Italiana' on the label. Today, Italy still sells three times as much oil as it produces.[45]

And it's not just olive oil:

> Four 'Italian' products in ten are actually foreign imports relabelled as Italian, often with false certificates of authenticity: over a third of pasta manufactured in Italy is made from imported wheat, half of mozzarella is produced with German milk and curds, and two-thirds of prosciutto comes from foreign hogs.[46]

HEART OF DARKNESS

While you're waiting to tuck into tasty tagliatelle in your nearest family-owned Italian restaurant, it's worth reflecting on the fundamental issue here. Whatever you may think of Bertolli or Silk Road or the Klan or *Adbusters* or BAE Systems, the fact of the matter is that they're outstanding brands. Judged in terms of their performance – rather than with regard to their morality – they can't be faulted. Harry Potter remains one of the biggest cultural brands in the world. Big Pharma is so profitable it's painful. Silk Road was described by one e-commerce authority as 'exceptional' (provided you ignore the products it sells). The Klan was a genuinely popular, grass-roots movement that employed best marketing practices to build its (undeniably prodigious) brand community.

Branding is hoisted by its own petard. Would it were otherwise but branding is blighted. When everything is regarded as a brand – just about – then branding principles must pertain to some pretty unpleasant things. If Beyoncé, Usain Bolt and Barack Obama are brands, according to today's anything goes attitude, why not Al Capone, Ted Bundy and Pol Pot? Why not well-known criminal gangs or terrorist organizations?

Although it may be excessive to suggest that branding's bounding success is turning it into a hellhound, there's no doubt that some brands are on the slippery slope. Just as Walter White, *Breaking Bad*'s brilliant anti-hero, slips from Mr Chips to Scarface, so too certain brands with the very best intentions become ever more monstrous through time. Take Google, aka Alphabet. When Larry Page and Sergey Brin set out to master the world wide web and make everyone's online life easier, they not only gave us their invaluable search engine *for free*, but made it available with one express intention: to turn the world into a better place. Fifteen years after the adoption of their admirable company motto, 'Don't be Evil', the organization is routinely described as Googzilla, the Evil Empire or worse. It has swallowed YouTube, devoured DoubleClick, hoovered up the contents of innumerable newspapers, magazines and public libraries – with nary a thought for intellectual property rights – and eaten large chunks of the advertising industry's lunch, thanks to AdWords, AdSense and analogous wiki-widgets. Thanks, moreover, to the runaway success of its Android operating system, Google has ingested a sizeable slice of the smartphone market. Google may not be Big Brother 2.0, as some privacy-preoccupied critics contend, but it has a reasonable claim to be the world's biggest Cookie Monster.[47]

For many concerned citizens, the goofy, geeky, free-gift grin that Google presents to the world – a wider world which loves and admires the organization, by and large – is an anti-corporate mask behind which lurks a dead-eyed, black-hearted beast, with a voracious appetite and venom-filled fangs. When Microsoft is accusing someone of monopolistic practices, News International is up in arms about IP pilfering, and Apple is angry over breaches of good faith, then it's clear that the genuinely noble aspirations of Google's founders have been torn asunder by the exigencies of tooth and nail competition and the insatiable demands of Wall Street, venture capital and media commentary on corporate performance. The degree of Google's darkness is moot, admittedly. But even its greatest admirers might concede that it's a couple of shades darker than when it started.

DARKNESS AT THE EDGE OF NIKETOWN

Contemporary branding, to summarize, is in an ontological quandary. On the one hand, the broadened branding concept – the basic idea that everything is a brand nowadays – can't exclude the Saddam Husseins, Sons of Sam and Gary Gilmores of this world (the latter, FYI, inspired Nike's Just Do It slogan). On the other hand, any attempt to assert that, say, brand KKK is admirable in its own terms is a step too far for most people. 'Admirable?' many might retort. 'Tell that to the innocent victims of Klan-instigated violence! Tell that to the lynched, the tortured, the raped, the intimidated, the run out of town, the firebombed, or indeed the students of the University of Notre Dame, who defended their institution against a full-scale Ku Klux Klan invasion in May 1924.' Such misbegotten actions presumably enhanced the Klan's image within its 'brand community'. But who among us is going to single it out for praise?

It would be a brave academic indeed who went to bat for the Klan. But the logic of the branding concept, as currently constituted, leaves no alternative. Perhaps it's time to distinguish between good bad brands (akin to the Klan or Silk Road) and bad good brands (à la New Coke or the Edsel). That's what literary critics do when they note the difference between good bad books like *Dracula* and *Fifty Shades of Grey* and bad good books like *Finnegans Wake* and *The Magus*.[48]

Or perhaps we should just face up to the fact that, when it comes to branding, we are never far away from what the great British poet John Milton called 'darkness visible'.[49] Although he was referring to Satan's noisome lair – in *Paradise Lost* – he could have been writing about branding. We can learn a lot from creative writers and artists.

BRAND TASK

In December 2014, Premier Foods was taken to task. The Bisto to Oxo branding powerhouse was accused of blackmailing suppliers. It had asked them for an 'investment payment' to support the conglomerate's future growth. However, this was spun by bad-news-sells-well newspapers into a tawdry tale of bully-boy tactics. Given that supermarkets demand slotting allowances and bookshops expect publishers to pay for in-store displays, what's so awful about Premier?

RECOMMENDED READINGS

Stephen Brown, Pierre McDonagh and Clifford Shultz, 'Dark Marketing: Skeleton in the Cupboard or Ghost in the Machine?', *European Business Review*, 24 (3), 2012, 196–215. Provides a reasonable overview of the topic, if I say so myself. More pertinently, it's a fairly succinct summary, which is a bit of a boon in an area where commentators pontificate at inordinate length.

Naomi Klein, *No Logo* (Picador: New York, 2000). A classic. You must read this. Although it's a root and branch critique of branding, it also serves as an excellent, if unbalanced, introduction to the subject. As a future brand manager, you may not like what she says, but she says it very eloquently.

Ben Goldacre, *Bad Pharma: How Drug Companies Mislead Doctors and Harm Patients* (Fourth Estate: London, 2012). Be afraid. Be very afraid. Seriously. This book is scarier than Stephen King at his most gruesome.

Ben Paynter, 'Suds for Drugs', *New York Magazine*, January 6, 2013, www.nymag.com. At first I thought this was a hoax. Then I surmised it was a superlative spoof. I finally concluded that it is simply amazing. See what you think. It's available as a free download.

CHAPTER 11
POP GOES THE BRAND

Overview

Branding is the bane of art. The b-word is a swearword. Or so the story goes. The old idea that authentic artists care naught for monetary matters no longer holds true. Some of the most creative branding achievements are found in the cultural sector. This creativity is attributable to the tension that still exists between the demands of commerce and the dreams of culture. The dreams, demands and determinants of cultural branding are considered below.

ROLLING IN THE DOSH

A couple of years ago, Adele was interviewed by *Vogue*. The mega-successful pop star – 30 million albums sold and counting – was asked about the Adele brand.[1] Affronted by the insinuation that she was somehow packaged or promoted, rather than an authentic artiste, Adele retorted, 'I am not going to act, not going to release an autobiography, not going to release a perfume, not going to design a range of clothes. I don't want to be a brand!'

Adele isn't the only artist to feel that way.[2] Jason Statham, the go-to tough-guy in many popcorn blockbuster movies – anything, basically, featuring fast cars, heavy weapons, kick-ass action and brain-dead dialogue – is equally adamant he isn't a brand.[3] When asked, in *Details* magazine, whether he viewed himself as a brand, he politely replied, 'Fuck no, why should I?' Equally politely, he added that he couldn't understand why people kept describing him as a brand. 'Fuck 'em,' he said, in keeping with his USP as Hollywood's hard man of the moment, 'I'm not a brand. Kim Kardashian's a fucking brand.'

Duffy no doubt shares Statham's scepticism. Because her brush with branding destroyed a promising career. When the blue-eyed soul sensation – and the first Welsh singer to top the charts since Bonnie Tyler – was approached by Diet Coke, she jumped at the opportunity. Who wouldn't want their career turbo-charged by a blockbuster brand? Unfortunately, the subsequent advertisement, which featured Duffy bicycling through a supermarket warbling *I Gotta Be Me*, was ridiculed by all and sundry. She was further mocked for her failure to wear protective headgear while pedalling down the beverage aisle. Accused of selling out, Duffy quickly disappeared into obscurity, her artistic credibility in shreds.

Unwarranted as it was, Duffy's total eclipse of the brand illustrates the antagonism that many artists feel toward branding and big business more generally. As the *Financial Times* famously conceded:

> In plenty of movies business is the bad guy; those featuring corporate heroes are far fewer. Even when the hero is in business, the film generally has an ambivalent attitude towards corporate life, since the villain often works there too … Negative portrayals of corporations and executives may stem from film makers' resentment of business curbs on their creativity. However, films are also aimed at mass audiences who instinctively think of businesspeople as rich and alien and nasty.[4]

To be sure, artists' hatred of The Man – the ad man in particular – goes back a long way. In the early 1980s, the acerbic stand-up comedian Bill Hicks had a much-admired routine where he urged marketers and advertisers to kill themselves: 'There is no excuse for what you do. You are Satan's little helpers. You are Satan's scum filling the world with bile and garbage. Kill yourselves.' Twenty years before that, The Doors' legendary lead singer Jim Morrison took a baseball bat to a Buick on stage because the car company used one of his songs in a commercial. Twenty years before that, Salvador Dalí smashed the plate glass windows of Bonwit Teller, a prestigious New York department store, after they'd rearranged one of his surrealist art installations without consultation.[5] How dare they? The philistines!

REBEL REBEL

This idea of the artist as rebel, as irreverent outsider, as a thorn in the side of the merchant classes, dates back to the Romantic movement of the mid-19th century.[6] That's when the notion of the 'starving artist in a garret' first emerged. Proper artists – artists with integrity, credibility, convictions – were prepared to live a life of poverty rather than compromise their principles by selling out. Their rallying cry was 'Art for art's sake'. Their ambition was to shock, subvert and scandalize the bourgeoisie.[7] It's an avant-garde ethos than runs all the way from the French Impressionists, past the writings of James Joyce and William Burroughs, through the punk rock explosion of the 1970s to the latter-day arrest of the Russian dissident rockers Pussy Riot by Vladimir Putin.

Raging against the machine sells records, luckily. The Sex Pistols were put together by a marketing mastermind, Malcolm McLaren, who also ran a retail store called Sex on the King's Road. The banning of James Joyce's racy novels was the making of them, more so arguably than the reading of them. The French Impressionists didn't do too badly out of their initial notoriety, nor did 'Avida Dollars' himself, Salvador Dalí.[8] As noted in chapter 6, sex sells, shock sells and shocking sex sells best of all. If further proof is needed, consider the *Fifty Shades of Grey* phenomenon:

> It has sold 65 million copies thus far. It has been translated into 37 languages and counting. It has spawned two equally successful sequels, *Fifty Shades Darker* and *Fifty Shades Freed*. It has stimulated a saturnalia of copy-cats, rip-offs and orgiastic parodies, such as the bestselling *Fifty Sheds of Grey* for frolicsome gardeners with tumescent tubers. It has given rise to all sorts of tie-in merchandise: music, apparel, jewellery, scents, sex toys, bed linen, package tours to the Heathman Hotel in Seattle, where most of the whip-cracking love action takes place and, presumably, a natty line in handcuffs, shackles, bondage gear-cum-butt plugs, *et cetera*. The only thing that's missing is a co-marketing arrangement with a leading brand of condiments. Fifty Shades of Grey Poupon definitely has a ring to it.[9]

For all the talk of artistic credibility, the 'clash' of culture and commerce is similar in certain respects to the battle between Coke and Pepsi or Adidas and Nike. It helps move the merchandise. Many might say there is something deeply cynical about artists who engineer outrage in order to sell stuff. But those who feel that way are living in a neo-Romantic dream world. The reality is that the rebel sell sells just as well as the docile sell that dominates marketers' customer-serving ideology. Badness sells better, in fact.[10] And anti-business badness better still. Just ask Naomi Klein. Or Russell Brand. Or *Adbusters*.

The Duffy debacle notwithstanding, some latter-day artists prefer to embrace the branding machine rather than rage against it. Victoria Beckham, former Spice Girl and current fashion designer, once stated that 'Right from the beginning, I wanted to be more famous than Persil Automatic.' When Cheryl Fernandez-Versini Cole, ex-Girl Aloud and *X Factor* judge, was appointed as a spokesperson for L'Oréal, she announced, 'I've always loved the brand and have always wanted to say the iconic phrase Because You're Worth It.' She might have been lip-synching, mind you. Def Leppard, the ageing hair-metal rock band that's still filling American enormodomes, recently explained their artistic vision: 'Sometimes you just gotta let it happen. But the other side of the equation is that the band is successful for a certain sound. It's a brand, like Coca-Cola, and you've got to give the people what they want.'[11]

For all Adele's huffing and puffing – and Statham's strutting and swearing – it's evident that ever more artists have accepted the fact that culture and commerce are joined at the hip.[12] For every graffiti artist like Banksy, who makes mock of the exploitative theme park industry with Dismaland, there's a celebrity baker akin to Paul Hollywood who rolls in the dough sold by Mr Kipling. For every scurrilous sculptor like Tom Sachs, whose *Prada Toilet* repurposes the luxury label's packaging to excremental effect, there's a superflat fine artist akin to Takashi Murakami who is more than happy to collaborate with Louis Vuitton. So much so, Japan's prodigal son recently confessed the following to the *Financial Times*: 'the theme my generation explored was the relationship between capitalism and art'. In Murakami's case at least, capitalism remains the dominant partner.[13]

THE ANTI-ANTI-BUSINESS BUSINESS

Nowhere is this transformation from selling out to selling output more apparent than in the telling change of terminology. These days, the sector is routinely referred to as 'the cultural industries', with an emphasis on industry. It is a business – a very big business – a crucially important element of the economy.[14] It is a sector where dying young is seen as an astute career move instead of a heartfelt cry for help by an anguished, unknown genius.

According to official government figures, the UK cultural industries are worth approximately £60 billion per annum. They employ 2.5 million people – 8% of the working population – in some 200,000 individual businesses. In Ireland, where the cultural sector is a crucial part of national brand identity, and where bona fide artists are given attractive tax breaks to live and work in the country, the proportions are considerably higher. In terms of direct employment, the arts are bigger than agriculture. When spin-offs are included, the significance of the sector is even more apparent. In addition to ancillary employment (roadies, security guards, box office attendants, etc.), the arts can act as vehicles for urban regeneration (the Tate Gallery in Liverpool's docklands, Hull's 'City of Culture' designation), and attract high net-worth tourists to town (consider the 2012 Olympics' impact on East London or the recently opened Turner Contemporary Gallery in Margate).

Cultural attractions are vast revenue generators in their own right, what's more. So much so, many leading museums operate chains of stand-alone retail stores in shopping malls and airports (the Metropolitan Museum of Art has twenty outlier outlets, for example). There's an intangible benefit too, insofar as culturally active hotspots are considered attractive places to live. Richard Florida, an American spatial scientist, has studied the residential choices of the creative classes and contends that they prefer to locate in cities that are culturally 'vibrant' (and tolerant of alternative lifestyles).[15] Given that such people are effectively footloose, where they choose to live and work has significant economic consequences. Prominent place brands like Barcelona, Berlin, Edinburgh, Sydney and San Francisco owe much of their global appeal to their cultural infrastructure. Tiny place brands like Austin (Texas), Park City (Utah), Bayreuth (Bavaria) and Wigtown (Dumfries) have been put on the map by their association with the SxSW music festival, the Sundance film festival, the Wagner opera festival and the Wigtown book festival respectively.

But what is meant by 'the cultural industries'? According to the official government definition, they comprise advertising, architecture, antiques, crafts, design, fashion, film, software, music, publishing and television/radio. There is one striking omission, though. sport. A prodigiously important part of popular culture, sports branding is a specialist subject in itself.[16] Suffice it to say that sports teams, and individual sports stars, rank among the most powerful brands on the planet. As Lewis Hamilton, the superstar racing driver, conceded a couple of years ago: 'My image, my name is a brand ... I am a brand ... I would like someone to help me grow as a brand.' You can send your CV to Brands Hatch, presumably.

GOLDEN BALLS

Lewis's loyalties, clearly, lie less with Brand Mercedes than Brand Hamilton. However, if he's looking for guidance, he could do worse than model himself on David Beckham.[17] For someone who, in the churlish words of George Best, 'can't dribble, can't tackle, can't head the ball and has no left foot', David Beckham parlayed his purportedly limited footballing skills into a globally admired sports brand. In addition to his advertisement/endorsement/sponsorship work for numerous blue-chip brands like Adidas, Gillette, Pepsi, Armani, Belstaff, Breitling, *Sky Sports* and H&M, he has released his own brand of personal care products and fragrances. The brand name 'Beckham' has been registered in eight different categories, as have 'Becks' and 'Golden Balls'. His tireless work on behalf of several charities including UNICEF is a model of corporate social responsibility. Such is the power of Beck's personal brand that when he joined America's MLS, average attendances rose 7%, replica shirt sales soared and television ratings took off too, especially among fourteen- to eighteen-year-olds, an attractive demographic for advertisers. It is estimated that Brand Beckham is worth approximately $75 million per annum, a figure that includes Victoria's vaunted fashion business. And while this is small beer beside Floyd Mayweather, who boxed his way to $300 million in 2015, it is far from trivial. Whatever his alleged limitations as a sportsman – or an actor, come to think of it – Beckham's marketing limitations are nil.[18]

If golden balls, the crown prince of Beckingham Palace, epitomizes the contemporary face of cultural branding, the old idea that commerce is crass hasn't gone away completely. Eminem, for instance, once stated that he knows little and cares less about the business side of the music business, even though he's named after a leading brand of chocolate confectionery. Banksy has built his graffiti-art brand by cocking a snook at the art world's egregious money-grubbing, just like Warhol, Haring, Basquiat and other art brand iconoclasts before him. AC/DC are as iconic a rock brand as it is possible to be. They are blessed with a unique sound, brilliant name, great logo, consistent look, reliable offer, fanatical consumers, fantastic mascot (the pneumatic Rosie), narratives aplenty (the post-Bon Scott comeback) and countless catchphrases (For Those About to Rock, We're On a Highway to Hell). But if you were to accuse Angus Young of being a brand, he'd probably take off his school blazer and punch you in the kneecap.[19]

Cultural branding, clearly, is somewhat paradoxical. On the one hand, more than a few creative types are careful to avoid the taint of commerce, the curse of selling out. On the other hand, much of today's most astute marketing is found in the creative industries.[20] Damien Hirst, the middle-aged superstar of the Young British Artist movement, is a master self-publicist (consider his shocking sculptures of dead sharks and disemboweled sheep), a master brand builder (consider his signature spot art, spin art and butterfly art), a master retailer (consider his invention of 'pop up' galleries in abandoned East London warehouses), a master sales manager (consider his DIY art auction in 2008, which cut out the middleman and generated world record prices on the very day that Wall Street imploded) and a master all-round businessman who not only designs bespoke brandy bottles and runs a restaurant, Pharmacy 2, but his work directly addresses the luxury brand obsessions of contemporary consumer society (see his £50 million diamond-encrusted skull, *For the Love of God*). It comes as no surprise to discover that Hirst is the son of a used car dealer and his mother owned a florist's shop.[21] However, his views on the customer remain wedded to the avant-garde ethos that artists with 'credibility' espouse:

> Fuck the customer. If you make great fucking art, fuck them. Fuck what they want. They'll buy what you fucking give them. If you're great, they'll buy it. If you're making great art, you don't have to think about the punters.[22]

Whatever way you look at it, cultural branding is riven with contradiction. These contradictions, though, aren't necessarily a bad thing. On the contrary, the power of cultural branding stems from its inbuilt tensions. Whereas, say, the branding of food and grocery products has become fairly standardized, with comparatively little scope for originality, that's not the case in the cultural realm, where creative conflict is the crucible of inspiration, innovation, imagination. According to Alex Shakar, who wrote a superb novel set in a market research agency, every successful brand has a paradoxical essence, a schismatic core where conflicting consumer desires coincide. Ice cream combines eroticism and innocence (Häagen-Dazs). Coffee offers stimulation and relaxation (Nescafé). Theme parks combine fear and reassurance (Alton Towers). Sneaker brands are in touch with the ground yet let their wearers soar free (Nike Jordan).[23]

FOREGROUNDING PERSPECTIVES

But that is by the by. When a helicopter view is taken of cultural branding, it's clear that there are four main schools of thought on the often fraught relationship between culture and commerce. The first of these is the *parasitic perspective*. This is the old idea that naïve artists, who are more interested in fame than in fortune, are systematically exploited by the cigar-chomping, double-dealing fat cat agents/executives/managers of legend. The music industry is especially notorious for its star makers and Svengalis, who make the brands and take the bucks.[24]

Perhaps the best example of the parasitic perspective is the hugely successful *X Factor* brand. Owned and controlled by Simon Cowell through his production company Syco, *X Factor* is one of the top-rated television programmes in the UK averaging 9 million viewers during its annual ten-week run.[25] The format has been sold to 51 different territories, including Australia, Angola, Argentina and Azerbaijan, as well as Nigeria, Iceland and the United States, where it famously failed to dislodge *American Idol* from the top of the talent show charts. Despite its US cancellation, the brand remains a licence to print money. It delivers sizeable audiences for television networks, which then sell the eyeballs to eager advertisers. The winners of the series are signed to Cowell's record label and their releases usually shoot to the top of the Christmas charts. Additional revenue streams include a hefty slice from the telephone voting pie, copious sponsorship deals, episode-by-episode music downloads, post-series ensemble arena tours and all sorts of tie-in merchandise from karaoke machines and glossy magazines to calendars and DVDs.

For many 'proper' artists – pop stars with credibility – Simon Cowell is Satan made flesh. 'He should be melted down and turned into glue', according to Coldplay. 'He has no recognisable talent, apart from self-promotion', says Sting. 'He is just cruel and that's all there is to it', Phil Collins observes. His devil child show, Sir Elton John hissed in 2010, 'is arse-paralysingly brain crippling'.[26] In reality, Old Nick Cowell is a showbiz shaman of sorts. As a group of star-struck scholars points out:

> Shaman Cowell has tapped into an inexhaustible public appetite for liminal ritual – and he markets it as an entertainment spectacle. In his iconic role as TV talent show judge, Cowell magisterially orchestrates the liminal rites of passage of countless hapless neophytes. His well-rehearsed one-liners carry the sacred authority of the jester, faultlessly expressing the collective need for moral judgments, and he serves as a shamanistic intermediary between the mundane world of dead-end jobs and the sacred space of superstardom ... He controls, patrols and provides safe passage across the seemingly impassable space between nonentity and celebrity, between penury and plenty, between karaoke and capitalism. Cowell judges and disciplines the participants but he also oversees their welfare in a paternalistic stance (which, coincidentally, also protects his investment).[27]

FIRESTARTER

No doubt many wannabe artists have their heads in the clouds and are thus soft touches for hard-headed businesspeople. Not all of them, however. Some, like the legendary rock band Kiss, are to the marketing manor born.[28] With sales of 100 million albums, the band is no slouch when it comes to music making. However, their sales owe much more to the POW factor of the Kiss brand – cartoon hard rockers in stack heels, elaborate costumes and grotesquely painted faces – than they do to power chords. Gene Simmons, the band's would-be Barnum, pretty much invented the band-brand business model as we now know it. More than 3,000 separate lines of trademarked memorabilia are available, including co-branding deals with Coca-Cola and Hello Kitty. These range from Kiss credit cards and Kiss Halloween costumes to Kiss condoms and Kiss coffins. 'We get you coming, then we get you going', Simmons smirks. Never tongue-tied about tie-in merchandise, Simmons also sells consultancy services to would-be rock brands and has written a bestselling brand management handbook, *Me, Inc.* Just like Damien Hirst, though, Simmons bristles at being called a sell-out. 'I sell out every night', he snaps.[29]

Kiss, then, typify the second school of cultural branding: the *Prodigy Perspective*. This posits that, far from presuming artists are exploited or royally ripped off by The Man, many creatives are canny businesspeople. Not only do they know what's what when it comes to branding, but some have more marketing flair than many MBA-garlanded brand managers (Think Box 22).

THINK BOX 22

Along Came an Ad Man

One of the areas where the prodigy perspective is particularly prevalent is publishing. Literature has traditionally been regarded as an elitist, otherworldly, art-for-art's-sake domain. Closer inspection reveals otherwise. Some of the savviest brand builders – let's call them authorpreneurs – are found in the books business. Charles Dickens, Mark Twain, Oscar Wilde and Agatha Christie, to name but a few, were brilliant self-publicists. A surprising number of literary high-fliers, what's more, worked in marketing or advertising before they became brand name authors. Tom Clancy, Elmore Leonard, Haruki Murakami, Roald Dahl, Dr. Seuss, Fay Weldon, Peter Carey, Salman Rushdie, Dorothy L. Sayers and F. Scott Fitzgerald, for starters.

Of all the authors with an upbringing in advertising, none has exploited his training better than the mega-selling thriller writer James L. Patterson. The youngest ever CEO of JWT, a blue-chip advertising agency, Patterson rose to stardom on the back of the Burger King account and coined at least one knock-em-dead slogan: I'm a Toys R Us Kid. To get away from the pressures of the job, he started writing novels in his spare time. Patterson's first work of fiction, *The Thomas Berryman Number*, was rejected by 26 publishers in the time-honoured manner but it went on several prestigious awards, if not mainstream acclaim. However, when he finally hit the big time with *Along Came a Spider*, the first Alex Cross police procedural, he did so on his own terms. Unhappy with his publisher's meagre marketing efforts, Patterson paid for a replacement front cover, self-funded a television advertising campaign and generally used his advertising acumen to flog his literary whopper. *Spider* became an instant bestseller and having established his fast-fiction franchise – very short chapters, non-stop action, all thriller no filler – he cranked them out in a manner that owes more to Dunkin' Donuts than Doubleday.

More impressive still is Patterson's hands-on management of his brand. Like most well-managed products, Patterson's novels come in clearly defined ranges – the *Women's Murder Club* series, the *Maximum Ride* series, the *Michael Bennett* series – and the production is outsourced to teams of co-authors, who do much of the grunt work. Unlike Dan Brown or Jo Nesbø or J.K. Rowling, who write a book every two years or so, the Patterson production plant delivers five or six blockbusters per annum. Movie and TV adaptation opportunities are also pursued enthusiastically, as are product placements, all of which combine to make Patterson the top-earning author in the world today. One-hundred-and-twenty-five bestsellers have been published thus far with worldwide sales of $80–100 million p.a. Nice work if you can get it.[30]

Thinking Outside the Think Box

Track down a copy of Philip Kerr's tongue-in-cheek novel, *Research*. It's a thriller about a bestselling author of thrillers who employs a team of nonentities to research and write the books, while he manages the brand. Is the novel good or bad publicity for Patterson? Is it proof of the old adage, attributed to Bob Dylan, that art is truer than the truth?

In this regard, it is noteworthy that the most creative responses to the recent crisis in the music industry have come from the musicians themselves rather than record labels. Radiohead, for instance, have released their last few albums in strikingly original ways, including an online honesty box where people paid what they considered appropriate. Trent Reznor, the brains behind Nine Inch Nails, sold his *Year Zero* album with the aid of an addictively interactive computer game. Moby, the pioneer of electronica, made waves by licensing every track on his *Play* album to advertising agencies, which did wonders for his profile. Daft Punk's mega-selling *Random Access Memories* was released with the aid of a brilliantly-orchestrated teaser campaign. Ditto David Bowie's *The New Day* and his pre-posthumous *Blackstar*. After the great man's passing, Bowie's former manager acknowledged that he was 'a so-so singer but a commercial genius'.[31]

Twenty years ago, such a statement would have been greeted with howls of protest. Today, it's fair to say, most artists have come to their senses about selling. They realize that the real money – the only money, in fact – is made on the concert circuit where revenue streams run deep. Katy Perry, Rihanna, J-Lo and Co. deliver blockbuster live shows which double as shop fronts/window displays for all sorts of high-margin ancillaries, not least the clothing ranges and eau de colognes that Adele allegedly abhors. Taylor Swift, no slouch she, has three different fragrances to her name. One Direction's tide of tie-in merchandise necessitated an entire store, 1D World, at the Mall of America. Daft Punk, meantime, made do with Get Lucky condoms, though at least they had the taste not to call them Random Access Members.

Lady Gaga, likewise, may not be the most gifted musician in the world – she trained as a dancer – but the power of her publicity machine is unsurpassed. As an art student, she did her dissertation on the brand that is Damien Hirst. The meat dress, let's be honest, had more than a whiff of Hirst about it. It also had a modicum of Madonna about it.

Indeed, if any musician exemplifies pitch perfect brand ambition that musician is Madonna.[32] Occasionally belittled because she, like Lady Gaga, began as a dancer rather than as a musician, Madonna Louise Ciccone has built one of the longest lasting brands in show business. She has sold 150 million albums, more than The Beatles and Elvis Presley. Her personal fortune is estimated at $650 million. Her tours are the highest grossing, pro rata, on the planet. She has her own lines of clothing-cum-beauty products, Truth or Dare and Material Girl. She runs a chain of fitness centres called Hard Candy. She has published several children's books, most notably the *English Roses* series. She was one of the first to come to terms with the music industry's need for a new business model (the ten-year, 360-degree contract with Live Nation). She is intimately involved with Tidal, the musician-driven streaming service designed to disrupt Spotify and Apple Music. She is a master of the headline-grabbing publicity stunt (kissing Britney at the MTV awards is one among many); she seizes opportunities to showcase her brand in front of huge global audiences (from Live 8 to the Super Bowl); she has an eye for strategic alliances (with Pepsi, Gap, H&M, Smirnoff, Jean-Paul Gaultier); she uses her concerts as a surrogate catwalk for sponsoring brands (the *Rebel Heart* tour of 2015/2016 features creations by Moschino and Alexander Wang among others); and she uses every trick in the book to keep her name at the forefront of public consciousness (such as the gold-plated dental brace, which she wears to 'piss everybody off'[33]). She is even a master of corporate social responsibility, through her charity work in Malawi (albeit the benefits to her brand likely far exceed those to African indigents).

POLARITY DANCING

Madonna may be the ice queen of pop, but when she started out back in the 1980s she was dismissed as a no-hoper, a talentless, lip-syncing, one hit wonder. Her lowly status back then testifies to the *polarity perspective* on cultural branding. Ever since the Romantics, a distinction has been made between high (elite) culture and low (popular) culture. The former is epitomized by opera and classical music (especially the heavies like Wagner, Mahler, Schoenberg, Bruckner), modernist literature and poetry (James, Joyce, Faulkner, Eliot), experimental theatre, abstract art, modern dance and cinematic auteurs (Brecht, Malevich, Rambert, Bergman). The latter consists of vulgar schlock targeted at the lowest common denominator: pop music, pulp fiction, reality TV, blockbuster movies, ballroom dancing, computer games. The list goes on and on. High art, allegedly, is challenging, profound and life enhancing; low art is simplistic, superficial and, if not quite spiritually degrading, an effective means of controlling the bovine proletariat. In other words, whereas a bestselling author like Marian Keyes or Stephen King is a 'brand', cranking out formulaic, cookie-cutter fast fiction, Jonathan Franzen or Joan Didion is an 'artist', a transcendent genius who cares not a jot for the bestseller list in his/her cosmic struggle to solve the riddle of human existence.[34]

Compare the K twins, Kinkade and Koons. The late lamented Thomas Kinkade was – and remains – the top-earning artist in the world. His kitsch paintings of twee landscapes with thatched cottages in bucolic settings are sold through retail stores in shopping malls across America. The unctuous images are made available at a variety of price points from cheap posters to hand-painted originals. They are reproduced, thanks to lucrative licensing deals, on coffee mugs, fridge magnets, key rings and T-shirts. Known as the 'Painter of Light', with accompanying streetlamp logo, Kinkade sells themed household goods, ranges of furniture and entire property developments. Until his recent untimely death – good career move, remember – he also had a profitable side-line in self-help books and wellbeing seminars.[35]

The Kinkade corporation, needless to say, is loathed by the artistic establishment. Jeff Koons, by contrast, is the darling of the art world, attracting the highest prices at auction of any living artist. His signature balloon dog sculptures – elephantine versions of the children's party standby in stainless steel, which sell for $60 million apiece – are on display in the world's preeminent art galleries and modern art museums. *Puppy*, his 43 ft tall topiary installation, guards the entrance to Bilbao's iconic Guggenheim museum. Koons, unlike dead and buried Kinkade, is a 'proper' artist. His corpus of kitsch collectables, advertising hoardings, submerged basketballs and multi-coloured vacuum cleaners is an ironic commentary on today's wretchedly commodified culture.

An unprejudiced viewer of their respective oeuvres, however, would find very little difference between them. Kinkade's work is cheesy, but so too is Koons'. The former was an astute marketing man but so is the latter. They are both brilliant marketers and smart self-publicizing businessmen (Koons was a Wall Street broker before becoming an artist). They are a matched pair of cultural brands. Kinkade's corporation is the Primark of the art world, Koons Corp. is the Prada. The Prada Evening Project, to be precise.[36]

The polarization of high art and low is often described as old hat. The distinctions, once described as a 'great divide', are increasingly blurred.[37] High art is used by advertisers (L'Oréal's Mondrian-style packaging) and advertising itself is art

(Mucha's posters for Moët & Chandon). Leading artists accept commissions from leading brands (Jeff Koons designs bottles for Dom Pérignon, Tracey Emin has done something similar for Beck's Bier) and leading brands collect the works of leading artists. The bedazzling Fondation Louis Vuitton in Paris, the Koolhaus-designed Fondazione Prada in Milan and Walmart's Crystal Bridges Museum of American Art in Bentonville, Arkansas, are typical of this art-mart meld.

Big-name museums, what is more, are embracing branding like long-lost brothers. Some, such as the Smithsonian, Guggenheim, Hermitage, Tate and Louvre, have expanded the brand by opening additional branches in carefully selected global cities. Many mount exhibitions of outstanding brands including Chanel, Armani, Tiffany, Cartier, Harley-Davidson and Alexander McQueen, whose *Savage Beauty* was a massive hit for the V&A in 2015.[38] Most contain gigantic museum shops that not only occupy prime space within the institutions – right by the main entrance – but sell reproductions of items held in the collections, not to mention tote bags, postcards, coffee mugs and more. Ever since Monet, cutting-edge artists have been incorporating brands and branding into their work and, a bit like Dorian Grey, have become brands themselves. The websites of leading artists are indistinguishable from any upmarket e-tail operation. You want Damien Hirst deckchairs decorated with his signature spot-art or butterfly-art motifs? They're yours at the click of a mouse. What about a digitally signed, limited edition screensaver by Dame Tracey Emin? It's only a download away. Fancy a Francis Bacon beach towel bearing the inscription 'I Believe in Deeply Ordered Chaos' or a silk scarf featuring his grotesque 'screaming popes'? Eat your heart out Hermès.

Stuck-in-the-mud artists may demur but the fact of the matter is that in today's difficult economic circumstances, when the budgets of arts organizations are being slashed, elite culture can't afford to distance itself from the common herd. Highly distinguished artistic companies like Northern Ballet, based in Leeds, are turning in desperation to 'sponsor a dancer' campaigns. London's Almeida theatre, famous for its challenging avant-garde productions, now rents out its premises for poker competitions and hen parties. The National Youth Theatre runs formal training pro-grammes and walk-in workshops for would-be thespians in China. Arts and Business, an organization that helps artistic types better communicate with businesspeople, is busier than ever. In a highly competitive world, where creativity is prized by corpo-rations as never before, who better to deliver off-the-wall thinking than rebellious artists? Duffy, Statham and Adele may not like it, but fellow artists the world over are lumping it. As Timberg concedes, 'each artist, regardless of temperament, must become his or her own producer, promoter, and publicist'.[39]

More to the point, though, Adele and Statham and Tom Sachs and Banksy's antiquated attitudes are predicated on the Romantic myth of the outsider and the Modernist myth of the artist as anti-bourgeois avant-garde. Yet history reveals that Lord Byron, the poster boy of Romantic poetry, not only penned advertising slogans for a bestselling brand of boot polish but his artistic persona was as carefully crafted and ably marketed as Justin Bieber's. Byron was a brand before branding began and the peerless Possum was its high modernist apotheosis (Think Box 23).

THINK BOX 23

Playing Possum

T.S. Eliot, the self-styled Possum of *Practical Cats*, is widely regarded as the highest of high modernists. He was, so the story goes, an especially challenging poet who reviled the money-grubbing merchant classes and the petit bourgeoisie more generally.

In reality, however, he was a very canny operator, an exceptionally astute author-preneur with business in his blood. He was the youngest son of a successful mid-western industrialist, who built the Hydraulic-Press Brick Company into a thriving regional brand. He began his first business venture at the age of eleven, a self-published magazine called *Fireside*, which contained spoof advertisements for popular brands of patent medicine, including the poetically named Dr. Pearce's Pleasant Pellets for Pink People. He salted his sophomore stanzas with luxury brands of liquor and his first published poem, *The Love Song of J. Alfred Prufrock*, got its name from a department store in Eliot's home town of St Louis. His later oeuvre was replete with matters mercantile, to say nothing of brand name-dropping, and drew heavily on purportedly loathsome popular culture. He was not only employed by Lloyd's Bank between 1917 and 1925 but he had a natural flair for finance and was promoted several times because of it. Unsurprisingly perhaps, he is aptly described by his latest biographer as 'a poet with a business brain'.[40] If Eliot were writing *The Hollow Men* today, he'd likely contend that the world will end not with a Bing but a Twitter.

Or possibly not. He might, though, point out that his mercantile-minded commercial nous is neither new nor unique. Shakespeare, after all, wrote for money. He was a theatrical impresario too. Mozart was pretty much dependent on patronage. He composed concertos for cash, like any tunesmith in Tin Pan Alley. Michelangelo and Leonardo were artists for hire, though the former was a better self-publicist than the latter and reaped more riches as a result.

Eliot might, if he were feeling especially frisky, relay the apocryphal story of his great contemporary and fellow high modernist, Pablo Picasso. Legend has it that an American visitor to the great avant-gardist's Parisian studio once stood, utterly bemused, in front of a characteristically confusing cubist canvas. 'What does it represent?' the American enquired politely. 'About twenty thousand dollars', Picasso replied without hesitation.

Thinking Outside the Think Box

Business needs creative minds but managers remain wary of what poets and so forth have to offer. Artists need to make a living, yet still harbour doubts about The Man. Make a business case for the arts and an artistic case for business. What measures would you put in place to benefit both?

PARADIGMATIC PRINCIPLE

If the inaugural Romantic poet was a marketing man manqué – and the modernist's modernist its ultimate expression – Adele et al. needn't worry too much about selling out. They can embrace the brand and sell out without denting their credibility. The *paradigmatic principle* might give them pause, though. It's premised on the idea that everything you need to know about branding can be found in the cultural sphere. Arts branding is all branding in miniature. Cultural branding encapsulates the totality. It is a distillate. The quintessence. Paradigmatic.

This idea of the macrocosm in the microcosm, the universal in the particular – that is, Blake's world in a grain of sand/and heaven in a wild flower – is a central premise of the arts.[41] The notion that a single work of art can say something deeply meaningful about the society that spawned it, and continues to speak to succeeding generations, is a widely accepted tenet of the cultural industries. Consider Homer's *Odyssey*, Shakespeare's *Hamlet*, Picasso's *Guernica*, or The Beatles' *Revolution*, which perfectly captures the hippie belief in rebellion based on peace, love and understanding.

The same basic idea can be applied to branding. Note, this does not mean that we can conveniently ignore the branding of fast-moving consumer goods or household appliances or information technology or the motor car industry or the fashion and luxury good sectors or the increasingly popular analyses of place branding, political branding, personal branding or whatever. It means that the branding issues evident in such sectors – cut-throat competition, disruptive innovation, brand expansion, etc. – are not only apparent in the cultural realm but apparent in heightened and exaggerated forms. Competition among supermarkets is never less than brutal. But it is nothing compared to that in the cultural industries where hundreds, often thousands, of talented actors, musicians, dancers and designers daily battle for limited numbers of positions. Standing out from the crowd of painters, poets, playwrights, performers, songwriters, screenwriters and so on is exceptionally difficult and attained by very, very few. For every Picasso and Matisse, Sue Roe shows, there were scores of gifted artists in Montmartre this time last century.[42] All since forgotten.

Failure rates, furthermore, are high in 21st century Silicon Valley, where bankruptcy is a badge of pride. However, compared to the cavalcade of catastrophes that is Broadway musicals, tech is a utopian land of milk and honey. For every box office bonanza like *Les Mis*, *Mama Mia* or *The Lion King* there are dozens of shows that go dark. The old Broadway saying, 'you can't make a living but you might make a killing' is no less true of music and literature, where tottering slush piles of unsolicited manuscripts and audition tapes have long been the bane of both and where even the biggest hits, including The Beatles and J.K. Rowling, are repeatedly rejected before getting a lucky break. Luck looms large in television, the theatre and movies too. The idea for *The Simpsons*, Groening reveals, was entirely serendipitous, a flash of inspiration while waiting to pitch to a network executive. Samuel Beckett's landmark play *Waiting for Godot* would not have been produced if it weren't for a grant from the

French government, which providentially arrived when Sam needed it most. Heavy metal, Sandbrook claims, owes everything to a 'lucky' industrial accident that sliced the fingertips off aspiring lead guitarist Tony Iommi, whose modified style became the mark of the beast that is Black Sabbath.[43]

Indeed, despite the reams of market research commissioned by the cultural industries, the old showbiz truism 'nobody knows anything' when it comes to predicting stinkers or sensations, is as true today as it ever was. Love them or hate them, the cultural industries are the model and template for business in general and branding in particular:

> Businesses that are sceptical about the value of marketing, and about the possibilities for creating consumer awareness rapidly, should look closely at how Hollywood manages to come up with new brands on a near-weekly basis. The key is to treat the marketing as a core part of the project, rather than as an afterthought.[44]

LOOKING BACK TO SEE AHEAD

Culture's universal-in-the-particular principle – also known as all-in-each – is equally applicable to the book you're reading. It can't have escaped your notice that more than a few of the cases in earlier chapters are drawn from works of popular culture, be it the Steve Jobs biopic, Jonathan Coe's description of identikit stand-up comedians or consumers letting themselves go when *Frozen* is playing in store. However, there's more to it than anecdotes. Almost every aspect of branding examined in chapters 1 through 10 is amplified in the cultural domain. Intellectual property is more rigorously policed by musicians, movie makers and their people than anyone in Apple's IP department. The Beatles outmanoeuvred Steve Jobs for years and Taylor Swift has browbeaten Tim Cook about copyright more recently.

The power of the brand name is nowhere better illustrated than in the case of the artist's signature. A few years ago, Rembrandt's entire oeuvre was officially reassessed and approximately half of the 600 extant works were denied autograph status. The artworks themselves were unchanged but the fact that they weren't 'by Rembrandt' caused prices to plummet precipitously.[45] When it comes to the COMPONENTS of branding, the taglines of movies, the logos of film studios, the charisma of pop stars, the overwhelming organoleptics of the heavy metal mosh pit are far from inferior to their FMCG counterparts. As for storytelling, branding is standing on the shoulders of giants.

The same is true of the living thing analogy outlined in chapter 5. Personification has long been a plaything of poets and novelists with their smiling sunbeams, babbling brooks and dancing daffodils. In the 19th century it was known as the 'pathetic fallacy' and seen as something best avoided. But few fallacies have proved more enduring than personification. Few brand fans, furthermore, are more fanatical than those of One Direction or Justin Bieber. And brands that wish to 'tease the customer' need look no further than the latest *Star Wars* trailer.

When it comes to the Ten Commandments of managing branding – avoiding failure, being different, getting lucky et al. – all are evident in the cultural industries, as is the importance of the past (movie remakes, retro music), periodicity (pop festivals, the original pop-ups), purpose (Live Aid, Comic Relief) and never-say-die perseverance. Brigit Riley, the brilliant British pioneer of Op-Art, struggled for twenty years before she stumbled on the black-and-white abstract images that made her name.[46] Riley expanded by contracting her palette (she was a colourist before Op-Art arrived) and thereby avoided the overexposure that can blight artistic careers when they expand to the point of ubiquity and suddenly collapse like a soufflé in *Bake Off*.

Although it may be a while before the Kardashians krash, it's worth noting that the disruptive competition discussed in chapter 9 was pretty much invented in the artistic sphere. Ever since the mid-19th century, avant-garde artists have set out to sweep aside the establishment and accepted ways of doing things. Every few years a new, radical, cutting-edge cultural movement – the Futurists, the Imagists, the Vorticists, the Surrealists, the modernists, the postmodernists, the post-postmodernists – sets out to purge the art world and, in so doing, become the most talked about brand on the block, the latest water-cooler cultural brand.[47] In between times, cultural brands engage in internecine warfare. For Coke versus Pepsi, read Blur versus Oasis. For Nike versus Adidas, read Bond versus Bourne. For Avis versus Hertz, read *Strictly* versus *X Factor*. Dirty tricks are not unknown in the cultural industries either. From shoplifting (Winona Ryder) to child sex abuse (Jimmy Savile), cultural brands are never far from the forefront of reprehensible behaviour. Stealing others' ideas – i.e. artistic industrial espionage – is their speciality, moreover. Celebrated copycats include Warhol, Elvis, Picasso, The Beatles, The Stones, Dangermouse, Philip Pullman, George R.R. Martin and Frank Lloyd Wright. As the Nobel prize-winner T.S. Eliot observed in *The Sacred Wood*, 'Immature poets imitate; mature poets steal.'[48] Just don't try stealing a quotation from his published works, if you know what's good for you. His estate will be on your case if you do. IP is the beating heart of cultural branding.

CULTURE VULTURES

Some readers might be having palpitations by now. Especially those who believe in 'representative' samples and 'rigorous' research and remain unconvinced by the all-in-each principle of cultural branding. It is incontestable, nonetheless, that there is an artistic side to brand creation, be it the poetry of the slogan, the eye appeal of the packaging or the rags-to-riches narrative of a brand's growth and development.

More importantly perhaps, the prevailing images of iconic brands often owe as much to popular culture as they do to the ministrations of their managers.[49] The outlaw persona of Harley-Davidson comes from the movies – *Easy Rider* in particular – not the brand's guardians. The same is true of Jack Daniels, which is irretrievably associated with rock 'n' roll excess. The Volkswagen's offbeat image in America wasn't just a consequence of creative advertising, the *Herbie* movies helped too. Niketown was inspired by *Back to the Future II*. Hermès' Birkin handbag is deeply indebted to *Sex and the City*. Doc Martens will be forever associated with *A Clockwork Orange*. The Brompton bicycle brand benefitted from its role as a running joke in the BBC sitcom, *W1*. Qantas's once impeccable reputation as the world's safest airline came courtesy of Dustin Hoffman in *Rain Man*. The Vespa's standing as a supercool scooter began in the Audrey Hepburn vehicle *Roman Holiday*. Tiffany's didn't do too badly out of her either. The Mini's name was made by *The Italian Job*, as was the New Mini's by the movie's 2003 remake. Hush Puppies' comeback in the late 1990s was triggered by *Forrest Gump*; FedEx was the real star of *Cast Away*; FAO Schwartz toy store became a major New York tourist attraction thanks to the fantastic piano sequence in *Big*. Colonel Sanders used to sell KFC franchises by borrowing a 'southern gentleman' persona sourced from *Gone With the Wind*. Michael O'Leary admits that Ryanair's rebellious routine was inspired by the punk rock of The Sex Pistols, as is BrewDog's brand of craft beer. Clark's desert boots kept their cachet because they were the footwear of choice among West Indian reggae musicians. The Levi's jeans brand reached its 20th century zenith when it featured on the front cover of Bruce Springsteen's blockbuster album, *Born in the USA*. The novels of Sir Walter Scott created the highlands 'n' heather image of Scotland that still forms the basis of its touristic place branding. New Zealand is not only Middle Earth, but nothing less than 100% Middle Earth, as its *Hobbit*-accompanying ads avowed.

Brands' appearances in popular culture greatly influence consumer perceptions. And managers must monitor these carefully. Failure to do so can prove deeply embarrassing. Nowhere more so than in the case of Titanic Belfast, the massive brand museum mentioned in chapter 1. Consumer perceptions of the *Titanic* tend to be predicated on James Cameron's multi-Oscar winning movie of 1997. Yet Titanic Belfast makes no mention of the movie, apart from a tiny tableau in the final gallery. It also contains an exact replica of the grand staircase, which featured prominently in Cameron's classic. However, visitors to the facility are denied access to the replica staircase, because it is situated in a banqueting suite which is closed to the general public. Therefore tourists turn up to Titanic Belfast, expecting to experience a Jack and Rose moment only to find that the I'm Flying lovebirds have flown the coop. The designers of the attraction failed to understand that it is the movie not the metal that fascinates today's consumers of Brand Titanic.

Managers, moreover, could do worse than employ creative artists as brand strategists. Creatives' record of predicting the future compares favourably with the forecasts of macroeconomics-minded scenario planners. Judith Krantz was writing about addictive shopping – and perfectly capturing its nuances – decades before marketing scholars. Alex Shakar's *Savage Girl*, mentioned earlier, anticipated the Diet Water craze by several years. Bret Easton Ellis's brand-bespattered protagonist in *American Psycho* was a harbinger of the 1990s, according to Arvidsson.[50] The late great David Foster Wallace predicted the rise of periodicity as a brand expansion tactic. *Infinite Jest*, his brilliantly funny blockbuster novel, takes place in The Year of the Depend Adult Undergarment, a P&G power brand.

When it comes to encapsulating brand expansion, however, the master forecaster is H.G. Wells. More than one hundred years ago, he wrote a novel about the branding and marketing of a proprietary patent medicine. Everything you need to know about growing a brand is contained in *Tono-Bungay*.[51]

So, even if you don't accept that the anarchistic '60s rock band The Grateful Dead successfully anticipated the freemium-based business model that currently holds sway in Silicon Valley, the sagacious views of Warren Buffet can't be ignored.[52] Arguably the preeminent venture capitalist in America – its richest man, no less – Buffet firmly believes that his brand, Berkshire Hathaway, is a majestic work of art on a par with the populist achievements of Norman Rockwell. Thus speaks the Thomas Kinkade of the Dow Jones Index. Are you listening, Adele? You're in denial, Statham! Where is Duffy when we need her?

BRAND TASK

Compare and contrast the James Bond and Indiana Jones cultural brands. Has Brand, James Brand, gone too far down the b-road with product placements and spin-offs? Why, by contrast, has whip-cracking Indie remained above the branding fray, with comparatively few ancillaries or sponsorships? Could Indiana Jones do more and, if so, what?

RECOMMENDED READINGS

John Weich, 'Banksy', in *Storytelling on Steroids* (BIS Publishers: Amsterdam, 2013, 85–93). There are many books about Banksy, the Oscar-nominated, anti-capitalist graffiti artist, including a coffee-table book by himself. This chapter in Weich's excellent text is as good a summary of the outsider artist as you'll get.

Daragh O'Reilly and Finola Kerrigan, eds., *Marketing the Arts: A Fresh Approach* (Routledge: London, 2010). Daragh and Finola are two of the leading lights in arts marketing. Their anthology contains chapters on everything from Damien Hirst to Miles Davis, all viewed from business and management perspectives. Don't try to read them all. Dip in and out as the fancy takes you. The chapter by Patterson on Liverpool's cultural-led makeover is especially cogent.

Andy Milligan, *Brand It Like Beckham* (Marshall Cavendish: London, 2010). This book is part of a series called Great Brand Stories, all well worth tracking down. Although Becks is the focus of this particular volume, the principles apply to any sports-star brand. The title alone is worth the price of entry.

Chris Hackley, Stephen Brown and Rungpaka Amy Hackley, 'The *X Factor* Enigma: Simon Cowell and the Marketization of Existential Liminality', *Marketing Theory*, 12 (4), 2012, 451–469. Chris is one of the best British writers on branding and advertising. Anything he writes is worth reading. In this paper, he lets rip on the *X Factor* phenomenon. My contribution to the article was minimal, you'll be relieved to hear.

CONCLUSION

CONCLUSION

CHAPTER 12
THE BRAND FINALE

Overview

Steve Jobs was a believer in brand magic. An i-Prestidigitator, he was often depicted pulling new products out of a top hat. Although the magical analogy is singularly appropriate to brand management, it isn't the only meaningful metaphor that's available. This chapter considers the importance and power of figurative thinking, then lists ten potential metaphors for branding going forward. Poetry, it posits, is perhaps the most promising.

BRANDACADABRA

Twenty years ago, I came up with a shopper typology. Though there's nothing unusual about that. Many classifications of consumers are in circulation. Identifying distinctive 'types' of consumers and developing brands/products/communication strategies to meet their needs is standard practice in marketing management.[1]

My typology was different, however. It was different in two respects. First, it identified twelve different categories of consumer. Back then, four to six types was the norm. So twelve was in POW territory for consumer typologists. I won't bore you with the details, but Shopper Type One was aggressive, demanding, impatient, impulsive; Shopper Type Two was slow, steady, deliberate, methodical; Shopper Type Three was capricious, flighty, undecided, indecisive; Shopper Type Four was grumpy, fussy, pernickety, stingy. You get the general picture.[2]

The second different thing about my 'new and improved' framework was that it generated a fair bit of feedback. This is very unusual for me. Normally, my books and articles are greeted with silence. But this particular shopper typology was different. Lots of marketing people got in touch, saying that they recognized the sorts of shopper I'd identified. Others wrote to me claiming that they, themselves, belonged to Shopper Type Seven or Type Eleven or whatever Type it was. 'I'm just like that!' was the overwhelming reaction. For the first time in my career I'd written something that really struck a chord.

There's a twist in the tale, admittedly. My shopper classification wasn't predicated on a representative sample of consumers or an elaborate questionnaire survey, the results of which were painstakingly extracted using multivariate statistical methods. Nor was it the outcome of careful qualitative research, based on focus groups, depth interviews and projective techniques involving inkblots, collages, sentence completion tests or dressing up in onesies for roleplay purposes.

It was, in fact, a spoof. Yes, a spoof. A spoof based on a book of star signs. I bought a second-hand book about astrology, poured over the supposed characteristics of Capricorns, Leos, Virgos, Sagittarians and so on, then imagined how these types of people would react in a supermarket checkout line at peak times or in an upmarket designer-brand boutique where the sales associates are snooty, indifferent la di dahs.

Looking back, mind you, the really weird thing about this tongue-in-cheek typology is that it resonated … it connected … it worked! As I said, the twelve-category classification I'd concocted got a reaction – an enthusiastic reaction, no less – from real-world brand managers and marketing practitioners. Weird or what?

So, what should we make of my youthful hocus-pocus? Was it fortuitous? Was it a fluke? A bit of fun? An uncanny coincidence? A rogue study that says more about the reprehensible state of higher education than the everyday reality of consumer behaviour and brand management? A warning of the lunacy that ensues when the narrow path of rigorous marketing research – the purported route to true knowledge – is abandoned for the twisty turnpike of pseudo-science and New Age nonsense?

Possibly.

Another possibility is that it's true. Perhaps shoppers *are* affected by the stars. Perhaps consumers have somehow convinced themselves that they're Arians or Pisceans or Scorpios and they act accordingly, be it in a brand flagship store, a busy supermarket checkout or anywhere else for that matter.[3] Perhaps my descriptions of shopper types were sufficiently ambiguous to trigger the so-called Barnum Effect (that is, where readers of horoscopes find something to believe about themselves in vaguely worded predictions for the days and months ahead).[4] As Barnum was one of the greatest marketers of all time, the latter possibility shouldn't be ruled out entirely.

Yet another possibility is that it was a sign of things to come (Think Box 24).

————————————— THINK BOX **24** —————————————

Mumbo Jumbo Maybe?

Twenty years ago, I described one particular shopper type as follows:

> Type Eleven is quite unlike any other shopper you'll ever meet, except of course for all the other shoppers just like him or her. Inventive, individual, idiosyncratic, knows what's best, has an incredible knack of finding the most unusual, original, bijou items in the most out of the way places, places that no-one else has heard of or patronised – restaurants, gift shops, galleries, jewellers, knick-knack shops etc. What's more, they have moved on to still more fashionable establishments before you've even got round to visiting the old one. Endowed with the most bizarre taste in clothes, furnishings, food and so on, they manage to combine the most incongruous elements to astonishing effect. Never found in the checkout line behind you, because he or she is either shopping elsewhere or has found an alternative way of avoiding the queues.

You don't need me to tell you that Type Eleven is an Aquarius. But what you may not know is that 21st century Aquarians are currently flocking to Selfridges in Oxford Street. There, Lucy Kellaway claims, enlightened shoppers 'can find their animal spirits, make a dream-catcher and have a crystal massage'.[5] Since October 2015, the department store has been running a Journey to the Stars event, where its display windows are devoted to different star signs and where a dedicated 'astrolounge' sells birth sign dresses, handbags, slippers, T-shirts, towels, makeup and more. The astrolounge, allegedly a bridge between the mystical and the material, also offers all sorts of enchanted experiential services, such as guided meditation and tarot readings and psychic enlightenment more generally. Presumably they also see shoppers coming.

Thinking Outside the Think Box

According to Heilbrunn, brands are the 21st century counterpart of 'love potions'. In what ways? Does this parallel only apply to brands that are ingested (food, drink, pharmaceuticals) or does it also apply, metaphorically, to perfumes, apparel, IT equipment, social media? Which, in your opinion, is the most potent potion out there?

MAKING MARKETING MAGIC

Regardless of what my irreverent act of necromancy really meant, or means, it draws attention to the magical character of commercial life. Many academic commentators have noted the inherent enchantments of the marketplace. Raymond Williams, the learned social theorist, called advertising 'the magic system'.[6] James Twitchell, a brand-fixated professor of English Literature who's written several bestselling books about marketing, repeatedly refers to the bewitching blandishments of luxury goods and designer labels.[7] Rachel Bowlby, whose highly regarded writings include *Just Looking* and *Shopping with Freud*, often waxes lyrical about the hypnotic, mesmeric, spellbinding character of shop windows and in-store displays.[8] Indeed, it is hard not to walk around, say, Jenners department store on Princes Street, Edinburgh, without feeling that you've stumbled into a consumer wonderland, a veritable BrandLand where products take on lives of their own.

And it's not just cloistered academics who feel this way. Unilever, one of the most hard-headed, number-crunching, research-driven, scientifically orientated branding behemoths on the planet, recently came up with a new corporate mantra: 'More Magic, Less Logic'. Steve Jobs, the imperious boss of Apple Inc., famously contended that new technologies are inherently magical and insisted, in one of his final diktats, that any future Apple TVs must be controlled by a 'magic wand', rather than the common-or-garden channel changer.[9] Back in the early days of Google, when the upstart search engine appointed its first marketing person, he listened attentively to the founders as they outlined their intention to revolutionize advertising, 'and protested, only half in jest, "You're fucking with the magic!" '[10]

Further evidence of this sorcerous state of affairs is supplied by creative writers. In *The Savage Girl*, a novel alluded to earlier, an employee of a cutting-edge market research agency considers the occult essence of branding. Brand name products, he claims, help consumers construct a wonderfully magical world above the mundane workaday world that they ordinarily occupy. It is a world of enchantment, allure and wish fulfilment:

> Our world exists only to hold up this other world, this ideal world. It's the world of our dreams, our desires. It's elaborate, it's heavy, and we carry it around with us everywhere. But we don't mind. The more that's up there, the better. Because up here is where we keep all that's best in us. The more that's up here, the richer our imagination becomes ... Products are the material we use to build our world above the world.[11]

This world above the world – the world that advertisers invoke and are largely responsible for – is a supremely magical world. It is a world of impossibly happy families, impossibly beautiful people, impossibly perfect holidays, impossibly empty roads, impossibly immaculate gardens, impossibly erogenous shampoos, impossibly healthy snacks, impossibly helpful insurers, impossibly kind-hearted banks, impossibly effective solutions to business problems. It is a world where polar bears quaff Coke, camels chat about cigarettes, green giants are inordinately happy, cars mutate into ice-skating Transformers and pink, battery-operated bunnies keep on going and going and going. It is a world where price reductions are 'unbelievable', customer service is 'fantastic', sales promotions are 'superhuman', value for money is 'incredible', special offers are 'beyond belief', and the latest product is simply 'amazing'.

It is a world where Walt Disney presides over a mouse-infested Magic Kingdom, where Marks & Spencer, the iconic British retailer, claims to sell Magic & Sparkle, where MAC makeup maintains it's the Magic of the Night, where the Panasonic brand of flat-screen TVs purports to be Mastering the Magic of Light, where Hitachi promotes its contribution to social innovation with the strapline 'Can't We Use Magic to Get There Faster?', where VisitLeeds sells its shop-till-you-drop city brand with the captivating words 'Magical Leeds, Where Shopping Begins' and where Lidl, the brand-devouring discount supermarket advertises its deluxe selection of fresh lobsters with the groan-worthy pun, 'A Lidl Bit of Magic'.[12]

It's a world, what's more, where marketing consultants *à la* Martin Lindstrom sell steaming cauldrons of hocus-pocus to anxious brand managers. Worried about what the future holds, many executives are happy to cross witchdoctors' palms with silver in return for good fortune going forward or getting lucky, like Kit-Kat in Japan:

> When Nestlé rolled out their candy in the Far East, locals couldn't help but notice how close the words 'Kit Kat' were to 'Kitto-Katsu', which roughly translates to 'win without fail'. In time, students began to believe that eating a Kit Kat before they took their exams would result in a higher grade, which is a major reason the Kit Kat brand is doing so well in Japan's overcrowded retail market. Nestlé went one step further by rolling out their Kit Kats in a blue bag – to make people think of the sky, as in Heaven – and printing the words 'Prayers to God' on the package. It seems that Kit Kats are scoring in Asia not just because they are considered good luck, but because on the Nestlé website, browsers can enter a prayer that they believe will be sent up to a higher power.[13]

THIS WAY TO THE WORLD ABOVE THE WORLD

And the enchantment doesn't stop there. Magic, like love, is a many-splendoured thing. There are countless forms, branches, strands and sub-fields of magical behaviour. These include Rosicrucianism, paganism, witchcraft, Satanism, cabbala, hermeticism, shamanism, spiritualism, mesmerism, palmistry, phrenology, theosophy, homeopathy, Wicca, wyrd, feng shui, geomancy, gematria, scrying, Tarot, Freemasonry and the stage/street magic practised by the Penn and Tellers, Siegfried and Roys, Derren Browns and Dynamos of this world.[14] Most if not all of these are discernible in the brand marketing sphere. In addition to astrology, outlined above, branding is replete with:

Spells and Incantations

One of the most striking things about branding is its love of spells and incantations. We call them slogans and catchphrases. They trip off the tongue. They are chanted constantly. Brand managers believe that if they are repeated often enough – and relentless repetition is central to magical ritual – they will bestow great wealth and good fortune on the organization responsible. From Drinka Pinta Milka Day via Clunk Click Every Trip to That'll Do Nicely Sir, brands intone incantations incessantly. This is as true of imaginary brands, incidentally, as it is of real ones. Duff Beer boasts: Can't Get Enough of that Wonderful Duff, It's Always Time for Duff, and The Beer That Makes the Days Fly By.

Symbology

Even the most casual reader of supernatural literature, or apathetic player of fantasy video games, can't have missed their profusion of magical symbols. These include pentangles, pyramids, sefiroth, zodiacs, ouroboroses, all-seeing-eyes and the major arcana of the Tarot. The same is true of branding. Only we call them logos. McDonald's arches, Nike's swoosh, Apple's apple, Shell's scallop, BMW's roundel, Playboy's bunny, Lacoste's crocodile, Google's candy-coloured homepage, and CBS's all-seeing-eye, beloved by conspiracy theorists, are more familiar to most consumers nowadays than the Titians, Rembrandts and Caravaggios that line the walls of the world's greatest museums. Museums have logos too.

Animism

As our 'living thing' discussion in chapter 5 demonstrated, animism is the act of breathing life into brands. It imbues inanimate companies, goods and services with anthropomorphic characteristics. Sometimes this is evoked by the brand name, such as Puma, Dove, Red Bull, Wild Turkey; sometimes it is linked to brand personalities, as per Disney's Mickey Mouse, Kellogg's Tony the Tiger, Budweiser's Clydesdale carthorses; sometimes it involves supernatural or otherworldly figures akin to Mr Muscle, Michelin's Bibendum, Pillsbury's Doughboy; and sometimes it includes recreations of 'real' people like Betty Crocker, Aunt Jemima, Uncle Ben, Ronald McDonald and the obstreperous Oxo family.

Divination

If the cross is the central symbol of Christianity, the archetypal occult object is a crystal ball. Soothsaying, foretelling, augury and prophecy are integral to the magical worldview. Business in general and marketing in particular is no different. Sales projections, marketing plans, strategic scenario forecasts and the sizeable retainer fees paid to futurists, trend spotters, cool hunters, et al. are proof positive that prognostication is not confined to the palmistry tent at the circus or tremulous tealeaf readings in the drawing room. Strategic storytellers are the seers of the C-suite nowadays.

Numerology

It goes without saying that magic requires words of power: abracadabra, alakazaam, open sesame, half-price sale, free gift inside, everything must go, I can't believe it's not butter. It also contains *numbers* of power, most notably lucky seven, unlucky thirteen, perfect ten, quintessential five and so forth. Once again, the same is true in commercial life, where thirteen (and fourteen) is routinely removed from hotel floor numberings, a Boeing 666 is so not going to happen and textbooks are filled with 3Cs, 4Ps, 7Ss and suchlike. Superstition even pervades the trading floor, insofar as Asian investors often avoid stock prices ending with a four (and underperform as a consequence).[15]

Alchemy

Although alchemy is conventionally associated with attempts to turn base metal into gold, this transformational process is increasingly understood in psychological rather than physical terms. The branding concept is likewise presented as a corporate philosopher's stone, something that turns the base metal of commodification into the 22-carat gold of spellbinding branding offerings, something that enchants consumers and enriches managers both. If, furthermore, the guidelines are carefully and painstakingly followed step-by-step, stage-by-stage, golden rule by golden rule – alchemy, like branding, is golden rule bound – then everlasting life is guaranteed.[16]

Shamanism

The shaman is a key figure in the magical tradition. Popularly portrayed as medicine men, shamans are people of extraordinary power and immense prestige. Often blessed with prodigious personal charisma, or *mana*, shamans perform traditional dances, participate in arcane rituals and preside over communal ceremonies that allow them to mediate between this world and the next, one state and another. It is no accident that management gurus like Jim Collins, Tom Peters and the late Peter Drucker are often described as witch doctors.[17] The same is true of the Martha Stewarts, Jack Mas and Karl Lagerfelds of this world. As Simon Cowell is our witness, shamanism sells.

Contagion

Whereas 'imitative' magic derives its power from physical resemblance – rhino horn is assumed to be an aphrodisiac, Jaguars are fast, sleek, stealthy modes of transportation – 'contagious' magic is associated with contact or juxtaposition. That is, being in the presence of a magical object, such as Stonehenge on midsummer morn. In branding contexts, the magical object is often a celebrity. Celebrity endorsement, as outlined earlier, is everywhere in branding, notwithstanding the attendant difficulties and human dramas that come with the territory. The basic assumption that their charisma, their presence, their greatness, rubs off on the brand – and thereafter the customer – is a central premise of 21st century branding understanding.[18]

Necromancy

A necromancer is not just another magician. Necromancers raise the dead. Many contemporary brand managers are necromancers in disguise. Because retrobranding is all around. The New Beetle, the inaugural retro automobile, has recently been given a makeover, which makes it the New New Beetle, presumably. Retro gaming is all the rage, as is retro food, retro fashion and retro photography, thanks in no small part to Instagram. As I write, *Star Wars* is being resurrected by J.J. Abrams, the *Man from UNCLE* has come and gone, and James Bond is not only back in fine fettle, but battling SPECTRE, a nefarious organization last seen in the early 1970s. Bolfeld's cat even makes a comeback. Can Goldfinger's great-grandson be far behind?

METAPHORS MATTER

Branding, then, is a manifestation of marketplace magic. From designer labels, which like lucky charms ward off the stigma of social disapproval, to the doppelgänger brands that imitate the market leader (such as the countless Starbucks clones), branding is bewitchment by another name.[19] Whether this bewitchment constitutes white magic or black magic is for you to decide.

Take Walmart's 'stomp the comp' behaviour, when it sets out to obliterate the independent retail stores – i.e. the mom and pop pharmacy, hardware and variety stores – of small town America.[20] Black or white? You decide.

Take the recent rapid rise of 'dark tourism', where places associated with murder, mutilation, malevolence and more are turned into brand name visitor attractions, complete with T-shirts and tie-in merchandise.[21] Black or white? You decide.

Take Elea Capital, a no-holds-barred hedge fund, which acquired the rights to Daraprim – a drug often prescribed to AIDS and cancer sufferers – then hiked the price of the pharmaceutical from $14 to $750 per pill.[22] Black or white? You decide.

Rather than take such a decision, you may of course reject the comparison completely. My contention that branding is magical is a *metaphor*, a figure of speech where one thing is compared to another. Time is money. Life is a journey. The mind is a machine. All three are examples of metaphorical thinking, as is Burns' celebrated simile 'my love is like a red, red rose', as is Forrest Gump's sagacious allusion 'life is like a box of chocolates'.

For many years, metaphors were regarded as literary devices found in fancy, high-falutin contexts. They represented unnecessary rhetorical flourishes that people used in order to impress others. More recently, linguists have come to realize that metaphors are pervasive in everyday conversation and learned discourse alike.[23] More than that, they shape and structure our thinking. We see the world through metaphorical viewfinders. People use, on average, six metaphors per minute of speech and marketing managers use more metaphors than most. As Caroline Tynan points out 'when we "launch" a new offering, describe a product as a "cash cow" or watch the adoption of our innovative new service "diffuse" across a market', we are engaging in figurative thinking.[24] Many of marketing's most deeply entrenched concepts are up to their necks, as it were, in metaphor. Viral marketing, the product life cycle, marketing myopia, the wheel of retailing, the globalization of markets, customer relationship management, buyer behaviour models, market segmentation-targeting-positioning, the trickle-down theory of fashion and the ingredients-based idea of the marketing mix are stocked in marketing's metaphorical pantry.[25] In the words of one over-exuberant academic, who's obviously trying to attract attention:

> The brute reality is that marketing thinking is inherently metaphoric, branding especially. Describing one thing in terms of another is what metaphors do (argument is war, life is a circle, paperwork is mountainous, etc.) and successfully branded products, services, organisations, countries, cities, celebrities and suchlike do exactly the same. Volvo is safety, BMW is performance, Virgin is fun, Marlboro is freedom, Levi's is rugged, Versace is sex, Paris is style, New York is energy, Brazil is samba, Scotland is canny, Madonna is metamorphic, Britney is bonkers. Just as metaphors often describe abstract constructs in concrete terms (America is a melting pot, bureaucracy is an iron cage) so too abstract characteristics become embodied in products and services (magic means Disney, refreshment is Coke, athleticism equals Nike). Some of these metaphorical transfers may be unanticipated by managers and are therefore decidedly unwelcome (McDonald's is arteriosclerosis, Microsoft is megalomaniacal, Las Vegas is sleazy), but such figurative imputations are the coin of the marketing realm.[26]

SIMILE SUMMARY

'So what?' some may say. What has this got to do with branding? Well, apart from the fact that it is unavoidable – and forms the basis of every concept you'll be exposed to as your degree progresses – it's integral to the book you've been reading. Every single chapter in *Brands and Branding* relies on an analogy, albeit some are more explicit than others. We began by positing that brands are properties. This is encapsulated in Hegarty's claim that a brand occupies the most valuable piece of real estate in the world, a corner of the consumer's mind. More than that, the brands-are-properties parallel is central to trademark law and brand valuation. Such things are open to all sorts of interpretations, as are metaphors more generally, but they keep IP attorneys in the moolah to which they're accustomed.

Chapters 2 to 4 are built on a building metaphor. They identified the component parts of the branding edifice and sought to show how they fit together like Lego. True, this section included subsidiary analogies, predicated on linguistics (Ps and Qs) and narratology (brands are stories). But the foundational metaphor is architectural rather than, say, culinary (the ingredients needed to cook up a brand), chemical (a periodic table of brand elements) or mechanical (assemble the branding machine and see it go).

The second section mixed our metaphors up again, beginning with the popular proposition that brands are living things (brand as animal). This expanded into an essentially ecological analogy, chapter 7's claim that brands are predators and consumers prey. After our branding bloodbath, a spiritual metaphor moved among us in chapter 7. We walked in the valley of the shadow of brand management noting the Ten Commandments that therein obtain.

Spiritual similes are hard to surpass, but cosmology is surely a contender. Hence the Big Brand Theory that detonated in chapter 8 and expanded in (eleven) different directions. Until the limits to branding kicked in – and off – in chapters 9 and 10. The former employed the familiar military metaphor of battling brand-to-brand warfare, whereas the latter raised the associated spectre of special forces, dirty tricks and underhand guerrilla tactics, as well as the dark side in all its grisly glory.

We followed this up on a more elevated plane, arguing that branding is a work of installation art. Chapter 11 further contended that we can learn much from artists and artworks, just as we can from the foregoing principles of magic. Wasn't it Picasso who proclaimed that making art was a kind of magic? Like many modernist artists, Picasso was preoccupied with the occult and loved nothing more than watching feats of prestidigitation by stage magicians.[27]

MIXING METAPHORS

This book, in short, comprises a pick 'n' mix of brand metaphors, a smorgasbord of similes. Literary purists might despair, since there is nothing worse – supposedly – than mixing metaphors. But the purists are wrong. They are wrong on three counts. First, the grammatical crime of 'mixing one's metaphors' usually refers to combining clashing analogies in the same sentence or paragraph. Sam Goldwyn's apocryphal 'bite the hand that lays the golden egg' is a well-known illustration of the problem, as is George Orwell's ironic classic, 'The Fascist octopus has sung its swan song, the jackboot is thrown into the melting pot'.[28] However, the mixing in the present book occurs at the chapter level, not within paragraphs or sentences.

Second, I would argue that my chosen metaphors, far from being indiscriminately mixed, are more like daisies on a chain. We started with a piece of property, on which we built a house, then filled it full of people with a penchant for raw meat barbeques despite their religious-cum-cosmological convictions. And although the family has some decidedly dirty habits, they're aspiring artists at the end of the day. So let's cut them some slack.

Third, the injunction against mixed metaphors is misplaced in any event. According to James Wood, a leading literary critic, the likes of William Shakespeare, D.H. Lawrence and Henry James mixed their metaphors with impunity.[29] The problem, he explains, is not mixed metaphors as such, but mixed clichés such as those called out by Stephen Pinker: 'The kind of writer who gets the ball rolling in his search for the holy grail, but finds that it's neither a magic bullet nor a slam dunk, so he rolls with the punches and lets the chips fall where they may while seeing the glass as half-full, which is easier said than done.'[30]

Mixing metaphors, if you ask me, is an indicator of creativity not a sign of lazy thinking. And, although it is true that business and management is infested with mixed clichés such as pushing the envelope up the flagpole of out of the box thinking to the next level of the learning curve ball where only proactive paradigm shifters survive no brainers going forward, let's not throw the baby out with the bathwater before each dog has its day and the fat lady sings.

Mixing metaphors is a good thing. Mixing them can spur further creativity. One of the reasons branding is burgeoning is because of its metaphorical plasticity. The metaphors mashed up in this book are only a fraction of those that have been employed by branding gurus. If you rummage through the textbooks, old and new, you'll discover that brands have been compared to all manner of inanimate objects including icebergs, pyramids, ladders, onions, funnels, chains, cogs, wheels, umbrellas, mountains, prisms, bicycles and stretchy strips of elastic. Animate objects are popular too, not just in branding but throughout the corporate jungle, where:

> ... animal analogies are essential if one deigns to dash off a management bestseller. Purple cows, black swans, inquisitive squirrels, dancing elephants, cubicle monkeys, indecisive mice, canny rats, lunatic lemmings, silverback CEOs, killer apes (sorry, apps), hares 'n' tortoises, hedgehogs 'n' foxes, spiders 'n' starfish, and strangely disembodied long tails are happily cavorting on the corporate Serengeti, where the consultancy waterholes are brimming and the retainer fee forage is inexhaustible.[31]

Now, this animate/inanimate dichotomy is interesting analytically. But, it is neither hard nor fast. Sometimes the tropes are successfully combined, as in the title of David Aaker's bestselling book *Building Strong Brands* (a mixed metaphor if ever there was one). More pertinent perhaps, is the secular trend that has become increasingly apparent in the past ten years or so. Namely, that our understandings of branding are more intangible than before. The concrete metaphors of yore – animate and inanimate both, be they chains, funnels, faces or physiques – are being superseded by cloudier conceptualizations. Twenty-first century brand gurus talk about brand gestalts, collages, bubbles, manifolds, myths, distillations, penumbras, black holes, spirit houses and so forth. The conventional idea of the brand as a clear, crisp, compact, coherent, consistent, coordinated and tightly-controlled *thing*, is giving way to nebulous, amorphous, diaphanous, essentially ethereal concepts of what it means to be a brand. The brand iceberg is melting. The funnel is a cyclone.

Clearly, these developments are related to the fact that we live in an increasingly experiential, ever more intangible economy (as the financial derivatives debacle a few years back is terrible testament). It is also related to the rise of social media, crowdsourcing, consumer co-creation, cloud computing, brand communities, user-generated content, etc. The traditional command-and-control concept of branding, where management calls the shots and communicates the message, is having to come to terms with consumer collectives' commentary, collaboration, censure and capture on occasion.[32] Whether managers like it or not:

> It is not hard to see why the old marketing magic is fading, in an age in which people can instantly learn truths (and indeed untruths) about the things they are contemplating buying. Online reviews and friends' comments on social media help consumers see a product's underlying merits and demerits, not the image that its makers are trying to build around it. The ease of accessing information makes consumers more likely to abandon their habitual brands because they have heard about something new, or learned that retailers' own-label products are much the same, except cheaper. Depending on your perspective, people are either increasingly fickle or ever more impermeable to marketing bullshit.[33]

Equally clearly, all this talk about ambiguous branding is unlikely to cut much ice with cut-the-crap brand managers. Nebulosity is not what they want to hear. They've been told for decades that brands must be clear, concise, precise, controlled, crystalline, pellucid. These guidelines, moreover, still appear in most mainstream textbooks and how-to guides for would-be brand builders. The big branding consultancies likewise continue to reiterate the golden oldie brand management message.

MORE METAPHORS

What we need is a new round of metaphorical reflection. We need to reimagine branding for our diaphanous age. For my own part, I feel the following figurative phenomena have conceptual potential:

Rainbows

Rainbows are remarkable physical things, simultaneously tangible (they're up there in the sky) and intangible (they're a trick of the light). They are multi-coloured magical objects, associated with all manner of myths and legends, including the pot of gold at rainbow's end. They are an awesome yet evanescent sight that raises the spirits of those who see them. Great brands do likewise.[34] Rainbows do what great brands do. It's no accident that, for a very long time, Apple's logo contained all the colours of the rainbow, albeit artfully rearranged in unconventional sequence. Think Different.

Lighthouses

The idea of 'lighthouse brands' is the intellectual property of Adam Morgan. In *Eating the Big Fish*, he draws attention to brilliant brands that shine out like beacons across the brandscape of undifferentiated products and services. These stand for something totally different and attract customers on that basis. Actually, Morgan's metaphor is similar to an earlier insight by a legendary literary theorist, who distinguishes between 'the mirror and the lamp'.[35] Mirror books, like customer-centric mirror brands, reflect the world as it is. Lamp works of literature, like lighthouse brands, show us how the world should be. It is no coincidence that eBay – a brilliant lamp brand to begin with – came about because of a laser pointer. Check it out on Wikipedia, another brilliant lighthouse brand.

Boomerangs

Boomerang brands, much like the Australian Aborigine weapon, return to the thrower. As such, they are an apt metaphor for the recent rise of retro brands, such as those mentioned earlier. Retro is all around these days and, although there is no shortage of age appropriate terminology (e.g. heritage brands, legacy brands, replicas, reproductions, classics, antiques), no one has come up with an apposite analogy. This is especially the case with completely new products that purport to be older than they are, such as the Chrysler P.T. Cruiser and Caffrey's Irish Ale. Their brand managers, in effect, hurled the products into the past and they returned coated in phony heritage. Just like boomerangs. They aren't so much nostalgic as newstalgic.

Ghosts

Ghost brands are equally evident of late. They comprise products that have come back from the dead, such as Dunlop Green Flash sneakers and Nike Air Max, as well as their individual body parts including names, slogans, packaging and mascots. The Tetley Tea Folk, McDonald's Hamburglar, Morris the Cat and the sainted Colonel Sanders are current cases in point. The tangible yet intangible nature of ghosts and revenants seems singularly appropriate to the amorphous essence of contemporary branding understanding. Ghosts, furthermore, are but one of many marketplace monstrosities ranging from vampire brands, zombie brands and werewolf brands to Frankenbrands, -zilla brands (à la Amazilla) and analogous creatures from the brand lagoon.

Icons

If ever a word has lost its power through overuse, that word is iconic. Ever since Doug Holt's book about iconicity, every brand in the street believes it's an icon in waiting.[36] All it has to do is tap into the cultural zeitgeist and Bob's your branding uncle. This debased interpretation of iconicity detracts from the idea of icons as religious symbols and therefore the spiritual side of branding. Real icons, Martin Kemp explains, are characterized by a combination of clarity and cloudiness.[37] That is, a simple symmetrical central image surrounded by a halo of penumbrous radiance. Iconic brands like *Titanic* exemplify this amalgam of clear core (the physical ship with four funnels) and all the strange stories, myths and legends that surround it (e.g. the curse of the Egyptian mummy stowed in the hold). Coke, similarly, is 'sparkling refreshment in an ice-cold can'. However, the brand is fuzzy as well as fizzy. What, for instance, does the 'it' in Coke is It refer to?

Games

Just as icon is becoming a dead metaphor – but with considerable scope for development – so too the sports and games parallel has been done to death. Retired sportspeople are a fixture on the brand consultancy circuit, where they extract lessons from their on-pitch experiences and apply them to commercial life. Gamification is one of the biggest buzzwords in branding right now, much like buzz marketing and viral marketing before it. Engaging app-happy consumers through fun-filled and rewarding computer games – such as Nike+ Fuelband, Magnum ice cream's Pleasure Hunt and the Axe/Lynx Fallen Angel Challenge – are typical of play-based brand building.[38] Indeed, if ever a brand epitomized the literal and metaphorical power of sport, that brand is surely Nike. Minecraft, though, might be a better metaphor for brand management in an increasingly virtual age. The painstaking building process, the existential threats posed by Enderman, the amazing executions that can result from builders' seemingly limitless ambitions are analogous to what brand managers do and aspire to. Mojang branding here we come.

Dolls

Games of course come in many shapes and forms. Although, as Kane explains, there is no rational let alone evolutionary basis for such activities, play appears to be a primal part of the human condition.[39] This predisposition is apparent from early childhood, where playing with dolls, toy soldiers and so on is an important part of growing up and personal development. A few years ago, when I was working on Harry Potter, I used a Russian Doll analogy to encapsulate the brand's astonishing consumer appeal. That is to say, the Harry Potter brand consists of stories within stories within stories within stories. Stories of the author, stories of the bookselling, stories of the movie making, stories of the theme parks, stories of the tie-in merchandise and of course the captivating stories of the boy wizard himself. I'm not sure how much additional mileage there is in my Matryoshka Marketing metaphor, but something similar was employed by Diamond et al. in their study of the brand gestalt of American Girl, whose fabulous flagship stores devoted to larger than life dolls have to be seen to be believed.[40] There may be more in the brands-are-dolls parallel. Play with it at your leisure.

Dance

Dancing is another intriguing possibility. Not only does it align neatly with the play paradigm, since dancing is nothing if not fun, fun, fun-filled, but it too is a deep-seated form of human expression that dates from the dawn of time.[41] Dance has a competitive element, what is more, as any episode of *Strictly Come Dancing* demonstrates. Cooperation and coordination are part of it too, something that is readily apparent in the crowdsourced, consumer co-created branding philosophy that currently prevails. A vision of manager and consumer in time, in tune, in step, in sync, in perfect harmony – going forward and sideways and backwards and kick! – is very much in keeping with contemporary sentiment. The branding-is-dancing metaphor seems to offer a sequined, spangled, spraytanned sashay with a swivel of the hips and a wiggle in its walk. Strictly Come Branding is the way to go. If nothing else, it offers an original update of the long-established living thing analogy. However, Tynan raises a key question that has to be answered: what kind of dance is branding? Is it 'a stately minuet, a seductive tango or even a wicked rave?'[42] Whatever it is, keeeeep branding!

BAP TILL YOU DROP

There are many art forms besides dance. If branding is an art, as Warren Buffet believes, then the question is: which one? It seems to me that whereas personal selling is a performance art, retailing is essentially sculptural, public relations is narrative driven and advertising is an overwhelmingly visual art, branding is poetry in motion. The above mentioned icebergs, onions, cogs and equivalent metaphors are literary devices.[43] And poetry is literature in excelsis. True, the brands-are-poems (BAP) trope isn't blindingly obvious. But if you think about it, especially in light of the foregoing discussion, the BAP comparison starts to make sense. Poems are simultaneously tangible and intangible. They are clearly identifiable things that accommodate ambiguities, multiplicities of equivocal meaning. Brands do too. Poems, furthermore, are very visually distinctive, insofar as they stand out on the page surrounded by white space. And standing out is paramount in branding. Poems are dynamic and driven, with their pounding rhythm and rhyme schemes. Just like the best brands. Poems work within constraints, especially traditional verse forms like sonnet or haiku, as do brands for the most part. And, last but not least, poems are comparatively compact. Compared to prose, they pack a lot into a little. They are thus very much in tune with today's limited-attention span society of tweets, texts, tags, one-liners, elevator pitches and summary 'takeaways' from lectures, seminars or short courses (Think Box 25).

THINK BOX 25

Cookin' the Book

At the start of this book, I stated that there were seven reasons why you should buy it. Similarly, there are seven things I want you to take away with you.

The first thing to remember about branding is the importance of being different. Branding is best defined as 'a mark of distinction' and distinction is what you must always aim for and aspire to. Don't be like everyone else. Be special. Be outstanding. Be different.

The second key point is that a brand is made up of many component parts, including name, logo, package, slogan, mascot, organoleptics, etc. All of these are important, not least the offer (the product or service itself), but an especially important component is the narrative or story. You must tell a tale to make the sale.

The third takeaway is that there is no point knowing all about branding if you don't understand the consumer. Knowing what makes customers tick is crucial and, in order to do so, research is often necessary. You have to study the customer if you want to sell to them. Many research tools and techniques are available, though they are far from infallible.

My fourth pearl of wisdom for you – and perhaps the most pertinent one – is that brands are living things. Some brands *really are* living things like sportspeople, celebrities and politicians. But most brands are living things in a metaphorical manner of speaking. It's vital to act *as if* they are living things. Treat them accordingly.

Fifth, never forget that brands are inclined to expand until they reach their elastic limit. No one knows where the limit lies, though. And no one knows whether an expanded brand will snap back into place or pop like an overinflated balloon. The secret of management is not to overstretch the brand, but the pressures to expand are prodigious and hard to resist.

Competition comes sixth. It is the single biggest constraint on expanding branding. However, competition can get very dirty very quickly. Battling brands can find themselves behaving in reprehensible ways. Little wonder many consumers regard brands and their managers as swindlers or scumbags or both. Consumers may like our products, our services, our adverts. But they don't like us.

The seventh point is that this anti-branding attitude is especially strong in the cultural sphere, where artists are opposed to the machinations of the merchant classes. In theory at any rate. In practice, creatives are canny brand builders. The very best branding these days is found in the cultural sphere. You can learn everything you need to know from popular culture. Never let on to your lecturers, though, some of whom hold candles for FMCG, B2B, financial services and so forth.

Thinking Outside the Think Box

Using the COMPONENTS inventory, analyse the present book as a brand. Give it a mark out of ten for every element. Compare these to the book's nearest competitors. Write a limerick that summarizes your findings. Send it to me. I'll reply with a two-word critique, the second of which is off.

Poems provide a way of capturing the essence of outstanding brands. The challenge, of course, is choosing the most appropriate poetic form – limerick, sestina, free verse, nursery rhyme, etc. – and then articulating the nature, the purpose, the spirit of the brand within that form. By boiling brands down to their basics, we can better understand them and see what they stand for. BAP helps cut through the buzzing, blooming confusion. As an illustration, consider Think Box 26, which uses the traditional ballad form to capture the experience of shopping at Hollister, aka HCo. It is based on 200 personal accounts of the Hollister encounter, consumers' quest for success in an icon of American apparel and supercool Sol-Cal style. Whatever you think of the poem, it better captures the spirit of the HCo brand than a lengthy research report, complete with a long list of references.

--- THINK BOX **26** ---

The Rime of the Hollister Follower

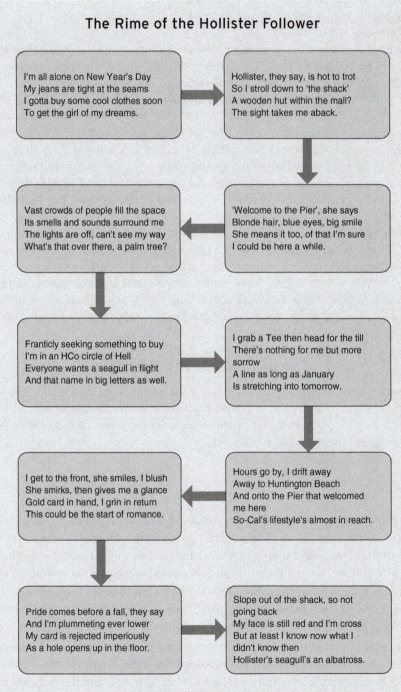

I'm all alone on New Year's Day
My jeans are tight at the seams
I gotta buy some cool clothes soon
To get the girl of my dreams.

Hollister, they say, is hot to trot
So I stroll down to 'the shack'
A wooden hut within the mall?
The sight takes me aback.

Vast crowds of people fill the space
Its smells and sounds surround me
The lights are off, can't see my way
What's that over there, a palm tree?

'Welcome to the Pier', she says
Blonde hair, blue eyes, big smile
She means it too, of that I'm sure
I could be here a while.

Franticly seeking something to buy
I'm in an HCo circle of Hell
Everyone wants a seagull in flight
And that name in big letters as well.

I grab a Tee then head for the till
There's nothing for me but more sorrow
A line as long as January
Is stretching into tomorrow.

I get to the front, she smiles, I blush
She smirks, then gives me a glance
Gold card in hand, I grin in return
This could be the start of romance.

Hours go by, I drift away
Away to Huntington Beach
And onto the Pier that welcomed me here
So-Cal's lifestyle's almost in reach.

Pride comes before a fall, they say
And I'm plummeting ever lower
My card is rejected imperiously
As a hole opens up in the floor.

Slope out of the shack, so not going back
My face is still red and I'm cross
But at least I know now what I didn't know then
Hollister's seagull's an albatross.

Thinking Outside the Think Box

Don't think. Feel. What are your feelings about brands now that you've studied the subject?

BAP, admittedly, is just one possibility among many. Whether any of the above will catch on remains to be seen. The cultural zeitgeist mentioned in chapter 4 applies to branding concepts as well as strategic brand stories. Those that connect with relevant consumers – brand managers, academics and students, in this instance – and help assuage the existential contradictions of the social group concerned, are the ones that will take branding forward. So let me conclude with two brief observations about the provenance of poetry. Call them ads for BAP, if you prefer.

According to one school of thought, poetry began with the customer-attracting cries of vendors, hawkers and stallholders in ancient marketplaces, who had to make themselves heard above the hubbub and whose sales pitches had to be better than those of their competitors.[44] According to an alternative school of thought, poetry's origins lie in ritual magic, ceremonial occasions in the pre-Christian world when words of power were uttered and deities invoked.[45]

It is not a case of either/or, however. The marketplace, as we have seen, is inherently magical. Bards bewitch. Brands do too. Sim Sala Bim.

BRAND TASK

Read the menu of takeaways in Think Box 25. Note the culinary analogy they're based upon. Is branding akin to cooking? In what ways? Are there branding equivalents of superfoods? Was Coco Chanel the Mary Berry of branding? Is James Dyson Heston Blumenthal?

RECOMMENDED READINGS

Elizabeth Hirschman, 'Metaphor in the Marketplace', *Marketing Theory*, 7 (3), 2007, 227–248. Beth Hirschman is the Nigella Lawson of consumer research, its domestic goddess incarnate. She's written tons of stuff, most of which is worth reading. In this piece, she elaborates on the place of metaphor in marketing and branding. I've written on this too, as has Ian Fillis. But Beth's the daddy.

Chris Miles, 'Persuasion, Marketing Communication and the Metaphor of Magic', *European Journal of Marketing*, 47 (11/12), 2013, 2002–2019. The magic of the marketplace is a topic that's attracted much academic discussion. Eric Arnould's writings are especially insightful. This paper, however, helpfully summarizes and astutely critiques the work of several scholars from different fields.

Alex Shakar, *The Savage Girl* (Scribner: London, 2001). If you intend to read one novel from the many novels I've mentioned in this book, make it this one. Naturally, I'd rather you read one of my novels (*The Marketing Code* is still available from all good charity shops and second-hand bookstores). But *The Savage Girl*, it pains me to admit, is much better for you.

Stephen Brown, *Wizard! Harry Potter's Brand Magic* (Cyan Books: London, 2005). If of course you're desperate to read more of my work – sick puppy that you are – you could always try this one. It includes both the doll and the rainbow metaphors mentioned above.

NOTES AND REFERENCES

CHAPTER 1: THE RUDIMENTS OF BRANDING

1. Evan Morris, *From Altoids to Zima: The Surprising Stories Behind 125 Famous Brand Names* (Simon & Schuster: New York, 2004, 1–2).
2. Stephen Brown, 'I'm Buying, Jack: Fooling Around an Ambiguous Brand', *Journal of Consumer Behaviour*, 13 (2), 2014, 108–121.
3. Stephen Brown, 'All Aboard the Unsinkable Ship! How Cultural Branding Relaunched a Myth-informed Metropolis', *Social Business*, 3 (2), 2013, 91–105.
4. Check out ipo.gov.uk for background information on intellectual property in general and trade marks in particular. See also Tom Blackett, *Trademarks* (Macmillan: Basingstoke, 1998) and Lionel Bently, Jennifer Davis and Jane C. Ginsburg, eds., *Trade Marks and Brands: An Interdisciplinary Critique* (Cambridge University Press: Cambridge, 2008).
5. John Mulgrew, 'Brewing Giant AB InBev Delivers Trademark Blow to Belfast Firm', *Belfast Telegraph*, March 3, 2015, www.belfasttelegraph.co.uk.
6. If it comes to fisticuffs, I know who I'll be betting on!
7. Mary Pilon, *The Monopolists: Obsession, Fury and the Scandal Behind the World's Favourite Board Game* (Bloomsbury: New York, 2015).
8. Vanessa Friedman, 'On the Vogue Brandwagon', *Financial Times: Life and Arts*, June 11, 2011, 4.
9. Though the word's association with burning marks of identification on the flesh of animals is related to contemporary usage.
10. Wally Olins, *Brand New* (Thames & Hudson: London, 2014, 105). For a good overview of brand valuation, see Jan Lindemann, 'The Financial Value of Brands', in Rita Clifton and John Simmons, eds., *Brands and Branding* (Bloomberg Press: Princeton, NJ, 2003, 27–45).
11. Stephen Brown, 'Marketing to Generation ®', *Harvard Business Review*, 81 (6), 2003, 16–17.
12. Naomi Klein, *No Logo: Taking Aim at the Brand Bullies* (Flamingo: London, 2000). To clarify, it was said that she trademarked the logo, something Naomi later denied. I suspect it was misinformation circulated by Klein's many enemies (see Chapter 10). She should've trademarked it, though. It's a terrific brand name.

13. Rachel Greenwald, *The Program: Fifteen Steps to Finding a Husband After Thirty* (Time Warner: London, 2004).
14. Quoted in Leslie de Chernatony, *From Brand Vision to Brand Evaluation* (Butterworth-Heinemann: Oxford, 2001, 21).
15. The sources are: Philip Kotler, *Marketing Insights from A to Z* (Wiley: Chichester, 2003, 8); John Miller and David Muir, *The Business of Brands* (Wiley: Chichester, 2004, 3); John Hegarty, *Hegarty on Advertising* (Thames & Hudson: London, 2011, 39); Susan Fournier, 'Consumers and their Brands', *Journal of Consumer Research*, 24 (March), 1998, 345; Winston Fletcher, *Powers of Persuasion* (Oxford University Press: Oxford, 2008, 255); Lucas Conley, *OBD: Obsessive Branding Disorder* (PublicAffairs: New York, 2008, 20); Don Schultz and Heidi Schultz, *Brand Babble* (South-Western: Mason, OH, 2003, 64); Sean Adams, in Debbie Millman, *Brand Thinking and Other Noble Pursuits* (Allworth Press: New York, 2013, 217); Melissa Davis, *More Than a Name* (Thames & Hudson: London, 2005, 57); Graham Hales, 'Branding', in Jeremy Kourdi, ed., *The Marketing Century* (Wiley: Chichester, 2011, 145); John Fanning, 'Tell Me a Story: The Future of Branding', *Irish Marketing Review*, 12 (2), 1999, 4; John Grant, *The New Marketing Manifesto* (Orion: London, 1999, 15); Wally Olins, in Millman, op. cit., 11; Jon Edge and Andy Milligan, *Don't Mess With the Logo* (Financial Times: London, 2009, 14); Tony O'Reilly, quoted in Richard Hall, *Brilliant Marketing* (Pearson: Harlow, 2012, 47); Neil Taylor, *The Name of the Beast* (Marshall Cavendish: London, 2007, 33); Phil Duncan, in Millman, op. cit., 52; Helen Edwards and Derek Day, 'Passion Brands', in Kartikeya Kompella, ed., *The Definitive Book of Branding* (Sage: New Delhi, 2014, 343); John F. Sherry, 'Brand Meaning', in Alice M. Tybout and Tim Calkins, eds., *Kellogg on Branding* (John Wiley: New York, 2005, 41). The de Chernatony article is: Leslie de Chernatony and Francesca Dell'Olmo Riley, 'Defining a Brand: Beyond the Literature with Experts' Interpretations', *Journal of Marketing Management*, 14 (5), 1998, 417–443.
16. Leslie de Chernatony and Malcolm H.B. McDonald, *Creating Powerful Brands* (Butterworth-Heinemann: Oxford, 1992, 18).
17. Wally Olins, *On Brand* (Thames & Hudson: London, 2003, 172).
18. Okay, okay, okay. I coined that one myself. It's not copyrighted so feel free to spread it around.
19. Lucas Conley, *OBD: Obsessive Branding Disorder*, op. cit., 196.
20. And while some puritans are deeply offended by all this 'conspicuous consumption', condemning branding is just another form of attempted differentiation: 'Look at me, I'm opposed to egregious overspending'.
21. Jean-Noël Kapferer, *The New Strategic Brand Management* (Kogan Page: London, 2012).
22. John B. Thompson, *Merchants of Culture* (Polity: Cambridge, 2010). On brand veneration in emerging economies, see Adam Arvidsson, *Brands: Meaning and Value in Media Culture* (Routledge: London, 2006).
23. Evolutionary psychologists are an odd bunch, mind you. See, for example, Geoffrey Miller, *Spent: Sex, Evolution and the Secrets of Consumerism* (Viking: New York, 2009).

24. John F. Sherry, 'Brand Meaning', in Alice M. Tybout and Tim Calkins, eds., *Kellogg on Branding*, op. cit.

25. Stephen Brown, 'The Failgood Factor: Playing Hopscotch in the Marketing Minefield', *The Marketing Review*, 7 (2), 2007, 125–138.

26. Mark Pendergrast, *For God, Country and Coca-Cola: The Unauthorized Story of the World's Most Popular Soft Drink* (Weidenfeld & Nicolson: London, 1993).

27. Jon Edge and Andy Milligan, *Don't Mess With the Logo*, op. cit., xi.

28. Jonathan Coe, *Number 11* (Viking: London, 2015, 145–146).

29. Quoted in Philip Kotler, *Marketing Insights from A to Z: Eighty Concepts Every Manager Needs to Know*, op. cit., 8.

30. Ryan Matthews and Watts Wacker, *What's Your Story? Storytelling to Move Markets, Audiences, People and Brands* (FT Press: Upper Saddle River, NJ, 2008).

31. Martin Lindstrom, *Buyology: Truth and Lies About Why We Buy* (Doubleday: New York, 2008).

32. David Derbyshire, 'So You Think You've Got a Nose for a Good Wine? Think Again', *The Observer*, June 23, 2013, 20–21.

33. Jonathan Gabay, *Brand Psychology: Consumer Perceptions, Corporate Reputations* (Kogan Page: London, 2015, 43).

34. John Lloyd, 'The Virtues of a Flawed Character', *Financial Times*, June 11, 2011, 19.

35. Peter H. Gleick, *Bottled and Sold: The Story Behind our Obsession with Bottled Water* (Island Press: Washington, DC, 2010).

CHAPTER 2: BRAND NAMES MATTER

1. Such is Amazon's product range nowadays, that it may well be selling medical supplies, embalming fluids and prosthetic body parts.

2. Slimeheads are now known as Orange Roughies, Mudbugs go by the name Crawfish and Pollock is Colin to you and me.

3. Phil can't have been too unhappy, since Nike sounds a lot like Knight.

4. Evan Morris, *From Altoids to Zima*, op. cit., 139.

5. Tom Blackett, *Trademarks*, op. cit., 13.

6. Marcel Danesi, *Brands* (Routledge: New York, 2006, 33).

7. Al Ries, 'The Essence of Positioning', in Kartikeya Kompella, ed., *The Definitive Book of Branding*, op. cit., 14.

8. Neil Taylor, *The Name of the Beast*, op. cit., 10.

9. Carol L. Bernick, 'Finding the Right Brand Name', in Alice M. Tybout and Tim Calkins, eds., *Kellogg on Branding*, op. cit., 289.

10. There's a famous marketing scholar in the States called Stephen W. Brown. To this day, I get emails from his fans saying how much they enjoy 'my' work. Naturally, I'm quite happy to take credit for his outstanding academic achievements!

11. Jean-Noël Kapferer, *The New Strategic Brand Management*, op. cit.

12. Steve Rivkin and Fraser Sutherland, *The Making of a Name: The Inside Story of the Brands We Buy* (Oxford University Press: Oxford, 2004).

13. The Budweiser dispute is not over, by any means. The company Anheuser-Busch acquired is only one of several using the disputed name in the Czech Republic, most notably Budweiser Budvar.

14. Belfast's Cipriani restaurant (as was) wouldn't see it that way, though. They suggested Sipriano as a compromise. But the last time I checked, it was called Settesoli.

15. Stephen Brown, *Wizard! Harry Potter's Brand Magic* (Cyan: London, 2005). You wouldn't believe the palaver we had to go through with HP's IP people. The Cruciatus Curse sprang to mind on several occasions ...

16. John Colapinto, 'Famous Names: Does it Matter What a Product is Called?', *The New Yorker*, October 3, 2011, www.newyorker.com.

17. Linda Woodhead, *War Paint: Helena Rubinstein and Elizabeth Arden, Their Lives, Their Times, Their Rivalry* (Virago: London, 2003). It's sometimes suggested that Arden's surname was sourced from a Tennyson poem, *Enoch Arden*. Woodhead shows otherwise.

18. Marty Neumeier, *The Brand Gap* (New Riders: Berkeley, 2005, 84).

19. Alex Frankel, *Word Craft: The Art of Turning Little Words into Big Business* (Crown: New York, 2004, 156). The Trojan horse remark surely qualifies as a Freudian slip, since America's leading brand of condoms goes by the name Trojan.

20. Christopher Johnson, *Microstyle: The Art of Writing Little* (W.W. Norton: New York, 2011, 62–63). Steve Jobs' infelicities on the naming front are discussed in John Arlidge, 'A Genius, Yes, But Steve Had Really Bad Ideas Too', *The Sunday Times*, June 3, 2012, 3.

21. Steve Rivkin and Fraser Sutherland, *The Making of a Name*, op. cit.

22. David McKie, *What's in a Surname? A Journey from Abercrombie to Zwicker* (Random House: London, 2013).

23. Or, as my mother used to say to me, 'brown by name, brown by nature'.

24. Steve Rivkin and Fraser Sutherland, *The Making of a Name*, op. cit.

25. Tom Blackett, *Trademarks*, op. cit., 15. This much-quoted passage is more like a rationalization than an explanation, because Eastman's fondness for the letter K owes much to his mother's maiden name, Kilbourn. After the premature death of his father, which plunged the family into penury, George's mother brought up the boy single-handedly. He never forgot the debt he owed to her and partially repaid it with one of the greatest brand names ever.

26. Alex Frankel, *Word Craft*, op. cit., 50.

27. Russell W. Belk, 'Las Vegas as Farce, Consumption as Play', *Consumption, Markets, & Culture*, 4 (2), 2000, 101–102.

28. Marcel Danesi, *Brands*, op. cit.

29. Tom Blackett, *Trademarks*, op. cit.

30. Note, the AGFA acronym is a bit of a swizz. It should really be AGAF. But AGFA's more euphonious, I'm sure you agree.

31. Remember the Cadabra story? Well, Consarc suffered from something very similar. When potential clients rang the consulting architects, many misheard the name and assumed they were speaking to something called Consort. An entirely different kind of professional service. Amazon escaped lightly by comparison!

32. Neil Taylor, *The Name of the Beast*, op. cit., 22.

33. Neil Taylor, ibid. See also Marty Neumeier, *Zag* (New Riders: Berkeley, 2006).
34. Although it sounds like a commemorative date, the name 4-7-11 derives from a street address in Cologne, where the makers of the fragrance were based.
35. Alex Bellos, 'Numbers Aren't Just for Counting – Why We Love Some and Hate Others', *The Observer*, April 13, 2014, 29.
36. 'A Curious Thing Called Cillit Bang', *BBC News*, June 11, 2015, www.bbc.co.uk.
37. Walt Kuenstler, *Myth, Magic and Marketing: An Irreverent History of Branding From the Acropolis to the Apple Store* (Zolexa Publishing: Havertown, PA, 2012, 49).
38. Ian Jack, 'If HSBC Reverts to Midland, it Will be a Small Victory in the Fight Against Hollow Brands', *The Guardian*, June 13, 2015, 31.
39. Jonathan Gabay, *Brand Psychology*, op. cit.
40. There aren't too many videotape rental stores these days. But Planet of the Tapes is such a good name, I couldn't resist including it. They don't make 'em like that anymore.
41. Evan Morris, *From Altoids to Zima*, op. cit.
42. Juliette Garside, 'Tom Tom Ready to Turn the Corner', *The Guardian*, November 25, 2011, 43.
43. Alex Frankel, *Word Craft*, op. cit.
44. Evan Morris, *From Altoids to Zima*, op. cit., 124. Morris's book also includes the Exxon story.
45. Laurent Muzellec, 'What is in a Name Change: Re-joycing Corporate Names to Create Corporate Brands', *Corporate Reputation Review*, 8 (4), 2006, 305–321.
46. Bill Bryson, *Made in America* (Minerva: London, 1995).
47. Matt Haig, *Brand Failures: The Truth About the 100 Biggest Branding Mistakes of All Time* (Kogan Page: London, 2003).

CHAPTER 3: LOGOS, SLOGANS, MASCOTS AND MORE

1. Rob Carney, ed., *50 Best Logos Ever: The Definitive Guide to the World's Greatest Logos* (Future Publishing: Bath, 2013).
2. Hannah Marriott, 'Fast-food Fashion – Is That Such a Good Idea When We're Suffering an Obesity Crisis?', *The Observer*, July 13, 2014, 7.
3. Naomi Klein, *No Logo*, op. cit.
4. Michael Evamy, *Logo* (Laurence King Publishing: London, 2007).
5. The same is true of the media, which tend to use the word brands when they're talking about logos and think about logos when they're writing about brands. Many managers likewise conflate the two.
6. Jon Edge and Andy Milligan, *Don't Mess with the Logo*, op. cit., xi.
7. For example: Comic Sans is the Kim Kardashian of fonts; note the nuanced drop shadows on Coke cans; the arrow-detail rebus in FedEx; the use of negative space on WWF's panda. And you thought the fashion industry was precious?
8. 'IBM is a monogram,' one says, 'Nike uses a symbol, both are trademarks but neither are logos' (Marty Neumeier, *The Brand Gap*, op. cit., 1).
9. Michael Evamy, *Logo*, op. cit., 15.

10. Marcel Danesi, *Brands*, op. cit., 79.
11. Jonathan Gabay, *Brand Psychology*, op. cit.
12. Michael Evamy, *Logo*, op. cit.
13. No, don't thank me. It's the least I can do in return for your custom. You did buy this book, didn't you? You better had, bro!
14. Anything that's too original, such as the striking cubist logo for the London Olympics, is liable to be berated by social media mavens.
15. Melissa Davis, *More Than a Name*, op. cit., 24–27.
16. Martin Lindstrom, *Brand Sense: How to Build Powerful Brands Through Touch, Taste, Smell, Sight and Sound* (Kogan Page: London, 2005).
17. Martin Lindstrom, *Buyology*, op. cit., 142.
18. Jeremy Clarkson, 'Spare me the 57 Varieties of Angela Who Think They Make a Better Ketchup', *The Sunday Times News Review*, July 19, 2015, 10.
19. Martin Lindstrom, *Brand Sense*, op. cit., 93–94.
20. Jonathan Gabay, *Brand Psychology*, op. cit.
21. It might be a while before Jo Malone does likewise.
22. Joel Beckerman, *The Sonic Boom: How Sound Transforms the Way We Think, Feel and Buy* (Houghton Mifflin Harcourt: Boston, 2014).
23. Neil Tweedie, 'Melody on the Menu: A Sprinkle of Mozart or Tchaikovsky Will Make Your Meal Sing', *The Observer*, April 5, 2015, 8–9. The same effect is apparent online. See 'Beware of Beethoven', *The Economist*, August 23, 2014, 60.
24. Diane Ackerman, *A Natural History of the Senses* (Vintage: New York, 1991, 127).
25. The seminal reference on 'taste', in a metaphorical sense, is Pierre Bourdieu's, *Distinction: A Social Critique of the Judgment of Taste* (London: Routledge, 1984).
26. Neil Munshi and James Fontanella-Khan, 'Kraft Heinz Will Have to Pass the Taste Test', *Financial Times*, March 28, 2015, 15.
27. Jeremy Clarkson, op. cit., 10.
28. Martin Lindstrom, *Brand Sense*, op. cit., 30.
29. Helen Edwards, 'Opinion: Wordcraft has Never been More Important to Brand Communications', *Marketing*, January 30, 2013, 26.
30. Helen Edwards, 'A Slogan is Forever', *Marketing*, May 11, 2011, 21.
31. Only joking, Ryanair! That said, the brand's recently-adopted slogan, which reflects Michael O'Leary's new-found commitment to customer care (Always Getting Better) was inspired by (aka ripped off from) Tesco's Every Little Helps.
32. Marcel Danesi, *Brands*, op. cit.
33. Steve Cone, *Powerlines: Words That Sell Brands, Grip Fans and Sometimes Change History* (Bloomberg Press: New York, 2008).
34. *The Sun*'s still at it: Gillette, We're Just Going to Keep Adding More Blades; iTunes, I Have Not Read the Terms and Conditions; Monopoly, A Great Way to Ruin Friendships; Pizza Hut, We Have a Salad Bar For Some Reason; Starbucks, Paying Tax Since, er, Recently; FIFA, In Partnership With PayPal (*The Sun*, July 9, 2014, 25).
35. Helen Edwards, *Marketing*, 2011, op. cit.
36. No, I'm not telling you what the brand is. Find out for yourself!
37. Ralph Kovel and Terry Kovel, *The Label Made Me Buy It* (Crown: New York, 1998).
38. Tom Espiner, 'Star Wars Toys on Show in YouTube Unboxing Marathon', *BBC News*, September 3, 2015, www.bbc.co.uk.

39. Matthew Goodman, 'Smoking Stuck in the Last Chance Saloon', *The Sunday Times*, January 25, 2015, 7.

40. The ultimate, admittedly, is the brand museum, which are often temples to the package. Guinness Storehouse in Dublin is an embodiment of the iconic pint. The World of Coca Cola in Atlanta has a giant glass bottle over the entrance. The Zippo Visitors Centre is surmounted by a vast cigarette lighter. McDonald's has built restaurants that look like enormous Happy Meals boxes.

41. Lucas Conley, *OBD: Obsessive Branding Disorder*, op. cit., 69–72.

42. Colour-coded nicknames aren't confined to sports brands like the Red Devils, the All Blacks, the Crimson teams of Harvard University. IBM, once the foremost computer maker in the world, is popularly known as Big Blue; CBRE, a famous firm of commercial property agents, is called the Mean Green Machine by competitors; *The Financial Times* is occasionally called 'The Pink 'Un'; and UPS, the parcels people, once tried to leverage its burnt umber livery with the deathless slogan, 'What Can Brown Do for You?' Not much, many consumers replied.

43. Satyendra Singh, 'Impact of Colour on Marketing', *European Journal of Marketing*, 44 (6), 2006, 783–789. Also useful is Jim Prior, 'What's in a Colour?', *Marketing*, October 10, 2012, 12.

44. Satyendra Singh, 'Impact of Colour', ibid.

45. Stephen Brown, 'Where the Wild Brands Are', *The Marketing Review*, 10 (3), 2010, 209–224.

46. Adapted from Olivier Darmon, *One Hundred Years of Michelin Man* (Hoëbeke Editions: Paris, 1997).

47. Stephen Brown, 'Mascot Mania: Monkeys, Meerkats, Martians and More', in Stephen Brown and Sharon Ponsonby-McCabe, *Brand Mascots* (Routledge: London, 2014, 1–16).

48. Stop Press! Phil Collins has just come out of retirement. Rumour has it he'll soon be going on tour. But who, fans ask, will be playing drums in his back-up band? It's gotta be the gorilla!

49. Stephen Brown, 'Wild Brands', op. cit.

50. Okay, you got me. I'm getting Cooly mixed up with Berlino, who was the mascot of the 2009 World Championships, held in Berlin. Check out Berlino's (and Cooly's) awesome athletic exploits on YouTube.

51. Rob Walker, 'Foreword', in Debbie Millman, *Brand Thinking and Other Noble Pursuits*, op. cit., viii.

52. 'Nuclear Experts Clean Radioactive Site with Cillit Bang', *The Daily Telegraph*, August 24, 2009, www.telegraph.co.uk.

53. Lisa Bachelor and Kara Gammell, 'Merry Little Christmas? How Festive Fare Got Smaller – On a Massive Scale', *The Observer*, November 16, 2014, 14–15.

CHAPTER 4: BRANDS TELL STORIES

1. Neal Gabler, *Walt Disney: The Biography* (Aurum: London, 2007).

2. Before you start searching high and low, checking up on my Walt story, I should explain that I've gilded the lily a tad (in keeping with the theme of this chapter).

The 'branding is for cattle' remark was actually made by Roy Disney, Walt's nephew, during the 'Disney Wars' at the turn of the millennium. However, he was channelling the spirit of the great man. See James B. Stewart, *Disney War: The Battle for the Magic Kingdom* (Pocket Books: London, 2006).

3. Tilde Heding, Charlotte F. Knudtzen and Mogens Bjerre, *Brand Management: Research, Theory and Practice* (Routledge: London, 2009).

4. Kenneth Roman, *The King of Madison Avenue: David Ogilvy and the Making of Modern Advertising* (Palgrave: Basingstoke, 2009).

5. David Ogilvy, *Confessions of an Advertising Man* (Athenaeum: London, 1963).

6. James B. Stewart, *Disney War*, op. cit.

7. Dorian Lynskey, 'Frozen-mania: How Elsa, Anna and Olaf Conquered the World', *The Guardian*, May 13, 2014, www.theguardian.com.

8. James B. Twitchell, *Branded Nation: The Marketing of Megachurch, College Inc. and Museumworld* (Simon & Schuster: New York, 2004, 4).

9. Barbara B. Stern, 'What Does *Brand* Mean? Historical-Analysis Method and Construct Definition', *Journal of the Academy of Marketing Science*, 34 (2), 2006, 216–223.

10. Mark Tungate, *Luxury World: The Past, Present and Future of Luxury Brands* (Kogan Page: London, 2009, 7).

11. John Williamson, 'Interview', in Melissa Davis, *More Than a Name*, op. cit., 34.

12. Stanley Hainsworth, 'Stanley Hainsworth', in Debbie Millman, *Brand Thinking*, op. cit., 133.

13. Tom Peters, 'Tom Peters', in Debbie Millman, ibid., 298.

14. Ajaz Ahmed and Stefan Olander, *Velocity: The Seven New Laws For a World Gone Digital* (Vermilion: London, 2012, 89).

15. Stephen Brown, *Fail Better!* (Marshall Cavendish: London, 2009).

16. James Ward, *Adventures in Stationery: A Journey Through Your Pencil Case* (Profile: London, 2014).

17. According to Brand Stone's *The Everything Store* (Corgi: London, 2014), Jeff Bezos insists that Amazon's internal memos are written story-style, not unlike press releases. Meetings commence with a period of silent reading.

18. Brian Collins, 'Brian Collins', in Debbie Millman, *Brand Thinking*, op. cit., 80.

19. Teressa Iezzi, *The Idea Writers: Copywriting in a New Media and Marketing Era* (Palgrave: New York, 2010).

20. Tom Peters, in Debbie Millman, *Brand Thinking*, op. cit.

21. Jeanne Willis and Dermot Flynn, *The Tale of City Sue* (Adams Foods Ltd: Leek, Staffs, 2015). See also Daniel Thomas Cook, 'Commercial Epistemologies of Childhood: "Fun" and the Leveraging of Children's Subjectivities and Desires', in Detlev Zwick and Julien Cayla, eds., *Inside Marketing: Practices, Ideologies, Devices* (Oxford University Press: Oxford, 2011, 257–268).

22. Aleksandr Orlov, *A Simples Life: The Life and Times of Aleksandr Orlov* (Ebury: London, 2010); Monkey, *Hero of Our Time* (Igloo Books: Sywell, 2013); Mr Tayto, *The Man Inside the Jacket* (Tayto: Dublin, 2009).

23. Christian Salmon, *Storytelling: Bewitching the Modern Mind* (Verso: London, 2010).

24. Walt Kuenstler, *Myth, Magic and Marketing*, op. cit., 44–45.

25. Evan Morris, *From Altoids to Zima*, op. cit.
26. Rob Carney, *50 Best Logos Ever*, op. cit.
27. James B. Twitchell, *Twenty Ads That Shook the World* (Three Rivers Press: New York, 2000).
28. I once wrote a story where the Spirit of Ecstasy was one of the characters, as were Betty Crocker and Bertie Bassett. Don't worry, I'll spare you the citation ...
29. 'Champions of Design: Cohiba', *Marketing*, August 15, 2012, 22.
30. 'Champions of Design: Toblerone', *Marketing*, July 18, 2012, 18. The secret knack of breaking the last two segments of the giant bar, BTW, is to push them together rather than pull them apart.
31. Axel Madsen, *Coco Chanel: A Biography* (Bloomsbury: London, 2009).
32. Vanessa Friedman, 'Why Are We So Cuckoo About Coco?', *Financial Times*, October 22, 2011, 4.
33. A helpful overview of charisma is found in Delphine Dion and Eric Arnould, 'Retail Luxury Strategy: Assembling Charisma Through Art and Magic', *Journal of Retailing*, 87 (4), 2011, 502–520.
34. Kevin Roberts, *Lovemarks: The Future beyond Brands* (Powerhouse Books: Brooklyn, 2006, 119).
35. See, for example, Helen Edwards and Derek Day, *Creating Passion Brands: Getting to the Heart of Branding* (Kogan Page: London, 2005).
36. John Hegarty, *Hegarty on Advertising*, op. cit., 102.
37. John Simmons, 'Guinness and the Role of Strategic Storytelling', *Journal of Strategic Marketing*, 14 (1), 2006, 11–18.
38. Anita Roddick, *Business as Unusual: The Triumph of Anita Roddick and the Body Shop* (Thorsons: London, 2000).
39. There's so much hagiography surrounding Branson, most of it self-generated, that it's salutary to read Tom Bower's *Branson* (Harper Perennial: London, 2008).
40. Virgin Galactic is puffed to infinity and beyond in Shaun Smith and Andy Milligan, *Bold: How to Be Brave in Business and Win* (Kogan Page: London, 2011).
41. Evan Morris, *From Altoids to Zima*, op. cit.
42. Grandiose words like grandiose don't help either, nor do orotund announcements like content is king, tales make sales, narrative's an imperative, etc. However, we'll pass over those in silence.
43. Douglas B. Holt, *How Brands Become Icons* (Harvard Business School Press: Boston, 2004, 36).
44. Christian Salmon, *Storytelling*, op. cit. Julien Cayla and Eric Arnould, 'Ethnographic Stories for Market Learning', *Journal of Marketing*, 77 (July), 1–16; Klaus Fog, Christian Budtz and Baris Yakaboylu, *Storytelling: Branding in Practice* (Springer: Berlin, 2005).
45. Christopher Booker, *The Seven Basic Plots: Why We Tell Stories* (Continuum: London, 2004). Sebastian Faulks, *Faulks on Fiction: Great British Characters and the Secret Life of the Novel* (BBC Books: London, 2011).
46. On the importance of conflict, see Albert Zuckerman, *Writing A Blockbuster Novel* (Sphere: New York, 1997).
47. Teressa Iezzi, *The Idea Writers*, op. cit., 156; Nick Paumgarten, 'Interesting', *The New Yorker*, February 7, 2011, www.newyorker.com.

CHAPTER 5: BRANDS ARE LIVING THINGS

1. Macintosh's comedy routine climaxed with the words: 'Never trust a computer you can't lift'. You had to be there, I guess.
2. I can also personally testify that Jobs' anthropomorphic beliefs about the Apple brand aren't especially eccentric. When the Apple II appeared, I was working in IT. A colleague of mine, who was convinced our DEC mainframe bore a grudge against him, bought one of the new-fangled Apples. And his love was unbounded. He adored the little creature. No one else was allowed to touch her. He carefully removed the plastic cover every morning to ensure her innards wouldn't overheat. Woe betide anyone who set a mug of coffee on his precious. I'm pretty sure he'd have married the Apple of his 'i' if such a civil partnership were possible.
3. Tim Nudd, 'Apple's Get a Mac: The Complete Campaign', *Adweek*, April 13, 2011, www.adweek.com.
4. For further information, check out the *Journal of Marketing Management*'s special double issue on anthropomorphism (Volume 29, Parts 1 and 2, 2013, 1–262).
5. The guy was called Stuart Baggs and, in fairness to him, he was treated very shabbily. He was an early exponent of self-branding, something that's not unusual these days. However he was hounded by the tabloids for his temerity.
6. And it's not only 'ordinary people'. Movie makers, novelists and sitcom writers concur. Consider Pixar's *Cars* and *Cars 2*, consider the *Herbie* movies, consider *Knight Rider*, consider Stephen King's *Christine*, consider the manic punishment meted out by Basil Fawlty when his car conked out at the worst possible moment (recently reprised in a TV ad for Specsavers).
7. Stephen Brown, 'It's Alive Inside', *Irish Marketing Review*, 21 (1–2), 2011, 3–11.
8. Martin Lindstrom, *Buyology: The Truth and Lies About Why We Buy* (Doubleday: New York, 2008, 32).
9. Philip Kotler, 'Foreword', in Martin Lindstrom, *Brand Sense: How to Build Powerful Brands Through Touch, Taste, Smell, Sight and Sound* (Kogan Page: London, 2010, ix).
10. Michael B. Beverland, *Building Brand Authenticity: Seven Habits of Iconic Brands* (Palgrave: Basingstoke, 2009, 2).
11. Nick Kendall, 'Introduction: How to Read This Book and Some Observations', in Nick Kendall, ed., *What is a 21st Century Brand?* (Kogan Page: London, 2015, 5).
12. Graham Hales, 'Branding', in Jeremy Kourdi, ed., *The Marketing Century*, op. cit., 141.
13. Dan Wieden, quoted by John V. Willshire, 'I Believe Communities are the Future of Brand Communication', in Nick Kendall, ed., *What is a 21st Century Brand?*, op. cit., 104.
14. Paul Feldwick, quoted by John Miller and David Muir, *The Business of Brands* (Wiley: Chichester, 2004, 151).
15. Hey, maybe they do. Who really knows what goes on once the shutters come down? Animated item in the bagging area! There's no shortage of brands on Facebook, that's for sure, all with their personal profiles, status updates and so forth. Just like you and me.
16. Don E. Schultz and Heidi F. Schultz, *Brand Babble*, op. cit., 29.

17. Rob Carney, ed., *50 Best Logos Ever*, op. cit., 108–111.

18. Yes I know it's a terrible poem, truly awful. But you'll be glad of it when you're sitting in an examination hall, trying to remember the eight elements of anthropomorphic branding.

19. An eponym, FYI, is the proper term for a place, building, institution, etc. which is named after a person. The Queen Victoria Centre (QVC) in Sydney is an example. St Petersburg is another. Selfridge's is a third. The Beetham Tower in Manchester is a fourth. And so on.

20. Delphine Dion and Eric Arnould, 'Retail Luxury Strategy', op. cit.

21. Caroline Scott, 'Come Fry With Me', *Sunday Times Magazine*, July 14, 2013, 20–24.

22. Martin Lindstrom, *Brandwashed: Tricks Companies Use to Manipulate Our Minds and Persuade Us to Buy* (Kogan Page: London, 2011).

23. Grant McCracken, 'Grant McCracken', in Debbie Millman, *Brand Thinking*, op. cit., 24–39.

24. Joel Beckerman, *The Sonic Boom*, op. cit.

25. James Watt, *Business for Punks: Break All the Rules – The BrewDog Way* (Portfolio Penguin: London, 2015).

26. Tony Allen and John Simmons, 'Visual and Verbal Identity', in Rita Clifton and John Simmons, eds., *Brands and Branding*, op. cit., 113–126.

27. A recent study of American man brands found that the following product categories are particularly strongly gendered: Apparel; Alcohol & Tobacco; Grooming Products; Tools & Equipment; Vehicles; Firearms. And each is characterized by a quintessential man brand. See Elizabeth Hirschman, *Branding Masculinity: Tracing the Cultural Foundations of Brand Meaning*, (Routledge: New York, 2016).

28. So lucrative, in fact, that some brands stand accused of overcharging for female versions of certain unisex products like razor blades. Known as the 'pink premium', these sexist surcharges range from 37% for personal care products to 50% for pastel-coloured ballpoint pens. See Claer Barrett, 'The Price of the Female Shoppers' "Pink Premium" ', *Financial Times*, January 22, 2016, www.ft.com.

29. James B. Twitchell, *Twenty Ads That Shook the World*, op. cit., 126–135.

30. Note, this is not a recent development. Androcentrism has been around from the outset. The famous Coca-Cola bottle, for instance, was deliberately designed in a fashionably female shape. It's known as the 'hobble skirt bottle' because dresses were cinched at the knee back in 1915 when the contour bottle was patented. When Virgin Cola was released back in the 1990s, in a vain attempt to knock Coca-Cola off its perch, the bottle was particularly bulbous at the top. Richard called it the Pammy bottle after Pamela Anderson, the pneumatic star of *Baywatch*. He wouldn't get away with that today.

31. Jill Avery, 'Defending the Markers of Masculinity: Consumer Resistance to Brand Gender-Bending', *International Journal of Research in Marketing*, 29 (4), 2012, 322–336.

32. These include a car with Toyota, a computer with Panasonic and a beer with Asahi. See Richard Rosenbaum-Elliott, Larry Percy and Simon Pervan, *Strategic Brand Management* (Oxford University Press: Oxford, 2015, 207).

33. Stephen Brown, 'It's Alive Inside', op. cit.

34. Stephen Brown, *Fail Better*, op. cit.

35. Giles Coren, 'The iPod Family is Unhappy in its Own Way', *The Times*, October 20, 2012, 32.
36. 'Don't Get Carried Away', *The Economist*, January 23, 2016, 64.
37. John Arlidge, 'Germany's Answer to Mini Mid-Life Crisis', *The Sunday Times*, January 26, 2014, 8.
38. Lynn B. Upshaw, *Building Brand Identity: A Strategy for Success in a Hostile Marketplace* (Wiley: New York, 1995, 151).
39. Jennifer Aaker, 'Dimensions of Brand Personality', *Journal of Marketing Research*, 34 (August), 1997, 345–357.
40. Teressa Iezzi, *The Idea Writers*, op. cit., 169–175.
41. Brian Boru, 'Ryanair: The Cú Chulainn of Civil Aviation', *Journal of Strategic Marketing*, 14 (1), 2006, 45–55.
42. Richard Rosenbaum-Elliott, Larry Percy and Simon Pervan, *Strategic Brand Management*, op. cit., 199–200.
43. Susan Fournier, 'Consumers and Their Brands: Developing Relationship Theory in Consumer Research', *Journal of Consumer Research*, 24 (3), 1997, 343–373.
44. Conversely, I've been a member of the Automobile Association for almost as long as I've been committed to Nike. I very rarely use their services. I don't think about the brand very much. But I stick with it in a kind of loveless marriage. Until last year that is, when they suddenly jacked up my renewal fee. When I queried it, their answers weren't very satisfactory and I was left with a strong feeling of betrayal. So I 'divorced' the brand.
45. 'Rooney and Gaga Among Car Nicknames', *The Irish Independent*, November 25, 2011, www.independent.ie.
46. Ribena Brown has a ring to it, mind you, as does Newcastle.
47. Stephen Brown, 'Wild Brands', op. cit.
48. Daniel P. Amos, 'How I Did It: Aflac's CEO Tells How He Fell for the Duck', *Harvard Business Review*, 88 (1), 2009, 131–134.
49. Stuart Guthrie, *Faces in the Clouds: A New Theory of Religion* (Oxford University Press: Oxford, 1993).
50. Sal Randazzo, *Mythmaking on Madison Avenue: How Advertisers Apply the Power of Myth and Symbolism to Create Leadership Brands* (Probus Publishing: Chicago, 1993, 26).

CHAPTER 6: CONSUMERS BEWARE

1. Wally Olins, *On Brand*, op. cit., 7.
2. Being burnt at the stake is an apt way to go, given the dictionary definition in chapter 1.
3. Pardon my typo. I wouldn't dream of accusing Wonga – a fine, upstanding organization, m'lord – of egregiously exploiting their customers.
4. Stephen Brown, 'O Customer, Where Art Thou?', *Business Horizons*, 47 (4), 2004, 61–70.
5. George Parker, *Confessions of a Mad Man* (Parker Consultants: Kindle Original, @ 73–74%).

6. Jonathan Bond and Richard Kirshenbaum, *Under the Radar: Talking to Today's Cynical Consumer* (John Wiley: New York, 1998, 92).

7. Rich Smith, 'Coke is an Idiot', *The Motley Fool*, June 12, 2006, www.fool.com.

8. Stephen Brown, *Wizard*, op. cit.

9. ibid., 148.

10. Philip Graves, *Consumerology: The Market Research Myth, the Truth about Consumers and the Psychology of Shopping* (Nicholas Brealey: London, 2010); Alan Mitchell, 'Make or Break for Market Research', *Marketing*, June 13, 2012, 30–32.

11. Stephen Brown, *Fail Better*, op. cit.

12. George Parker, *Confessions of a Mad Man*, op. cit.

13. Stephen Brown, 'Mascot Mania', op. cit.

14. Stanley Hainsworth, 'Stanley Hainsworth', in Debbie Millman, *Brand Thinking*, op. cit., 139. See also John Hegarty, *Hegarty on Creativity: There Are No Rules* (Thames & Hudson: London, 2014, 94–95).

15. Wally Olins, *On Brand*, op. cit.

16. Before I describe Cialdini's principles, it is necessary to note that these things *influence* consumer behaviour, they do not *determine* consumer behaviour. The fundamentals interact, furthermore. They are neither free standing nor clear cut. Please also note that I've adapted Cialdini's principles to suit my purposes.

17. Robert B. Cialdini, *Influence: Science and Practice* (Pearson: London, 2000, 22).

18. Russell W. Belk, 'Studies in the New Consumer Behaviour', in Daniel Miller, ed., *Acknowledging Consumption: A Review of New Studies* (Routledge: London, 1995, 58–95).

19. In case you're wondering, this is a true story. I'm still living with the consequences.

20. And then, of course, there's the legendary BOGOF, Buy One Get One Free.

21. Lauren Mack, 'Chinese Culture: Chinese Gift-Giving Etiquette', About.com, December 10, 2014, www.chineseculture.about.com.

22. Dan Ariely, *Predictably Irrational: The Hidden Forces That Shape Our Decisions* (HarperCollins: London, 2008, 54, 62).

23. Noah J. Goldstein, Steve J. Martin and Robert B. Cialdini, *Yes: 50 Secrets from the Science of Persuasion* (Profile: London, 2007).

24. Robert B. Cialdini, *Influence*, op. cit., 59.

25. Black Friday is the day after America's annual Thanksgiving holiday (last Thursday in November). It's the day when Christmas shopping starts in earnest and when many retail stores move into the black (after spending most of the year in the red). So crucial has it become for retailers that it is now a major promotional occasion, with tempting bargains all over the shop. The idea spread to the UK in 2012, where it was introduced by Asda, a subsidiary of the US giant Walmart. The occasion is not without controversy. And fisticuffs, furthermore. See Zoe Wood, Sarah Butler and Rupert Neate, 'They're Going to Need a Bigger Boot ... Black Friday Brings Shopping Frenzy', *The Guardian*, November 29, 2014, 5.

26. Stephen Brown, *Free Gift Inside* (Capstone: Chichester, 2003).

27. Russell W. Belk, *Collecting in a Consumer Society* (Routledge: London, 2001).

28. Nina Diamond et al., 'American Girl and the Brand Gestalt: Closing the Loop on Sociocultural Branding Research', *Journal of Marketing*, 73 (May), 2009, 118–134.

29. It also applies to students' insatiable desire to sit in the same seat every week in the lecture theatre (plus or minus a few seats or rows on either side, depending on how crowded it is).

30. George K. Zipf, *Human Behaviour and the Principle of Least Effort* (Addison-Wesley: New York, 1949).

31. You don't need me to tell you that MAMILs are Middle-Aged Men in Lycra.

32. Stephen Brown and Rhona Reid, 'Shoppers on the Verge of a Nervous Breakdown', in Stephen Brown and Darach Turley, eds., *Consumer Research: Postcards from the Edge* (Routledge: London, 1997, 79–149).

33. Byron Sharp, *How Brands Grow: What Marketers Don't Know* (Oxford University Press: Oxford, 2010).

34. Dennis W. Rook, 'The Ritual Dimension of Consumer Behaviour', *Journal of Consumer Research*, 12 (December), 1985, 251–264.

35. Martin Lindstrom, *Buyology*, op. cit.

36. Patricia L. Sunderland and Rita M. Denny, 'Consumer Segmentation in Practice: An Ethnographic Account of Slippage', in Detlev Zwick and Julien Cayla, eds., *Inside Marketing: Practices, Ideologies, Devices* (Oxford University Press: Oxford, 2011, 137–161).

37. See Jon Ungoed-Thomas and Hannah Summers, 'Royal Warrant Holder Rakes in £66m Profit', *The Sunday Times*, December 13, 2015, 1, 9. Royal allure still works, mind you. Consider the 'Duchess of Cambridge effect' on apparel brands and maternity wear.

38. Another frequently-encountered example is police officers who appear in public service ads to remind us about driving carefully, respecting the speed limit and resisting the siren call of mobile phones while at the wheel.

39. Now, I know what you're saying to yourself: that doesn't apply to me. I wouldn't dream of following the crowd. You're deluding yourself, my friend. Check out Mark Earls' book, *Herd: How to Change Mass Behaviour by Harnessing Our True Nature* (Wiley: Chichester, 2007).

40. Stanley Hainsworth, 'Stanley Hainsworth', op. cit., 136–137.

41. Stephen Brown, John F. Sherry and Robert V. Kozinets, 'Sell Me the Old, Old Story', *Journal of Customer Behaviour*, 2 (2), 2003, 133–147.

42. Bernard Cova, Robert V. Kozinets and Avi Shankar, *Consumer Tribes* (Routledge: London, 2007).

43. James H. McAlexander and John W. Schouten, 'Brandfests: Servicescapes for the Cultivation of Brand Equity', in John F. Sherry, Jr, ed., *Servicescapes: The Concept of Place in Contemporary Markets* (NTC Business Books: Chicago, 1998, 377–401).

44. Stephen Brown, John F. Sherry and Robert V. Kozinets, 'Teaching Old Brands New Tricks: Retro Branding and the Art of Brand Revival', *Journal of Marketing*, 67 (July), 2003, 19–33.

45. Philip Delves Broughton, *Life's a Pitch: What the World's Best Sales People Can Teach Us All* (Penguin: New York, 2013).

46. Stephen Brown, 'It's Alive Inside', op. cit.

47. Stuff and nonsense, I hear you say. Flatterers? Pah! No way, Jose. People like you can see through people like that. Or so you imagine. Don't flatter yourself. We're all susceptible.

48. That said, if you approach the average brand or marketing manager, they'll be completely nonplussed by this cozen-the-customer caricature. Most brand managers, I've found, truly believe in customer care, customer satisfaction, customer sovereignty, in the old saying that the customer is always right. But many consumers beg to differ.

49. Vance Packard, *The Hidden Persuaders* (Simon & Schuster: New York, 1957).

50. Dan Ariely, *Predictably Irrational*, op. cit.

51. Rob Walker, *I'm with the Brand* (Constable & Robinson: London, 2008).

52. Russell Belk, 'Sharing', *Journal of Consumer Research*, 36 (5), 2010, 715–734.

53. Andrew Lih, *The Wikipedia Story: How a Bunch of Nobodies Created the World's Greatest Encyclopaedia* (Aurum: London, 2007).

CHAPTER 7: BRAND MANAGEMENT

1. John Hegarty, *Hegarty on Advertising*, op. cit., 45–48.

2. Ibid., 47.

3. John F. Sherry, Jr. 'Brand Meaning', op. cit.

4. Stephen Brown, *Wizard*, op. cit., 145.

5. Stephen Brown, 'The Devil has All the Best Brands: Raising Hell in a House of Horrors', in Diego Rinallo, Linda Scott and Pauline Maclaran, eds., *Consumption and Spirituality* (Routledge: London, 2013, 94–105).

6. Russell W. Belk and Gülnur Tumbat, 'The Cult of Macintosh', *Consumption, Markets and Culture*, 8 (3), 2005, 205.

7. Douglas Atkin, *The Culting of Brands: When Customers Become True Believers* (Portfolio: New York, 2004, 116–117).

8. Albert M. Muñiz, Jr and Hope Jensen Schau, 'Religiosity in the Abandoned Apple Newton Community', *Journal of Consumer Research*, 31 (4), 2005, 737–747.

9. The names in this Think Box have been changed to protect the innocent.

10. Stephen Brown, 'The Failgood Factor: Playing Hopscotch in the Marketing Minefield', *The Marketing Review*, 7 (2), 2007, 125–138.

11. Ted Levitt, *Thinking About Management* (Free Press: New York, 1991, 35).

12. Tim Harford, 'Learn From the Losers', *Financial Times Magazine*, November 29, 2014, 53. See also Robert Booth, 'From Potato Salad Making to Sailing Round the World: Crowdfunding's Hits and Misses', *The Guardian*, December 27, 2014, 3; 'Crowdfunding: The Stars Are the Limit', *The Economist*, February 14, 2015, 63.

13. Carl Franklin, *Why Innovation Fails: Hard-Won Lessons for Business* (Spiro Press: London, 2003).

14. Stephen Brown, *Fail Better*, op. cit.

15. Patti Waldmeir, 'Great Leap Backwards at Li-Ning', *Financial Times*, January 25, 2015, 15.

16. 'The Failure Issue', *Harvard Business Review*, 90 (4), 2011.

17. The Dasani debacle didn't begin and end with its hapless slogan, Bottled Spunk. That was just the start of it. For the full horror, involving both the source (tap water from Sidcup) and the bottling process (contaminated by bromate, a carcinogen),

check out Bill Garrett, 'Coke's Water Bomb', *BBC News*, June 16, 2004, www.news.bbc.co.uk.

18. Douglas Atkin, *The Culting of Brands*, op. cit., 128.

19. Michael E. Raynor, Mumtaz Ahmed and Andrew D. Henderson, 'Are Great Companies Just Lucky?', *Harvard Business Review*, 88 (4), 2009, www.hbr.org.

20. Stephen Brown, 'Science, Serendipity and the Contemporary Marketing Condition', *European Journal of Marketing*, 39 (11–12), 2005, 1229–1234.

21. Stephen Brown, *Fail Better*, op. cit., 119.

22. Stephen Brown, 'The Failgood Factor', op. cit., 136.

23. Evan Morris, *From Altoids to Zima*, op. cit.

24. John Hegarty, *Hegarty on Advertising*, op. cit., 164–165.

25. Ibid., 166.

26. 'Obituary: Burt Shavitz', *The Economist*, July 25, 2015, 82.

27. Alfredo Marcantonio, John O'Driscoll and David Abbott, *Remember Those Great Volkswagen Ads?* (Enterprise Millennium: New York, 2000).

28. Kevin Lane Keller, *Strategic Brand Management: Building, Measuring and Managing Brand Equity* (Pearson: London, 2012).

29. Jonas Ridderstråle and Kjell Nordström, *Funky Business: Talent Makes Capital Dance* (Financial Times: London, 2005).

30. Youngme Moon, *Different: Escaping the Competitive Herd* (Crown: New York, 2011).

31. Jay Rainer, 'Heston Blumenthal Interview: The Fat Duck Flies Again', *Observer Magazine*, August 23, 2015, www.theguardian.com.

32. In case you're wondering where POW comes from, I'm afraid I must bear full responsibility. I have no learned citations to back up my contribution. It seems to me, though, that POW's a natural extension of Keller's POPs and PODs.

33. Quoted in Shaun Smith and Andy Milligan, *Bold: How to Be Brave in Business and Win* (Kogan Page: London, 2011, 141).

34. Henry Mintzberg, Bruce Ahlstrand and Joseph Lampel, *Strategy Safari: A Guided Tour Through the Wilds of Strategic Management* (Financial Times: London, 1998).

35. Martin Reeves, Knut Haanæs and Janmejaya Sinha, *Your Strategy Needs a Strategy: How to Choose and Execute the Right Approach* (Harvard Business School Press: Boston, 2015). See also 'A Palette of Plans', *The Economist*, May 30, 2015, 66; 'The Creed of Speed', *The Economist*, December 5, 2015, 23–26.

36. W. Chan Kim and Renée Mauborgne, *Blue Ocean Strategy: How to Create Uncontested Market Space and Make the Competition Irrelevant* (Harvard Business School Press: Boston, 2005).

37. Note, Diageo sold Bushmills to Mexico's Casa Cuervo Group in December 2014. The latter paid £275 million, plus its half-stake in Don Julio, the premium tequila brand. For the full story, see Samantha McCaughren, 'Cast Adrift', *The Sunday Times*, November 9, 2014, 7.

38. Tim Bradshaw and Hannah Kuchler, 'The Start-up That Never Grew Up', *Financial Times*, August 1, 2015, 9. All quotes are from this article, bar the Noto statement below.

39. Charles Arthur, 'It's Fast, Global, Engaged and Very Influential – So Why Isn't Twitter Flying?', *The Observer*, August 2, 2015, 41.

40. Susan Fournier and Jill Avery, 'The Uninvited Brand', *Business Horizons*, 54 (3), 2010, 193–207.

41. John Hegarty, *Hegarty on Advertising*, op. cit., 156; Philip Graves, *Consumerology*, op. cit., 169.

42. Nicola Clark, 'Testing the Wisdom of Crowds: Brands are Embracing Crowdsourcing But is it a Viable Alternative to the Ad Agency?', *Marketing*, July 14, 2010, 13.

43. Andrew Lih, *The Wikipedia Revolution*, op. cit., 122–130.

44. David Hannah, Michael Parent, Leyland Pitt and Pierre Berthon, 'It's a Secret: Marketing Value and the Denial of Availability', *Business Horizons*, 57 (1), 2014, 49–59. See also the special issue 'The Magic of Secrets', *Business Horizons*, 58 (6), 2015, 589–696.

45. As Ed himself said, 'I want to be the guy where they say "I fucking love him" or "I fucking hate him".' See, Dorian Lynskey, 'Ed Sheeran: Wembley Stadium, London', *Q Magazine*, September 2015, 96–99.

46. Youngme Moon, *Different*, op. cit., 175–177.

47. Stephen Brown, *Fail Better*, op. cit., 17.

48. Teressa Iezzi, *The Idea Writers*, op. cit., 164–169.

49. Vicki Owen, 'Yes, We Were Naïve at First – Now Even Wars Can't Stop Fairtrade', *The Mail on Sunday*, August 24, 2014, 83.

50. Rupert Neate, 'Sex Doesn't Always Sell: Falling Sales Could Push American Apparel off High Street', *The Guardian*, August 22, 2015, 5.

51. Ashlee Humphreys and Craig J. Thompson, 'Branding Disaster: Re-establishing Trust through the Ideological Containment of Systemic Risk Anxieties', *Journal of Consumer Research*, 41 (December), 2014, 877–910.

52. David Mitchell, *Talking About It Only Makes It Worse: And Other Lessons from Modern Life* (Guardian Books: London, 2015, 90–91).

CHAPTER 8: EXPANDING THE BRAND

1. Jim Bell and Stephen Brown, 'Tyrone Crystal: Striking Out in Japan', *Irish Marketing Review*, 4 (2), 1989, 23–32.

2. Apropos this chapter, never forget that the 4Ps framework has itself been expanded. Jim Blythe delivers a laugh-out-loud riff on the subject in *A Very Short, Fairly Interesting and Reasonably Cheap Book About Studying Marketing* (Sage: London, 2006).

3. Igor Ansoff, 'Strategies for Diversification', *Harvard Business Review*, 35 (5), 1957, 113–124.

4. Tom Blackett, 'What is a Brand?', in Rita Clifton and John Simmons, eds., *Brands and Branding* (Bloomberg Press: Princeton, 2003, 13–25).

5. Karl Moore and Susan Reid, 'The Birth of the Brand: 4000 Years of Branding', *Business History*, 50 (4), 2008, 419–432.

6. Wilson Bastos and Sidney Levy, 'A History of the Concept of Branding: Practice and Theory', *Journal of Historical Research in Marketing*, 4 (3), 2012, 347–368.

7. Since writing this chapter I've discovered that bottles of Canadian mountain air have recently gone on sale in China. Called Vitality Air, it costs C$19 (£9) for a three-litre canister. Sales are soaring, apparently. See Will Pavia, 'Canadians Sell Air to Smog-hit China', *The Times*, December 19, 2015, 51.

8. Big beverage brands urge their consumers to 'Drink Sensibly' and strive to battle social scourges like alcoholism and binge drinking. Woe betide the brand managers, though, who preside over a fall in sales.

9. Lucy Kellaway, *Sense and Nonsense in the Office* (FTCom: London, 2000, 121–122).

10. Youngme Moon, *Different*, op. cit. Bum Fresh, BTW, is a fictional brand of toilet tissue that features in David Walliams' comic novel *Billionaire Boy* (HarperCollins: London, 2011).

11. 11 factorial, in case you're wondering about my figures, which comes to a grand total of 39,916,800. Or forty million to the likes of you and me.

12. 'Ferrari's IPO: Wheel Spin-off', *The Economist*, October 17, 2015, 74.

13. David Runciman, 'Where are the Clever People?', *The Guardian Review*, May, 17, 2014, 6.

14. Mark Tungate, *Luxury World: The Past, Present and Future of Luxury Brands* (Kogan Page: London, 2009).

15. Ashlee Vance, *Elon Musk: How the Billionaire CEO of SpaceX and Tesla Is Shaping Our Future* (Virgin Books: London, 2015).

16. This is the famous Wheel of Retailing theory, though the basic idea is applicable to all sorts of sectors besides retailing: motels, hamburger chains, low-cost airlines, laptop computers, space rockets, razor blades and, latterly, cosmetics. The classic reference is still Stanley C. Hollander, 'The Wheel of Retailing', *Journal of Marketing*, 25 (1), 1960, 37–42.

17. 'Cheap and Cheerful', *The Economist*, January 24, 2015, 64.

18. Lucas Conley, *OBD: Obsessive Branding Disorder*, op. cit. See also Jack Grimston, 'We're No Mugs, We've Sold Our Faces', *The Sunday Times*, March 4, 2012, 11.

19. I live in hope. A fine summary of product placement, and the issues arising, is found in Chris Hackley, Rungpaka Amy Tiwsakul and Lutz Preuss, 'An Ethical Evaluation of Product Placement: A Deceptive Practice?', *Business Ethics*, 17 (2), 2008, 109–120.

20. Wally Olins, *Brand New*, op. cit.

21. Bryan Appleyard, 'Adblock-alypse Now', *The Sunday Times Magazine*, November 29, 2015, 30–39. See also Simon Duke, 'Tech Giants Go to War Over Ad Blockers', *The Sunday Times*, November 15, 2015, 6.

22. Thomas L. Friedman, *The World is Flat: The Globalized World in the Twenty-first Century* (Penguin: London, 2005).

23. There are dozens of books, and hundreds of articles, on place branding. See, for example, Simon Anholt, *Competitive Identity: The New Brand Management for Nations, Cities and Regions* (Palgrave: Basingstoke, 2008).

24. Tony Patterson, 'Extreme Cultural and Marketing Makeover: Liverpool Home Edition', in Daragh O'Reilly and Finola Kerrigan, eds., *Marketing the Arts: A Fresh Approach* (Routledge: London, 2010, 240–256).

25. CRC, 'Chain Reaction Cycles: Our Story', www.chainreactioncycles.com (accessed 29 December 2015). CRC was taken over by arch-rival Wiggle in February 2016.

26. Wu Zhiyan, Janet Borgerson and Jonathan Schroeder, *From Chinese Brand Culture to Global Brands: Insights from Aesthetics, Fashion and History* (Palgrave: Basingstoke, 2013).

27. Youngme Moon, *Different*, op. cit., 66–67.

28. Jan Lindemann, 'The Financial Value of Brands', op. cit., 30–31.

29. Laura Chesters, 'East's Yen for UK Icons', *The Daily Mail*, October 23, 2015, 81; Oliver Shah, 'I Like Britain So Much That I Can't Wait to Buy More of It', *The Sunday Times Business*, November 1, 2015, 6; Scheherazade Daneshkhu, 'Foreign Groups Step Up Raids on UK Larders', *The Financial Times*, November 8, 2014, 19.

30. Al Ries and Laura Ries, *The 22 Immutable Laws of Branding* (Collins Business: New York, 2002, 75).

31. See for example, David A. Aaker, *Building Strong Brands* (Simon & Schuster: London, 2002).

32. The principal obstacle, I suspect, was James Bond's IP lawyers.

33. Simon Reynolds, *Retromania: Pop Culture's Addiction to Its Own Past* (Faber & Faber: London, 2011, xvii–xviii).

34. Stephen Brown, 'When Innovation Met Renovation: Back to the Future of Branding', *Marketing Intelligence and Planning*, 33 (5), 2015, 634–655.

35. John Simmons, *Innocent: The Inside Story of Innocent Told from the Outside* (Marshall Cavendish: London, 2011).

36. Periodicity also makes its presence felt in the groves of academe. Popular constructs like 'moments of truth', 'speed to market' and 'critical incident research' are all predicated on periodicity.

37. Kadhim Shubber, Scheherazade Daneshkhu and Malcolm Moore, 'Dinner is Served – Morning, Noon and Night', *Financial Times*, April 11, 2015, 17.

38. Chris Edger and Andrew Emmerson, *Franchising: How Both Sides Can Win* (Libri Publishing: Faringdon, Oxfordshire, 2015).

39. Andrew Levy and Judy Bartkowiak, *Secrets of Success in Brand Licensing* (MX Publishing: London, 2011).

40. Evgeny Morozov, 'Where Uber's Über-Powerful and Amazon Rules: Welcome to the World of the Platform', *The Observer*, June 7, 2015, 24.

41. At $420 billion, Alibaba's sales already exceed Amazon and eBay combined. See 'Alibaba: Clicks to Bricks', *The Economist*, August 15, 2015, 66–67.

42. Porter Erisman, *Alibaba's World: How a Remarkable Chinese Company Is Changing the Face of Global Business* (Macmillan: Basingstoke, 2015).

43. Ironically, the demon brew that they drank in Jonestown wasn't actually Kool-Aid. It was Kool-Aid's copy-cat rival, Flavor Aid.

44. The legal nuances of 'genericide' are discussed in Lionel Bently, Jennifer Davis and Jane C. Ginsburg, eds., *Trade Marks and Brands*, op. cit.

45. The marketing angle is covered in: Bernard Cova, 'Rebranding Brand Genericide', *Business Horizons*, 57 (3), 2014, 359–369.

46. Richard Rosenbaum-Elliott, Larry Percy and Simon Pervan, *Strategic Brand Management*, op. cit., 276.

47. Noah J. Goldstein, Steve J. Martin and Robert B. Cialdini, *Yes: 50 Secrets from the Science of Persuasion*, op. cit., 25–28.

48. David Robertson, *Brick By Brick: How Lego Rewrote the Rules of Innovation* (Random House: London, 2013).

49. The four styles of IKEA are: Scandinavian, Modern, Country and Young Swede. That said, the imperious Swedish brand is in the middle of a strategic rethink. See Richard Milne, 'Ikea Store Planners Think Outside the Big Box', *Financial Times*, December 5, 2015, 18.

50. Note, these six items don't include In-N-Out Burger's 'secret menu'.

CHAPTER 9: THE BRAND STOPS HERE

1. Let's be honest, Amazon's All Hands is an improvement on the corporate anthem that IBM employees used to stand and sing lustily. Composed by Vittorio Giannini in 1939, it was called *Hail to the IBM*.

2. Mike Daisey, *Twenty-one Dog Years: Doing Time @ Amazon.com* (Fourth Estate: London, 2002, 98–99).

3. Sorry, make that every decimal place of every percentile of every fraction of every iota of market share.

4. Monopolistic utility companies are an exception to the rule and, of course, few managers would admit that they steer their course by the competition (customer care is their lodestar, don't you know). The reality, though, is that competitors loom largest in corporate psyches.

5. The classic text is Barrie G. James, *Business Wargames: Business Strategy for Executives in the Trenches of Market Warfare* (Penguin: London, 1985). But there are dozens of others. For a solid summary of the field, see Aric Rindfleisch, 'Marketing as Warfare: Reassessing a Dominant Metaphor', *Business Horizons*, 39 (5), 2002, 3–10.

6. Fiona Gilmore, *Brand Warriors: Corporate Leaders Share Their Winning Strategies* (HarperCollins: London, 1999).

7. If you think that's impressive, try James Watt of the belligerent Scottish beer brand BrewDog, who rolled a decommissioned Russian tank on to the lawn of the London Stock Exchange. The publicity helped his IPO, though.

8. I recounted the Ellison story in *Free Gift Inside*, op. cit., 171–173.

9. Only kidding! It's bad enough being harangued by Harry Potterites. The last thing I need is grumpy military historians giving me grief.

10. *Batman v Superman: Dawn of Justice* is coming soon to a cinema near you. I fear a franchise in the making. Providing, of course, *BvS* beats *Captain America* at the box office. They're scheduled for release on the same day. Postscript update! It was a dead heat. Both earned approx. US $800 million world-wide.

11. Emily Steel, 'Super Bowl Kicks Off World's Largest Ad Game', *Financial Times*, January 31, 2014, 1–2.

12. The dog-eat-dog ethos is evident in science as well. See Michael White, *Rivals: Conflict as the Fuel of Science* (Vintage: London, 2002).

13. Lindsay Whipp and James Shotter, 'Adidas Kicks Off US Drive to Close in on Nike', *Financial Times*, August 9, 2015, 13.

14. Mark E. Babej and Tim Pollak, 'Boeing Versus Airbus', *Forbes*, 24 May, 2006, www. forbes.com. See also 'Aircraft Makers: Keep Seatbelts Fastened', *The Economist*, June 20, 2015, 68. Airbus, incidentally, is edging ahead in the short-haul market sector, where the A320 Neo is outselling the 737 Max by two to one.

15. Raf Simons, funnily enough, was the first to blink. He quit Dior, pleading pressures of work, in October 2015. Slimane followed suit in March 2016.

16. Such was the disparity in relative market shares (in all five cases) that it wasn't so much a case of David defeating Goliath as David's little sister beating Goliath's big brother.

17. Adam Morgan, *Eating the Big Fish: How Challenger Brands Can Compete Against Market Leaders* (Wiley: Chichester, 2000).

18. Robert Lea, 'Today It's Norway, Tomorrow the World – The Airline Intent on Challenging the Budget Giants', *The Times*, May 18, 2013, 52.

19. Søren Askegaard and Fabian F. Csaba, 'The Good, the Bad and the Jolly: Taste, Image and the Symbolic Resistance to the Coca-Colonisation of Denmark', in Stephen Brown and Anthony Patterson, eds., *Imagining Marketing* (Routledge: London, 2000, 124–140).

20. Adam Morgan, *Eating the Big Fish*, op. cit.

21. Mindi Chahal, 'The Power of Disruption: The New Challenger Brands Changing Your Industry', *Marketing Week*, May 14, 2014, www.marketingweek.co.uk; Jill Lepore, 'The Disruption Machine', *The New Yorker*, June 23, 2014, www.newyorker. com; John Naughton, 'The Theory of "Disruption" has been Disrupted. Can We All Move on Now, Please?', *The Observer*, July 13, 2014, 21.

22. Mark Ritson, 'Should You Launch a Fighter Brand?', *Harvard Business Review*, 87 (10), 2009, 86–94.

23. John Naughton, 'Big Bad Tech: How America's Digital Capitalists are Taking Us All for a Ride', *The Observer*, November 23, 2014, 39.

24. See, for example, Robert Lea, 'Russian Sanctions Hit Rolls-Royce', *The Times*, October 18, 2014, 47; 'Russia's Food Embargo: Bonfire of the Vans of Cheese', *The Economist*, August 15, 2015, 30; Stephen Burgen, Stephanie Kirchgaessner and Alec Luhn, 'Med's Russian Lament: We Wish You Were Here', *The Guardian*, September 5, 2015, 25.

25. Shaun Walker, 'Russians Dismayed as Outlaw Cheese Destroyed by Bulldozer', *The Guardian*, August 8, 2015, 20.

26. 'European Carmakers: Too Many Cars, Too Few Buyers', *The Economist*, February 18, 2012, 61–62.

27. Not so long ago, Arvidsson reports (*Brands*, op. cit., 4), the Chinese new rich were so taken with western brands that they left the price tags on and swanked around displaying their expensive wares.

28. John Arlidge, 'What's Happened to the Great Malls of China?', *The Sunday Times*, January 24, 2016, 22–23; 'China: Beyond Bling', *The Economist Special Report on Luxury*, December 13, 2014, 11–12; 'China's Wealthy No Longer Putting on the Ritz', *Financial Times*, November 21, 2015, 17.

29. Gareth Rubin, 'You are Single and Looking for a Date in the New Year: So Who Will you Call?', *The Observer*, December 28, 2014, 25; Matthew Goodman, 'Our Eyes Met Across a Crowded Room … And My Phone App Did the Rest', *The Sunday Times*, February 8, 2015, 9.

30. That said, the alterations to accountancy rules in the 1980s were no less instrumental in branding's imperious ascent. See Jan Lindemann, 'The Financial Value of Brands', op. cit.

31. For full details of the scheme, see European Commission Geographical Indications and Traditional Specialities, www.ec.europa.eu/agriculture/quality/schemes.

32. Deirdre Hipwell, 'It Takes More Than a Noodle Crisis to Leave Nestlé's Boss Tied Up in Knots', *The Times*, August 15, 2015, 51; 'Nestlé in India: Instant Karma', *The Economist*, July 4, 2015, 55.

33. Jon Ronson, *So You've Been Publically Shamed* (Picador: London, 2015). A visceral evocation of the online hate mob can be found in Jonathan Coe's recent novel, *Number 11*.

34. Richard Rosenbaum-Elliott, Larry Percy and Simon Pervan, *Strategic Brand Management*, op. cit., 229.

35. It was just the two of them, with hand-painted placards, protesting outside their local Sears store. This was in the days before social media, but it proved no less effective.

36. Rupert Neate, 'Sex Doesn't Always Sell', op. cit., 5; Sarah Butler, 'American Apparel: Paula Schneider's "Wild Ride" to Revive the Brand', *The Guardian*, November 10, 2015, www.theguardian.com; Oliver Shah, 'Sex, Threats and Lawsuits: It's Just Another Day at American Apparel', *The Sunday Times*, November 15, 2015, 7.

37. When Unilever, one of the biggest branding machines on the planet, was endeavouring to catch up with P&G's new and improved Ariel washing powder, it rush-released an enzyme enriched product called Persil Power. Unfortunately, Persil Power's prodigious enzymes were so powerful that they destroyed the clothing they were supposed to be cleaning.

38. Adam Morgan and Mark Barden, *A Beautiful Constraint: How to Transform Your Limitations into Advantages and Why It's Everyone's Business* (Wiley: Chichester, 2015).

39. I recount the Boo.com debacle in *Fail Better*, op. cit., 18–19. Boo.com shouldn't be confused with Boohoo.com, the superfast fast fashion e-tailer.

40. Adam Morgan and Mark Barden, *A Beautiful Constraint*, op. cit., 3.

41. The Howard Gossage story is summarized in George Parker, *Confessions of a Mad Man*, op. cit. A fuller account is contained in Steve Harrison, *Changing the World is the Only Fit Work for a Grown Man* (Adworld Press: London, 2012). Ogilvy's 'tight brief' remark also comes from Parker.

42. The Bill Bernbach quotation is trotted out in every attack on rigorous research methods. George Parker, *Confessions*, ibid. is a case in point.

43. A terrific brand name, Hypnos carries clever echoes of stage mesmerists murmuring, 'You are Feeling Sleepy, Sleepy'.

44. Wilson Bastos and Sidney Levy, 'A History of the Concept of Branding', op. cit.

45. Gillian Tett, *The Silo Effect: Why Putting Everything in its Place isn't Such a Bright Idea* (Little, Brown: London, 2015).

46. Nicholas Ind, 'Living the Brand', in Kartikeya Kompella, ed., *The Definitive Book of Branding*, op. cit., 200.

47. Robert B. Cialdini, *Influence*, op. cit.

48. Apple, by contrast, paid $60 million for the use of its domain name in China.

49. Michael Tonello, *Bringing Home the Birkin: My Life in Pursuit of the World's Most Coveted Handbag* (William Morrow: New York, 2008). The brand's allure wasn't undermined by the revelations, incidentally. See Suna Erdem, 'Handbags at Dawn', *Sunday Times Style*, December 26, 2015, 18–19.

50. A recent example of the Anna Karenina Principle is the *E. coli* outbreak that has stricken the Chipotle Mexican restaurant chain. The brand has not only become the butt of jokes – 'Breaking News: Chipotle to begin serving e.coli all day!' – but its share price has plunged by 35% in a matter of months.

51. Hamish Pringle, *Celebrity Sells* (Wiley: Chichester, 2004).

52. Wally Olins, *Brand New*, op. cit.

53. Teressa Iezzi, *The Idea Writers*, op. cit, 10). YouTube views currently stand at 15 million, with 86,000 comments.

CHAPTER 10: THE DARK SIDE OF THE BRAND

1. Alun isn't bitter. Although he lost everything when Oakvale bit the dust, he still lives in the big house on Beach Road, Penarth, thanks largely to the perspicacity of his indomitable wife, Sherlie.

2. Stephen Brown, *Free Gift Inside*, op. cit., 171–173.

3. Porter Erisman, *Alibaba's World*, op. cit., 159–160.

4. 'Wine Vandalism: Draining Mystery', *The Economist*, December 8, 2012, 72.

5. Deborah Cadbury, *Chocolate Wars. From Cadbury to Kraft: 200 Years of Sweet Success and Bitter Rivalry* (HarperPress: London, 2011). See also John Bradley, *Cadbury's Purple Reign: The Story Behind Chocolate's Best-Loved Brand* (John Wiley: Chichester, 2008).

6. The going rate is $15 per thousand likes. See Charles Arthur, 'Like it or Not? Why Internet Thumbs-up May be Fake', *The Guardian*, August 3, 2013, 5.

7. Ben Laurance and Aimee Donnellan, 'The Two Faces of HSBC', *The Sunday Times Business*, February 15, 2105, 5; Iain Dey, 'RBS in Dock for Mercy Killings', *The Sunday Times Business*, December 1, 2013, 7; Leanna Byrne, 'Would I Do it to My Mammy?' *The Sunday Business Post*, November 16, 2014, 25.

8. David Charter, 'Ikea Admits Forced Prison Labour Made its Furniture', *The Times*, November 17, 2012, 61. On Ferdinand Porsche's war record, see https://mondediplo.com/1998/01/11volkswag.

9. Alexi Mostrous, 'Retailer Accused of Making £50m from Airports Ruse', *The Times*, August 22, 2015, www.thetimes.co.uk.

10. Jodi Kantor and David Streitfeld, 'Inside Amazon: Wrestling Big Ideas in a Bruising Workplace', *The New York Times*, August 15, 2015, www.nytimes.com; Leslie Hook and Shannon Bond, 'Amazon Rebuts New York Times Exposé', *Financial Times*, October 19, 2015, www.ft.com.

11. Emma Howard, 'Requiem for the Arctic: Church to Join Protests over Shell's Drilling Plan', *The Guardian*, August 22, 2015, 15.

12. Jonathan Soble, 'The Olympus Affair: A Camera-maker Obscura', *Financial Times*, October 22, 2011, 8.

13. 'An On-line Fraud Scandal in China: Alibaba and the 2,236 Thieves', *The Economist*, February 22, 2011, www.economist.com.

14. Nicola Smith and Robin Henry, 'Stores Spurn Fund for Factory Victims', *The Sunday Times*, January 12, 2014, 13; Sarah Butler, 'Bangladesh Factory Deaths Give Impetus to Safety Drive,' *The Observer*, June 23, 2013, 39.

15. 'Italian Punters: An Offer They Couldn't Refuse', *The Economist*, October 3, 2015, 42.

16. 'Female Viagra Pill Gets Go-ahead in the States', *BBC News*, August 19, 2015, www.bbc.co.uk.

17. Stephen Brown, Pierre McDonagh and Clifford Shultz, 'Dark Marketing: Ghost in the Machine or Skeleton in the Cupboard?', *European Business Review*, 24 (3), 2012, 196–215.

18. 'Shredding the Rules', *The Economist*, May 2, 2015, 64. All of the examples following come from this article, except SpaceX, which derives from Ashlee Vance, *Elon Musk*, op. cit. The indictment of Thomas Watson is likewise covered in numerous biographies of IBM's imperious founder. See, for example, Richard S. Tedlow, *The Watson Dynasty* (HarperBusiness: New York, 2003).

19. James Freund and Erik S. Jacobi, 'Revenge of the Brand Monsters: How Goldman Sachs Doppelgänger Turned Monstrous', *Journal of Marketing Management*, 29 (1–2), 2013, 175–194.

20. Naomi Klein, *No Logo*, op. cit. See also Lena Corner, 'New World Order?', *The Independent on Sunday*, November 20, 2011, 32–35.

21. Naomi Klein, 'The Best Brand on Earth', *The Guardian*, January 16, 2010, 2.

22. Vincent-Wayne Mitchell and Joseph Ka Lun Chan, 'Investigating UK Consumers' Unethical Attitudes and Behaviours', *Journal of Marketing Management*, 18 (1–2), 2002, 5–26.

23. Well, you are one of the few who feel that way. You are an angel in human form. Most brands don't deserve you, not even The Body Shop or the Catholic Church.

24. Before you ask, Hello Kitty boxer shorts really do exist.

25. In fairness to Burberry, I should acknowledge that they've recently announced plans to open a new factory (for trench coats) in Leeds.

26. Roxanna Magee and Audrey Gilmore, 'Heritage Site Management: From Dark Tourism to Transformative Service Experience?', *The Service Industries Journal*, 35 (15–16), 2015, 898–917.

27. John Lennon and Malcolm Foley, *Dark Tourism: The Attraction of Death and Disaster* (Continuum: London, 2000). See also Tony Seaton, 'Thanatourism and its Discontents', in Tazim Jamal and Mike Robinson, eds., *The Sage Handbook of Tourism Studies* (Sage: London, 2009, 521–542).

28. Margarette Driscoll, 'Oh No, We're Not Shoplifting, Just "Liberating" ', *The Sunday Times*, January 15, 2012, 11; Carole Cadwalladr, 'Who's the Thief Here Tesco?', *The Observer,* January 15, 2012, www.theguardian.com.

29. Ronald A. Fullerton and Girish Punj, 'The Unintended Consequences of the Culture of Consumption: An Historical-theoretical Analysis of Consumer Misbehaviour', *Consumption, Markets and Culture*, 1 (4), 1998, 403.

30. Charles Cumming, 'Times Modern', *The Times*, January 14, 2011, 5.

31. Wolff Olins, *The New Guide to Identity: How to Create and Sustain Change Through Managing Identity* (Gower: Aldershot, 2007). See also Wally Olins, *The Brand Handbook* (Thames & Hudson: London, 2008).

32. Lucas Conley, *OBD: Obsessive Branding Disorder*, op. cit., 54.

33. Sarah Butler, 'Shops Hope for Wicked Halloween Sales Record', *The Guardian*, October 31, 2015, 19.

34. Ben Paynter, 'Suds for Drugs', *New York Magazine*, January 6, 2013, www.nymag.com.

35. John Weich, *Storytelling on Steroids* (BIS Publishers: Amsterdam, 2013, 110).

36. Sean Adams, 'Sean Adams', in Debbie Millman, *Brand Thinking*, op. cit., 219–220.

37. Vioxx was withdrawn from sale in September 2004 after revelations concerning increased risks of heart attacks and strokes among users (evidence that was withheld by Merck for more than five years). Vioxx was a very widely prescribed drug at the time, with approximately 80 million users worldwide.

38. Ben Goldacre, *Bad Pharma: How Drug Companies Mislead Doctors and Harm Patients* (Fourth Estate: London, 2012); Andrew Ward, 'Big Pharma: Storehouse of Trouble', *Financial Times*, April 12, 2014, 9.

39. The best history of the KKK is Wyn Craig Wade, *The Fiery Cross: The Ku Klux Klan in America* (Oxford University Press: New York, 1998).

40. Note the judicious use of the 'k' sound that we've noted on several occasions. Note also, the Klan still exists but it's a fraction of its former size and influence. See Iain Dey, 'Resurgent Klan Fans America's Flame of Hate', *The Sunday Times*, October 26, 2014, 32.

41. Lucy Moore, *Anything Goes: A Biography of the Roaring Twenties* (Atlantic: London, 2008).

42. Carole Cadwalladr, 'How I Bought Drugs From "Dark Net" – It's Just Like Amazon Run by Cartels', *The Observer*, October 6, 2013, 36.

43. I wonder if the Silk Road brand name is trademarked? Just a thought …

44. Tom Mueller, *Extra Virginity: The Sublime and Scandalous World of Olive Oil* (Atlantic Books: London, 2012).

45. Alex Renton, 'Big Business and a Bitter Harvest', *The Observer*, January 13, 2012, 40.

46. Tom Mueller, *Extra Virginity*, op. cit., 46.

47. Ken Auletta, *Googled: The End of the World as We Know It* (Virgin Books: London, 2011).

48. First published in November 1945, 'Good Bad Books' is a famous essay by George Orwell. It's anthologized in *George Orwell: Essays* (Penguin: London, 2000, 318–321).

49. 'As one great furnace flam'd, yet from those flames/No light, but rather darkness visible/Serv'd only to discover sights of woe'. *Paradise Lost*, Book 1, Lines 62–64.

CHAPTER 11: POP GOES THE BRAND

1. Jonathan Van Meter, 'Adele: One and Only', Vogue, February 13, 2012, www.vogue.com.
2. She hasn't changed her tune in the intervening years. In the interviews that accompanied the release of 25, Adele restated her anti-branding stance: 'What have I said no to? Everything you can imagine. Literally every-fucking-thing. Books, clothes, food ranges, drink ranges, fitness ranges … That's probably the funniest.' See Tom Lamont, 'Hello From the Other Side', The Observer Music, November 15, 2015, 8–13.
3. Ivan Solotaroff, 'Jason Statham: The King of Action Films', Details, April 1, 2012, www.details.com.
4. 'Monsters Inc.' Financial Times, January 29, 2010, www.ft.com.
5. What Dalí's artwork was doing in the display window of a department store is another matter entirely. On Salvador's marketing savvy, see Ian Fillis, 'The Endless Enigma or the Last Self-Portrait (or, What the Marketer Can Learn from the Artist)', in Stephen Brown and Anthony Patterson, eds., Imagining Marketing, op. cit., 52–72.
6. The classic text on this topic is Colin Wilson, The Outsider (Gollancz: London, 1956). A more recent statement on the outsider archetype is Robert Kelsey, The Outside Edge: How Outsiders Can Succeed in a World Made by Insiders (Capstone: Chichester, 2015).
7. Check out Jonathan Schroeder, 'Edouard Manet, Calvin Klein and the Strategic Use of Scandal', in Stephen Brown and Anthony Patterson, eds., Imagining Marketing, op. cit., 36–51.
8. Stephen Brown, 'The Brand Stripped Bare by its Marketers, Even', in Daragh O'Reilly and Finola Kerrigan, eds., Marketing the Arts: A Fresh Approach, op. cit., 257–266. Salvador Dalí was nicknamed Avida Dollars by Andre Breton, an anagram that alluded to the great artist's unseemly cupidity.
9. Stephen Brown, 'The Books Business: Fifty Shades of Grief', in Daragh O'Reilly, Ruth Rentschler and Theresa A. Kirchner, eds., The Routledge Companion to Arts Marketing (Routledge: London, 2013, 275–276).
10. Joseph Heath and Andrew Potter, The Rebel Sell: How the Counter Culture Became Consumer Culture (Capstone: Chichester, 2006).
11. The Leppard quotes come from an interview in Classic Rock Magazine ('The Industry Can't Kill Us', March 2014, 5).
12. Peter Aspden, 'Art's Revenge on Commerce', Financial Times, June 23, 2012, 10; Will Gompertz, Think Like an Artist … And Lead a More Creative, Productive Life (Penguin: London, 2015).
13. David Pilling, 'Lunch with the FT: Takashi Murakami', Financial Times, June 20, 2015, 3.
14. James Ashton, 'Road to Recovery: Creative Industries', The Sunday Times Business Section, May 1, 2011, 7–10.
15. Richard Florida, The Rise of the Creative Class, Revisited (Basic Books: New York, 2012).

16. Matthew D. Shank, *Sports Marketing: A Strategic Perspective* (Pearson: Upper Saddle River, NJ, 2009).

17. Andy Milligan, *Brand It Like Beckham* (Marshall Cavendish: London, 2010).

18. 'The Becks Effect', *The Economist*, November 19, 2011, 54; Ben Smith, 'Brand Beckham: Where Next for Pioneer David?', *BBC Sport*, www.bbc.co.uk/sport/; Matthew Syed, 'David Beckham: My Next Career Move', *The Times Magazine*, September 5, 2015, 18–24.

19. While we're on the subject, AC/DC doesn't exactly stint on the tie-in merchandise, which ranges from pillow cases and fine wines to flashing devil's horns. Hell's bells!

20. Daragh O'Reilly and Finola Kerrigan 'Marketing the Arts', in Daragh O'Reilly and Finola Kerrigan, eds., *Marketing the Arts: A Fresh Approach*, op. cit., 1–4.

21. Stephen Brown, *Free Gift Inside*, op. cit., 115–117.

22. Damien Hirst and Gordon Burn, *On the Way to Work* (Faber & Faber: London, 2001, 105).

23. Alex Shakar, *The Savage Girl* (Scribner: London, 2001).

24. Celebrated examples include, Colonel Tom Parker (Elvis), Andrew Loog Oldham (Rolling Stones), Brian Epstein (The Beatles), Freddy DeMann (Michael Jackson), Simon Fuller (Spice Girls), Louis Walsh (Westlife) and Simon Cowell (One Direction). See Johnny Rogan, *Starmakers and Svengalis* (Futura: London, 1989) and Gareth Murphy, *Cowboys and Indies* (Serpent's Tail: London, 2015).

25. Charlie Gray, 'If it Was Easy, Everybody Would Do it', *Financial Times Magazine*, October 11, 2014, 14–19. Note, *X Factor* audiences fell significantly during the 2015 season (to its lowest ratings since 2004). Whether this is a temporary blip or the beginning of the end remains to be seen.

26. Quoted in Stephen Brown and Chris Hackley, 'The Greatest Showman on Earth: Is Simon Cowell P.T. Barnum Reborn?', *Journal of Historical Research in Marketing*, 4 (2), 2012, 290–308.

27. Chris Hackley, Stephen Brown and Rungpaka Amy Hackley, 'The X Factor Enigma: Simon Cowell and the Marketization of Existential Liminality', *Marketing Theory*, 12 (4), 2012, 451–469.

28. Gene Simmons, *Kiss and Make-Up* (Arrow: London, 2003).

29. Iain Dey, 'Kiss and Sell: Rick's Giant Cash Machine', *The Sunday Times*, December 7, 2014, 9.

30. Nick Wroe, 'The Books Interview: James Patterson', *The Guardian*, May 11, 2013, 12–13; Stephen Brown, 'And Then We Come to the Brand: Academic Lessons from International Bestsellers', *Arts Marketing: An International Journal*, 1 (1), 2011, 70–86.

31. Sean O'Neill, 'Bowie the Business Genius Tops Charts', *The Times*, January 16, 2016, 35.

32. Stephen Brown, 'Material Girl or Managerial Girl? Charting Madonna's Brand Ambition', *Business Horizons*, 46 (4), 2003, 2–10. See also Tom Whipple, 'How Do You Turn $35 into $400m? Ask Madonna', *The Times*, March 17, 2012, 4–5.

33. David Hutchison, 'Madonna at the Grammys', *Digital Spy*, January 27, 2014, www.digitalspy.com.

34. Stephen King admits to being the booklover's equivalent of a Big Mac, though I reckon Burger King's a better analogy. King's the home of the whopper, after all.

35. Jonathan Schroeder, 'Aesthetics Awry: The Painter of Light and the Commodification of Artistic Values', *Culture, Markets and Consumption*, 9 (2), 2006, 87–99; David Randall, 'A Light Goes Out as "King of Kitsch" Dies Aged 54', *The Independent on Sunday*, April 8, 2012, 29.

36. Prada Evening Project is the bespoke line of apparel at the very top of Miuccia Prada's range. It's way beyond the budget of you and me. Jeff Koons can afford it, though.

37. Andreas Huyssen, *After the Great Divide: Modernism, Mass Culture, Postmodernism* (Indiana University Press: Bloomington, 1986).

38. *Savage Beauty* attracted 500,000 people to the V&A during its 21-week run in 2015.

39. Scott Timberg, *Culture Crash: The Killing of the Creative Class* (Yale University Press: New Haven, 2015, 7).

40. Robert Crawford, *Young Eliot: From St Louis to* The Waste Land (Jonathan Cape: London, 2015, 42); Stephen Brown, 'Selling Poetry by the Pound: T.S. Eliot and *The Waste Land* Brand', *Consumption, Markets and Culture*, 18 (5), 2015, 411–426.

41. The most eloquent exponent of this perspective in marketing and consumer research is Morris B. Holbrook. All his books and articles are outstanding. Some of the best are gathered together in an anthology, *Consumer Research: Introspective Essays on the Study of Consumption* (Sage: Thousand Oaks, 1995).

42. Sue Roe, *In Montmartre: Picasso, Matisse and Modernism in Paris, 1900–1910* (Penguin: London, 2015).

43. Dominic Sandbrook, *The Great British Dream Factory: The Strange History of Our National Imagination* (Allen Lane: London, 2015).

44. 'Creative Capitalism: Other Industries Have a Lot to Learn from Hollywood', *The Economist*, November 1, 2014, 78.

45. Richard Rosenbaum-Elliott, Larry Percy and Simon Pervan, *Strategic Brand Management*, op. cit., 98–99.

46. Will Gompertz, *Think Like an Artist*, op. cit.

47. David Cottington, *The Avant-Garde: A Very Short Introduction* (Oxford University Press: Oxford, 2013).

48. T.S. Eliot, *The Sacred Wood: Essays on Poetry and Criticism* (Faber & Faber: London, 1997, 105).

49. Douglas B. Holt, *How Brands Become Icons*, op. cit.

50. Adam Arvidsson, *Brands*, op. cit., 2–3.

51. H.G. Wells, *Tono-Bungay* (Collins: London, 1909).

52. Christopher Goodwin, 'Think Different, Man!', *The Sunday Times Magazine*, August 1, 2010, 46–51. See also Edward Helmore, 'Selling Out? The Grateful Dead's Farewell Tour Hits a Controversial Box Office High', *The Observer*, May 17, 2015, 17.

CHAPTER 12: THE BRAND FINALE

1. Stephen Brown and Rhona Reid, 'Shoppers on the Verge of a Nervous Breakdown', op. cit.

2. Stephen Brown, *Songs of the Humpback Shopper (And Other Bazaar Ballads)*, www.sfxbrown.com, 1998.

3. Vincent-Wayne Mitchell and Sarah Haggett, 'Sun-sign Astrology in Market Segmentation: An Empirical Investigation', *Journal of Consumer Marketing*, 14 (2), 1997, 113–131.

4. FYI, I discuss the Barnum Effect in Stephen Brown, *Marketing – The Retro Revolution* (Sage: London, 2001, 71). It's a well-established psychological propensity.

5. Lucy Kellaway, 'Get into the Christmas Spirits', *The Financial Times*, November 28, 2015, 6.

6. Raymond Williams, 'Advertising: The Magic System', in Simon During, ed., *The Cultural Studies Reader* (Routledge: London, 1993, 320–336).

7. James B. Twitchell, *Adcult USA: The Triumph of Advertising in American Culture* (Columbia University Press: New York, 1996).

8. Rachel Bowlby, *Shopping with Freud* (Routledge: London, 1993), *Just Looking: Consumer Culture in Dreiser, Gissing and Zola* (London: Methuen, 1985).

9. Steve, characteristically, 'borrowed' the technology-is-magical idea from sci-fi novelist Arthur C. Clarke, whose 'third law' states that any sufficiently advanced technology is indistinguishable from magic. Driverless cars would be a contemporary example, as would the new generation of virtual-reality headsets.

10. Ken Auletta, *Googled: The End of the World as We Know It* (Virgin Books: London, 2010, 9).

11. Alex Shakar, *The Savage Girl*, op. cit., 51.

12. Anthony Aveni, *Behind the Crystal Ball: Magic and Science from Antiquity to the New Age* (Newleaf: London, 1997).

13. Martin Lindstrom, *Buyology*, op. cit., 97.

14. Stephen Brown, 'Double, Double Toil and Trouble: On the Equivocal Magic of Marketing', *Journal of Customer Behaviour*, 8 (2), 2009, 163–175.

15. 'Superstitious Investors: Black-cat Market', *The Economist*, August 30, 62; 'Tetraphobia: Nothing to Fear', *The Economist*, December 5, 2015, 51.

16. Stephen Brown, 'It's A Kinda Magic: Adventures in Alchemy', in Philip Kitchen, ed., *Marketing Metaphors and Metamorphosis* (Palgrave: Basingstoke, 2008, 88–101).

17. John Micklethwait and Adrian Wooldrige, *The Witch Doctors: What the Management Gurus Are Saying* (Crown: New York, 1996).

18. Delphine Dion and Eric Arnould, 'Retail Luxury Strategy', op. cit.; Hamish Pringle, *Celebrity Sells*, op. cit.

19. Craig J. Thompson, Aric Rindfleisch and Zeynep Arsel, 'Emotional Branding and the Strategic Value of the Doppelgänger Brand Image', *Journal of Marketing*, 70 (1), 2006, 50–64.

20. Bill Quinn, *How Walmart Is Destroying America (and the World) and What You Can Do About It* (Ten Speed Press: Berkeley, 2000).

21. John Lennon and Malcolm Foley, *Dark Tourism: The Attraction of Death and Disaster* (Continuum: London, 2000).

22. David Crow, 'A Provocateur in the Pharma Wars', *Financial Times*, September 26, 2015, 13; David Crow and Gina Chon, 'Highs and Lows of Pharma Sector's Whizz Kid', *Financial Times*, December 19, 2015, 17.

23. Elizabeth Hirschman, 'Metaphor in the Marketplace', *Marketing Theory*, 7 (3), 2007, 227–248.

24. Caroline Tynan, 'Metaphors and Marketing: Some Uses and Abuses', in Philip Kitchen, ed., *Marketing Metaphors and Metamorphosis*, op. cit., 10.

25. Philip Kitchen, 'Marketing Metaphors and Metamorphosis: An Introduction', in Philip Kitchen, ed., *Marketing Metaphors and Metamorphosis*, ibid., 1–9.

26. Stephen Brown, 'Are Marketing's Metaphors Good for it?', *The Marketing Review*, 8 (3), 2008, 211.

27. Sue Roe, *In Montmartre*, op. cit.

28. George Orwell, 'Politics and the English Language'. Originally written in 1946, this seminal essay on the art of writing is republished in *Inside the Whale and Other Essays* (Penguin: London, 1962). The mixed metaphor appears on page 151.

29. James Wood, *How Fiction Works* (Jonathan Cape: London, 2008).

30. Stephen Pinker, *The Sense of Style: The Thinking Person's Guide to Writing in the 21st Century* (Penguin: London, 2014, 46).

31. Stephen Brown, 'Metaphorical Myopia', in Pauline Maclaran, Mike Saren, Barbara Stern and Mark Tadajewski, eds., *The Sage Handbook of Marketing Theory* (Sage: London, 2011, 268).

32. Burberry, BP, Nestlé and Nike all know what it's like to have their brand misappropriated and maligned by consumers. This doesn't mean that managers must capitulate to the kidnappers, merely that they would do well to negotiate brand meanings with them.

33. 'It's the Real Thing', *The Economist*, November 14, 2015, 77.

34. Stephen Brown, *Wizard*. op. cit., 162–168.

35. M.H. Abrams, *The Mirror and the Lamp: Romantic Theory and the Critical Tradition* (Oxford University Press: Oxford, 1953).

36. Douglas B. Holt, *How Brands Become Icons*, op. cit.

37. Martin Kemp, *Christ to Coke: How Image Becomes Icon* (Oxford University Press: Oxford, 2011).

38. Tim Jones, 'I Believe in Gaming Your Brand', in Nick Kendall, ed., *What is a 21st Century Brand?* (Kogan Page: London, 2015, 65–69).

39. Pat Kane, *The Play Ethic: A Manifesto for a Different Way of Living* (Macmillan: Basingstoke, 2004).

40. Nina Diamond et al., 'American Girl and the Brand Gestalt', op. cit.

41. Alexei Sayle, 'Tango & Cash', *The Guardian*, November 29, 2014, 17.

42. Caroline Tynan, 'Metaphors and Marketing', op. cit., 13.

43. John F. Sherry and John Schouten, 'A Role for Poetry in Consumer Research', *Journal of Consumer Research*, 29 (2), 2002, 218–234.

44. James Fenton, *An Introduction to English Poetry* (Penguin: London, 2003).

45. S. Musgrove, 'Poetry and Magic', *The Australian Quarterly*, 18 (1), 1946, 102–114.

INDEX